CultureShock!
A Survival Guide to Customs and Etiquette

San Francisco

Frances Gendlin

Marshall Cavendish
Editions

This third edition published in 2011 by:
Marshall Cavendish Corporation
99 White Plains Road
Tarrytown, NY 10591-9001
www.marshallcavendish.us

Text Copyright © 2011, 2007, 2001 Frances Gendlin
Design Copyright © 2011 Marshall Cavendish International (Asia) Private Limited
All rights reserved

No part of this publication may be reproduced, stored in a retrieval system or transmitted, in any form or by any means, electronic, mechanical, photocopying, recording or otherwise, without the prior permission of the copyright owner. Request for permission should be addressed to the Publisher, Marshall Cavendish International (Asia) Private Limited, 1 New Industrial Road, Singapore 536196. Tel: (65) 6213 9300, fax: (65) 6285 4871. E-mail: genref@sg.marshallcavendish.com

The publisher makes no representation or warranties with respect to the contents of this book, and specifically disclaims any implied warranties or merchantability or fitness for any particular purpose, and shall in no events be liable for any loss of profit or any other commercial damage, including but not limited to special, incidental, consequential, or other damages.

Other Marshall Cavendish Offices:
Marshall Cavendish International (Asia) Private Limited. 1 New Industrial Road, Singapore 536196 ■ Marshall Cavendish International. PO Box 65829, London EC1P 1NY, UK ■ Marshall Cavendish International (Thailand) Co Ltd. 253 Asoke, 12th Flr, Sukhumvit 21 Road, Klongtoey Nua, Wattana, Bangkok 10110, Thailand ■ Marshall Cavendish (Malaysia) Sdn Bhd, Times Subang, Lot 46, Subang Hi-Tech Industrial Park, Batu Tiga, 40000 Shah Alam, Selangor Darul Ehsan, Malaysia

Marshall Cavendish is a trademark of Times Publishing Limited

ISBN: 978-0-7614-5876-0

Please contact the publisher for the Library of Congress catalogue number

Printed in Singapore by Times Printers Private Limited

Photo Credits:
All photos by San Francisco Convention & Visitors Bureau except page 60 (Age Fotostock/Adam Jones); page 66 (Age Fotostock/Renaud Visage); page 134 (Eleanor Burke); pages xiii, 21, 27, 33, 62, 167, 198, 322, 345 (Photolibrary). ■ Cover photo: Photolibrary.

All illustrations by TRIGG. Map on page xvi by John Zaugg.

ABOUT THE SERIES

Culture shock is a state of disorientation that can come over anyone who has been thrust into unknown surroundings, away from one's comfort zone. *CultureShock!* is a series of trusted and reputed guides which has, for decades, been helping expatriates and long-term visitors to cushion the impact of culture shock whenever they move to a new country.

Written by people who have lived in the country and experienced culture shock themselves, the authors share all the information necessary for anyone to cope with these feelings of disorientation more effectively. The guides are written in a style that is easy to read and covers a range of topics that will arm readers with enough advice, hints and tips to make their lives as normal as possible again.

Each book is structured in the same manner. It begins with the first impressions that visitors will have of that city or country. To understand a culture, one must first understand the people—where they came from, who they are, the values and traditions they live by, as well as their customs and etiquette. This is covered in the first half of the book.

Then on with the practical aspects—how to settle in with the greatest of ease. Authors walk readers through topics such as how to find accommodation, get the utilities and telecommunications up and running, enrol the children in school and keep in the pink of health. But that's not all. Once the essentials are out of the way, venture out and try the food, enjoy more of the culture and travel to other areas. Then be immersed in the language of the country before discovering more about the business side of things.

To round off, snippets of basic information are offered before readers are 'tested' on customs and etiquette of the country. Useful words and phrases, a comprehensive resource guide and list of books for further research are also included for easy reference.

CONTENTS

Acknowledgements vi
Note vii
Dedication viii
Introduction ix
Map of San Francisco xvi

Chapter 1
First Impressions — 1

Chapter 2
Overview of the City and its History — 8

The City by the Bay	9
Climate	11
Earthquakes	13
Thinking about Place	14
District by District: Finding Your Own	16
Yet Questions Persist	49
And Around the Bay	49

Chapter 3
The People by the Bay — 54

So, What Are They Like?	57
A Sense of Humor	58
Gays in the City	60
Making It Work	63

Chapter 4
Socializing in San Francisco — 64

Finding Your Social Niche	65
The Ethos	67
Some Helpful Hints	68

Chapter 5
Settling In — 71

Formalities for Foreigners	72
Finding Your Nest	82
Making Yourself at Home	99
A Child's World	118
The Student Life	136
To Your Health!	146
Up and Down the Hills	157
Shopping at Your Door	181

Chapter 6
Food Lovers' Haven — 199

Gastronomic Superlatives	200
Eating Out in Asia	231
Gourmet Dining at Home: The Markets	242
Watering Holes	258

Chapter 7
Enjoying the Good Life — 271

The Sporting Scene	272
Culture—High and Low!	287
Films	300
National Holidays and Local Events	304
And More Around The Bay: The Wine Country	310
Over Land and On The Sea	320

Chapter 8
Learning the Language — 331

English in the City	332

Chapter 9
Business and Employment — 335

Work and Business on the Pacific Rim	336
Starting a Business	337
The Job Search	342

Chapter 10
San Francisco at a Glance — 347

Some Well-known Americans	352
Abbreviations, Acronyms... ...and Slang	356
Culture Quiz	357
Do's and Don'ts	365
Resource Guide	368
Further Reading	378
About the Author	380
Index	381

ACKNOWLEDGEMENTS

San Franciscans, as you will come to understand, are an opinionated lot. My friends and colleagues in The City By the Bay cheerfully gave me helpful suggestions for information to be included in the first edition of this book, and they were no doubt either gratified or disappointed upon reading it. (None said they were disappointed. I didn't ask.) Nonetheless, I truly did appreciate their comments, their willingness to try new restaurants and to drive around the far reaches of the city with me, and to participate with me in my musings about what makes San Francisco tick. In these regards, I was especially appreciative of Fred Allardyce, Eleanor Burke, Helen Cohn, Jean Coyner, Robert Domush, Jaem Heath-O'Ryan, Allan Jacobs, the late Edith Jenkins, Faye Jones, James Keough, Sarah Keough, Andy Leakakos, Peter Linenthal, Ann Magennis, Ronda Nasuti, Les Plack, Candida Quinn, Ken Rosselot, Newby Schweitzer, Linda Sparrowe, Patricia Unterman, Al Williams, and John Zaugg. And for this current edition, I am grateful to the San Francisco Convention and Visitors Center, whose materials were timely and helpful. Marsha Felton, Diane Johnson and John Murray, Mary Duncan, Jim Iwersen, and Joy Eckel also made the task easier, so I thank them, as well.

With so much varied and detailed information, all guide books, no matter how current, suffer from suddenly outdated information or an error or two. So, regardless of all our efforts, there may be a mistake here and there concerning a business that has suddenly disappeared or a neighborhood that has changed perhaps almost overnight. If there are any such errors, they are, of course, mine alone. Some things are sure, however. There is an old joke among chauvinistic San Franciscans, that "one of these days there will be a big earthquake here, and the rest of the country will fall into the sea." But as of the book's publication, at least, the city was intact: the "big one" had not hit and San Francisco and the rest of the continent were still firmly attached. So, if other things have changed, as of course they must, or if something more expensive has replaced what once was, take it in stride. Just enjoy San Francisco for what it is—on that particular day. The next day it might be something different, after all.

NOTE

Readers may be surprised to find some spelling inconsistencies and should understand that this has more to do with the American psyche than a malfunction of the word processor. Although our American ancestors rebelled against the British and forged their own language and spelling of certain words—"theater" and "center," for example—some current Americans seem to find British spelling more elegant. Thus there will appear here a "shopping centre" or two and a "theatre" or two amid the centers and theaters, but it doesn't matter, for they are American in every important regard. The same holds true for the word "cafe," which is American, but which may variously be spelled "caffè" or "café," depending on the nationality or whim of the owner of the establishment.

Where services or shops will be sought out owing to their location (e.g. bakeries), they are listed by the neighborhood closest to them; where the services might be needed no matter where they happen to be (e.g. churches), they are listed alphabetically or by category. Also, Internet addresses have been included for information that readers might reasonably want to access online—such as housing options, visa formalities, business advice—but not for every Internet address in this totally cyber-friendly city. When possible, do check the websites for the most current information.

Readers should note that guidelines about regulations, addresses, and Internet sites were current as of Spring 2010, to the best of our research and knowledge. The author and publisher bear no responsibility for any changes in immigration laws (which have been strengthened considerably since 2001 and continue to change without notice), prices that have risen since this writing, quality of products or accommodations, the disappearance of a shop, the occasional bad meal (yes—rare but true even in San Francisco) or any other inconvenience that might arise. San Franciscans may be faithful, but they are also fickle and spontaneous, and the city changes day by day

DEDICATION

To Newby

INTRODUCTION

Welcome to San Francisco, certainly the most open and probably the most tolerant city in the United States. This is a city where you can not only openly be who you are, you can also try being whatever it is you want to be. Just about anything goes, whether you have come to make a fortune or to squander one, whether you have decided to join the established culture or any one of the myriad counter-cultures that call San Francisco home. Just think of the city's changing nicknames. In the 1850s the city was called "The Barbary Coast," when rowdy gold miners recalled the old-time Barbary pirates. For a time it was even called "Baghdad by the Bay," when that city was still exotic and untouched. Current appellations, however, demonstrate the city's pride in what it has accomplished: "The City That Knows How," or even the proud "City by the Bay." But most San Franciscans just call it "The City," as though it were the only one—as for many residents it is. One nickname it does not ever have—at least for locals—is Frisco. Do not call the city Frisco.

A San Francisco Year
- 16.4 million visitors
- US$ 8.5 billion spent by visitors (US$ 22 million per day)
- US$ 527 million in tax and fee revenues for the city
- 77,856 jobs supporting the visitor industry
- 32,866 hotel rooms
- 14 percent hotel tax
- 1,432 licensed taxicabs
- 7.9 million cable car rides
- 39 million vehicles cross the Golden Gate Bridge

About 16 million visitors a year come to "everyone's favorite city." You might think the reasons obvious: San Francisco is the most beautiful—ravishing—cosmopolitan city in the United States, with clean air, sparkling water on three sides, steep hills rising in the middle of the city, and breathtaking views. Quaint cable cars clang up and down the hills, and exotic aromas waft through the streets. People are outgoing and friendly. And when the sun shines and the sky is bright blue, it feels as though there is no other city in the world where you would want to be. But although beauty and charm stretch far, they do not tell the entire story. The deeper story unfolds as you come to understand the city and its residents, as time goes on.

Some of San Francisco's substance, of course, is in plain view. Perched on the Pacific Rim, the city is home to some of the most important banks and trade institutions in the country. It is the northern focus of Silicon Valley—an area that may not appear on any map, but which nonetheless commands much of the world's high technology development and trade. It is a port for passenger cruises. It has an outstanding opera company, symphony orchestra, and ballet, plus impressive art museums and galleries. It has excellent universities, hospitals, and research institutions. It has a glorious climate and beautiful parks and promenades from which to enjoy it all. And it has some of the best restaurants in the country.

You can find all this in a standard tourist guide, of course. Such guides describe the city and its unique attractions in detail, review restaurants, and suggest hotels of all categories. Each has its own approach to capturing the spirit of this enchanting city by the sea—and in the most eye-catching manner possible. All, however, have one thing in common: they are designed only for people visiting for a short while—visitors who think that what they see in a week is what the city is all about.

It is true that you can get a general idea of the magnetism of this city in a short time, and that is a good start. Certainly, many of the things you have heard about The City by the Bay do ring somewhat true. Definitely it is charming at its core, always vibrant, ever pushing toward the future. And its beauty does stretch far. That Tony Bennett has sung to the world "I left my heart in San Francisco" is no mistake. But it is also odd, offbeat, perhaps even outrageous in some ways, and its outright iconoclasm contributes a great deal to its delicious mystique. When you begin to understand the city's acceptance of the unusual and its constant search for any next frontier, you will realize that it wholeheartedly embraces the new, which should be important to you if you are coming for a longer stay, perhaps even to settle in.

And, if you are here for a while, you will need that extra look, those extra clues as to how The City works. This book, thus, although offering information for the first-time visitor, also focuses on where tourism ends and where daily life begins. Whether your stay is for a month or two or a year or two, the type of information you need for a successful stay is different—deeper and more detailed than that found in the standard tourist guides. How to choose a neighborhood that suits you, where to find the most interesting markets and shops, how best to get up and down the hills or commute in from other towns, how to cope with the difficulties of finding (almost) affordable housing or the right school for your children, and, of course, how to find out what is going on at any day of the year—these are just a few examples of basic information that should help you maneuver comfortably within the San Francisco scene.

So, what will you find here? A city to take seriously, no matter what you have heard about the eclectic lifestyles and iconoclasm of its residents. As in any city in the world, daily life rules: if San Franciscans are known for playing hard, they work hard, too. In the soaring office buildings of the Financial District and in the funky warehouses of the Inner Mission (sometimes called Multimedia Gulch), workers earn salaries that, on average, are among the highest in the country; more than half of the city's residents hold college or professional degrees. Locals spend their dollars in almost 13,000 retail businesses and eat out in more than 4,000 restaurants, all of which must appeal to a population that demands creativity and excellence—and something ever new to tickle its fancy for novelty. Even the municipality itself has done its best to make its urban life attractive and rewarding. Where other cities have seen their downtowns collapse as people fled to the suburbs, San Francisco has conscientiously upgraded its own with the Moscone Convention Center, Yerba Buena

Gardens, Museum of Modern Art, the light rail system, the refurbished waterfront, and the vibrant downtown AT&T Baseball Park.

Businesses that manage to capture the changing, eclectic tastes of San Franciscans tend to succeed. Yet those that do not often see failure as an opportunity to start again, to reinvent themselves with a different—even more novel—approach. The city has always been known for its creative energy, and, since Gold Rush times, for taking risks. If the area is on the cutting edge of technology and finance now, think back to 1853 when Levi Strauss came to San Francisco to work with his brother-in-law. By 1871, they had received a patent for securing the seams of their duck twill work pants with copper saddlebag rivets. Now the headquarters of the multi-million dollar Levi Strauss & Company sits in its own lovely green park along the Embarcadero, and the company provides more than 1,000 people with work.

On the other hand, there is a lot not to take seriously in The City by the Bay. What contributes to the very energy and essence of San Francisco is the attitude that makes living here downright fun. This book also describes the area's myriad sporting opportunities, the friskiness of the population, the varying Chinese cuisines and their eateries—both upscale and definitely not—and some cultural—and decidedly non-cultural—events. What it cannot impart in detail—but you will soon find out for yourself—is how the light-hearted and quirky nature of the city's population contributes to what makes San Francisco the way it is, a place like nowhere else.

The city, of course, has its problems. Although it is often rated near the top of "quality of life" surveys, and its workers earn above the national average, the cost of living in the Bay Area also ranks among the highest in the country and is the highest in the state. This is owing to a lack of affordable housing, brought about by a shortage of housing in general and the willingness of well-paid professionals to pay high rents and purchase prices. Housing in the Bay Area—for both purchases and rentals—costs significantly more than in most areas of the country, and San Francisco has

Union Square. Dating from the 1850s, this beautifully modernized public plaza is the focal point for the downtown shopping area.

been rated as one of the country's most overpriced cities. Although prices may have fallen somewhat during the recent financial crises, they are still much higher then the national average, and some people are concerned that San Francisco may in the future become a city dominated by the interests of the rich. And it is true that families with children are finding life in other regions of the Bay Area more affordable and just about as pleasant. And, San Francisco is not very far away.

Other top problems facing the city's residents are a public transportation system that has not always transported well, and, as in other major urban areas, there are too many homeless people on the streets. A succession of mayoral candidates has used homelessness as a campaign issue, and those elected come into office with big plans, only to find that, without being able to address the causes of homelessness, few "Band-Aid" solutions actually work. Mayors also set out to address the problems of transportation and parking, affordable housing, and more serious crime, and occasionally it seems—at least temporarily—that some progress is being made.

San Francisco also has its undesirable elements, its occasional robberies and muggings. Yet women need take only the usual precautions of staying on well-traveled streets and jogging in the parks with friends on designated paths and in daylight hours. And there should be no reason at all for anyone to enter the Tenderloin alone at night—that area between Union Square and the Civic Center that might in other cities be termed "skid row"—or Hunters Point to the south. Some other neighborhoods that are trendy in some spots—the Mission, Western Addition, Lower Haight—also occasionally have their pockets of problematical areas. But these areas are few, and they too have their agreeable streets and attitudes.

All in all, as you will shortly discover, San Francisco is—and it also is not—just like any other city. This book should help you find that out as you begin to make your way. Scout out the neighborhoods it describes, stroll the outdoor markets, experiment with unfamiliar dishes in offbeat Asian eateries. Get to know your neighbors and your colleagues at work, for San Franciscans are welcoming folk. Volunteer in your community. Spend Sundays in one of the city's beautiful parks, go whale watching not far offshore, and find the view that best makes your own heart soar. San Francisco's Convention & Visitors Bureau says that the three commandments when visiting San Francisco are to "explore, experience, and enjoy." When you join long-time San Franciscans in following these "commandments," soon you too will understand what led the city's beloved writer Alice Adams to term San Francisco "the last lovely city." Welcome home.

MAP OF SAN FRANCISCO

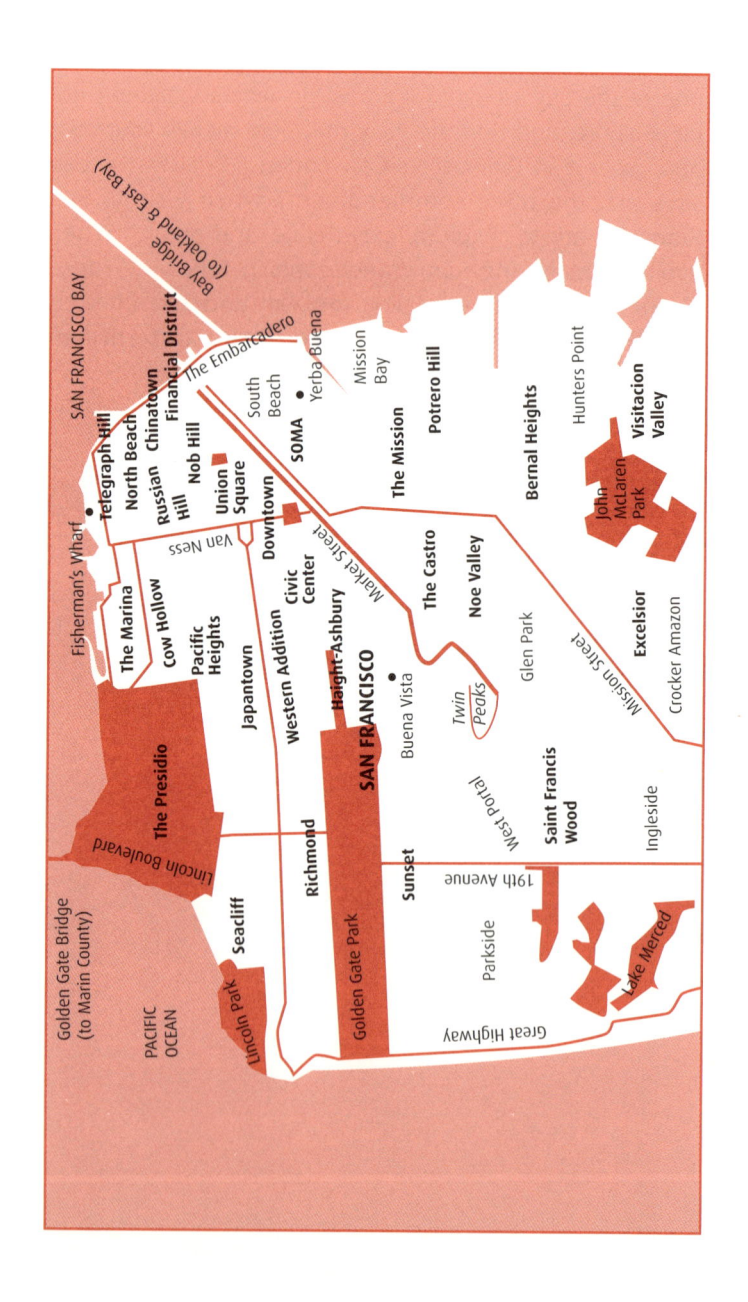

FIRST IMPRESSIONS

CHAPTER 1

'No city invites the heart to come to life as
San Francisco does.'
—William Saroyan

ON THE SUMMER MORNING your plane arrives in San Francisco, you've already been wondering if everything you've heard about the city is true. Is it really the most beautiful city in the United States? The most cosmopolitan, like a European city? Well, you're here for a meeting and have come two days early, just to find out. So, after your cab has deposited you at a downtown hotel on what looks to be a cool, cloudy day and you've checked in, you set out to see for yourself, city map in hand. You'll start with the Union Square area downtown, then see if you can find Chinatown to get a bite to eat, and perhaps go to North Beach on one those cable cars that seem to be symbolic of the city. You've heard that the Italian cafés in North Beach not only have good coffee, they're excellent for "people watching," too. You carry a jacket—just in case.

And then as you start your walk, the wind hits you full force. Unrelenting, damp. It's whipping along the canyons of tall office buildings as you forge your way through the Financial District up to Union Square. You can't see the tops of the buildings for the fog. So, you've got your jacket on, zipped up, and are glad that you read somewhere that only uninformed tourists wear shorts and sandals in "summery" San Francisco. People talk about the lovely climate here. Surely, they can't mean this.

You cut through the Crocker Galleria, three levels of open balconies with shops and cafés that look interesting, and you make a mental note to come back. And then ahead you see Union Square, up some steps. A group of colorfully-dressed Latin American musicians are playing their pipes, creating a lively air. One of the musicians nods at you as you pass by on your way up. And suddenly you are charmed. The old plaza—no matter how modernly restored—is captivating, overlooking its bustling surroundings. There's a human scale, the buildings are low, and there aren't any fogbound skyscrapers here. You can imagine what it must have looked like a century ago. Down the steps again, you circle the square to browse the windows of Saks, Tiffany, Nieman Marcus, and Macy's, and you even wander in to look at the lobby of the famous Saint Francis hotel. The cable car is clanging by as you come out, and people even seem to be hanging off the sides. Watching as it works its way up a steep hill, you decide that yes, this isn't to be missed.

Chinatown is marked on the map, so you turn on Grant Avenue, glancing right and left, seeing that this downtown area offers a lot but is not overwhelming. You look up, straight ahead. And there it is: the Chinatown Gate! Spanning Grant Avenue where it narrows, it's a tall welcoming entrance with a tiled roof like a pagoda, painted red and green, the Chinese colors of prosperity. So here you are, possibly being beckoned into another world. You quicken your steps, not minding the upward incline. At first there are gift shops to the right and left: the windows show jade and gold, silks, artworks, and Chinese tourist kitsch, of course. But buying souvenirs for the family is for another day, so you walk on. It's not so cold now, and a bright blue sky is showing through in patches as the fog is beginning to lift. In fact, you're almost ready to take your jacket off.

And then the restaurants appear, their wafting aromas trying to lure you in. "Eat where the Chinese do," your boss advised, so you look in. But there are Asians in all of them, so you keep on. You turn up steep Washington Street and see that the signs are all in Chinese! Now on Stockton it doesn't seem like America any longer. Ancient-looking women with their shopping bags are shouting in Chinese to the fruit vendors, gesturing at piles of vegetables, the likes of which you've never seen before. The descriptions are in Chinese but the prices are not, and they are incredibly cheap. The fish markets, open to the sidewalk, also have their lines, if this pell-mell assortment of people can be called a line. Buckets of fish line the floor below those above that are in cases or on ice. Some of the women in mismatched clothes and black cloth sandals—they could even be great-grandmothers—have fabric slings tied firmly across their chests, with a baby snuggled, almost swaddled, behind.

Now you notice there are so many little eateries you don't think you could make a choice. So, you just go into the next. There are cooked, crispy ducks hanging in the windows, and a huge vat of what must be soup is bubbling on a burner, as well. And it's clear that no one is speaking English, not one word.

The waiter zipping by points to a large round table where five businessmen in suits are talking in Chinese while eating their lunch, chopsticks in one hand, rice bowl in the other. They don't look up as you take the remaining seat. There's a pitcher of water on the table, and at your place a handwritten menu that, thank heavens, has English translations under the listings in Chinese. There are also a yellow plastic glass, chopsticks, and a paper napkin, but no fork. You look to see what the men are eating. Are those chicken feet? And what is that meat in brownish sauce? The guy next to you is shoveling it in, so it must be good. You've heard about authentic Chinese food in San Francisco. It looks like you've come to the right place.

So when the waiter halts just briefly in front of you, although you had been thinking of that delicious-looking duck, you point to what your neighbor is having. And instead of tea, which all the others are drinking, you take a chance and order a Diet Coke. It may be China, but it's America, too, is it not? And in almost the blink of an eye, an enormous meal is thrust in front of you—first soup and then the main course with rice, along with the Coke. The man next to you gives you a quick nod of approval, but then looks down to his rice bowl once again. You don't know exactly how to describe your meal—"beef and vegetables" doesn't do it justice—but you'd come back for it again, any day. Being here reminds you that there's a celebrated Asian Art Museum, a must for tomorrow, the last free day before your meeting begins. Finally, when the bill is set before you, you can't read it, for it's scrawled in Chinese, but since it's only US$ 6.50 including the Coke, you couldn't care less. On the way out you give your own nod of approval at two other tourists who have come in and are now looking around, wondering what to order. That's all.

And when you're back on the sidewalk, contentedly replete, something is different. You realize that the entire sky is clear and the air is warm. In fact, the sky is of a blue so startling it almost takes your breath away. The street seems to sparkle as you walk up to Mason Street to wait for the cable car. You realize as you climb, that you've walked just about across the whole downtown, and that San Francisco is a "walking city," despite the hills you've climbed and see just ahead. You don't wait long, but when the cable car arrives, it's full, or so you think. Yet people adjust themselves to make a space for you, so you jump on, finding a pole to hold on to to steady yourself. The gripman rings his bell, and off you go.

North Beach is too close, so you ride until the end of the line, only a few streets from the famous Fisherman's Wharf. The meeting organizers have planned for a group dinner out here one night, so instead of stopping here, you stroll along the promenade, noticing a brightly colored antique-looking trolley car discharging passengers for their own afternoon at the Wharf. But you're going to Pier 39 where you've heard that there are actually sea lions living right in the city, and darned if it isn't true! Only a few today, but they're basking and barking and lounging on their piers, and an official sign cautions people against bothering them in any way. Along with everyone else, you take a picture or two. Then, before doing anything else, you get a cup of coffee and walk around to the end of Pier 39.

And there at the end is the most incredible panorama a city could ever have! Unbelievable! The glistening bay, the Golden Gate itself, mountains across the water, and the glorious unending sky, still that piercing blue, the air now quite warm. You lean against the rail, sip your coffee, never wanting to move, almost overawed. Finally, you whisk past the tourist shops, you glide along the moving walkway of the Aquarium, and then you are out once again onto the street. You're thinking tiredly of the long walk back to your hotel, and perhaps of a nap.

But San Francisco accommodates, and there approaching the corner is one of those colorful trolley cars, and you— along with several others—flag it down, somewhat relieved to catch the ride. The tracks run along the Embarcadero, the broad boulevard that parallels the bay, and with stately palms guiding the way, you're soon back downtown; And tight asleep on a comfortable bed only a few minutes after that. A fresh sea breeze, a healthy walk, and a delicious lunch are all it took.

Later, in the hotel lobby you run into a colleague also arriving for the meeting, so you agree to spend the evening together. Outside, it's still quite balmy, and the breeze has died down. What will it be? North Beach and an Italian evening, or a walk down Market Street to the Ferry Building? No, you agree to meet there early in the morning to take in the Farmers Market and then the ferry, perhaps to visit Sausalito. And later, the Asian Art Museum for you and the Museum of Modern Art for your friend. There's clearly too much to do, and too little time. You've both got your jackets at the ready, and you decide to take the cable car from its starting point at Market Street and get to North Beach.

For the first few streets, it's flat, but as the car reaches Kearny Street it gets steep, and then steeper and steeper yet. And the car is climbing and everyone is smiling. You pass Grant Avenue where you had walked earlier in the day, and finally you get off at Powell, where your friend hails another bell-clanging cable car that is coming up the hill. This one is heading north, and as the other chugged up, this one—after a few minutes—glides down, and then down some more. The cable cars are a National Landmark, and you can see why.

When you are once again on foot, at Saint Francis Square, you stroll around and look at the works at an art fair there. You chat with a photographer, thinking to buy his photo of the sea lions, but you don't, for you want to see how your own come out. And then you walk south on Columbus, past the famous coffee houses and perhaps as many Italian restaurants as there were Chinese earlier in the day. Your friend has heard of a place that specializes in garlic, the Stinking Rose. That suits you just fine, and the place turns out to be as good as advertised. An hour or so later, when you come out (with several business cards in your pocket to give to friends back home), it's cooling off and you put your jacket back on. Suddenly you remember something else you once heard about San Francisco, that it does have four seasons, but they all just happen in one day! You tell your friend, and you both nod in agreement and laugh.

Strolling back to the hotel, you look at the streets, into the restaurant windows, wishing there were more time. And then you hear a low blast of noise. It's a real foghorn, clearly announcing the fog starting to come back in. But now you understand and can't wait for that afternoon warm blue sky. And, just before you end this first day, you decide to have a drink at the top of your hotel whose lounge boasts of a spectacular view of San Francisco and the bay. The lights of the city are twinkling below the fog that is now drifting in, and you and your friend sit rather quietly with your glasses in front of you—a California Cabernet that the waiter has recommended. You look out at the lights, and you mull over what you've seen on this first day, and whether San Francisco lives up to its reputation for charm.

And if this first day at the city had been yours, what would you conclude?

OVERVIEW OF THE CITY AND ITS HISTORY

CHAPTER 2

'San Francisco is 49 square miles surrounded by reality.'
—Paul Kantner (Jefferson Airplane)

THE CITY BY THE BAY

Then …

When the founding fathers of the United States were signing the Declaration of Independence in 1776, what is now San Francisco had only recently been discovered and was still wild lands and sand dunes as far as the eye could see. That people date this "discovery" to 1769 by Spanish soldiers looking for Monterey Bay of course doesn't take into account the thousand years the area had already been inhabited by the native Miwok, Ohlones, and Wintuns, hunters and gatherers who were quickly subjugated by the intruders and then overcome by their domination and diseases. The soldiers and missionaries coming to control and convert these native peoples very shortly did them in.

One wonders whether those Spanish soldiers were as awed by the beauty of their find as we are today. The sandy shoreline they took over was backed by soaring cliffs. Rocky hills were covered with live oaks and sweet-smelling grasses, and the ever-shifting sand dunes reached toward little inland marshes and streams, borne by the constant ocean breeze. But, as with the native peoples, even the bay we currently see, spectacular as it is, is not as the Spaniards found it, for some 40 percent has been filled in. Bay waters originally came as far as what is now Montgomery Street, lapping at Kearny Street, and the Marina was dredged only for the 1915

Panama-Pacific Exposition. By Francisco and Taylor Streets there once was a protected sandy cove called North Beach, but now all that remains is the name.

The Spanish named the area Yerba Buena, after those herbal grasses on the hills. By 1776, Juan Bautista de Anza and his contingent of 200 Spanish soldiers had established the Presidio, a fort that commanded a strategic overlook of both ocean and bay, and it remained a military base until a little more than a decade ago. By 1776, too, the priest Junipero Serra had founded the sixth of the Franciscan missions that stretched up the 600-mile Alta California coast, several years later dedicating what is now known as Mission Dolores, an adobe building which still stands.

Although the areas that are now the Mission District and the Presidio were the first to be settled, the original village of Yerba Buena was founded along the city's easternmost waterfront. Yerba Buena Plaza, now Portsmouth Square in Chinatown, was the heart of the village, which was first Spanish, then Mexican, and finally, in 1846, American. The town also rolled down the hill to the waterfront and today the old brick buildings on streets with names such as Balance Street and Gold Street still attest to their role during the Gold Rush, a century and a half ago.

It may be that only a few buildings remain, but the spirit of a city determined by the 1849 discovery of gold persists today. While thousands of adventurers seeking quick fortunes came to the Sierra foothills, clever merchants of all sorts readied their wares to take some of that fortune for themselves. Restaurants, bordellos, hotels and rooming houses, groceries, baths, and laundries almost exploded overnight around the Barbary Coast. Banks and financial services set themselves up toward Montgomery Street. Levi Strauss started producing his trousers. And a sleepy town that a short while before had counted only 500 residents with one newspaper became a city of 35,000 with twelve dailies on the country's western edge. The discovery of silver—the 1859 Comstock Lode—brought more speculation and wealth, immigrants, and workers and services to keep them all. By the end of the century the city held ten times that 35,000, and today, with the population having doubled from that, the frontier spirit holds—in the soaring steel and glass downtown office buildings, with this century's financial adventurers looking out, this time over the Pacific Rim.

San Francisco's colorful history may not be long—just over 200 years—and earthquakes and fires have taken their toll. But the city's background is still visible in some of its streets, and it is also evident in its residents' continuingly iconoclastic attitudes toward life, focusing on opportunities seen and grasped, whether at work or at play.

And Now ...

Today, the City of San Francisco makes up the entire San Francisco County, the most important of the nine counties comprising the Bay Area. Yet it is the smallest of the nine, and almost half of it is water, most of it San Francisco Bay. In fact, it is the smallest county in the state. Situated on about the same latitude as Tokyo and Washington D.C., the beautiful, hilly, wind-swept city sits at the top of a peninsula, and its land area encompasses 46.7 square miles (121 sq km), just 7 miles (11.3 km) across. Only since 1937 has the city been connected to the north and east by its two famous bridges, and ferries that have long brought people to the city still traverse the sparkling bay. The city itself swells like the ocean tides: each day it accommodates 200,000 workers who commute in from around the Bay Area, plus, over the course of a year, 16 million visitors—tourists and conventioneers—who filter through.

CLIMATE

To simplify what is truly complex, the city's climate is determined by the ocean, by the 40 or so hills that break or conduct the ever-present wind, and by the long Central Valley that cuts down the middle of the state. When the Central Valley swelters in the summer and the foothills are golden and dry, the hot air rises, as it must. This forces cold ocean air to whip through the natural opening of the Golden Gate to cool the eastern valleys, but bringing to the city foggy days and brisk winds that move bitingly through the streets. Sometimes the fog burns off by late morning and early afternoons can be clear and warm. Other times, however, the fog hovers and does not move for days, leaving visitors surprised that they need a jacket in mid-summer and residents amused by the tourists in their shorts and tee shirts, hunched against the wind. Conversely, when the Central Valley cools off in September and October, San Francisco can have its sunniest summer days, with its temperatures even reaching about 90°F (32.2°C) for a day or two. This is when diehard San Franciscans complain the most, bemoaning the absence of their beloved fog.

Winter itself is cool and damp, but not really cold. Although climate is changeable in San Francisco, as it seems to be everywhere these days, there has traditionally been a winter "rainy season" and a summer "dry season," but there is never a season of snow. Rains can be gentle or hard, but there are rarely thunderstorms, and usually part of each day is clear. With the city rarely seeing temperatures below freezing, flowers bloom outdoors in the winter, athletes play tennis in shorts and sweatshirts, office workers eat their sandwiches at outdoor tables, and people walk to work wearing light wool jackets—perhaps carrying an umbrella, just in case. On those rare occasions when a flake or two of snow does appear, so do the amazed telephone calls: "Did you see the snow?" People love snow, though, as long as it is in the Sierra, so they can head past the vivid green hills, up to the mountains to ski.

> Get the extensive *San Francisco Visitors Planning Guide* at the Visitor Information Center, 900 Market Street, downstairs at Hallidie Plaza. Or download it at http://www.nxtbook.com/nxtbooks/weaver/sfovg208/

Within San Francisco are about a half-dozen separate microclimates, depending on which side of which hill or valley you are looking at and the patterns of the winds. No matter where, however, the climate is bracing and the average annual temperature is about 55°F (12.8°C). Generally, the areas near the ocean are the foggiest and most cool, as are the summits of the highest hills. Areas away from the ocean and on the lee sides of hills—SoMa, the Mission, Noe Valley, and the Castro, for instance—are often sunny when other parts of the city are socked in or enshrouded by fog, and in fact, these are the warmest parts of town.

EARTHQUAKES

It is a fact one has to admit: San Francisco sits above the intersection of several of the earth's tectonic plates. Earthquakes regularly assault the entire Bay Area, owing to adjustments in the rifts of those nearby plates: the famous San Andreas and Hayward faults, as well as the San Gregorio, Greenville, and Calaveras faults. Two major tremblers, two "big ones," are still remembered with awe: the 1906 quake, registering 8.0 on the Richter scale, whose fiery aftermath all but destroyed the city; and the lesser one in 1989, registering 6.9, which caused great damage and a restructuring of the downtown waterfront.

No matter how long people have lived here, everyone talks about the occasional minor quakes and tremors, and few people get used to the even more rare large seismic jolts. Despite nervous jokes about "waiting for the big one," the dangers earthquakes present do not seem to drive people away. All recently constructed apartment and office buildings in the city must be "earthquake-proof," which means they might sway during a quake, but should not collapse.

Nonetheless, earthquakes remain dangerous, and if they worry you, you might consider living away from the faults in one of the other counties of the Bay Area where the risk is perhaps somewhat less. Scientists are now saying there is a 70 percent chance of a major quake within the next 30 years, and although no one knows exactly when the next "big one" will come, everyone knows that it will.

But earthquakes, for better or worse, bring new beginnings. After the 1906 "big one" destroyed some 25,000 buildings in the eastern part of the city, a modern, well-planned city rose from the ashes, today's downtown districts. And after the 1989 Loma Prieta quake damaged the freeway that hid the city's waterfront, San Franciscans—who had always wished the eyesore would somehow just go away—voted to demolish it and to refurbish the three-mile strip, reclaiming it beautifully for their own. Now the Ferry Building and clock tower that withstood both "big ones" are visible at the foot of Market Street and can once again be a symbol of city pride.

THINKING ABOUT PLACE

San Francisco is, by and large, a residential city. Its major businesses and largest banks cluster in the eastern portion that became the city's financial hub during the Gold Rush, and the rest—extremely diverse residential areas—maintain the local services and shops that residents of each area would expect. The city calls its widespread areas "districts," and their names often reflect their history, such as the Mission or Cow Hollow. Yet the hills and their microclimates, and the lifestyle each area has molded, have created myriad little neighborhoods with names of their own, and it should not be surprising that in such an individualistic city each area has its own character, often fiercely defended. Some of these neighborhoods may take more understanding than others, and some may display distinctly different characteristics even just from block to block, such as in the Mission or Western Addition. Many are charming and welcoming. Some are warm, sunny, and relaxed, some foggy, wind-swept, and brisk. Some are known for their social activism, some clearly defined by their ethnicity. Some are slightly more reasonably priced than others, but in any neighborhood worth considering, this will not last. And only a very few are not worth considering at all.

Some San Franciscans regard the eastern part of the city as urbanized and progressive and the western parts as more suburban and conservative. It is true that although neighborhoods overlap and populations change as prices rise and older districts become gentrified, people still tend to be characterized by the districts they call home. This, however, is beginning to change. In fact, the ethnic and social population is diffuse, and the city's balanced cultural diversity constitutes a great part of its cosmopolitan charm. While Pacific Heights is known to be predominately wealthy Caucasian, the Castro gay, Chinatown Chinese, the Mission Latino, and the Western Addition African-American, in general there is a pleasing—and sometimes surprising—ethnic distribution throughout the city. Asians are now predominant in the area around Clement Street, and a diverse mix of San Franciscans has been moving into the Mission, Bernal Heights, Potrero Hill, and The Haight—all areas where people took advantage of the few remaining reasonably priced homes—of course now having driven the prices up. In fact, young professionals—unmarried and childless—with an abundance of discretionary dollars to spend on housing are moving into all the different neighborhoods, bringing life and color to those areas that were once uninspired, or, conversely, that were once considered only private enclaves of the rich.

As in any city, some districts are more open, beautiful, or well-kept than others. No matter where you live, however, you will have access to open space, whether it is the sandy strips that form the miles of ocean beaches or the wide concrete promenade that runs alongside the Bay. If the eastern half of the city, destroyed in the 1906 earthquake, does not see as many leafy streets as its western counterpart, green squares and large landscaped plazas nonetheless pleasantly dot the area, allowing spectacular views of the nearby mountains and the often bright blue, almost iridescent, sky. Away from downtown, large parks, both sculpted and wild—Buena Vista, Glen Canyon, McClaren, and Harding—offer as many attractions, in their own ways, as the city's two most famous, the Presidio and Golden Gate Park.

Each district, naturally, abuts at least one other. Sometimes there is a dividing boulevard or street or a hill, but sometimes just a subtle sense of change. In some areas, just one small street will mean the difference between an area you would consider for housing and one you might not. Although all the districts are given a broad look on the next pages, some mini-neighborhoods may not be mentioned, only partly for lack of space. Some are too small to describe and, given the overwhelming need for housing, some are in the process of change or rebirth; these may lose their longtime flavor to gentrification, or they may not, if residents of those areas have their way. In any case, change is what San Francisco is all about.

DISTRICT BY DISTRICT: FINDING YOUR OWN

Downtown

Until just about a decade ago San Franciscans characterized their city as "North of Market" or "South of Market," for these areas that bordered the long bisecting Market Street were quite distinct—both in commercial feel and in their residents' approach to life. Now, of course, the downtown still encompasses the old Union Square to the north of Market Street, and it is still the focal point of the central part of the city. But it also encompasses a dozen streets or more to the south of Market Street, in an area called SoMa (South of Market), which has added a new vivacity and trendiness to what was once a staid commercial set of blocks surrounding the square. The south side of Market Street itself now boasts two enormous modern shopping malls, and just behind there are some of San Francisco's major cultural attractions—The Museum of Modern Art, Yerba Buena Gardens, the Moscone Convention Center, and the Metreon cinema complex. Even more, there are the new Marriott and St. Regis hotels, fashionable restaurants, and bars, and a lively late-night spirit that pervades. So now, Union Square itself, influenced almost by default by its bustling neighbor a few streets to the south, is becoming more modern, much less staid in itself.

Named after the pro-Union rallies held here during the Civil War, the Union Square area remains San Francisco's downtown shopping and theater district. A century ago this area that nestles around the 2-acre (0.81-ha) square was wealthy residential, but when the cable car made the steep hills more accessible, the wealthy moved up or out toward the new elegant residential district along Van Ness. Yet the high-quality shops and artisans that had served the residents stayed on when the neighborhood changed, and after the 1906 fire, commerce moved back as soon as it could. Today the pleasantly landscaped green square is ringed by luxury hotels and modern department stores; most of the original shops are long gone, but one or two—such as Shreve's Jewelers—still exist. The hotels and theaters cluster near Geary, and some of the city's most chic restaurants—catering to locals as well as tourists—nestle in the side streets, along with small, interesting boutiques.

In terms of residences, however, although there are some pleasant rental apartments north of Geary and on the southern foothill of Nob Hill, others may be shabby, and some may be too close to the seedy Tenderloin, which stretches out toward Polk Street. Yet, a Vietnamese community has established itself around Larkin Street, and some students are drawn to the reasonable rents here and easy access to public transportation. New apartments are appearing and small restaurants, clubs, and exotic shops are being found by San Franciscans. So soon, no doubt, the currently still rather depressed area between Theater District and the Civic Center to the West will increase in desirability—and also in price.

To the west of Union Square, past the problematic Tenderloin and straddling Van Ness Boulevard, is the Civic Center, with its beautiful Beaux Arts buildings, the city's center for government and culture. In addition to City Hall and government offices in the surrounding buildings, are the opera house and concert hall. the main library, and famous Asian art museum (*see page 290*). Just across Market Street, reviving that area, are the soaring Federal Building and luxurious Intercontinental Hotel. With all this activity, this area that ends at Van Ness Boulevard still qualifies as downtown, in a way, and even if residential living has not quite caught up with the atmosphere of the area, have no doubt—it will.

Van Ness Boulevard itself is helping the process along. It is interesting that a century after the 1906 fire destroyed it, the Van Ness corridor is once again an upscale residential area, with its condominiums, supermarket, and multi-screen theater, and chic restaurants in all directions. To the west of the Boulevard is a small community called Hayes Valley, that until the freeway was torn down had little to say for itself, but now in the open has blossomed and shown its true character to the world. Of course this Hayes Valley side of Van Ness cannot be considered downtown. But concert-goers come here to dine, the city's bureaucrats lunch in the restaurants, neighbors visit in the afternoon over a cup of tea, and shoppers check out unique shops and stores selling handcrafted products. Hayes Valley is in the perfect position to accommodate them all.

Streets that heretofore had been hidden under the freeway have cleaned themselves up, and now, despite the presence of some housing projects, Hayes Valley—stretching out to Octavia Street—is home to little restaurants, upscale boutiques, art galleries, and refurbished apartments. So, perhaps for some it is an extension of the Civic Center and to others it is its pleasing for its cultural buildings and pre-theater restaurants, but in truth it is a lively neighborhood in itself.

Financial District

Back to Union Square, though, and "North of Market." Stretching east to the Bay from Union Square is the Financial District, the "Wall Street of the West." As people hurry down the windy corridors of Montgomery and Sansome Streets, they probably do not think about the early days of San Francisco, when everything east of Kearny was mud flats, and the waters of the bay came up to what is now Montgomery Street. Having solidified its hold on the city's commerce during the Gold Rush, the Financial District (along with Los Angeles) is now the Western capital of the Pacific Rim, and some 300,000 people work here in about 50 million square feet (4.7 million sq m) of office space. The Financial District—with just a few steel-shell buildings remaining from before the 1906 earthquake—is home to almost all of the city's modern high-rise office buildings. A few have appeared in SoMa, but basically the new buildings there are apartment complexes, transforming that sunny area into a mixed-use residential-business-entertainment-sports area, leaving nothing out.

In the Financial District, however, the wind can whip through the concrete canyons, and here quite often is a "neighborhood" deserted when the corporate types go home after work. A few restaurants thrive on lunchtime customers and close early in the evenings (but not in upbeat Belden Street), and these may close on weekends. But because so many people work in this area, it is filled with little treasures of restaurants and shops; the closer to Union Square they are, the more expensive they become. If this is not a residential area, at least there are some interesting places to live in within easy walking distance in any direction except east.

Nob Hill

To the west, Nob Hill overlooks downtown. Perhaps the best known of the city's hills, Nob Hill still houses some of San Francisco's wealth, but not in any of the palaces ostentatiously constructed at the end of the last century by San Francisco's "Mother Lode" and railroad tycoons. The opulent lifestyle that allowed for 50-room homes came to an end in 1906, and today only one old mansion remains, now a private club whose facade allows us a glimpse at what once was.

Today, residents at the summit live in elegant apartment buildings, sharing the impressive views with the imposing Grace Cathedral and fashionable hotels. The little park in the middle holds a playground for the area's children, but except for this slight nod to residents of this expensive aerie, conveniences for daily living are found down the hill to the west.

The summit of Nob Hill, dominated by Grace Cathedral.

Until the end of the 19th century, Nob Hill was too steep for horse-drawn carriages, and it was workers who built little cottages along the lower slopes. But although cable cars allowed the tycoons to claim the summit, after the 1906 earthquake most rebuilt on safer terrain. Small frame apartment buildings began to appear, and many of these buildings—refurbished and modernized—remain convenient today for people working in the Financial District or Chinatown. High-rises appeared at the summit in the Fifties, but here, as in other areas, height limits were instituted, limiting the amount of skyline that could be blocked. Now there is a six-story limit on new construction, but that does not affect those fortunate few who are already there, enjoying the view.

The bus and cable car have made this steep hill convenient for Asians, as Chinatown expands up Clay and Sacramento from the north. On the west, low-rise apartment buildings line the narrow streets heading down to the Polk Gulch corridor. You probably will not find housing available on the top of

Overview of the City and its History

Nob Hill itself, although on its slopes apartments do become available from time to time.

Chinatown

Down Nob Hill to the north is Chinatown. You may not want to live here, but no discussion of San Francisco would be complete without a bow to this colorful, iconoclastic area that—the Mission and military Presidio aside—formed the original settlement of Yerba Buena and that in its own way dominates much of the spirit of the modern city.

Chinatown, that used to extend from Bush to Broadway and from Kearny to Powell, now crosses over Broadway into North Beach and up Russian and Nob hills. The Chinese community has also expanded out to Clement Street and into the Sunset, but Chinatown remains home base; no matter where people live, many come back on a Sunday for shopping and a family lunch. Although residents complain that their traditional area is becoming too homogeneous in its commercial effort to lure tourists, Chinatown is still a

On Grant Avenue at Bush Street, just a few blocks north of Union Square, is the Dragon Gate that marks the entry to Chinatown.

crowded warren of streets and alleys, of small exotic-looking shops and apartments above, perhaps with an open window and laundry waving in the breeze. In fact, behind some of the shabby, unmarked doors in the little alleyways is where the most interesting—and quietly private—business of this sometimes-secretive community takes place. The tantalizing aromas from the restaurants, coversations and audible bargaining in Mandarin and other Chinese dialects, and the inexpensive markets crowded with elderly women carrying their grandchildren on their backs in cloth sacks also conspire to give Chinatown an air of other-worldliness.

Although only about half of the city's Chinese population lives here, this 24-block area is one of the city's most densely populated districts. Its constant bustle is perhaps at least slightly reminiscent of the original Chinese quarter founded in the 1850s, when Cantonese immigrants flocked to these shores. During the Gold Rush they were cooks, launderers, and shopkeepers, even brothel keepers, and then workers on the railroad. By 1881, some 25,000 Chinese were resident in the city, and so many were coming to the United States that the Chinese Exclusion Act of 1882 was passed to stop the influx, meaning that until its repeal in 1943, the Chinese population became older—and poorer. Only in the post-World War II period did immigration begin once again and did the Chinese come again to Chinatown.

The main local shopping streets are to the west, on Stockton and Powell, which leaves Grant to the tourists looking for gifts. But the spiritual heart of the community is Portsmouth Square, which as Yerba Buena Plaza was originally only one street away from the shoreline. Until commerce moved east to Montgomery Street, this was the center of town, and it was at Yerba Buena Plaza that the discovery of gold was announced.

Rents in Chinatown are reasonable, but conditions may not be particularly agreeable. This is not the cleanest part of the city by any means, nor is there anything leafy green. Many of the area's renters are poor and elderly, speaking no English, and some live in substandard housing without understanding the recourse to city agencies that could help

The Wonders of North Beach

When you are on Telegraph Hill in North Beach, perhaps on your way up to Coit Tower, do not be surprised to hear and see hundreds of colorful wild parrots swirling loudly about and then landing into the trees. These cherry-headed conures and canary-winged parakeets may well be descendants of household pets that decades ago escaped—or more likely were released owing to how extremely noisy they were. Now they range around the city, but primarily on Telegraph Hill and near the Embarcadero by the Ferry Building Park. San Franciscans are as proud of their North Beach parrots as they were of the sea lions at Pier 39.

As to Coit Tower on the top of Telegraph Hill, it was built in 1933, funded by the widow Lillie Hitchcock Coit. Soaring 210 feet above Telegraph hill, the Art Deco fluted column of Coit Tower has extraordinary Diego Rivera-inspired murals with Socialist-realist images. Take the elevator to the top or walk around the perimeter of the area and experience sublime views of the city and the bay. The Bay Bridge, the Golden Gate Bridge, the city skyline, Alcatraz Island, and the glistening surface of the water accentuate the beauty that is San Francisco.

---

them. Yet this is certainly the most exotic and fascinating part of the city, and although you might easily enjoy living nearby—in an apartment complex along the Embarcadero, up Russian Hill, or in North Beach—consider carefully if Chinatown appeals. Chinatown is another planet, deep in the heart of San Francisco.

The North Embarcadero

Down along the Bay, as the working piers head north toward Pier 39 and Fisherman's Wharf, the North Embarcadero is a pleasant mixed-office/residential area on its inland side. Long in decline, the area took on a new life in the 1960s, when an old produce market was demolished and warehouses were restored to hold offices, television studios, and art galleries. At Jackson Street, the Golden Gateway Center added more than one thousand living quarters in apartments and townhouses, creating an instant neighborhood. Expensive though it is, the Golden Gateway is convenient to the massive four-building office, shopping, cinema, and restaurant complex of the Embarcadero Center—an extension of the nearby Financial District—which is almost a city in itself.

Here is the flat land-filled area that was once the Barbary Coast, its dance halls, boarding houses, and bawdy night life catering to the boisterous gold miners down from the hills. Now the surviving red brick buildings dating from the 1860s have been turned into antique shops and art galleries in an area called the Jackson Square Historic District. With supper clubs and cinemas open late, the area is once again offering succor to those looking for fun. That the old Ferry Building has been renewed and charmingly transformed—market stalls and restaurants abound—is the cap that makes this area a prized place to be.

There are several open plazas in this sunny area, in addition to the splendid promenade that runs along the Bay. Sidney Walton Park, with its sculptures and fountain, brings office workers to its grassy knolls at lunchtime. Overlooking the park are the Golden Gateway Commons, spacious red brick condominiums built around private landscaped walkways. These town homes are sometimes rented out by their owners; when put up for sale, their prices are extremely high.

Farther along to the north, nestled below the eastern granite outcropping of Telegraph Hill, several condominium complexes bring quiet residentiality to an area that was enhanced by the construction of Levi Strauss Plaza, with its fountains, streams, and grassy lawns. Some of these condominiums along Lombard or Montgomery are rented out by their owners, and some come up for sale. The prices are what one would expect. Unfortunately, as yet, there are few commercial services, and residents must head over to Bay Street or back toward Jackson for a supermarket and pharmacies. Up Telegraph Hill—on the sheer eastern side that no car can traverse—are the Filbert Street Steps, a landscaped walkway with enchanting clapboard cottages along lanes and terraces that might seem precarious, but that (at least so far) have survived earthquakes, rains, and whatever else the San Francisco climate (or politicians) might inflict.

Two Hills and a Valley

Over the top of the hill is North Beach, a sunny valley nestled between the western slope of Telegraph Hill and the

The eastern side of Telegraph Hill is too steep for roads and cars. On the top of the hill is the famous Coit Tower, a landmark of San Francisco.

eastern edges of Russian Hill. One hundred and fifty years ago there were a few docks and a little beach along the northern waterfront. Fishermen lived close by, some Basque and Portuguese, but primarily it was the Italians in what came to be called Little Italy who gave the area its flavor, one that still remains. Italian restaurants, coffee houses, bakeries, and delis draw the crowds, and old Italian-American gentlemen sit in the sun at Washington Square, the heart of the community, watching the passers-by. That this working class area of cheap rents was also home to the "Beat" poets in the fifties brought a rather bohemian feel to the area, but prices today are no longer cheap. And the atmosphere has also changed: Chinese restaurants and groceries have crossed their erstwhile boundary at Broadway, and now along Stockton they compete noisily for attention, while in the early morning Washington Square is taken up with devotees of tai chi. The result is an agreeable mix, one that tourists and San Franciscans appreciate to their full. North Beach is one of the most treasured areas of the city.

As a residence, North Beach is popular with people who work in the Financial District, as it is only a 15-minute walk away. Low-rise apartments hover above interesting shops and restaurants. On the east, the quiet residential neighborhood of Telegraph Hill rises slowly, and as it does, many of the three- and four-story apartment buildings command excellent views. Long-term residents live in cottages or in old buildings that new arrivals would love to get their hands on to refurbish. Some properties do become available from time to time, and their prices vary from expensive to the more expensive, according to the view provided and the redecorating or restoration work needed. Not all of these buildings have garages, and even with a residential parking permit, finding a space on North Beach streets is always a challenge, to say the least.

Heading up the winding road to Coit Tower, private homes of all sizes and apartment buildings command prices that are as steep as the hill's gradient; the hill is on bedrock and its buildings less liable to damage during earthquakes, and the views can be grand. The old beach itself may be gone, but a beach town it remains: keep your windows open at night and you will hear the foghorn piercing through and perhaps even the barks of sea lions, if they choose to return.

This holds true, too, for parts of steep Russian Hill, which climbs up from North Beach to the west. Its location could not be better. With trendy Polk Street on the west, North Beach to the east, Cow Hollow down past the western slope, and Chinatown to the south, Russian Hill is ringed by every convenience one could want. If the area took its name from

For twenty years, hundreds of sea lions basked and barked on the docks at Pier 39. But just after Thanksgiving of 2009, they all just swam away. Now San Franciscans are asking, "Where did they go?" and "Will they ever come back?"

the Russian seal hunters who 150 years ago were said to have buried their dead up here, the area is now very much alive.

People do not talk much about Russian Hill, and few tour buses labor up the hill—which suits the residents very well. The small businesses and restaurants on Hyde Street cater to locals, and in general this is a rather peaceful district with many enchanting pockets of almost-hidden charm. On Russian Hill, you can probably find an apartment either for rent or sale. It just takes patience.

What everybody finds is a well-kept residential community with an active community association to keep it so. People may live in small apartments above neighborhood shops, in large buildings that push up against the fog, in luxurious condominiums on little landscaped lanes, or even in single-family homes—small, large, or enormous—that persist despite the desire of development to encroach. Some streets have Mediterranean villas or simple redwood homes, and some cul de sacs even have houses with gardens in front. Russian Hill seems to have it all.

West of Van Ness

Past North Beach and the commercial Fisherman's Wharf area, the exquisite, residential Marina sits on marshland dredged for the 1915 Panama Pacific Exposition celebrating the opening of the Panama Canal. If the Exposition was designed to show the world that the city was once again on its feet after the 1906 earthquake, the quake of 1989 that damaged so much of this landfill district showed how fragile that footing actually was. Nonetheless, defying nature's whims, most Marina residents decided to stay, rebuilt their homes, and are today enjoying spectacular views of the Bay, the Golden Gate Bridge, and the distant hills—at least until the next "big one" hits.

Looking majestically out over the broad, grassy strip of the Marina Green, a line of elegant Mediterranean-style private homes stands as entry to the peaceful, often fog-shrouded neighborhood within. Grand stucco houses, smaller homes, and gracious Art Deco apartment buildings that impose on broad or winding wind-buffeted streets are home to a smart set of young professionals or yuppies—many singles but also some with families—who enjoy the proximity to the activities at Fort Mason, the greensward called the Marina Green, the eucalyptus-fragrant Presidio, and also to Chestnut Street, the area's effervescent commercial and nightlife scene. The area here may be flat, but the prices are quite steep.

Across Chestnut and the broad, commercial Lombard Street, Cow Hollow bridges the Marina below to aristocratic Pacific Heights above. An area of tranquil dairy farms more than 150 years ago, the restaurants and nightspots of Union Street—from Franklin to Divisadero—are today a playground for the upscale singles crowd. Interesting apartments and homes line just about every street, and climbing the steep hill up to Pacific Heights, the houses along Green and Vallejo are generally Victorian. On Union Street itself, the old Victorians have been converted into offices and trendy shops.

Combined, the Marina and Cow Hollow are great areas for living and hanging out. It is hard to park in these areas, so if you are interested in living here, it will be good to have a garage for your car. Yet services, supermarkets, and shops are all within walking distance, and public transportation to the Financial District is so convenient that you may not need a car.

The Presidio

How many cities have a National Park right in their heart? San Francisco does: the Presidio, a 1491-acre (603.4-ha) multi-use expanse which, as already mentioned, was among the original settled parts of the city, a military base for more than 200 years. In 1994 it was decommissioned and turned into a multi-use park, including a residential program, and lucky indeed are the people who get to live here.

The Presidio is jointly managed by the National Park Service and the Presidio Trust, a U.S. government corporation. They must make the park financially self-sufficient by 2013, and this may require new development, which is being met with some objections. Nonetheless, it would take some doing to destroy what is one of the most beautiful pieces of real estate in the country, and no one is about to let that happen. Undeveloped areas abound and are officially preserved, including gorgeous Crissy Field—wetlands and open space that are populated by migrating birds, joggers, picnickers, and windsurfers to name a few—plus hiking and bike trails, and miles of beaches that everyone enjoys. And if you play golf, you do not have to go far, with a par 72 course in your own backyard.

The park has some 800 buildings, many of them already refurbished and in use. Almost three thousand people currently rent homes here, in apartment duplexes and single family homes formerly used by military personnel. More families will move in when a new hospital opens, and they can play tennis at beautiful Mountain Lake Park while their kids play at the playground. This may well be the best of all worlds: living in a lovely park in a lovely city, with San Francisco Bay to one side and the Pacific Ocean on the other. And they will have the The City itself: The

Marina abutting to the east, and Pacific Heights and Presidio Heights to the South, so that there are restaurants, shops, and schools only a few minutes away from the city's woods, fields, and waves.

Pacific Heights

Just up the hill from the Marina, Pacific Heights is the costliest residential district in the city. In Pacific Heights, luxurious apartment buildings near Broadway and Fillmore quickly give way to beautiful single-family homes, and even these soon give way—as the broad streets head west toward Divisadero and Presidio—to the exquisite mansions of the truly rich. The tranquil, empty streets climb hills and dip into valleys, making the outer part of Pacific Heights a rather removed enclave, with little to disturb its serenity. Once seen as almost a suburb of San Francisco, the area does feel remote in certain places. Properties occasionally come on the market here, and the prices soar above the unbelievable.

Yet streets to the sides of Fillmore, although still decidedly Pacific Heights in character, harbor rental apartments nestled among large private homes. This area is less removed, more in touch, as residents are seen with their children at Alta Plaza or Lafayette Park, or walking their dogs. Upper Fillmore Street itself, from Washington to Pine, is becoming trendier and livelier by the day (if possible), with restaurants, chic boutiques, an international cinema, a popular supermarket that sells high-quality products, and crowds of people strolling and browsing the shops.

Presidio Heights

An extension to the west, Presidio Heights is perhaps slightly less aristocratic in demeanor than Pacific Heights, but the stately houses lining Clay, Washington, and Jackson nonetheless offer extremely gracious living in the heart of the city, with tree-lined streets, few passers-by, and the security that a rather suburban lifestyle might provide. Proximity to shopping in Laurel Village and to the Sacramento/Presidio intersection makes the area feel connected to city life, while the leafy Presidio and its edge of Mountain Lake Park make it feel less so. A few apartment buildings ring the edges, but vacancies are rare and prices are high. Primarily, it is the domain of one beautiful home after another; the houses do come up for sale from time to time and they sell quickly and well. Presidio Terrace—backing onto the Presidio itself—is one of the most secluded and beautiful enclaves in the city.

Starting at California and reaching to Geary are the almost hidden, overlapping communities of Laurel Heights and Jordan Park, whose broad, clean streets are often swept by fog and wind. Quiet neighborhoods of apartments and private homes, they are rather underrated, except by those fortunate enough to live there. Now that the shopping mall at Geary and Masonic has established itself, and the crowded Trader Joe's is just a few streets away, there are some bustling commercial opportunities that residents can enjoy—or deplore.

Moving South

From Geary, though, there is the Western Addition, stretching to the Panhandle of Golden Gate Park. Although parts of it—in the New Fillmore (around O'Farrell and Fillmore) and near the Panhandle or Alamo Square—offer pleasant apartments and welcoming communities, the entire area is in transition and has always seemed to have been so, in one way or another. Its image and populations may change, but it has long been controversial, riddled by problems. Perhaps it is finally now on the way to some solution.

Originally, Japantown (to the east of that great concrete swath of Geary Boulevard) was considered a part of this district, but now it has a character of its own. By the end of the 19th century, while the Chinese population was diminishing, the Japanese population increased. Many Japanese immigrants lived south of Market, but others moved out to the Western Addition, buying small houses and settling in the area they called Nihonjimachi, or "Japanese people's town." After the Chinese Exclusion Act, the Japanese bore the brunt of racism, setting the atmosphere for the infamous Order 9066, during World War II, when Japanese

Americans were sent to "relocation centers," forcing them to abandon their homes. By 1942, ship workers—many African Americans—found the now-empty buildings, heard of the low rents, and settled in. Ultimately the Western Addition became known as a "Black neighborhood."

When the Japanese came back, most settled in the Richmond and the Sunset. Only a small percentage of the city's Japanese residents lives in Japantown, now separated from the rest of the Western Addition by Geary's concrete. But the area is once again the central focus of the community: the 5-acre (2.02-ha) Japan Center shopping, cinema, and restaurant complex at Post and Fillmore draws people from all over, but Nihonjimachi remains firmly and locally Japanese.

But across Geary, the Western Addition was an area that had long been poised to go downhill. Fillmore Street near McAllister, the commercial center of town after the 1906 devastation, was more or less abandoned by 1912, when commerce moved back downtown. The lovely 1890s Victorians on Alamo Square—and just about all the others—went to seed. Eventually the area became known only for its shabby housing projects, dilapidated homes that lined the once-tranquil streets, and for crime and drugs.

Finally, urban renewal stepped in, as did people looking for affordable homes. The Victorians on the once again chic Alamo Square were restored to their brightly-colored glory. The development of a shopping center and several large modern apartment complexes just south of Geary brought stability and vivacity to the area, and people throughout began sprucing up apartments and single-family homes. This new atmosphere, of course, has brought restaurants of all levels, and more services are moving in.

The Haight

Across the Panhandle from the Western Addition, starts the Lower Haight that then, a few streets west at Masonic Boulevard, turns into The Haight, famous for decades as the Haight-Ashbury and for an attitude that in one way or another manages to persist. The Haight is still identified by

Alamo Square's colorful Victorians, sometimes called "San Francisco's painted ladies," with the urban skyline in the background.

its most celebrated moment—the "flower children" of 1967's Summer of Love, when psychedelic hippies found the place they felt they could best exist. But if young seekers still flock to the Haight—which they do—it is the Lower Haight, today at its funkiest best, that draws the locals, with great bars and barbeque joints, ethnic eateries, and reasonable rents for the apartments that hover above.

Haight Street itself does not seem to have changed—a street with cluttered storefronts and this generation's anti-establishment youth lounging the sidewalks. These young people easily mix with—or more likely ignore—the new homeowners who are refurbishing the Victorians that line the side streets and the Panhandle. So, the Sixties have moved on, and unusual shops and eateries are coexisting with upmarket boutiques and restaurants that are gentrifying an area that had become extremely seedy. One can only hope the area will not lose its unique character as gentrification tries to pervade.

In fact, the district around Haight and Ashbury has a rather surprising appeal. The neighborhoods that abut—Upper Haight, Cole Valley, Parnassus Heights, Buena Vista—offer an extremely appealing mix of large and small private homes on tree-lined, sometimes winding, streets. These are still inhabited by long-term residents, by young couples who value the backyards for their children, and by faculty members and researchers at the UC Medical Center, for whom this area is prime. Rentals are available throughout the district. In terms of purchase, although this is not one of the city's most expensive areas, the homes are often large and thus prices can be steep.

The Haight's attraction for the "flower children" is not hard to understand. This area along the Panhandle was once quite fashionable, as the Victorians attest. But during the economic depression of the 1930s, it was hard to maintain the large homes, and during the war some were split into apartments with cheap rents. When North Beach became too popular and expensive, many Beat Generation poets and "beatniks" (their followers) moved here, and by 1962, the entire area was rather Bohemian. By 1967, very hippie. But years of decline took their toll. Finally the City stepped in to subsidize the refurbishing of buildings and to limit the building of new units, which encouraged people sensing bargains to buy and restore the lovely old homes.

All these areas are near Golden Gate Park and the hilly Buena Vista Park, with its cypress, pines, and redwoods. They are also near commercial but charming Cole Street, and down the hill toward 9th and Irving, a vibrant part of a vast section of town loosely called "the avenues."

The Avenues

To the west of Arguello Boulevard (Richmond District) and Stanyan Street (Sunset District) are "the avenues," grid-like streets that start at 2nd Avenue and go west until they can go no more. They stretch on both sides of Golden Gate Park, and it is the park that divides its two adjacent districts, the Richmond and the Sunset, which have much in common, although slightly less as time goes on. In terms of climate, these are the foggiest districts in the city, and on some days when downtown areas are still basking in the sun, the Outer Richmond and the Outer Sunset are shrouded in mist, buffeted by wind. Both these large residential areas were developed only in the 1920s and 1930s; pleasantly culturally diverse, they are solidly middle class, known for their two-story, stucco, pastel-colored homes, sitting side by side, street after street. In each district, however, there are gems of luxury, of magnificent views, of exquisite homes—to be had at a price. These roomy communities—safe, comfortable, and well-kept—are seen by some as far from the city life, and some residents rarely feel the need to go downtown.

The Richmond's eastern edges—from Presidio Terrace (really still in Presidio Heights) all the way out to exclusive Seacliff remind one of Pacific Heights, with their mansions standing stately in the fog. Just across California Street, however, the Richmond is increasingly Asian: some 35 percent of the Chinese community has settled here, making Clement Street the focus of a "new Chinatown." Geary, its neighbor to the south and one of the city's longest commercial thoroughfares, has long been the stronghold of the Russian community, marked by the impressive gold-domed Cathedral of the Holy Virgin; all along Geary there are Russian delicatessens, bakeries, and stores, firmly ensconced in the increasingly Asian strip. So, this particular set of avenues is multi-cultural at its core.

South of Geary begin the alphabetically consecutive streets, starting at Anza. Residentially, there are low-rise homes and apartments on wide, straight, rather bland streets. As the area heads out toward the ocean, however, it begins to feel like the wild beach town it is. At the very edge of the continent, past the tourist attractions at Cliff House, the condominiums of Ocean Beach sit along the Great Highway, behind the sandy dunes.

South of Golden Gate Park, in the Sunset, the avenues begin again and so do the alphabetical streets, taking up again at Lincoln and ending far to the south at Wawona.

Years ago, the sleepy intersection at 9th and Irving (which is actually in the Inner Sunset) held a few shops, restaurants, and local services, but not much else. Now, despite the fog that whips in early, it is one of the city's liveliest scenes. As with many other areas that have been discovered, however, small businesses are being forced out as rents are raised, allowing chain eateries and cafés to move in. Yet residents of this area—students, faculty, artists, and young Asian families who live in low-rise apartments or two-story stucco homes—have fought back, forcing businesses to keep the scale and size of stores appropriate to their sites. Several large chains were rejected, and at present the area remains an extremely popular commercial nexus.

Yet in a few streets west, the atmosphere of 9th and Irving begins to fade, and the straight broad streets carry on as far as they can to the west into the chilling fog. Despite seemingly endless rows of small, undistinguished single-family bungalows and semidetached homes, the Outer Sunset has some attractions, including Asian commercial districts on Irving and Noriega, especially around 19th Avenue. With access to beaches and several large parks, and close to the major Stonestown Galleria and San Francisco State University, the residents seem content. All along the westernmost stretches, past 19th Avenue and surrounding the long Sunset Avenue greensward, a few of the discreet, pleasantly residential communities—Parkside, Pine Lake Park—seem part of a more tranquil world. Prices here are reasonable in relation to the rest of the city.

The Southwest

Just south of the "avenues" and still in proximity to the university and Stonestown sits the Oceanview Merced Ingleside (OMI) set of Western Neighbourhoods. These green, fragrant areas are often totally socked in by fog, but their residents enjoy the coastal winds and the smell of the sea. Revolving around Ocean Avenue and 19th Avenue, these are really three middle class neighborhoods trying to form a cohesive whole. In general, they are known for pleasant, single-family homes with neatly kept yards. Some apartment areas exist around Stonestown, inhabited by both long-term local residents and students who come and go. Park Merced, adjacent to the university, is an extensive apartment and townhouse complex.

To the west, near the university in its wooded and garden-like setting, near large Harding Park and near Lake Merced, and close to the ocean with its crashing waves, the area begins to take on the aspect of the coastal town it is. Lining the western side of the lake, along John Muir Drive, a large complex of rental units can be seen in a community known as Lakeshore.

Ocean Avenue, the northern border of the district, is gently residential to the west of 19th Avenue, but commercial to the east. This is one of the commercial areas that service Ingleside Terrace, known for the looping residential Urbano Drive that follows the course of the long-gone Ingleside Race Track. The comfortable, well-kept houses here exude the atmosphere of suburban living, and, fortunately, one may occasionally come up for rent.

Yet Ingleside and Oceanview themselves continue in a transition that started some time ago. Years ago, when the decaying Fillmore districts were being redeveloped, African American families were evicted with a promise they could return to new housing. Instead, many families migrated outward to the OMI and affordable homes, as the formerly entrenched White communities bought automobiles and moved to suburban living. Decades later, centralized shopping centers and large cinema complexes forced small local businesses to close, and the area declined. In recent decades, however, an active citizens' effort has strived to bring the area back to its residents, with rebuilt and expanded public facilities and an overall sense of renewal.

The Southeast

Also at the south, but on the city's eastern edge, are several districts that seem not to fit into the vibrant San Francisco mold. Separated from Bernal Heights by Interstate 280, Portola is a generally lower-middle class melting pot. Originally an Italian neighborhood, then Jewish, it is now truly multicultural, as evidenced along San Bruno Avenue, with its Latin American establishments, Italian butchers, and Asian restaurants of all kinds. People buying their first homes often settled here, but now prices are rising as they are everywhere else, and especially so in this area so near Bernal Heights.

Surrounding the large John McLaren Park are several neighborhoods—Excelsior, Visitacion Valley, and Crocker Amazon—that are generally characterized by middle-income and working class families living in undistinguished single-

McLaren Park

The 318-acre McLaren Park is a hilly natural treasure. While you are strolling on the trails or picnicking with your family, keep your eye out for the wildflowers on the grasslands, the Coastal Redwoods and Monterey Cypress trees, the California quail, and especially the Great Horned Owl, which also enjoys the park from time to time.

family homes. Originally Italian, these areas now see more Latinos and Asians. Yet, the foggy, rather uninspired streets with their rows of little houses are convenient to Daly City, to San Francisco State, and to the city by BART (Bay Area Rapid Transit). With older housing ready for refurbishment, neighborhoods are poised to come back. And Crocker Amazon has some slightly newer homes on more interesting streets such as Chicago Way.

But just across the Highway 101 corridor are Hunters Point, an area of city-wide concern, and Bayview, which seems now to be considering an upturn. During World War II military shipyards here bustled with some 35,000 workers. Now, however, with much of the city's public housing—some of it still in use since the war—these are the areas most beset by poverty and crime. Yet, Silver Terrace, close to the thriving Bernal Heights district is coming up, and perhaps even here San Francisco is moving on.

South of Market

And now we come, finally, to what is called South of Market, to old communities and new, each with its own character and ethos, and each as different from those in North of Market as can be. Those streets that abut Market Street to the South—that begin the vital area called SoMa—are still an extension of Union Square, in a way, in their cultural and commercial appeal. The outstanding Museum of Modern Art, the unique Yerba Buena Gardens, elegant hotels, entertainment of all sorts, and one new exciting restaurant after another, strain the imagination. And now even more hotels and luxurious apartment buildings are going up, and one wonders what more could possibly come. No doubt the wondering will not go on for long. These few blocks—from Market south to the ball park—will continue to entice San Franciscans with something new for years.

A new neighborhood in a city that has nowhere to expand? Actually, this area was here all along, waiting to be remembered and reborn. After the "big one" of 1906 destroyed what had been a wealthy residential district, this area was left to wither, becoming a seedy area of industry, shipyards, and cheap rooming houses. This atmosphere only increased during World War II, with the influx of men who came to work in the yards.

Hunters Point
The Hunter family that lived near here in the 19th century knew what they were doing: this area has one of the warmest climates in town. After a half-century of squalid decline and seemingly insurmountable problems and gnawing concerns, a slow but steady upswing should eventually reclaim Hunters Point.

But no longer. San Franciscan voters were wise to vote for a downtown baseball park, for this, together with the opening up of the south Embarcadero after the freeway was demolished, encouraged SoMa to expand to the south—down as far as China Basin, to King Street where the train station and the freeway onramp once stood at the border of the industrial streets, isolated in the sun.

New condominiums and rental apartments exploded onto the scene, restaurants found old abandoned warehouses, San Franciscans found lofts in others, and a new neighborhood rose—almost literally—out of that rather desolate industrial area that had lost its appeal after the 1906 earthquake did it in. A new light-rail transportation network has made apartment living in this area both convenient and fun, a chic neighborhood that has taken on a life of its own. Now with Safeway, Whole Foods, and Walgreens, as well as Borders Books, this area is set to feel like a real neighborhood, at last. Real estate prices for the new residential complexes do vary, but nothing is cheap anymore.

Even more is yet to come at Mission Bay, past China Basin and AT&T Park, at a 303-acre (122.62-ha) development that has clearly begun to retake an area of industry and railroad yards between Potrero Hill and the Bay. This sunny area that was long ago the hunting grounds for the native peoples will eventually hold some 6,000 homes, schools, 49 acres (19.8 ha) of parks, and a supermarket and stores, all anchored by the 43-acre (17.4-ha) research complex of the University of California, San Francisco. It encompasses an area called Central Waterfront and is just beyond the Mission

Creek enclave of houseboats, whose residents are fiercely protective of their neighborhood and have successfully sought legal protection so that they may stay. The light rail network already has streetcars gliding by, and as locals look out as they ride, perhaps they will one day think of coming here to stay.

Benefiting from all of this is a previously forgotten area called Dogpatch, centering around 3rd Street and Mariposa. Having survived the 1906 fire only to decline, it is now designated a Historic District. A new breed of residents and chic restaurants have found what turned industrial, and the area is already showing new life.

But not every part of SoMa is yet moving up. As the streets stretch west from about 7th Street to 13th Street where the overhead 101 freeway marks the boundary of the Mission District, the scruffy atmosphere that SoMa replaced farther east still exists. Some major megastores line 13th Street— Costco, Best Buy, Office Max, and Sports Authority, as well as the popular health food supermarket Rainbow Foods. But between SoMa and the Mission, refurbishment is sorely needed, and knowing San Francisco's dynamic vigor, it will, without a doubt, come.

The Mission

The Mission is another of the sections of town that you should understand well before choosing: some pockets of the Mission are charming and some will be charming soon, but a few others are still not charming at all, or at least not yet.

But remember that this is where it all started, and where, after more than 200 years, it seems to be renewing once again. Since the Spanish priests established their mission here in 1769, the area has maintained a Latin tone, despite waves of other nationalities that have left their mark on the Mission. Some 60,000 people currently live in the Mission, in a melting pot of races and nationalities, yet it is the 65 percent Latino population that gives the area its colorful, uninhibited flavor.

Mission Street, which centuries ago linked Mission Dolores to the port at Yerba Buena, is the city's longest; as it cuts to the southwest, it takes on the character of each surrounding neighborhood. Here it is a Latino main street, with businesses displaying their wares on the sidewalk, taquerias offering inexpensive meals, and neighborhood folk volubly carrying on an outdoor life. The 24th Street intersection is the heart of the barrio. Many of the side streets are uninspired, with three-story, bay-windowed flats and other low-rise apartments perched over the neighborhood stores. Although now in the process of a great upturn, this has long been—and still is—a poor, working class area. Some streets are noisier and dirtier than others, and occasionally there are turf battles between gangs of differing outlooks and intensities.

This had not always been a poor neighborhood: toward the end of the 19th century, it was solidly middle-class. Yet this was one area that did not benefit from the advent of the cable car, for when the hills became accessible, many people moved up. As industry developed near the waterfront, Irish, German, and Italian workers flocked to this sunny area from which they could walk to work. Although the area had been international for decades, what defined it as Latino was the establishment of international fruit and coffee companies that dealt with Latin America.

Many people think of the district as solely Mexican, yet from the early 20th century it has had a mix of Latin cultures. Unfortunately, despite the bilingual ballots and campaign materials, this neighborhood has traditionally voted less than many others, and its political clout has been low.

Now, however, the Mission has been rediscovered by San Franciscans, especially by young entrepreneurs who see an area ripe for investment and for a refurbishment of old, decaying houses. The Mission is a booming town. Drive around the district and you will be convinced. Hundreds of restored large Victorians and small bungalows line side streets between Valencia and Guerrero. Ride along well-maintained grassy Dolores with its Canary Palms, on Fair Oaks with its Chinese elms, and down streets such as Capp Street or Hill Street with Italianate Victorians on one side and Stick Victorians on the other. Many are already brightly restored. Chula Lane to Abbey Street is a cul-de-sac of Victorians as well. Crossing over Cesar Chavez, the Precita Park area that backs up on Bernal Heights Park is a community of small homes on short streets that is suburban in feel. These are all areas home buyers are looking for, and when you look around you will see beautifully restored homes perching majestically over some that look as though they would fall over in the next breeze, as well as modern apartment complexes rising in any inch of space.

Rents and purchase prices in the Mission may still be more reasonable in comparison to those in other parts of town, but that does not mean that they are cheap. Chic non-Latin restaurants, hip bars, galleries, and charming boutiques are following the affluence, causing real estate prices to rise, especially around the now trendy Valencia Corridor. Some traditional businesses are being forced out by the rise in rents. In addition, the rent for a two-bedroom apartment may now approach US$ 1,900, and this may ultimately mean a displacement of low-income families. But this may not happen in the near future, and the Mission remains a melting pot of cultures like nothing else in the city, for better or for worse. Again, if this area appeals to you, make sure you understand it well.

Potrero Hill

East of the Mission, sunny Potrero Hill was traditionally a working class district, removed from San Francisco's downtown more in spirit than in distance. Few early tourists braved the hill and the wind, and in fact, there was little to explore in what was a rather sedate, residential quarter settled by Scottish and Irish shipbuilders. Yet a few decades ago, as prices around the city escalated, this area became ripe for gentrification. Now artists and professionals, straight and gay couples, and young families are mixing pleasantly with old-timers in a neighborhood that many regard as an easy commute to the Financial District. Houses here are in demand, especially those "fixer-uppers" that consequently increase in value, although people who come to live on Potrero Hill tend to stay. A rather iconoclastic ambience still persists, but for how long?

Although industrial sites, furniture shops, and offbeat businesses dominate the northern flats, local commerce is clustered up and down the 18th Street hill. Residential areas that follow the hill's contours seem quiet, and lining the leafy streets are small clapboard houses, large spaces converted into lofts, multi-story Victorians, attached single-family homes, and apartment buildings—a pleasant mix that looks sunnily out over other parts of the city that may already be enveloped in fog. Potrero Hill is bordered on the east by several public housing projects, and their proximity to the hill has contributed over the years to robberies and auto break-ins. Yet, a condominium complex has transformed the southern section near 24th and Wisconsin, and ongoing building and restorations are making this area increasingly attractive. Potrero Hill is the kind of neighborhood its residents swear never to leave.

There are no supermarkets or banks on the hill, but the Potrero Center down on the flat at Potrero Boulevard is a neighborhood hangout. Multimedia businesses have taken hold out here, and their proximity to the Mission makes some people call this area Baja Mission; but except for the hilly Utah Street with its little houses, this area is not residential—yet. What much of it is, at least today, is a superficially arid stretch of warehouses and old buildings that house some of the city's popular restaurants and breweries, avant-garde theaters, and multimedia businesses. It will be interesting over the years to see which of the districts—Potrero or the Mission—claims this area as its own.

The Castro and Noe Valley

Certainly no discussion of San Francisco would be complete without some understanding of the Castro. In San Francisco geography it is actually Eureka Valley, although no one calls it that any more. Originally part of a large ranch owned by José de Jesùs Noe, whose name remains on the next valley over, this multi-colored rainbow district that begins around Market and 16th Street, and climbs up the steep hill to its south, is known simply as the Castro, although little of the Castro is simple at all.

Until the end of the 19th century, this was one of those hilly areas that was seen as remote by San Francisco's elite, and so it remained rural and agricultural longer than its neighbors closer in. But when the cable car made the hill with its 18.4 percent grade (gradient of slope) habitable, real estate speculators laid out a grid of streets, built Victorian houses and peak-roofed cottages and sold them to the working-class Irish, Scandinavians, and Germans, who created a traditional Catholic neighborhood—or so they thought.

Look at the Castro today. To outsiders it may look like the city's "gay ghetto," but to most San Franciscans it is much more than that. It truly is a small town with its own set of urban pleasures and problems, its local services and shops, its particular sense of what a community should be. Look at the thriving shops, the crowded cafés, the bright, rainbow-striped flags waving from windows, and you will understand this community's pride and solidarity. Both light-hearted and serious, this is a community that will no longer be anything but bold.

Some of the Irish population still lives in the warm, sunny Castro, but most moved away as the neighborhood changed, leaving the then-shabby Victorians their families had inhabited for almost a century. The white-collar workers and professionals then stepped in, refurbishing the houses, setting up shops. This is what gregarious Harvey Milk did in the Seventies, and his subsequent rise in city politics and tragic assassination drew together what had been a rather disparate community, one that has stood its ground ever since. Do not underestimate its political clout; politicians now understand that, like everyone else, gays need public transportation, affordable housing, and reasonable zoning laws. Unlike everyone else, however, they often get out to vote as a bloc. Now, although gays—like all San Franciscans—live anywhere they can afford, the Castro is the community's spiritual and political home. Castro Street is bustling with men doing their daily shopping and errands, cruising, frequenting the late-night clubs, or going to the Castro Theater, along with other San Franciscans who come for the film festivals and for the trendy restaurants nearby.

As a residential area, the center of the Castro is a sunny valley. Steep hills shelter the small houses, and flowers bloom in backyard gardens or in pots on the sunny decks. As the streets rise steeply toward Twin Peaks, the homes become larger—Victorians and Queen Anne cottages—and these, when they are put up for sale, are snapped up in the blink of an eye, no matter the cost. Rentals are also climbing: at the time of this writing, the average price for a rental apartment in the Castro is above US$ 2,000.

Street Fairs

What better way to get to know San Francisco's neighborhoods than to attend their annual street fairs? Each district has its own characteristics and so do their neighborhood celebrations. All feature food, most have arts and crafts, and some kind of music and other entertainment. So, make a note to go…and enjoy! Check the newspapers for exact dates, for they change from year to year. And do not forget that all of San Francisco is a year-round festival; consult the calendar of national holidays and local events on pages 304–309, so you can celebrate too, in your own way.

JUNE
- Union Street Festival between Gough and Steiner
- Sixth Street Fair around Sixth and Minna
- North Beach Festival on Grant Avenue at Green
- Haight Street Fair

JULY
- Fillmore Street Jazz Festival

AUGUST
- Nihonmachi Street Fair in Japantown

SEPTEMBER
- Folsom Street Fair

OCTOBER
- Castro Street Fair

Across Market, up toward Corona Heights and Buena Vista Parks, the Castro's suburbs have large, well-landscaped homes on winding, hilly streets. This is a more traditional, less noticeable area, agreeable and calm, and prices are rising considerably here. And farther in is the Duboce Triangle, less wealthy but always in demand.

Just to the south, Noe Valley takes and gives to both the Castro and the Mission, but is in fact a village unto itself. Some old German and Irish still live here, as they do in the Castro, but it is now one of the most sought-after areas of town by young couples, by lesbians and gays spilling over from the Castro, and by artists and others with a bohemian outlook. Protected from the fog by three steep hills, this sunny valley is one of the city's most popular areas for young families; mothers pushing their children in strollers do their shopping on 24th Street or sit with their friends at outdoor tables in front of any of the area's charming little cafes. Twenty-fourth and Church is the main shopping intersection, but the shopping district really stretches from Diamond to Dolores. Since the J-Church streetcare line comes here, Noe Valley is a convenient commute for those who work downtown.

The entire area is relaxed in feel, less frenetic than the Castro, more solidly comfortable. Streets are fairly wide, and the small houses that line them are painted in light colors. The streets leading up to Diamond Heights are steep and the large Victorians have exceptional views, although the higher the climb, of course, the denser the fog. The residents of Noe Valley value their village and are trying to keep out the big businesses and chains. They have been doing so somewhat successfully so far.

Only a few years ago you would not have paid much attention to Noe Valley's neighbor at the southern edge of the Mission Valley, a rather placid, uninspired—sometimes rundown—area of small private homes nestled on low-rising hills. Now, however, sunny Bernal Heights is much in demand. The area's excellent location—with borders also on Diamond Heights and the Mission—meant that it was a logical expansion for those neighborhoods, as well as for men and women who might also have thought of the lively

Castro or Inner Mission as their home. Pleasantly winding streets heading up low-rising hills, several welcoming green parks, gentle breezes, and lovely views from Bernal Hill drew a new generation of San Franciscans, ready to remake the Victorian bungalows and Queen Anne cottages, many of which were suffering from neglect. Bernal Heights is now an area with its own cachet.

Fortunately, the area has not lost its traditional multiracial, multi-ethnic character, but it took the work of community activists opposed to excessive gentrification to keep it that way. It is true that new businesses and restaurants are moving in, but so far the neighborhood ambience persists, even on Cortland Avenue, the district's main commercial street, which offers to residents all the conveniences and services that a small town would want. Private homes still have gardens, the renewed Holly Park is a treasure for families, and neighbors chat together in Bernal Park while letting their dogs romp and play.

Bernal Heights thus remains an area of satisfying proportions. Old-timers still inhabit their homes, lesbians, families, young professionals, and artists are fixing up cottages throughout, and Latino families are finding their way out from the crowded Mission to homes that are still within financial reach, both for rental and purchase. But the good prices here will not last long. Home prices increased nearly 18 percent in just one recent year. Rent control means that a long-term renter might be paying US$ 900 per month, but a young professional who is just moving in might pay US$ 1,900. So, Bernal Heights is expanding in a way, annexing perhaps the area known as Silver Terrace on the edge of the problematical Bayview Area, which itself is on the way up. Clearly, Bernal Heights is a neighborhood to value, and fortunate is the person who can seize an opportunity here.

The Mountainous Center

To the south and west of Noe Valley the highest hills in the city impose themselves over a dozen interesting communities. Wind-swept and foggy for the most part, Twin Peaks, Mount

Davidson, and Mount Sutro command the city's geographical center; many of their neighborhoods are blessed with exquisite views and park-like settings, some a bit sheltered from the cold ocean wind. Despite the winding and dead-end streets, each area is convenient to—or overlaps—another of interest, and all are in proximity to the city's major universities, making them attractive to faculty and students. There are mansions and private homes, small cottages, and well-maintained apartments, but what you will find depends on where you look, for each area has its own character.

Diamond Heights, which is the major district on the eastern slopes of Twin Peaks, was developed in the 1960s, and its modernity shows in its large apartment complexes and well-designed, single-family homes. Its proximity to its eastern neighbors makes it ever more desirable, as prices in Noe Valley and the Castro soar. Being "discovered" also is the attractive hilly Glen Park district to the southeast, with its many rental apartments, Victorians, and almost reasonably priced homes, although it had long been a sedate, well-kept neighborhood. And the Glen Park BART Station makes the Financial District even more quickly accessible than some areas closer in. Nearby, the steep Glen Canyon Park offers a wilderness park, although playgrounds, tennis courts, and a baseball field have tamed it somewhat.

Mount Davidson's summit is foggy and wild, but on its western downslopes are some incredibly beautiful neighborhoods, almost a surprise in this outer part of the city. That they are near the university and the Stonestown shopping area makes them very much in demand. Drive around Sherwood Forest and Saint Francis Wood, for example, to see the lovely homes on impeccably landscaped grounds. Houses occasionally come up for sale here, but as in Pacific Heights, the prices are astronomical. The pleasant homes of West Portal bridge toward the more ordinary Miraloma Park, Westwood Highlands, and Westwood Park, where some areas and streets are more appealing than others.

Just above the UC Medical Center, Mount Sutro and its fragrant eucalyptus forest may be the city's best-kept secret. On the hill's eastern edge, within walking distance of the hospital, the charming enclave of Sutro Heights backs on the forest, and here are several of the most beautiful and flowery streets in the city, especially Edgewood Avenue, which is paved in red brick.

Circling the hill, wild, foggy Sutro Forest sees private homes and apartments in addition to institutional housing for medical students. And around the hill to the west is Forest Knolls, a grouping of more than one hundred small, uniform homes on winding streets, each facing the forest itself.

YET QUESTIONS PERSIST

This overview of the city should help you get a feel for it as you explore it on your own. As you do, you will discover that San Francisco retains its little mysteries, and it always will. Old ones will be resolved and new ones will show up. Will the charming enclave of private homes around the University of San Francisco continue to be considered part of the nearby Western Addition, which is forging a new identity of its own? Will new residents actually create a neighborhood at the enormous mixed-use area now being developed at Mission Bay? Will Polk Gulch rename itself to Polk Village, as merchants in that area hope? Will the name NoPa for the area north of the Panhandle really catch on? And will the Van Ness corridor, now sparkling with new condominiums, supermarkets, and theaters, coin a name for itself? The answers to these particular puzzles will certainly soon unfold while others appear. In any case, the architect Frank Lloyd Wright summed up his own understanding: "What I like best about San Francisco is … San Francisco," he said. For all in all, as San Franciscans believe, the city is unique.

AND AROUND THE BAY

A Different Style of Living

The eight outlying counties of the Bay Area stretch about 50 miles (80.5 km) south toward the major metropolis of San Jose, east past the industrial port of Oakland, and north to Sonoma, up toward what is known as the Delta. Bay Area counties are generally referred to by their position in relation to the Bay: the North Bay (Marin, Sonoma, Napa, and Solano counties), the South Bay whose farther reaches are called the Peninsula (San Mateo and Santa Clara counties), and the East Bay (Alameda and Contra Costa counties). Thousands of people commute to the city from the nearer portions of these counties, and now even some of the farther reaches are beginning to be regarded as within commuting distance.

People choose to live in the greater Bay Area rather than in San Francisco for a variety of reasons: the preference for a tranquil suburban or even rural lifestyle, lower housing costs (in some places), access and proximity to good public and private schools, low crime rates, fewer earthquakes, or perhaps even a more "normal" climate. Although the details of the towns and villages of the Bay Area are beyond the province of this book, they are well worth considering in terms of residence.

Unlike San Francisco, much of the Bay Area sees four distinct seasons. While San Francisco is enjoying its natural summer air conditioning, it is warmest inland, away from the bay. Temperatures in the rest of the Bay Area can soar in the summer, but even in these areas, winter climes are mild,

Overview of the City and its History

with perhaps a touch of snow in Sonoma, on the peaks of Mount Diablo, or on Mount Tamalpais.

If you want major cities with stores, excellent transportation, and cultural diversity, consider the always up-and-coming Oakland in the East Bay or its famous intellectual neighbor Berkeley. Both are just across the Bay Bridge in Alameda County, which has the highest population of the Bay Area. Formerly seen as less desirable than Marin to the north or San Mateo County to the south, the East Bay now holds its own. In the North Bay, Sausalito exudes charm, but Mill Valley has it all: conveniences of every sort and a gentle way of life. And to the south, as you head to San Jose, known as the focal point of "Silicon Valley" and its Internet entrepreneurs, do not miss San Mateo or lovely Palo Alto, home to Stanford University and just about anything you could want.

All the adjacent counties are dotted with delicious little towns, gentle and leafy green, linked by country roads and, for the most part, touched by major highways. Living here, thus, requires keeping a car, perhaps more if two people in a household are working, or if a child needs to be taken to school.

> In the North Bay, Marin is two counties in one: east of the coastal mountains are lovely towns with fashionable homes and elegant, peaceful living. To the west of the coastal mountains, is rugged coastline, cliffs, and surf. A quarter of a million people live in Marin, from corporation executives who commute to The City from their multimillion-dollar homes, to solitary artists and writers who leave their cottages to brave the winds and stroll the beaches, but who rarely want to come out "over the hill." Up the coastal, winding coastal road are Stinson Beach and Bolinas. On the bay, the old fishing village of Sausalito now exhibits expensive charm, and Mill Valley, San Anselmo, and San Rafael are fashionable family towns.

If living outside the city appeals to you, think about living along the BART line, which goes from San Francisco under the bay to the east, and somewhat toward the south. (*See page 169.*) Commuting by car during rush hours is slow and tedious, but the BART is reliable and fast. From the North Bay, commuting is most often by car, crowding the lanes of the Golden Gate Bridge; there too, however, the public commuter buses and even ferries are reliable and practical. And from the south also come the buses, train, and BART (from Colma), and, unfortunately, long lines of cars.

Taking a Tour

Tours are especially good for an in-depth understanding of a particular site or culture. Many of the tours are to be made on foot, so wear comfortable shoes, and do not forget to bring a jacket.

- All About Chinatown Walking Tours; tel: (415) 982-8839; website: http://www.allaboutchinatown.com. Lively tour, ending with a dim-sum lunch. Call to reserve and for the meeting place.
- Audiosteps; 2590 Greenwich, Suite #1, San Francisco, California 94123; tel: (415) 346-2604; website: http://www.audiosteps.com. Purchase and download an audio tour of San Francisco to your MP3 player and explore the city at your own pace.
- Blazing Saddles Bike Tours; 2715 Hyde Street at Fisherman's Wharf and other locations; tel: (415) 202-8888; website: http://www.blazingsaddles.com. This well-established bicycle rental and touring company provides daily guided bike tours. You may also take a guided audio tour on your own using an MP3 player.
- Blue & Gold Fleet Sightseeing Tours; Hour-long cruise on the Bay, seeing Alcatraz, the Golden Gate Bridge, and Sausalito. Tickets may be purchased online, over the phone, or from yellow ticket box offices located between Pier 41 and Pier 39. Cruise boats leave from Pier 39; tel: (415) 773-1188; fax: (415) 705-5429; website: http://www.blueandgoldfleet.com.
- Chinese Culture Center of San Francisco; 750 Kearny Street, 3rd Floor; tel: (415) 986-1822; fax: (415) 986-2825; website: http://www.c-c-c.org. Docent-led tours of Chinatown and a narration of and introduction to the city's Chinese culture.
- Cruisin' the Castro Tours; 584 Castro Street; tel: (415) 255-1821; website: http://www.cruisinthecastro.com. If you want to know everything about the Castro, this tour gives you the history and attractions of the country's largest "gay mecca."

Taking a Tour

(Continued from previous page)
- San Francisco Fire Engine Tours & Adventures; The Cannery; tel: (415) 333-7077; website: http://www.fireenginetours.com. Tour from the Cannery, over the Golden Gate Bridge, and then back, in a restored, classic, open-air, bright red fire engine.
- San Francisco Electric Tours; 757 Beach Street, at Hyde Street; tel: (415) 474-3130; website: http://www,electrictourcompany.com. Take a tour of the city on a Segway (a gyroscope-enabled, self-balancing two wheeler).
- Victorian Home Walk; 2226 15th Street; tel: (415) 252-9485; website: http://www.victorianwalk.com. Tour Pacific Heights, and see colorful Victorians, beautiful gardens, historical houses, and the inside of a period home. Check the website for time and meeting place.

Rents and purchase prices vary from the merely expensive to the outrageous, depending on the size of the home and its views of the bay, as well as the town's amenities. Some of the communities have new subdivisions with planned developments of single-family and multi-family homes, some clustered around golf courses. Whereas the towns close to San Francisco were considered an easy commute to the City, now communities as far north as Petaluma or Novato, or as far east as Concord are being developed and considered within traveling distance. Whatever the price range, the beauty and lifestyles of these more relaxed areas are considered by many—especially young families—to be essential for a well-balanced life. Towns around the Bay Area are never called suburbs, but life there is truly suburban. Check them out.

THE PEOPLE BY THE BAY

CHAPTER 3

'A mad city—inhabited for the most part by perfectly insane people whose women are of remarkable beauty.'
—Rudyard Kipling

CERTAINLY WHEN YOU COME TO SAN FRANCISCO and look around at the people you encounter on the streets, next door, or at your job, you will be wondering just what these San Franciscans "are like." How can you understand them, get to know them, figure out where you belong? After all, in some cities and countries this is easy: in France most people are French and in Beijing they are Chinese. But in multicultural San Francisco, such classifications may not be so simple. It might well be harder to categorize the population of the City that Knows How, but this diversity and cosmopolitanism might also make it easier for you—no matter your nationality or cultural orientation—to find yourself at home. Some people say that San Francisco does not fit into any specific mold. But perhaps it is that there is a mold for everyone, and if yours is not evident, then there is probably room for you to create it, yourself.

San Francisco's demographics tell it all: more of its residents were born overseas than here. About 40 percent of San Franciscans were born in another country, 25 percent were born in another state of the United States, and only 35 percent were born in California itself. And, it is Asians—not European Caucasians—who are the primary source of international immigration to San Francisco. In 2004, 60 percent of all immigrants came from Asia, with 20 percent coming from China, alone. So, although you will see more Caucasians in business suits than any others as you walk in the Financial District, this is just one district out of many, and each neighborhood has its own vibrant ethnic or cultural ethos, waiting for you to discover.

New arrivals compare San Francisco to their own city and others they have seen, saying, "San Francisco is so European," or "so Asian," or "it's not like home at all." And they are right, or partly so: San Francisco does carry hints of other cultures on every street, but it is indeed like home, because it is home to more than 800,000 San Franciscans—of all ethnic backgrounds, religions, political persuasions, and sexual preferences—who have created this wonderful city in their image, on their own terms. San Franciscans—whoever they are and wherever they have come from, or whoever they have decided to be—are in love with their city, adore its views (visual, political, and social), appreciate its eclectic population, and in general are convinced they live in the best, most exotic city in the United States, if not the world. (And, sometimes tediously, they never stop telling everybody so.)

Another way to think about this diverse mix of people is to understand that it is a city of minorities, for no ethnic, religious, or societal group dominates. Of the 800,000 inhabitants, there are approximately 195,000 Asians, 65,000 Latinos, sizeable populations of Russians, Italians, and African Americans, and throughout all these ethnic groups, some 90,000 gays and lesbians. This leads standard tourist guides to devote separate sections to Chinatown, Japantown, the Mission, or the Castro, describing them to people passing through. But no such delineation can really help you understand the populace, for these people and their areas are each just a part of the overall scene. Part of what makes San Francisco so interesting is that each separate residential area is open enough that anyone can feel welcome, but tight enough not to lose its sense of community and identity.

So, stereotyping does not work in San Francisco. But some generalities might prove helpful as you look around. The Chinese community—like most of the other immigrant communities—tends to be close-knit, grouped in extended families, private (but not entirely closed) toward outsiders, welcoming and friendly within. And, apart from the older generations, the children—born in San Francisco, most likely—on the buses on their way home from school speak Mandarin to each other, preserving their sense of community, but also genuinely acknowledging their larger community by perhaps shouting in English, "See you tomorrow," as they get off the bus. The Latinos in the barrio seem to be, as one might expect of people coming from warm climates, more open, teeming in the streets, laughing with friends. If you have something in common with any of these cultures—those of your heritage or outlook on life—you will understand them. But what of the rest?

SO, WHAT ARE THEY LIKE?
Despite the delicious assortment of cultures, when people talk about what San Franciscans are like, they are generally referring to the people who work to keep the city prosperous or to further the business of the Pacific Rim, to people who own shops, buy the books, go to the ball games and the gyms, or those who explore all the superb cuisines and libations the city has to offer. Many of these are the "financial types," the "yuppies" (young urban professionals), the "metrosexuals," or the "dot.comers" that San Francisco is known for, and if we are talking about them, then we can surely give some clues as to who they are.

If you have not noticed it by now, you will soon. San Franciscans like to play. They may love (or hate) their work and strive to succeed, but their lives outside their jobs define more of who they are. They eat out often, go to films, spend discretionary dollars on fitness and sport, look for the trendiest cocktail of the moment—downing quite a few—and, liking to look good, they shop. (They do not smoke, for the most part—and they will not hesitate to chide you if you do!) Yes, the "dot.com" bubble burst and a recession hit worldwide, but somehow San Francisco remains itself. Wages in San Francisco rose 30 percent in the last decade, whereas in the rest of the country they rose only 18 percent. And if the cost of living is also higher here, somehow it seems not to matter to these people, or not much. As families with children move away to where raising children is more affordable, young professionals are still sliding right in to take their place.

As already mentioned, the climate is agreeable year-round, and the views are exquisite. Acquaintances are friendly and open, and the best of everything is not hard to find. No wonder people seem light-hearted and ready for themselves and everyone else to have fun. And they have come to the right city, for there is something about San Francisco, itself, that makes it all work.

A SENSE OF HUMOR

If Americans have found that it is easier to get along together by avoiding talk of politics, sex, and religion—San Francisco begs to differ. A sense of humor is important, and San Francisco encourages its lovers to think that anything—and anybody—can be teased, even themselves.

Where else would you have found the citizens of a city irreverently twitting a rather imperial mayor Willie Brown by referring to him as "His Williness?" Where else would you find a group of gay men forming an "order" of nuns, "The Sisters of Perpetual Indulgence," with one of those men—Sister Boom Boom—running for a seat in the Board of Supervisors, as "nun of the above?" (This happened in 1982, and although some 23,000 voted for him, the votes were not enough for him to win.) And where else would the electorate have countermanded the police department's prohibition, voting that a friendly policeman could carry a ventriloquist's dummy wearing a little police uniform on his beat? These all happened over the years, and these stories quickly go into the city's legends and lore.

Should you find some of the humor distasteful, just roll your eyes and shake your head, for San Francisco's enjoyment of the outrageous goes far back and it has encompassed all strata of the city's society. Take the case of one Joshua Abraham Norton.

The Sister Boom Boom Law

Encouraged by the support he garnered while campaigning for a seat in the Board of Supervisors in 1982, a young gay astrologer, better known as Sister Boom Boom, decided to run for mayor the next year. His candidacy as "Nun of the Above," and the resulting excessive declarations of nicknames in the campaigning led to the imposition of a new law, dubbed as the Sister Boom Boom Law, which requires all candidates running for offices in San Francisco to use their legal names.

Having left San Francisco in the mid-1850s a financial failure, he returned just a few months later styling himself as "Emperor of the United States and Protector of Mexico." His proclamations were published in the newspapers, and he became the "darling of everybody in town." For 20 years Emperor Norton sported regal finery, was fed for free at various establishments around the city, and pontificated at corporation board meetings. When he died in 1880, he was given a fittingly royal funeral, to which 10,000 of his "subjects" came.

Two of Emperor Norton's Noteworthy Decrees

It was Emperor Norton who first admonished the citizenry never to call their city Frisco.

"Whoever after due and proper warning shall be heard to utter the abominable word 'Frisco,' which has no linguistic or other warrant, shall be deemed guilty of a High Misdemeanor."

His quirky yet brilliant vision of having a bridge constructed over the bay was disregarded and realized only in 1937—a milestone in San Francisco's existence—when the world-renowned Golden Gate Bridge was opened.

San Francisco's iconic Golden Gate Bridge, completed in 1937, a symbol of human ingenuity. With the Pacific Ocean to its west and the Bay to the east, it spans the Golden Gate, discovered by Spanish soldiers in 1769.

And a century later, in 1999, when gay politician Tom Ammiano was sworn in as President of the Board of Supervisors, his predecessor gave him a tiara and feathered scepter she had received at the beginning of her term, and declared him "queen of the realm." Acknowledging the change in the city's leadership and in societal tolerance, Ammiano responded by quoting from *The Wizard of Oz*, a movie favorite, "We're not in Kansas anymore."

GAYS IN THE CITY

In fact, San Francisco from its beginnings was a town of men: the priests and soldiers who adventured north to Alta California to settle the area two centuries ago, the Chinese men fleeing famine who sailed the Pacific, and the adventurers who flocked to the California frontier in 1849 seeking gold. That the miners also sought booze and bawdy women convinced some moralists that the city should be punished, and after the 1906 earthquake they thought it had been. (Not likely!) But a port city it was and it remained, welcoming more sailors after the opening of the Panama Canal in 1914 and ship workers through World War II. During the war, San Francisco was a military port of embarkation, where eagle-eyed officers mustered out men who were homosexual, many of whom then decided to stay. By the 1960s, when it was said that the 70,000 gays who lived here frequented "decadent" gay bars, national newspapers stereotyped the city as a haven for sexual deviates. Far from having the desired effect, the news spread throughout the country that this was a place for gays and other iconoclasts to feel at home. And when gay San Francisco Supervisor and activist Harvey Milk was assassinated in 1978, the gay community mobilized itself and has since become a potent political force.

For quite some time the city has had a precedent-setting, official stance on affording equal rights to domestic partners of any persuasion. And, when Gavin Newsom was elected as mayor in December 2003, he declared gay marriages to be legal. But he was ahead of his time. In 2008 the anti-gay marriage bloc carried the majority and voted that marriage in California is "between a man and a woman." The state Supreme Court upheld the vote, but declared that the 18,000 marriages already performed were valid. Yet the campaign isn't over: one can only say at this point, as they do on television, "stay tuned."

If The City was once primarily the province of male gays—in the Haight and Polk Gulch, and of course the Castro—and lesbians were more prominent across the Bay in Oakland, this has been changing for some time. In recent decades, the lesbian community has been establishing itself solidly throughout the city, especially in the Inner Mission, Noe Valley, Bernal Heights, and Glen Park. And now, the dynamic district of SoMa is happily welcoming to the entire city.

Unfortunately, "hate crimes" occur from time to time in America, but they are rare here, for San Franciscans tend to get along in harmony. That you can find a beautifully dressed society matron at the opera sitting just one row away from a Rastafarian sporting dreadlocks and wearing blue jeans is not a paradox. That you can find a middle-aged straight couple

Towers of commerce cluster together in the Financial District, leaving residential districts with a human scale.

eating a delicious dinner at Asia SF, a transvestite "gender illusion" café, is not unusual. That you can find one of the best martinis in town at a bar in the seedy Inner Mission does not keep anyone away. And that a distinguished looking gentleman driving a Mercedes can order take-out ribs from a shack called Brother-in-Law's #2, in the Western Addition, means only that he has good taste. (And no one cares that there is no Brother-in-Law's #1.) Since its beginnings, San Francisco has carried the country's vision of the "melting pot" where differing societal cultures and attitudes enrich the whole. What is different about San Francisco is that each mini-society in its own way embraces this vision and is—at least for the most part and on most days—proud of it.

MAKING IT WORK

Even more unlike some other cities in this emerging century, San Francisco is managing to triumph, in its own unique way. The intensity San Franciscans bring to their lives translates into a civic activism that cuts through all levels of society. As that former Mayor Brown once said, "Here in San Francisco, you have more than 750,000 people, and each and every one of them is informed, interested, and has an opinion on everything." It is true. Residents volunteer at food banks that feed the homeless, at non-profit cultural institutions, for environmental and political causes, and at organizations for needy children. They form groups to protest injustice and to call for reform. They insist volubly on better transportation, more parking, and more affordable housing. They vote in higher percentages than in most other major cities, and if it appears that San Francisco is at the far side of "liberal," look at the most talked-about issues and see that residents vote for the very things that make their city work: good social programs, preservation of cultural institutions, improvement of the downtown areas, and equality and tolerance for all.

And again: where else would all levels of society flock to an elegant restaurant on the Embarcadero (Delancey Street) that is staffed entirely by former drug addicts and felons who, having hit bottom, are now on their way back up? And where else would a Methodist church (Glide Memorial) in the gritty Tenderloin district that feeds hundreds each day at its soup kitchen also draw more than a thousand San Franciscans of all strata and religious beliefs on Sunday mornings to its rafter-raising, rocking, gospel message?

So all this is quintessentially San Franciscan, and it is the San Franciscans who have made it and continue to make it so. You will discover all this for yourself as you settle in. Look around. This eclectic population known as San Franciscans, whether they say so or not, hope—no, they assume—that you will find your place among them. And, no doubt, you will.

SOCIALIZING IN SAN FRANCISCO

CHAPTER 4

'I have always been rather better treated in San Francisco
than I actually deserved.'
—Mark Twain

FINDING YOUR SOCIAL NICHE

First Encounters

Your own attitudes plus a bit of fortitude will play a large part in how your life in San Francisco unfolds. That is probably true in moving to any new city, but in this one, the myriad social structures and mini-structures—as open and deep as in many other cities combined—ensure that if you reach out, you will find the communities that suit you best. Yes, "communities" in the plural, for there is no reason to fit yourself into just one group. In this eclectic city, groups manage to keep their identities while complementing, merging, and overlapping with others, forming that ever-fluid and delicious whole called San Francisco. But fortitude also plays a part. Assimilating and being accepted will require a conscious effort: the ability and willingness to look around and observe how each community functions within its own value system, to see how best you can fit in, and to patiently let time take its course as you interact.

Many people make their maiden journey to The City with no family or job to come to. All they have are names of people from their communities at home—friends of friends, perhaps—and they will meet them first and no doubt be warmly met and orientated. In fact, knowing people from the same background who have already adjusted to The City's ethos but who still feel bound together can help you

Two friends enjoying some tortilla chips at a Mexican restaurant in the eclectic neighborhood of the Mission.

integrate and start feeling at home. Even if these people do not ultimately become your best friends, they will—either explicitly or not—show you the San Francisco ropes. And, if you do not know where to look for these welcoming folk, call your consulate (or access its Internet site) and ask about cultural groups you might attend. There is no need—as the American saying goes—for you to "feel like a fish out of water" in San Francisco, even at the start.

In fact, immigrant and other special interest communities tend to cluster together and to stay close-knit—even while taking in newcomers. They celebrate their own holidays with their comfortable traditions from home (and other San Franciscans often join in). Yet with their friends they also celebrate American holidays and San Francisco's own festivals, and they enjoy what anyone in San Francisco does. Younger Asians do try a Mexican burrito from time to time; Latinos in the barrio of the Mission District will down a spicy Hunan dinner or a plate of Japanese sushi; Christian communities have joint projects with Jewish groups, and everyone goes to the San Francisco film festivals, no matter the cultural theme.

Civic Activism

If you do not know a soul when you get here, see pages 115–118 and see if there is a religious denomination listed that mirrors your own beliefs and attitudes. (And if not, look in the *Yellow Pages*, where there are many more.) Even if you are not a religiously observant person, people of any faith will be welcoming. Religious congregations in San Francisco certainly have worship services, but they also help feed the homeless and work with disadvantaged groups. They hold potluck suppers and conduct other social events, and they mix with different denominations' congregations, as well. They take part in city life, and there is no better way for you to do so, than to participate with these groups, yourself. (*Also look at the* Resource Guide *for networking groups you might consider joining*.)

Observe and learn where their interests lie, whether they are cultural or artistic or political or sportive, or—in other words—how their activities mirror your own interests. The groups in San Francisco cover just about anything the city enjoys.

THE ETHOS

In fact, throughout all the groups, you will find that appreciation of the San Francisco lifestyle runs high. Perhaps, in fact, the unofficial motto of San Francisco should be "enjoy yourself," for that is what most people strive to do, each in their own way. In San Francisco it is pretty easy to do that, since the opportunities seem endless in their variety and quantity. A few decades ago, during what was sometimes termed the "me generation," younger Americans were being chided for thinking only about themselves, for wanting to focus their lives on fun, for wanting all the conveniences of life—perhaps without working as hard for them as their parents had. Northern Californians, as they would, turned this into humor, poking fun at themselves and at those who were doing the chiding. People of the Bay Area started sporting stickers on the back bumpers of their cars that proclaimed, "Honk if you want it all, now!" And other drivers laughed and waved and honked their car horns in response.

But, none of this means that San Franciscans are not serious, for they are—when it suits them. They are serious about their work, whether because they believe in it or even just because it supports the lifestyle they so enjoy. They are serious about their social activism, and they are serious about socializing with their likeminded friends. So, participating with your new colleagues on work projects or studying in a school where other students also have the desire to learn, will also help you fit in.

SOME HELPFUL HINTS

Expect the unexpected when it comes to fitting in with San Franciscans—no matter who they are or where they came from. This even includes people from your own country, in whose homes you might think to expect the utmost in traditions. But they too are living in San Francisco and have made adjustments to the culture, the climate, the seasons, and even the agricultural bounty (including the wines). So, as they have done, look around and see how each group comports itself, and then, to use a favorite American expression, "When in Rome, do as the Romans do."

There are, after all, some attitudes of the populace that translate into a cultural ethos. Perhaps they are not "rules" for behavior, but understandings that help people get along. You will add them to others you have discovered, make adjustments in groups that do not seem to follow them—and after a while you will find that you are as flexible, adaptable, and easy-going about life in The City as anyone else.

- Generally, San Francisco is an "early" town. Since stockbrokers and other financial types adjust their hours to the opening of the Stock Exchange in New York, they go to work sometimes before dawn and go to sleep early. If you go to the theater or a concert, you will no doubt dine before, not afterwards. And, on weekdays you may find people socializing right after work. One of the most favorite occasions is "happy hour," after work, when co-workers gather at a bar for a couple of drinks and snacks (provided by the bar with the drinks), hang out together for a while, and then head for home. "Happy hour," in fact may last from

5:00 pm, when most offices close, until 7:30 pm or so, and does not last just one hour, although it is often pretty happy indeed.
- If you are invited to someone's home, arrive close to the time specified. Being "fashionably late" may be the norm in some cultures, but not here. Depending on your hosts, bring a token of gratitude for the invitation: a bottle of wine, a box of artisan chocolates, a popular book you think your host might be interested in reading—something you have thought about and know your host will like. In some homes, pre-dinner hors d'oeuvres are served in the living room with a glass of wine or cocktail. At the table, praise the meal served, and feel free to accept seconds when offered. You will no doubt be served a California wine and also water. Savor the wine for the flavor but slake your thirst with the water. Then, take your cue from others—your hosts and other guests—as to how late to stay. Guests often linger over their coffees at the dining table, and shortly thereafter begin to take their leave.
- If you go to a restaurant with friends, arrive at the time for which the reservation was made. When your meal arrives—each course that you have ordered—be prepared to offer a taste of yours to your dining partners and to taste their meals as well. This is normal in America. (But feel free not to taste something you do not want to.) Also, people like to split their appetizers or main courses, either allowing them to eat less, or giving them the opportunity to sample several different dishes. And last—unless you have been invited to a particular function or party—understand that the bill will probably be divided equally, even if your dinner cost less than the others. In a group, people do not usually look at each item on the bill to determine who pays how much more or how much less.
- If you are included at a weekend brunch, be prepared to stay for a while. Brunch? The word indicates a combination of breakfast and lunch, but what it means is a social occasion that might start with a mimosa (champagne and orange juice cocktail) and then continue with any combination of eggs and sausages, sauces, rolls and pastries, fruits

and desserts, and espresso or cappuccino—or whatever else the trendiest places are concocting that day. People remain for hours over a weekend brunch, especially in a restaurant that has a view, that offers live music, or that has the most or the best of something that they want.

- If you are with a group of sporty friends, you might go on a hike on the weekends, or take a bike ride together in the hills outside the city. Do not forget that your friends will probably work out in a gym during the week, or take a jog in the mornings before or the afternoons after work. Think about these things for yourself, for keeping fit, besides being good for your health, will help expand your social horizons!
- And on weekend evenings—especially Friday and Saturday nights—younger San Franciscans like to party. Each group will hang out with likeminded friends, doing whatever suits them best. Across the groups, however, they might like to try the newest eatery to appear on the scene, to drink the most fashionable cocktails at the noisiest bar, to hear the hottest music, or even to bring a six-pack beer to somebody's flat. And—early town or not—they stay out late. Enjoyment is what San Francisco is about.

And last, make the effort to be "in the know." Consider at the outset some of the suggestions in this book. Learn about your new home. Explore the areas beyond The City. Taste some California wines, either in San Francisco or in the charming Wine Country towns. Keep abreast of current events. Know which film festivals appear in which months, and when the neighborhood street fairs take place. Be positive. Be a person your new friends find interesting and well informed. Relax and enjoy yourself. And if you do these things, you will be well on your way to being a San Franciscan yourself.

SETTLING IN

CHAPTER 5

'Arrival in San Francisco is an experience in living.'
—William Saroyan

FORMALITIES FOR FOREIGNERS

Immigration

Perhaps the streets of the United States were not paved with gold as so many immigrants imagined when they came to these shores, but America has nonetheless been seen, since its earliest days, as a land of opportunity. Whether people came to escape poverty or persecution, America has always seemed to be—and often has been—the world's most beneficial haven. America, in fact, truly gained its strength by being a "melting pot" of cultures and becoming the world's most successful multi-ethnic nation.

Although both American citizens and the government believe that diversity enriches society, the country has always had mixed feelings toward immigration. During the last decade, the population of the United States grew by only 8 percent, but the percentage of foreign-born residents grew by some 30 percent. Thus, the subject of limiting immigration has always come up during economic downturns, for—whether true or not—it has been widely held that immigrants take jobs away from low-skilled American citizens. Also, since the terrorist attacks of September 11, 2001, the question of unlimited immigration and even tourist entry into the United States has been revisited, and regulations continue to be tightened.

The problem is also compounded by illegal immigrants, and immigration policy, a highly volatile issue, is currently under review by the government. Some 11 million people are estimated to be living illegally in the United States, most of them Mexicans who have slipped across the 700-mile (1,100-km) border between Mexico and the United States. The border is difficult to police, but administration proposals for securing it have not yet met with success in the Congress or with approval by Americans, who have—led by coalitions of immigrants—demonstrated in the streets around the country. At the time of this writing, new plans are still under consideration, but nothing has been resolved.

Thus, immigration laws are changeable and will no doubt remain very complex. The information provided in this chapter should be helpful, but it is important to consult the American Embassy in your country (or the consulate nearest to you) long in advance of your desired trip (or emigration) and to receive the most up-to-date information.

One thing is sure: compile as much documentation as possible concerning your personal history, health, qualifications, financial condition, and plans for your stay in the United States. These are sure to be carefully checked and scrutinized.

Arriving in the United States

If you have not come to the United States in the last five years or so, you will notice that some of the security documentation regulations for entering the county have changed. Everyone—short- or long-term visitors—must comply with tight rules, many of which were promulgated after 9/11. And whether you are coming for a tourist visit or for work—sponsored by your prospective employer—you will still have to comply with all the visa requirements as set forth by the State Department.

The following are some websites for general guidelines. To inform yourself fully of the requirements, contact either the American embassy or consulate near you, or access any of the governmental Internet sites, below. For student visas, refer to pages 137–139.

- For visitors: website: http://travel.state.gov/visa/temp/temp_1305.html

- For visa policies: website: http://www.unitedstatesvisas.gov/visa/questions/questions_4433.html
- For electronic visa application forms: website: http://evisaforms.state.gov/
- For immigrants: website: http://travel.state.gov/visa/immigrants/immigrants_1340.html
- For immigrant visas: website: http://travel.state.gov/visa/immigrants/types/types_1326.html
- For U.S Citizen and Immigration Services: website: http://www.uscis.gov/graphics/index.htm

Passports

All people entering the United States must hold a machine-readable (biometric) passport. This now also includes Canada. A biometric passport includes a digital photograph on the data page, plus several lines of machine-readable biographical information on the bottom of the page.

The United States is now issuing an "e-passport," in which data is embedded in an electronic chip. The chip is inside the rear cover, and it contains the same data as on the front inside page. Whichever type of passport you have, it will be scanned by the Customs official when you enter and leave the country.

Visa Waiver Program

The Visa Waiver Program (VWP) basically allows qualified citizens of designated countries (plus Canada) to enter the United States (for business or tourism purposes) for stays of up to 90 days without holding a visa. Currently, the 27 countries that participate in the program are: Andorra, Australia, Austria, Belgium, Brunei, Denmark, Finland, France, Germany, Iceland, Ireland, Italy, Japan, Liechtenstein, Luxembourg, Monaco, the Netherlands, New Zealand, Norway, Portugal, San Marino, Singapore, Slovenia, Spain, Sweden, Switzerland, and the United Kingdom.

Even if you qualify under the VWP, you will still have to comply with all other requirements, such as having an e-passport with biographic data and a digital photograph. You will still be screened as you enter the country, having filled out the Form I-94 provided to you when you arrive and you will still be subject to the Department of Homeland Security's US-VISIT program. (*See section* US-VISIT Program *for more details*.)

Getting a Visa

If your country does not participate in the VWP, you will need a visa. The most common visas are the B-1 for business travelers and the B-2 for people who come for pleasure or medical treatments. Most likely you will need a personal interview at the American embassy or consulate nearest you when applying for the visa, so schedule your appointment well in advance of your trip. It may take some time, depending on the season and how many applications are ahead of you. Inquire as to the necessary procedures you have to complete, for each embassy has some discretion in arranging its services.

US-VISIT Program

The US-VISIT Program is a security measure that tracks the identity of every visitor to the United States, and keeps a record of when they have departed. The program requires fingerscans and digital photos of visitors, and these are matched when the traveler enters and leaves the country. You may obtain more details at http://www.dhs.gov/us-visit.

If you are not from a VWP country and thus require a visa, you will have the fingerscans done at the time of the personal interview during your visa application. Both index fingers will be scanned and a digital photo taken. People who qualify for the VWP will have these done at Customs upon arrival in the United States.

When you arrive in the States, be prepared to wait in line at the immigration booth, to show your passport, visa, and return ticket, and to explain the reason for your visit. Here the fingerscanning is repeated to ensure that you are the same person who was issued the visa. If you need help, immigration officers at the airport have the information you require. In dire situations, you may wish to call your country's embassy in Washington, D.C. or a consulate near your port of entry.

Upon leaving the country, you will need to verify your departure. At some airports, automated machines make the process easier. The information is retained on your travel records, kept and checked at your next application to enter the country. You will also turn in the stub of Form I-94, which you were given when you entered the country—and which you have kept with you during your stay. Keeping the I-94 stub is important, for if you do not turn it in, you will likely be identified as an "overstay," meaning that you may be denied re-entry into the United States.

Employment-based Visas

Do not expect to enter the United States and then to look for a permanent, legal job. Nor should you expect to come and be illegally employed, despite tales from your friends of how easy it is to find work in a restaurant or bar. Employers face stiff fines if caught employing non-documented foreigners. Immigration laws are tightening, and the demand for this kind of labor is drying up.

There are, however, a variety of options for coming to the United States to work, depending on your skills, abilities, and experience. It also often depends on how much an employer needs your particular services. If a company is hiring you for a temporary position, the potential employer will fill out Form I-129 (form for non-immigrant work visa). For immigrant worker visas, the would-be employer must file Form I-140, which is mandatory for the application for the visa. (*Access one of the Internet sites listed in section on* Arriving in the United States *on pages 73–74 for more information.*)

Trusted Traveler Programs

- "Global Entry" is a new program to facilitate the entry into the United States of pre-approved travelers—American citizens and permanent residents, as well as citizens of some other countries. After passing a background check, travelers will use an automated kiosk to clear passport control, thereby avoiding the long lines. So far, the program is available at major international airports, such as John F. Kennedy, Dulles, Miami, Atlanta, Los Angeles, Houston, and Chicago. More airports should be added shortly.

- "NEXUS" facilitates pre-screened American and Canadian travelers between those two countries, at airports, automobile, and marine ports of entry. "SENTRI" is the same type of program, that facilities easier entry at borders for frequent travelers between the United States and Mexico.

- The "FAST COMMERCIAL DRIVER" programs between the United States and Canada and Mexico, allow citizens or permanent residents of these three countries to drive into the United States, using a "Fast Commercial Driver Card."

In all programs, you must be admissible into the United States under current laws. And for the FAST programs, you must also have a valid driver's license. For more information and criteria about how to apply and set up an appointment, access the Customs and Border Protection website: http://www.customs.gov, and click on "Trusted Travelers Programs."

Diversity Immigrant Visa Program

The Diversity Immigrant Program is an annual lottery that offers 50,000 American residence visas. The program is divided into six regions: Asia; South America, Central America, and the Caribbean; Europe; Africa; Oceania; and North America (the Bahamas). No one country receives more than 3,500 visas in any year.

Applications for a visa date of two years in the future are generally due in October. Inquire at the consulate nearest you for current information or access the Internet site at this http://travel.state.gov/visa/immigrants/types/types_1322.html. All applications must be filed electronically. A digital photograph—either new or scanned—must accompany the application.

USCIS

The San Francisco District Office of the Bureau of U.S. Citizenship and Immigration Services (USCIS) is located at 444 Washington Street, near Sansome (tel: (415) 705-4411). It is open from 7:00 am to 3:00 pm weekdays except Wednesday, when it closes at 2:30 pm.

With the exception of obtaining forms, everyone must make an appointment through INFOPASS, accessed at http://infopass.uscis.gov/. Forms may be ordered by telephone if you know the number of the form you need (tel: (800) 375-5283), or from the office on Washington Street. If you need a passport, immigration photographs, or fingerprint documentation, try the two shops listed below and located across from the USCIS building. Both are open on weekdays only.

- Leetone Photo Center, 615 Sansome Street; tel: (415) 391-9890
- Corning Gold Photography, 501 Washington Street; tel: (415) 392-2223

Foreign Consulates

In the United States, all foreign embassies are situated in Washington, D.C., but countries with many residents or visitors in certain areas maintain regional consulates as well. San Francisco has many consulates, and they are most helpful during times of crisis: they replace lost passports and help in medical or legal emergencies by making referrals to appropriate doctors, dentists, or lawyers. They do not, however, help people get out of jail. Yet in all emergencies, they act as liaison between you in the United States and your family at home. It is therefore a good idea to carry the telephone number of the consulate in your wallet.

Embassies or consulates also renew passports, record births, marriages, and deaths, and advise on matters pertaining to citizens of their country. Sometimes they offer information on local services, including lists of doctors and attorneys who speak your language, as well as translators.

Most consulates are open for consular affairs on weekday mornings only. Some open their telephone lines for a few hours in the afternoons. Find out when your consulate is open before visiting it. On the national holidays both of the United States and of your own country, the consulate will no doubt be closed. The contact details of all embassies in Washington can be obtained at http://www.embassy.org/embassies. For a list of relevant consulates in San Francisco, see the *Yellow Pages* under Consulates & Other Foreign Government Representatives.

Customs and Border Protection

It is U.S. Customs and Border Protection (CBP) that screens you and your goods or baggage when you enter the country, whether these are hand-carried or checked-in (website: http://www.cbp.gov). The information CBP provides can be extremely helpful as you prepare for your relocation. Access their Internet site, where you will find online publications and a variety of subjects concerning entering the United States, as well as a list of hundreds of answers to common importation questions (website: http://www.customs.gov).

Bringing Your Belongings…

If your appropriate visa for residency is in order, you may bring your personal effects into the United States if you have owned them for more than one year (refer to Publication

0518 on the CBP website). There is no duty on these imports; antiques are also free of duty if they are more than 100 years old.

Your shipment of goods must be cleared through Customs at its first port of arrival. Customs does not notify you when the goods have arrived, so your mover must do so within 15 days of their arrival. Generally someone must clear the goods through Customs, providing an inventory of the goods on CBP Form 3299.

...Your Appliances

Electricity in the United States is 110–120 volts, 60 hertz. Importing European appliances may be more trouble than it is worth, for appliances—large and small—are fairly inexpensive in America, and discount shops are found in every city. Most apartments and houses are equipped with stoves and refrigerators, and some have clothes washers and dryers. To import appliances may mean dealing with converters and adaptors, and putting your appliances into spaces that were not designed for them.

...Your Car

All cars and vehicles coming into the country must conform with U.S. safety, bumper, and emission standards; you will have to have written certification that the vehicle meets the set requirements before it may enter the country. This may either be in the form of a statement from the Environmental Protection Agency (EPA), or a manufacturer's label in English that is affixed to the inside front door of the car. For information, call the EPA Import Hotline and ask for the Automotive Imports Facts Manual, (tel: (202) 343-9240; website: http://www.epa.gov/otaq/imports/quikover.htm).

When it comes to Customs, you will have to declare the car to a CBP officer when it arrives in the United States (Refer to Publication 0520 on CBP website.). You will need the shipper's original bill of lading, the bill of sale, foreign registration, and any other documents that cover the vehicle. The undercarriage of the car must be free of foreign soil, which can be accomplished by having the car steam-cleaned before shipment. Make sure you know in advance from your shipper the date the car will arrive, so that Customs can clear it. If the car has not been in your possession for a year, you will have to pay a duty based on the purchase price or "blue book" value (the accepted value of that car when offered for sale, used).

...Your Money
There is no limit to the total amount of monetary instruments—cash, traveler's checks, or negotiable securities—that may be brought into the United States. But if you bring in more than US$ 10,000 (or if you receive that amount), you must file this with the Customs Service, using The Report of International Transportation of Currency or Monetary Instruments, Form FinCEN105.

...Your Medications
To bring any medications that contain habit-forming drugs or narcotics (prescription-strength cough medicine, diuretics, heart drugs, tranquilizers, etc) into the country, make sure all are properly identified and that you have a physician's prescription or written statement that the medicine is used under a doctor's direction. Bring an amount that will tide you over until you can get a new prescription in the United States. The Customs Department recommends bringing a supply for no more than 60 days.

...Your Pets
All dogs and cats being brought into the country will be examined at the port of entry. This also applies to pets that were taken out of the country and are being brought back in. Every dog must be accompanied by a health certificate stating that it is free of diseases communicable to human beings. Both dogs and cats must be vaccinated against rabies at least 30 days before entry into the United States (except for animals under three months old). If the dog has been living in an area free of rabies, no rabies certificate is required; otherwise the dog should have a valid rabies vaccination certificate.

FINDING YOUR NEST

Getting Started: Hotels

If you are coming to San Francisco for a visit, you will first need to find somewhere to stay. Even though San Francisco has more than 200 hotels and some 32,000 hotel rooms, it also has about 16 million visitors a year and is a favorite convention destination. So, finding a hotel that meets your needs and your budget should be an early priority of your traveling planning. Book the accommodation that you want as soon as you can.

San Francisco is well-visited all year round and tourism is not seasonal, so prices for hotel rooms do not fluctuate as much as they might elsewhere. And prices can be steep. Nonetheless, even the most sought after hotels do offer special "packages," and you should make sure to ask about them.

Instead of accepting the "rack rate" (the published price, and the one initially quoted to you), inquire about corporate, family, or weekend rates. Specify any discounts you might be entitled to: AARP, AAA, or your airline benefits, for instance. Your travel agent usually has access to the best deals and should tell you about them. When calculating costs, remember that taxes are not included in the price of the room: you will have to add 14 percent state and city taxes, and if you are bringing a car, you will also have to add the hotel's comparatively hefty fee for its "valet parking"—the service provided when a hotel employee parks your car for you and then brings it back to you when you want it—charged on a per-day basis. The motels on Van Ness or on Lombard Street are reasonably priced and have easier accommodations for an automobile.

Nob Hill and Union Square are the two most expensive areas, and rack rates of rooms in the famous hotels may begin at about US$ 250 (plus 14 percent) or even higher. Away from these areas are many hotels that are reasonably priced (some under US$ 100), but make sure you understand the neighborhood, for just a few streets away from the from the Square to the west and just past the adjacent Theater District, for example, you might find yourself in the problematical Tenderloin district. There the ambiance varies from street to street.

Smaller boutique hotels—some of them in restored Victorian houses—may offer more charm as well as more affordable prices. B&Bs, (bed and breakfasts), which in addition to breakfast (and sometimes a glass of wine in the afternoon) also usually include a more personal welcome (Check out the Archbishop's Mansion and the Red Victorian.). Some hotels that look old on their facade—with a preserved older San Francisco nostalgic ambiance—have also undergone renovation and upgrading in the past few years, and they are well worth considering. Most will indicate in their descriptions online if they have been restored or renovated.

Starting the Search

There are hundreds of global Internet sites such as http://www.expedia.com or http://www.opodo.co.uk that list hotels all around the world. There are also websites for hotel chains—Holiday Inn, Best Western, Westin, Marriott and Hilton, for example—that have several locations in San Francisco, with varying price rates and levels of service. Usually their website address is http://www.*addthehotelname*.com. The following site are especially good for San Francisco.

- SF Convention and Visitors Bureau: recommendations for some hotels and basic tourist information; website: http://www.onlyinsanfrancisco.com
- Kimpton Hotels: Nine typically San Francisco downtown hotels; website: http://www.kimptonhotels.com
- Personality Hotels: Seven hotels near Union Square; tel: (800) 533-1900; website: http://personalityhotels.com
- San Francisco Reservations; tel: (800) 737-2060; website: http://www.hotelres.com
- California Hotels; website: http://www.californiahotels.com
- Hotels.Com: good listing of discounts and deals; website: http://www.hotels.com
- Joie de Vivre Hospitality; a group of charming smaller hotels, and the stunning new Vitale, on the Embarcadero; website: http://www.jdvhospitality.com
- Bed and Breakfast San Francisco; tel: (415) 899-0060; website: http://www.bbsf.com
- Bed and Breakfast International; website: http://www.ibbp.com

The following are two hotels with Japanese amenities and atmosphere:

- Nikko San Francisco, 222 Mason Street near Union Square; tel: (415) 394-1111; website: http://www.hotelnikkosf.com
- Kabuki Hotel at 1625 Post Street, in Japantown; tel: (415) 614-5498; website:http//www.jdvhotels.com

And last, if the buffeting winds of the ocean appeal to you, there is Seal Rock Inn at 48th Avenue and Geary; tel: (415) 752-8000; website: http://www.sealrockinn.com. It is just a five-minute walk down to the waves.

Short-term Home Exchange

Yet, hotels are not the only option. The least expensive way to stay in San Francisco for a few weeks is to exchange your home for one here. International home exchange companies list homes available worldwide (in brochures and on the Internet). Members pay to list their own locations and can search for those in the city of their choice, specifying the dates available. In your listing, you also describe your home, and its surroundings and amenities. You correspond with

the people who answer, provide photos of the property, compare experiences of previous people who have been in that apartment, and reach an agreement. To know more about such home exchanges, visit the following:
- Homelink International; website: http://www.homelink.org
- Intervac U.S.; website: http://www.intervac.com
- HomeExchange.com; website: http://www.homeexchange.com

Short-term Rentals

If you are staying in The City for more than a week, especially for an extended stay, consider a residence hotel or corporate apartment. For short-term stays, furnished suites generally combine the comforts of an apartment with the amenities of a hotel. Suites are of various sizes and include cooking facilities. Prices vary of course, but the marginal cost of your stay, when taking into consideration the number of nights you will actually be staying and the amount saved from not having to eat every meal in a restaurant, will generally be lower than at a prestigious hotel. And indeed, a furnished apartment is also the most comfortable way to spend a month or so, while you search for long-term lodgings.

Some companies' Internet sites list multiple opportunities for temporary quarters for extended stay:
- Synergy Corporate Housing, 685 Folsom Street; tel: (800) 600-1115; website: http://www.synergyhousing.com
- Executive Suites, tel: (415) 776-5151; fax: (415) 776-5155; website: http://www.executivesuites-sf.com

And individually managed residence hotels dot the city.
- **Downtown**—The Steinhart, 952 Sutter Street (tel: (415) 928-3855; (800) 553-1900; website: http://www.steinharthotel.com. An older, restored, landmark building on the foothill of Nob Hill. Studios and one-bedroom furnished apartments, maid service.
- **Fisherman's Wharf**—Suites at Fisherman's Wharf, 2655 Hyde Street; tel: (415) 771-0200; website: http://www.thesuitesatfishermanswharf.com. A resort near the Wharf, good for families.

- **Nob Hill**—Grosvenor Suites, 899 Pine, at Mason; tel: (415) 421-1899; (800) 999-9189; website: http://www.grosvenorsuites.com. Studio to two-bedrooms, fully equipped. Parking available.
- **Van Ness**—The Kenmore, 1570 Sutter Street, near Gough; tel: (415) 776-5815; website: http://www.kenmorehotel.us. Residence club near Civic Center. Close to public transportation, supermarket, restaurants. Breakfast and dinners included, brunch on Sunday. (website: http://www.kenmorehotelsf.com)
- **Van Ness**—The Monroe, 1870 Sacramento Street; tel: (415) 474-6200; website: http://www.monroeresidenceclub.com. Full breakfasts and dinners six days a week; brunch on Sunday.

The Long-term Housing Situation

The good news is that as small and compact as it is, San Francisco offers a wide range of housing, from elegant mansions and single-family homes with gardens to semidetached row houses; from high-rise complexes to low-rise apartments over neighborhood stores, to flats in two-story homes. Thousands of charming Victorian houses and small homes coexist peaceably with the few tall modern structures, and each of the almost thirty distinct neighborhoods has its own eclectic blend.

In general, San Franciscans are apartment dwellers. Of the more than 330,000 residences in the city, some 229,000 are multi-units, and only about 105,000 are single or semidetached one-family homes. And, fortunately, San Francisco is a city of renters. Some two-thirds of the population rent their homes, while only slightly more than one-third own theirs.

But unfortunately, San Francisco is a city whose boundaries are fixed by water, and its expanding commercial areas have reduced residential possibilities. That the city has decided to keep its residential ambience and put height restrictions on new building construction has created a low inventory of available apartments. And increasing demand over the last decade—until the "tech bubble" of nearby Silicon

Valley burst—fueled a difficult price situation, for many of the newly-rich preferred to live in San Francisco and were willing to pay whatever it took to do so. This held true for both purchase and rental units. All of this pushed prices up to the point where the city was rated—and still is—as one of the least affordable housing markets in the United States.

At mid-decade, for example, the rate of only 15 percent of California households could afford a median priced home (US$ 543,980), each needing an estimated income of US$ 128,000 to support it. Compare this with the general U.S. figures, which showed a median-priced home to be US$ 212,000 and an income needed of US$ 50,000.

In the Bay Area, however, the rate of affordability was even lower, at 12 percent, as median property and rental prices were higher. In fact, San Franciscans themselves consistently rate the lack of affordable housing and the city's high rents as the city's most pressing problems. The median home price currently stands at US$ 716,000, almost quadruple the aforementioned national median of US$ 212,000. Rental vacancies hover around 4.5 percent, and the average cost for a rental apartment in the city is currently US$ 1,667.

The Housing Problem

The problem began with the construction boom after World War II. Just about all the high-rent commercial skyscrapers in the city were built during what critics called the "Manhattanization of San Francisco," which stopped only because there was no more space downtown. Small businesses were driven to the outer reaches, some lower-end apartments were demolished to build hotels or upscale apartments, and some former rental units themselves were converted to expensive condominiums.

And, an important part of why housing costs are so high is that despite a commute to Silicon Valley, many of the "dot.com" entrepreneurs of the Nineties preferred to live in San Francisco; sometimes San Francisco itself seemed a bedroom community as cars created a new, southbound morning rush hour. That these people could ignore traditional purchase procedures forced the market ever higher. Although the bubble burst and prices dipped for a while, the market has once again become overheated.

It is beginning to hold true, as some people say, that in San Francisco nothing worth living in is inexpensive. Do not be shocked, do not be upset. It is just the way it is. Finding the right home at the right price is not an easy matter, but eventually you will find one, especially if you understand that you will have to compromise. But do not expect to arrive in San Francisco and move into the perfect inexpensive apartment with a spectacular view after a short stay in a hotel of about two or three days. San Francisco does not work that way. Expect instead to find a short-term apartment or residence hotel, and to spend several months in search of a home.

Yet the news is not all bad. Although the cost of living in San Francisco is higher than that of the United States average, income levels in the Bay Area are generally commensurate. In other words, salaries are also higher here than in regions where costs are lower. Costs other than housing are not particularly high: the mild climate allows residents to spend less on household utilities than in some other cities, for instance, and San Franciscans are always happy to say how little they paid for something, whether clothing bought at a discount or a delicious meal in an Asian restaurant. For cost of living comparisons, access any of the "cost of living calculators" on the Internet (website: http://www.bestplaces.net).

The Internet will be your best bet in determining neighbourhoods you can afford, either to buy or to rent. Check especially http://www.hotpads.com, and agency that lists median prices for purchase and rental by neighbourhood, plus availability and prices of individual properties.

Rent Control

Another plus is that renters do have some protection under San Francisco law. Apartment rental in San Francisco has been controlled since 1979, meaning that rents for tenants with leases may only be raised a certain percentage each year, determined by a formula tied to the Cost of Living Index. Currently, the rate of increase is 2.2 percent. Rents may be raised to "market levels," however, when a tenant leaves and before a new tenant moves in; this sometimes encourages landlords to force tenants out under one pretext or another, or to insist on month-to-month contracts, rather than leases.

In some apartment complexes, tenants who have held leases for 20 years are paying only a fraction of what a new tenant pays. This may seem unfair, but without some regulation to protect existing tenants, rents in San Francisco would be even higher than they are. Although some people claim that rent control is forcing the higher rents of new tenants and that a free market would bring rents down, statistics have not shown this to be true. In fact, the Board of Supervisors is constantly struggling with the rental issues, endeavoring to be fair to renters and landlords alike.

Speaking of Rent...

Rental units are strewn throughout the city; the areas to the north and east have more apartments, and to the west and south, more private homes. Their rental price, of course, depends on the apartment itself, and also the neighborhood, and the view; the more central or trendy the neighborhood, the higher the price. Even areas that were once seen as lower-priced are no longer so, and this at least benefits the long-term tenants who are protected under rent control. It is said that fewer than one-third of the people who moved to an apartment in the Mission just five years ago could afford to today; even in this formerly low-rent area, the current average rent for a two-bedroom apartment that cost US$ 1,600 five years ago costs US$ 2,200 now. Nonetheless, you should be able to find housing within your price range, but it might take some time and compromise.

It is hard to predict the type of rentals in any given area. Older apartments may be found in newly trendy areas, and some recent construction may be found in areas thought of as traditional. And some reasonably priced rentals may be just on the edge of higher-priced districts, in areas called the Outer Mission, Lower Haight, or Upper Market. Except for a few areas near the Tenderloin and down by Hunters Point, there are practically no areas of the city that are not appropriate for the apartment search. Although some parts of other neighborhoods—in the Western Addition, for example—will require some thought, they should not automatically be ruled out.

Starting the Rental Search

You can begin to understand the San Francisco rental market in advance of arrival by looking online. Some listing services charge a small access fee, usually good for three months; these services, however, allow searches by location or by housing requirements (number of rooms, elevator, etc), and they often offer advice on moving and landlord requirements. (*Refer also to section on* Roommates *on page 140*)

- Apartment Guide: http://www.apartmentguide.com
- Craigslist; website: http://www.craigslist.org
- Apartments For Rent.Com: http://www.forrent.com
- Rent Tech: San Francisco and East Bay rental listings; website: http://www.renttech.com

Once in San Francisco, you can read the local publications and walk around the neighborhoods you are interested in to spot the "for rent" signs in apartment windows, each of which gives a telephone number to call. If you can afford it, however, work with a real estate agent who knows what is available in particular neighborhoods. You will have to pay a commission, but it may be worth it to streamline the search. Although most real estate agents handle rentals (*see list on page 95*), Hill & Co, at both 1906 (rentals) and 2107 Union Street, as well as 1880 Lombard Street, is especially known for its rental properties (tel: (415) 921-6000; website: http://www.hill-co.com).

The *San Francisco Chronicle* is an excellent source for rentals, but if you see something you like, act immediately. Fast-spreading news of the availability of a good apartment may mean that by the time an advertisement appears in the paper, the apartment might well have been taken.

- *San Francisco Chronicle*; website: http://sfgate.com
- *San Francisco Weekly*; website: http://www.sfweekly.com
- East Bay: *East Bay Express*; website: http://www.eastbayexpress.com
- Oakland and East Bay: *Oakland Tribune*; website: http://www.oaklandtribune.com
- East Bay: *Contra Costa Times*; website: http://www.contracostatimes.com
- Marin County: *Marin Independent Journal*; website: http://www.marinij.com
- San Jose: *San Jose Mercury News*; website: http://www.mercurynews.com
- San Mateo County: *San Mateo County Times*; website: http://www.insidebayarea.com/sanmateocountytimes

The Apartment

San Francisco real estate makes a distinction between an apartment and a flat. A flat is an entire floor of a small apartment building or two-story house, and it has its own entrance. Thus, you might walk up an outdoor flight of stairs to your door, and inside, the entire floor is your own. An apartment, however, is one of several—or many—on a single floor. Foreigners should understand that, in the United States, the first floor is really the ground floor, and the second floor is the next floor up.

If you are bringing in a car, pay attention to the parking situation. Although new buildings must include some off-street parking, older dwellings may have no garages, and parking in San Francisco is generally a problem in all but the western neighborhoods. Some areas have public garages that rent spaces by the month; in addition to price, which varies from district to district, inquire about hours of access. If you intend to park your car on the street, you will probably need a city-issued parking permit. (*Refer to page 178.*) You should also determine the closest access to public transportation. Even people with cars often take public transportation or walk to work.

Landlords generally ask for an application fee, which covers the cost of a credit check, plus the first and last months' rent, and/or a security deposit when the application is approved. Be prepared to provide a credit reference and the names of your past and current employers and landlords. Identification might include your driver's license, bank account numbers, and Social Security number. Many places do not allow pets, but it is illegal for a landlord to prohibit children.

A lease must specify a beginning date and termination date (not when you are required to move out, but when the lease must be renewed). If there is no termination date, the contract is not a "lease," but an "agreement." And an agreement runs month to month indefinitely and may be terminated by either party at any time, which, of course, is beneficial to the landlord. It is not wise to accept an oral agreement, which has no legal validity.

Before signing, ask your landlord for an explanation of the necessary procedures for breaking a lease, should you need to move. In general, you should give as much notice as possible, in writing, and expect to pay the entire remainder of the lease should a new tenant not be found.

Security deposits are used to cover or compensate for any damage to the apartment (deducted upon your departure). Thus, when you are returning the signed lease, check for any irregularities in the apartment, and specify them in writing—every crack in the walls or chip on an appliance—so that upon leaving you will not be charged for damage. If you are applying for a furnished apartment, inquire about some of the items you require, such as a desk, Internet access, or a microwave oven. Ask the landlord for a detailed inventory of all objects in the apartment, and make sure everything listed is actually there.

Apartment Complexes

For permanent housing, some large apartment complexes handle their own rentals. These generally have a management office on the premises, which—at least theoretically—should make it efficient for repairs and service. In addition to considering these for long-term leases (if there are apartments available) you might also consider one of these complexes for the short term, so you can have a place to live while looking for permanent housing. Some offer six-month leases or month-to-month contracts; in fact, taking several months to find or decide on satisfactory permanent housing—especially if you are planning to buy—is not uncommon.

If you are interested in living in the Presidio, contact the John Stewart Company at 558 Presidio Boulevard (tel: (415) 561-5454; website: http://www.presidio.gov/leasing/residentialleasing). Depending on what is currently available, the options are for 2-3-4 bedroom apartments, townhouses, single-family homes, and duplexes.

Trinity Management Services at 333 Bay Street manages apartment buildings on the north side of San Francisco—Nob Hill, Russian Hill and Telegraph Hill, North Beach, the Marina (tel: (415) 433-3333; website: http://www.trinitymanagement.com). They handle both short- and long-term apartments, furnished and unfurnished.

Avalon Communities also manages several full-service rental properties (tel: (415) 284-9080; website: http://www.avaloncommunities.com). Their holdings are in the Sunset, in SoMa, on Nob Hill, at Mission Bay, and in Diamond Heights.

Archstone manages apartments all around the Bay Area; website:http://www.archstoneapartments.com. In San Francisco, one building is at Third and Harrison Streets; tel:

(877) 525-7299; another is Fox Plaza, on Market Street near Van Ness; tel: (877) 270-4346.

- **Embarcadero**—Golden Gateway Center, 460 Davis Court, at Jackson; tel: (415) 434-5700; website: http://www.goldengatewaycenter.com. Luxury apartments and townhouses, with a fitness center, tennis courts, and a swimming pool. Parking garage is another plus.
- **Embarcadero**—Bayside Village, The Embarcadero at Brannan; tel: (415) 777-4850; website: http://www.baysidevillage.com. Studio to two-bedroom units, parking. Free shuttle bus to Financial District. Swimming pools and a fitness center.
- **Lake Merced/San Francisco State**—Parkmerced, 3711 19th Avenue; tel: (877) 243-5544; website: http://www.parkmerced.com. Moderately priced single-family townhouses and apartments in a large development near San Francisco State.
- **SoMa**—Marina Apartments, 2 Townsend Street; tel: (415) 495-4119; website: http://www.sbma-sf.com). One- and two-bedroom apartments, pool, sauna, tennis courts, parking.
- **SoMa**—Rincon Towers:88 Howard Street; tel: (9415) 615-9200; website: http://www.rinconresidential.com. Furnished and unfurnished apartments on the Embarcadero.
- **Western Addition**—Webster Tower and Terrace, 1489 Webster Street, at Geary; tel: (415) 931-6300; website: http://www.webstertower.com. Modern studios, one- and two-bedroom apartments, and penthouses, both furnished and unfurnished.
- **The New Fillmore**—The Fillmore Center, 1475 Fillmore Street; tel: (415) 921-1969; website: http://www.thefillmorecenter.com. Studios to three-bedroom apartments, penthouse, townhouse. Health club on premises. Shopping convenience.

Purchasing a Home

Since most homes for sale are listed in the centralized database of the San Francisco Board of Realtors' Multiple Listing Service, real estate agents have access to the broadest range of available housing. In San Francisco, agents usually receive a 6 percent commission, which is paid by the seller.

The "fair market value" of a home is what a buyer will pay and a seller will accept. Generally, a home sells at a price within the price range of similar homes on the market in its area, and your real estate agent should be able to give you an estimate of what each neighborhood's homes are going for. Price ranges fluctuate over time: when the stock market is rising (and the Pacific Rim entrepreneurs are doing well), a seller may receive multiple ever-higher offers, and when the stock market "corrects," these bidding wars may slow.

Work, if possible, with an agent with experience in the San Francisco market and with solid references; recommendations from friends and colleagues should help. Be specific with your agent about your price limits and your needs; also indicate on which items you might be willing to compromise. Ask also about their relocation services. The following are a few well-known agencies. There are many others (including Hill, mentioned above), offering homes with a range of prices, depending on location, square footage, and the market conditions. Check the websites; most have several branches.

- Tri-Coldwell Banker, 1699 Van Ness;
  tel: (415) 474-1750; fax: (415) 771-1264;
  website: http://www.tricoldwellbanker.com
- McGuire, 2001 Lombard; tel: (415) 929-1500;
  17 Bluxome Street; tel: (415) 546-3100
  website: http://www.mcguire.com
- Pacific Union, 601 Van Ness; tel: (415) 474-6600;
  website: http://www.pacunion.com

Your real estate agent should inform you of the weekend "open houses" that are held in the neighborhoods you are considering. By visiting these and looking at what is available in different areas and price ranges, you should quickly begin to understand property values and how you may need to modify your own positions.

Understanding the Market

Most apartments for sale are condominiums in which each unit is privately owned along with a percentage of the common space. The few "community apartments" are what other cities call cooperative apartments, where residents share in the corporation that owns the building. These apartments are generally in buildings constructed in the 1920s, and as that was a time when real estate was inexpensive, these co-ops had large, open floor plans. Today, however, only a few of the condominiums may measure 2,500 square feet (232.3 sq m) in floor area, and in general a new one-bedroom apartment averages 800–900 square feet (74.3–83.6 sq m) and a two-bedroom about 1,200–1,300 square feet (111.5–120.8 sq m).

Small, stucco single-family bungalows line the streets in the western sections of the city, and large, well-designed homes (some are really mansions) are found in the northern districts of Pacific Heights and the Marina, farther out at Seacliff, and in enclaves such as Cole Valley, Diamond Heights, and Sherwood Forest. There are low-rise apartment buildings in every area, high-rise apartment complexes in some, and some semidetached row houses in just about all.

Victorian houses are San Francisco's pride. Although thousands disappeared in 1906, some 14,000 survived the fire and have been preserved, primarily throughout the Mission, Cow Hollow, Pacific Heights, and Alamo Square districts. Victorians may be garish or gracious, they may appear in a number of styles such as Queen Anne, Italianate, or Stick, they may be single-family homes or two-flats, or—as along Union Street—they may have been converted into stores and offices. Regardless of their state, Victorians are always sought after and do not come cheap; a few still needing restoration are left, but for the most part they have already been refurbished and decorated in the glorious colors that have earned them the name of "San Francisco's painted ladies."

But Victorians, famous and expensive as they may be, are not all the city offers. If you are interested in historic houses, look also for the Brown Shingles popular in the 1890s, single-family homes built in reaction to the ornate Victorians. Made of natural materials, used simply and liberally, with cedar shingles and window trims of plain broad planks, they were still fairly Victorian in attitude. It was not until the early part of the following century that the one-story Craftsman Bungalow led the city away from its previous era. By the twenties, the compact California Bungalow, with its front porch and stucco walls, had become predominant in the then-developing western portions of the city. All these interesting styles still exist in the city and are occasionally put up for sale.

Thinking About Price

San Francisco rates among the most expensive housing markets in the country. You should therefore figure out where the best resale locations in the city are. Check out if they are in good school districts, in sunny areas, or in upcoming parts of the city—although these of course are the most expensive. Some districts—the Marina, Pacific Heights, Noe Valley, the Castro—are always in strong demand. Others are in upward transition, both in atmosphere and price—Hayes Valley, Potrero Hill, Bernal Heights. Note that most neighborhoods have their own improvement associations—local residents who are vigilant about keeping the character of the area intact—which will, of course, maintain the value of real estate as well as that area's lifestyle. A general rule in the property market is "the better the view, the higher the price; the farther out into the fog, the lower the price."

A few years ago, for instance, homes in Pacific and Presidio Heights had a range of US$ 1.5 million to US$ 20 million, while houses in the Sunset had a range of

---

Views of the City

"If you're alive, you can't be bored in San Francisco. If you're not alive, San Francisco will bring you to life." —William Saroyan

"You wouldn't think such a place as San Francisco could exist." —Dylan Thomas

"East is east, and West is San Francisco." —O. Henry

"You must think of the city as your best girl and treat her well." —James Rolph (mayor of San Francisco, 1912)

US$ 500,000 to US$ 1.43 million. And to accentuate the varied range of prices in just one area, Telegraph Hill's range of prices was between US$ 625,000 and US$ 8.75 million; and Cow Hollow's range was between US$ 825,000 and US$ 7.5 million. Even though the median price of a single home in the city declined by US$ 100,000 between May 2008 and May 2009, it is still no wonder that at about US$ 740,000, only about 12 percent of the populace can afford such a home here. But these ranges should serve as a guide as you assess the different areas for a potential home to buy. If a job is the reason for your relocation to an area, inquire of the Human Resources department as to whether the company offers housing incentives or a relocation package. Some do.

The Purchase: Step by Step

- Determine your preferred location, type of housing (condominium, house, etc), and your budget.
- Find the real estate agent you have confidence in.
- Identify (with your agent) the best bank for your mortgage.
- Begin the process of applying for a loan.
- Begin the search, based on your criteria; find a place you like.
- Review with your agent the "disclosure package" of the seller.
- Review comparable sales in neighborhood (determining reasonable offering price).
- Negotiate with seller (perhaps making a higher or lower offer, and then receiving a counter offer from seller).
- Accept offer; give deposit.
- Within two weeks, receive reports from home inspector, pest control inspector, etc.
- Make final offer (negotiate again with seller, based on inspectors' reports) or reject property.
- Complete financing; bank appraises property.
- Title and escrow company prepares closing package: loan documents, closing costs, government-required documents.
- Buyer and seller sign and signatures notarized (at title company office).
- The home is yours! Move in and open a bottle of California sparkling wine!

Yerba Buena Gardens
There is no better place to alleviate the stress of settling into a new home than Yerba Buena Gardens, at Mission and 4th Streets (website: http://www.yerbabuenagardens.com). No matter what makes you relax, you will probably find it here. Five and one-half acres of meadows, trees, flowers, falling water, public art, and museums, plus entertainment for the whole family and many small cafés. There is a striking waterfall memorial honoring Martin Luther King, and a beautiful wooden tribute to the Ohlone Indians that centuries ago might have lived on these grounds. The Rooftop has a Children's Garden with 100,000 square feet (929 sq m) of gardens and streams, an antique carousel, a play circle, a labyrinth made of hedges, and an interactive play center. The Center for the Arts has a gallery with changing exhibitions, and performances at the Center for the Arts Theater range from music festivals to operetta. So, come to Yerba Buena Gardens once—and then come back often again. Everyone does.

Retirement Living

If you are planning to retire to San Francisco, as many people do, you might consider one of the attractive urban complexes that offer independent-living apartments plus assisted living and medical care programs. These complexes—in which you purchase your own apartment—are convenient with respect to cultural events, the city's restaurants, and downtown shopping. Others dot the Bay Area, up into the Sonoma and Napa Valleys. *San Francisco* magazine occasionally runs an advertising section on retirement living. Some retirement apartments that can be found:

- San Francisco Towers, 1661 Pine Street; tel: (415) 776-0500; website: http://www.ehf.org/sft/
- The Sequoias, 1400 Geary Boulevard, near Gough; tel: (415) 922-9700; website: http://www.ncphs.org
- Coventry Park, 1550 Sutter Street; tel: (415) 921-1552; website: http://www.coventryparksf.com

MAKING YOURSELF AT HOME

Now that you have found a place to live, you have got to get your new home ready to move in. What comes next? Whether you have rented or bought a place, you will need to arrange for the electricity to be registered in your name, for your telephone service, and for your cable television and Internet access. There are other things you will want to know, as well, as you settle in, about household and earthquake insurance, and where to find certain services. In San Francisco it is not difficult. You just have to know where to look. (*For household furnishings and appliances, see pages 184–189.*)

And for official information, access the Internet site of the The City and County of San Francisco (website: http://www.sfgov.org—click on "Residents"). Information is offered in English, Chinese, Spanish, German, French, and Korean.

Electricity Hookup

In most rental homes you will be expected to pay for your use of electricity and gas, but in some they are included in the rent. The electric utility industry in California has been deregulated, meaning that homeowners may choose their own electricity provider. PG&E (Pacific Gas and Electric), formerly the public monopoly in the state, however, continues to maintain the poles and lines for all electric service in California, and it is still the major provider of residential electricity and gas. Call PG&E (tel: (800) 743-5000; website: http://www.pge.com).

Note that in the United States electricity is 110 volts, 60 hertz, and appliances brought from abroad that run on 220 volts will not work. Fortunately, all housing comes with major appliances such as refrigerators and stoves, and sometimes clothes washers and dryers are included, as well. Appliances in the United States are not particularly expensive anyway, so it would be most efficient just to plan on purchasing what you need here.

Water

If you rent an apartment, the water will be turned on when you move in, and the utility cost is included in the rent. If you are purchasing a home, you will need to have the water service transferred to your name. Call the San Francisco Public Utilities Commission at 1155 Market Street (tel: (415) 551-3000; website: http://sfwater.org)

Telephone Service

Deciding on which telephone service is not as simple as it used to be when there was just one provider. But the multitude of possible providers now means that you can choose whichever option suits you best and that the price will probably be lower than it was even yesterday or the day before.

Local telephone service is provided by AT&T. To connect your residential telephone, consult the telephone book, which details the rates, hookup and repair procedures, and all options such as call-waiting and voice mail; then call AT&T. (tel: (800) 310-2355; website: http://www.att.com) Customer service is available in English, Cantonese and Mandarin, Spanish, Korean, Vietnamese, Filipino, and Japanese; refer to the telephone book under AT&T for their language-specific telephone numbers.

Long Distance Communication

Long distance service may be handled by any one of a number of providers. Rates and services among carriers vary widely, so shop around; advertisements appear regularly in the media. Owing to inexpensive options and the advent of the Internet for cheap digital calling (*see below*), rates are dropping rapidly. This includes AT&T, which also provides options and alternatives to its standard service.

- AT&T; tel: (800) 288-2020; website: http://www.att.com
- GTC Telecom; tel: (800) 486-4030; website: http://www.gtctelecom.com
- MCI; tel: (800) 444-3333; website: http://www.mci.com
- Sprint; tel: (800) 777-4646; website: http://www.sprint.com
- Verizon; tel: (800) 483-4000; website: http://www.verizon.com

VoIP

All this said, you really do not need to have standard telephone service at all, although most people do, at least at present. If you have internet, you might decide to use one of the voice over Internet protocol (VoIP) providers and to use a cell phone for local calls. VoIP allows you to make phone calls over any Internet connection. If you call another member of your particular service it's free; to non-members it's not at all costly.

Basically, you talk from your computer. If you have a built in speaker and microphone you will not need any external equipment. Otherwise, you might need a headset or external microphone. Some providers now also have specially-adapted telephones, and you can also call from your cell phone, or hand-held device if you have one that connects to the Internet, capable of downloading the VoIP software.

VoIP service usually includes voicemail, call waiting, and just about all the other options you are used to with traditional service. And, whenever you are connected to the Internet, your calls will be routed to your same account.

One caveat is that VoIP may not support calls to 911, the nationwide emergency number, Also since VoIP uses standard household electricity, if your computer does not automatically switch to a battery during a power outage, your service may be interrupted for a while. Some of the traditional phone companies are adding in digital services. Currently the three VoIP poviders below are among the most well-known:

- Skype; website: http://www.skype.com
- Sun Rocket; website: http://www.Sun-Rocket.com
- Vonage; website: http://www.vonage.com

Also check out MagicJack, (website: http://www.magicjack.com), which offers free local and long distance calling after an initial purchase of the MagicJack USB key (website: http://www.MagicJack.com). Insert your telephone plug into the MagicJack, and use your telephone as usual. All calls in North America are free, and there is a low annual cost, currently around US$ 20. MagicJack supports standard telephone features, such as 911 calls and call-forwarding.

Mobile Phones

Mobile phones in the United States work on the 1900 GSM frequency. Americans will, of course, have no trouble in

San Francisco, for all the major wireless companies have coverage here. For people who are just arriving in the United States, though, service will depend on your phone. If you have a tri- or quad-band mobile phone, it should work on an American provider. Ask your original provider if it has an agreement with an American company, and when you arrive, switch your settings to that partner. Unfortunately, roaming costs are high, so it is best to find a new American provider as soon as possible.

Because competition is fierce among service providers, and price plans can be inexpensive, some newcomers do not bother to hook up a landline at all, but use only their mobiles. On the other hand, people who do not subscribe to a mobile line very often can purchase a "pay as you go" option and pay only for the minutes used—topping up the prepaid account when it is low in airtime value.

The companies listed on the next page provide service to San Francisco. Most have outlets around the city. Check the providers listed below and the phone book for the stores nearest you. There are also stores that handle information, phones, and plans for several different services providers. And Radio Shack, a chain of small electronics stores, can be helpful with telephone equipment and information, and purchase plans. In addition to AT&T, consider the following providers:

- MetroPCS; tel: (888) 863-8768; website: http://www.metropcs.com
- Sprint; tel: (800) 866-7509; website: http://www.sprint.com
- T-Mobile; tel: (800)-866-2453; website: http://www.t-mobile.com
- Verizon; tel: (800) 922-0204; website: http://www.verizonwireless.com

Area Codes and Dialing

The area code for the city and county of San Francisco is 415. For all other telephone numbers, you must dial the number 1 and then the area code before the telephone number itself. Calls to numbers that start with 800, 888, 877, and 866 are toll-free, but those starting with 900 charge by the minute. Some impose a minimal fee.

Telephone Books

If you choose AT&T for your local telephone service, its telephone books will be delivered when your new service is hooked up. New telephone directories are issued annually in September, and are generally left in the lobbies of apartment buildings or delivered to the doors of private residences. Informational pages at the beginning of each book are multilingual, in English, Chinese, and Spanish. You can also pick up phone books at Safeway stores.

The *White Pages* include the names and telephone numbers of all businesses and of people who want their contact numbers listed for all to see. If you prefer not to list your number publicly, you may arrange for an "unlisted number" when you hook up a phone line. Or, you can list your name and number but not your address. The *White Pages* also list the numbers of the offices for the city, county, and federal government, and these can be quite helpful as you settle in.

The *Yellow Pages* list, by alphabetical category, all businesses that pay to be included. Not all do, so if you are looking for a particular business, if it is not in the *Yellow Pages*, look in the regular telephone book.

Many special interests publish their own "yellow pages," and they are generally free. You can usually find them in shops that cater to that particular clientele. Certainly there are more than the two representative examples listed below, so keep your eye out in the shops, gyms, or churches you frequent for those that suit your needs.

- *The GGBA Pride Pages*, a publication of the Golden Gate Business Association, is a directory that lists hundreds of LGBT-friendly businesses in San Francisco.
- *The Natural Pages* detail natural food restaurants and shops, green products, holistic health care, and other natural services available in San Francisco.

Television and Radio

Since June 2009. all the television broadcasts in the United States are digital, not analog, allowing high-defintion programming. Thus, if your television is analog, you will not be able to receive with just an external anenna; you will need either a cable or satellite service. Consider buying a digital TV. The large chain stores such as Best Buy and Costco (see page *186*) have competitive prices.

For cable service, call Comcast Cable, which also has digital voice and Internet services; tel: (877) 863-3175; website: http://www.comcast.com. On one Comcast channel, the current and upcoming programs are scrolled on the screen. Otherwise, you might buy *TV Guide*, which is available at supermarkets and elsewhere.

With some 80 radio stations in the Bay Area, you can probably find just what you are looking for, in whatever language. FM reception may depend on what side of a hill you are living on, and you may need an external antenna. AM reception is generally clear. The newspapers list the radio stations.

Accessing the Internet

You will be able to access your e-mail at home once you arrange for a connection to the Internet, either by telephone (ADSL) or cable (broadband). To connect to the Internet using your telephone line, arrange for it when you connect your phone. For Internet access via cable, call Comcast. Until then, try any of the hundreds of cafés in the city that offer free wireless access. There is usually a sign outside that says "Wifi." The FedEx-Kinko's chain has outlets in the city, and they all have computer stations and Internet access. The current mayor is planning to transform San Francisco into a "wireless city," meaning that wherever you are in San Francisco, you would have access to WiFi.

Mail Delivery

The United States Postal Service delivers mail addressed to you at your new address without official notification, although you will have no doubt submitted a Change of Address card to your previous post office. There is one mail delivery per day, except Sundays and holidays.

Until you have a permanent mailing address you may have mail sent to your name at General Delivery, San Francisco CA 94142. Pick it up at the Civic Center, 101 Hyde Street, at Golden Gate Avenue; Opening days and hours: Monday–Saturday, 10:00 am–2:00 pm. Bring identification with you.

Each postal "zip code" has a post office. All are open weekdays from 8:30/9:00 am to 5:00 pm; most, but not all, are open Saturdays for some portion of the day. For the post office nearest you, call the toll-free Postal Service telephone number or access its Internet site; tel: (800) 275-8777; website: http://www.usps.com.

The Postal Service has an Express Mail service (tel: (800) 222-1811) with pickup and delivery. And these international shippers below are convenient; you can call for pickup, but they also have stores throughout the city.

- Federal Express; tel: (800) 463-3339; website: http://www.fedex.com; At FedEx-Kinko.
- UPS; tel: (800) 742-5877; website: http://www.ups.com;. At UPS Stores and at Office Depot.
- DHL; tel: (800) 225-5345; website: http://www.dhl.com; In DHL and independent mailing shops.

Household Insurance

If you are buying a home, homeowner's insurance is required as part of the process of obtaining a mortgage. The insurer will check for fire resistance (wood frames cost more than masonry) and assess the risks of living in the location; risk considerations such as whether it is a high theft area or located a great distance from a fire station will be factored in.

Ask about deductibles: the higher the deductible, the lower the premium. If you are insuring a car, then having both policies with one insurer may lower the cost. But even if you are renting an apartment, you should consider homeowner's insurance to protect yourself against theft or liability if someone is injured in your home.

For information on insurance, contact the California Department of Insurance; tel: (800) 927-4357; website: http://www.insurance.ca.gov.

For a comprehensive list of insurance agents, refer to the *Yellow Pages*.

Many Californians take out policies with the California State Automobile Association, (part of the American Automobile Association) which has several offices in San Francisco for insurance.

Earthquake Insurance

Homeowners may want to take out earthquake insurance, as part of the homeowners' insurance policy; inquire of your insurance agent. The California Earthquake Authority (CEA) "minipolicy" is available through many insurance agencies (telephone numbers: (916) 325-3800; (877) 797-4300; website: http://www.earthquakeauthority.com). Your insurer can add earthquake insurance to your policy, and there is usually a 10–15 percent deductible based on the value of the home.

Speaking of Earthquakes…

On a practical note, no matter where you are in the Bay Area, you should keep a working flashlight in your home and perhaps some candles, a portable radio with extra batteries, a standard, non-electric telephone, non-perishable food supplies, and a few gallons of water—just in case. Always keep enough medication and a small reserve of cash to tide you over. Stores around the Bay Area sell earthquake kits.

Many children are taught to "duck, cover, and hold" should an earthquake hit. This series of safety responses is important in the event of even small tremblers, as well as for those that can be identified as precursors to a big one. When tremors are felt, get under a table or doorway. Cover your head and face in case debris starts to fall. And hold on to something stable in case your surroundings begin to move. Stay away from windows, and never go into an elevator or stairway. If you are in a car, pull over to the curb and stop. Wait until the shaking of the ground stops. And if you are outside, in a park for example, stay away from trees and power lines. Stay calm.

Once the quake is over, check your home. Fill your bathtub, in case the water gets turned off. Listen to the local radio news for advice and instructions (if this is, indeed, the "big one," and there is a lot of damage).

Identification Cards

For obtaining a California Driver's License, see page 176. If you do not intend to drive, however, you may wish to obtain a state identification card. Like drivers' licenses, these are issued by the Department of Motor Vehicles. Bring your birth certificate or passport, and Social Security or taxpayer identification number.

Registering to Vote

There are no time-linked residency requirements for voter registration; all citizens over the age of 18 with proof of a permanent address may vote. Call the Department of Elections located at 633 Folsom Street, Room 109, for a registration form up to one month before an election; tel: (415) 554-4375. Otherwise, before each election or primary there are usually people outside supermarkets registering voters.

Opening a Bank Account

Opening a bank account is easier here than it is in some other countries. You will only need to provide a picture identification, an address, and enough money to make your initial deposit. When choosing a bank or a savings or loan association, make sure it is part of the federal insurance systems FDIC or FSLIC, to ensure that your funds will not be at risk. Consider a credit union, for they often offer good terms, both on accounts and fees, and on interest paid on time deposits and savings accounts. And, choose a bank that is within proximity to your home or workplace. Those listed below have branches throughout the city. Look in the phone book for their specific locations.

Inquire as to all options open to you, especially their charges; some offer no-fee checking, or a cheaper account if you do your banking online and with the automated teller machines (ATMs). Banks are affiliated with major networks such as CIRRUS or PLUS, which allows withdrawal of cash from the ATM, but your bank may charge you if you are using the ATM of a different bank. Shops and groceries accept bankcards, which, unlike charge or credit cards, debit your expenditure from your account immediately.

You will be asked whether you wish to apply for a Visa/Master Card. Inquire as to the rates of interest charged, for rates vary and low-interest cards are available. It is illegal in California for merchants to use your credit card as identification; they may not write its number down on your check. Do not let this happen.

- Bank of America; website: http://www.bankofamerica.com
- Bank of the West; website: http://www.bankofthewest.com
- Chase: website: http://www.chase.com
- Citibank; website: http://www.citibank.com
- Wells Fargo; website: http://www.wellsfargo.com

Currency Exchanges

If you need to exchange your foreign currency for dollars, you can use a "currency exchange," if that is your only option. You will get a better rate of exchange, however, if you have a bank or credit card and can use an ATM machine. These are generally linked to banks and give the bank's competitive rate of exchange. With currency exchanges, however, be sure to ask about fees and the rate for the amount you wish to exchange.

Bank of America has several locations for exchanging foreign currencies (Information hotline: (415) 953-5102). The most central is situated at Powell Street, at the cable car turnaround.

- American Express, 455 Market Street; tel: (415) 536-2600; website: http://www.americanexpress.com
- Pacific Foreign Exchange, 533a Sutter Street; tel: (415) 391-2548
- Associated Foreign Exchange, 221 Sansome Street; tel: (800) 525-2339; website: http://.afex.com

Taxes

If you are earning income in the United States, you will no doubt be required to file a tax return. This requires you to have a Social Security number (website: http://www.ssa.gov), or a Taxpayer Identification number. You should approach either the American Embassy in your home country or your employer for help with these.

If you are from a country that has a bilateral agreement with the United States, a portion of your income may be exempt from taxes here. Contact the Internal Revenue Service (tel: (800) 829-1040; website: http://www.irs.gov) should you need answers to any questions.

As a resident of California, you will also have to pay California state tax. Both federal and state taxes are due on April 15th every year.

If you have questions about California state taxes, you can call the State Franchise Tax Board or visit its website for more information (telephone numbers: (800) 852-5711; (916) 845-6500; website: http://www.ftb.ca.gov).

House Cleaning Services

If you need an occasional house cleaner, you can ask one of your neighbors if they could recommend a domestic helper or cleaner, or consider one of the professional cleaning services. The cleaning company will send a cleaner to your home when you want one, they provide the cleaning supplies, and their rates are reasonable. If, however, you need a fulltime housekeeper, then you will be responsible, as any employer is, to report wages paid to the Social Security Administration. For occasional house-help, try the following or check out the *Yellow Pages*.

- Merry Maids; tel: (415) 221-6243
- The Clean Team; tel: (415) 621-3678

Finding a Laundry

If your apartment does not come with a washer and dryer and there are none in your building, you will need to find a laundromat. Fortunately, laundromats are in every district, so look around as you stroll your new neighborhood.

Washing machines generally accept quarters only. Although many sell soap powder, it is better to bring your own; this way, it saves you money, and you can choose the kind you like. The two laundromats listed below are well-known and provide entertainment, always a plus when you have to fold your sheets.
- Brain Wash, 1122 Folsom, between 7th and 8th Streets; tel: (415) 861-3663
- Star Wash, 392 Dolores Street at 17th; tel: (415) 431-2443

Dry Cleaners

Ask your neighbors for recommendations for dry cleaners, for there are many good ones offering reasonable prices. Cleaning of standard items generally takes about three days, but most cleaners have "early bird specials." Clothes that are brought in before a certain time (8:30 am o°r 9:00 am) may be picked up the same day after 5:00 pm; many offer home pickup and delivery. Hard-to-clean items take longer, as do items that require repair. Cleaners that advertise "hand finishing" or "French cleaning" do well with more delicate items. This service of course costs more. Cleaners generally do laundry and finishing of shirts. These high-quality cleaners generally have good reviews:
- Locust Cleaners, 3587 Sacramento Street; tel: 346-9271
- Meaders, established in 1912, has two locations; 1877 Geary Boulevard, tel: (415) 922-3300; 1475 Sansome Street; tel: (415) 781-8200
- Pacific Heights Cleaners, 2437 Fillmore Street; tel: (415) 567-5999
- Peninou French Laundry and Cleaners, 3707 Sacramento Street; tel: (415) 751-7050; 3063 Laguna Street; tel: (415) 351-2554
- Union French Cleaners,1718 Union Street; tel: (415) 923-1212

Storage Lockers

If your new home is smaller than you had imagined and you need to store some belongings, consider a self-storage locker. Sizes range from those that would hold a few items to those

in which you might store all your furniture while looking for housing. In these dry, well-maintained warehouses, there is 24-hour security; you retain the key to your own locker and have daily access. Sometimes there are waiting lists, but lockers do come available, and new warehouses are opening up. There are others in the East Bay and Marin.
- Attic Self Storage, 2440 16th Street; tel: (415) 626-2510
- American Storage Unlimited, 600 Amador Street; tel: (415) 824-2388
- Public Storage; Self-storage facilities throughout city; website: http://www.publicstorage.com
- Crocker's Lockers, 1400 Folsom Street; tel: (415) 626-6665
- SoMa Self Storage, 1475 Mission Street; tel: (415) 861-5500

Trash Collection

Almost all apartments and houses have in-sink garbage disposal units to handle most food waste. For people living in large apartment buildings, both trash collection and recycling of paper, glass, and metal are taken care of by the management. In small buildings, tenants themselves may have to place trash bins and the blue recycling boxes by the curb on the days specified for that neighborhood. If you live in a house, you will have to arrange for garbage collection. Ask your neighbors or the previous owner of your home which scavenger company is used in your area or access the combined websites: http://www.goldengatedisposal.com; and http://www.sunsetscavenger.com.
- Golden Gate Disposal & Recycling; tel: (415) 626-4000
- Sunset Scavenger; tel: (415) 330-1300

Getting Your Hair Cut

Many of the city's hair salons are unisex. Prices vary widely, depending primarily on location, with salons near Union Square charging more than a local hairdresser in one of the outer districts. Tips are not included in the price, and every person—shampoo person, hair stylist, coat check—gets a tip based on the level of service provided. Of course, the quality varies from hairdresser to hairdresser at any salon, so you just have to experiment until you find someone you like.

One of the city's most famous landmarks and a popular tourist attraction is the Castro Theatre along Castro Street, San Francisco's gay district.

The Conservatory of Flowers in Golden Gate Park is known as the "oldest public growing house in California". The building was shipped from London to San Francisco in 1875.

San Francisco is an interesting blend of the old and the new. The Sentinel Building, built after the devasting 1906 earthquake and fire, stands near the soaring modern Transamerica Pyramid built in 1972.

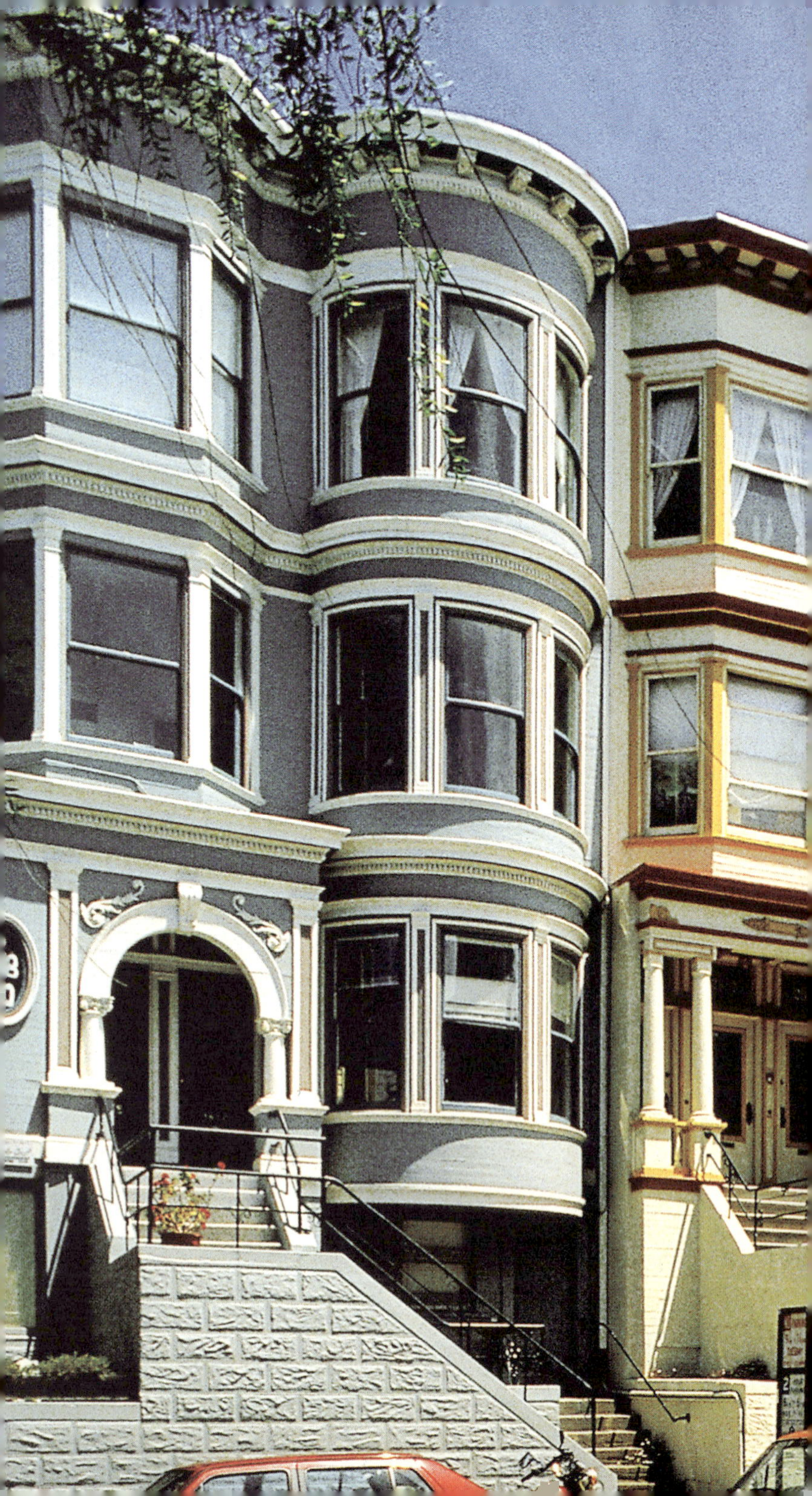

A row of 'Painted Ladies" or Victorian style houses. These shown here are in the Italianate design, popular between 1850–1875, and are characterised by bay windows with side windows slanting inward, pipe-stem columns flanking the front door and flat crowns.

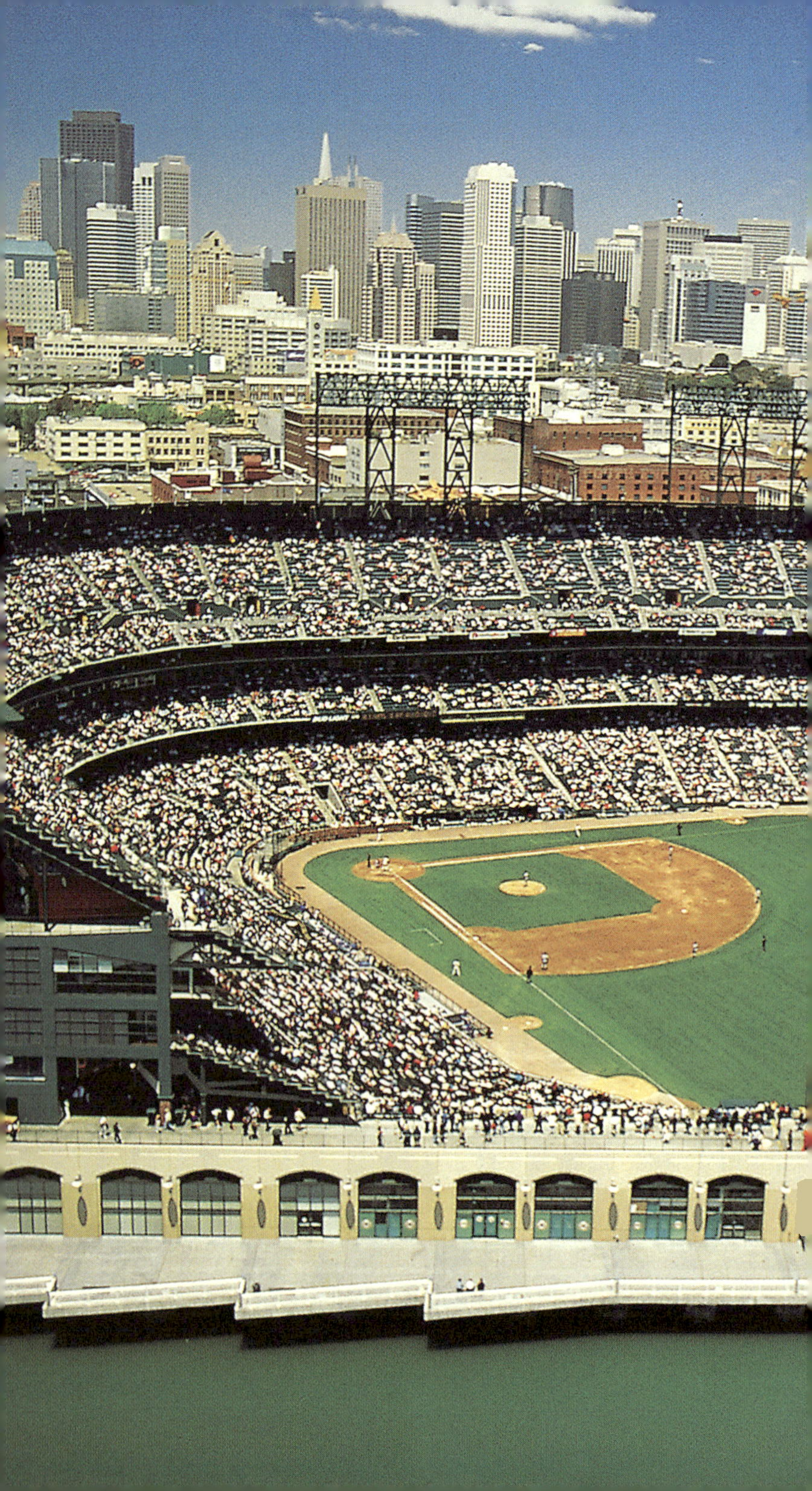

Aerial view of AT&T Park, home to the San Francisco Giants baseball team. The 48,000 capacity waterfront stadium helped revitalize the South of Market area that was destroyed during the 1906 earthquake.

San Francisco offers a wide variety of dining options. Statistics released by the San Francisco Convention & Visitors Bureau indicate that over 25 percent of the visitors come for the food.

Spa salons may offer more services than you are used to: massage, music, art exhibits, and so on. For a true "San Francisco experience," try one of these listed below. But before you make the appointment, check the prices for the services you want. Luxury does not come cheap.

- Elevation Salon & Café, 451 Bush Street; tel: (415) 392-2969. Full service elegant salon—hair, skin, and nails—plus a café in the back that serves light lunches and desserts.
- Spa Bar, 246 Second Street; tel: (415) 975-0888. Chic total beauty salon and spa, offering hair, body, facial, and nail treatments. Night spa open until 10 pm.
- Festoon, 9 Claude Lane, at Bush Street; tel: (415) 421-3223; (888) 357-2566. Another of San Francisco's artistic, elegant salons. Trendy, modern. Closed on Mondays.
- Kamala Day Spa & Hair Salon, 240 Stockton Street (7th floor); tel: (415) 217-7700. Lavish Indian décor, exotic furniture. Massage, hands, feet, facials, body treatments salon services. "Inner peace, outer beauty."
- Vidal Sassoon, 359 Sutter; tel: (415) 397-5105. Popular salon, part of a nationwide chain.
- Yosh for Hair, 173 Maiden Lane; tel: (415) 989-7704. Among the top styling salons in the city. Japanese thermal reconditioning to smooth curly, frizzy hair.

Haircuts for Kids

Neighborhood salons cut children's hair as well as adults'. These two, however, are known for their welcoming atmosphere for kids.

- Peppermint Cuts, 1772 Lombard Street; tel: (415) 292-6177
- Snippity Crickets, 3562 Sacramento; tel: (415) 441-9363

Keeping Up with the Times

San Francisco has one daily newspaper, the *San Francisco Chronicle*. The *Oakland Tribune* and the *Berkeley Barb* serve the East Bay, as does the *Contra Costa Times*. In the South Bay, the *San Mateo County Times* and the *San Jose Mercury News* are the standards, and in the North Bay, the *Marin Independent*. All are available for subscription to be delivered to your door before dawn, as are such national newspapers as the *New York Times* and the *Wall Street Journal*. Many can now now also be read online.

Some of the most interesting and popular local newspapers, however, are free. *The Bay Guardian* (now only online) is a liberal weekly that covers issues of interest throughout the Bay Area and reviews events and cultural activities. The *San Francisco Weekly*, issued on Wednesdays, is free and can be found in news boxes on street corners. And the daily *San Francisco Examiner* is also free.

Look for the free tabloid of your own community, most of which are monthly, and all of which carry articles of local interest and advertisements for neighborhood services. The *Nob Hill Gazette* covers Nob Hill, and *Northside* covers Pacific heights, the Marina, and North Beach.

Various ethnic communities have their own newspapers. *Korea Times* and *Asian Week* can be found at news boxes on city streets. In Japantown look for *Nichi Bei Times*, a Japanese-English daily. The national *Sing Tao Daily* has an extensive section on California and is read by 100,000 Asians. *El Mensajero* is the bilingual weekly for the Latino Community, and *El Latino* is only in Spanish. *San Francisco Bay View* is a free weekly newspaper for the African-American community. There are others. And, leading the list of gay publications are *Bay Area Reporter* and the *San Francisco Bay Times*. *San Francisco Spectrum* (http://www.sfspectrum.com) and *Gloss Magazine (*http://www.sfgloss.com) are tabloids for the gay communities of Northern California. Both are distributed in sites around the Castro and can be read online.

Look also for *San Francisco*, the city's monthly magazine that has articles of interest to San Franciscans, reviews, and lists of upcoming performances and events.

Foreign Periodicals

European and Asian publications and some American hometown newspapers are found in a few shops around the city, and Borders on Union Square has a good selection. Chinatown's newsstands sell a good selection of Chinese papers, and you may find the free Chinese TV Guide tabloid in some restaurants and Chinese shops. Kinokuniya Bookstore

in the Japan Center has an outstanding selection of Japanese publications (*See also section* Foreign Bookstores.).
- **Chinatown Gate**—Café de la Presse, 352 Grant; tel: (415) 398-2680
- **Financial District**—Fog City News, 455 Market Street; tel: (415) 543-7400
- **Haight**—Booksmith, 1644 Haight Street; tel: (415) 863-8688
- **North Beach**—Cavalli Italian Bookstore, 1441 Stockton; tel: (415) 421-4219
- **Pacific Heights**—Juicy News, 2453 Fillmore Street; tel: (415) 441-3051

Finding Your Spiritual Home

Finding the right place of worship should not be difficult. Generally the city's churches and synagogues are welcoming of anybody who wants to worship, whether affiliated with that religion or not. San Franciscans practice their religion the same way they do everything else—according to their own reasons and tastes—and it is said that only some 35 percent of the population is identified with a major religious denomination. Nonetheless there are multilingual options for daily or weekly worship for just about any faith. Most churches and synagogues sponsor social programs for their congregants and educational opportunities for the children.

There are so many faiths that listing all of them here would be impossible: traditional denominations, evangelical, messianic, and those that worship in their own ways, such as the well-attended Church of Saint John Coltrane, an African Orthodox church that "preaches the gospel of jazz and love" in its liturgy (1286 Fillmore Street; tel: (415) 673-3372). And there are so many worship sites that they, too, would be impossible to mention. Instead, this small sampling should serve to show the diversity of opportunities in San Francisco. See the *Yellow Pages* under Churches or Synagogues. Some print their worship schedules.

Whether you are religious or not, and no matter your religious traditions, you should know about Glide Memorial United Methodist Church, 330 Ellis Street, at Taylor (tel: (415) 647-6000). In the heart of the Tenderloin, Glide is the city's most celebrated religious gathering place. Sunday services are always crowded—more than 1,000 people come. This is the church most known in the city for social activism, feeding and providing job training for the poor and homeless, and more.

- **Baptist**—Third Baptist Church, 1399 Mcallister Street; tel: (415) 346-4426. People of all faiths and cultures are welcome. First Chinese Baptist Church; 15 Waverly Place; tel: (415) 362-4139. Bilingual and bicultural. For a complete listing of Baptist, Baptist Conservative, General Conference, Independent, Independent Fundamental, Missionary, and Southern Baptist churches, see the *Yellow Pages*.
- **Buddhist**—Zen Center, 300 Page Street; tel: (415) 863-3136. Buddhist temple and information point for Buddhism in the Bay Area. Also, San Francisco Buddhist Center; 37 Bartlett Street; tel: (415) 282-2018; website: http://www.sfbuddhistcenter.org
- **Catholic**—The major Catholic cathedral is The Cathedral of Saint Mary, at 1111 Gough Street, at Geary; tel: (415) 567-2020. Mission Dolores; 3321-16th Street; tel: (415) 621-8203. Masses are conducted in both English and Spanish, in the oldest building in San Francisco. For information on the Catholic community, schools, and churches, contact the Archdiocese office at 1 Peter Yorke Way; tel: (415) 614-5500; website: http://www.sfarchdiocese.org
- **Christian Science**—First Church of Christ, Scientist, 1700 Franklin Street; tel: (415) 673-3544. Call for details on other places of worship and reading rooms.
- **Episcopal**—Grace Cathedral, 1100 California at Taylor; info tel: (415) 749-6300. In addition to regular, scheduled worship, this "modern Gothic" cathedral hosts lectures, concerts, and much more. Evening prayer, Evensong on Thursdays, with carillon recitals and concerts.
- **Greek Orthodox**—Cathedral of the Annunciation, 245 Valencia; tel: (415) 864-8000; website: http://www.annunciation.org. Many religious and social events are conducted for the community.

- **Islam**—For information on worship, call the Islamic Society of San Francisco, 20 Jones Street; tel: (415) 863-7997.
- **Jewish (Reform)**—Congregation Emanu-El, 2 Lake Street; tel: (415) 751-2535; website: http://www.emanuelsf.org. The largest congregation in San Francisco. For information on Judaism in San Francisco, call the Jewish Community Federation at 121 Steuart Street; tel: (415) 777-1411. Inquire about *Resource*, its guide to Jewish life in the Bay Area; website: http://www.sfjcf.org
- **Lutheran**—Saint Mark's, 1111 O'Farrell; tel: (415) 928-7770; website: http://www.stmarks-sf.org. For more than 150 years, Saint Mark's active ministry has been committed to social outreach in the San Francisco community.
- **Methodist**—Park Presidio United Methodist Church, 4301 Geary Boulevard; tel: (415) 751-4438. Services are conducted in English, Chinese, and Korean. The congregation is involved in community projects. For more on Methodist churches, see the *Yellow Pages*.
- **Presbyterian**—Noe Valley Ministry, 1021 Sanchez, at 23rd Street; tel: (415) 282-2317; website: http://noevalleyministry.org. The de facto community center for Noe Valley, this church is an interfaith gathering point, organizing social events, meetings, and concerts.
- **Quaker**—Friends Quaker Meeting, 65 9th Street; tel: (415) 431-7440. Unprogrammed meeting. Socially active.
- **Unitarian**—First Unitarian Universalist Church, 1187 Franklin Street; tel: (415) 776-4580. Congregation has worshiped here since 1888.
- **Vedanta**—The Vedanta Temple, 2323 Vallejo Street at Fillmore; tel: (415) 922-2323; website: http://www.sfvedanta.org. Source of Hinduism, based on the Upanishads, and spiritually affiliated with the Ramakrishna Order. Lecture services are held on Sunday mornings and Wednesday evenings as well.

Gay and Lesbian Worship

San Francisco's churches and synagogues are openly welcoming of gays and lesbians, singles, or couples. Yet, although active and integrated into the city's spiritual life, gays and lesbians are also forming supportive spiritual groups and worship sites of their own. Progressive in outlook, these communities are usually open to people of all sexual identities.

- **Catholic**—Dignity San Francisco, 1329 7th Avenue at the Presbyterian Church; tel: (415) 681-2491; website: http://www.dignitysanfrancisco;org; Catholic worship since 1973, for GLBT Catholics and their families.
- **Interfaith Christian**—Metropolitan Community Church, 150 Eureka Street; tel: (415) 863-4434; website: http://www.mccsf.org; A house of prayer for all people and a "home for queer spirituality."
- **Jewish**—Congregation Sha'ar Zahav, 290 Dolores Street; tel: (415) 861-6932; website: http://www.shaarzahav.org; Progressive Reform synagogue founded in 1977.
- **Evangelical**—Freedom in Christ Evangelical Church, 1111 O'Farrell Street at the Urban Life Center, Saint Mark's Square; tel: (415) 970-8149; website: http://www.freedominchrist-sf.org; Evangelistic, charismatic, gay affirming, reaching the LGBT community with the Gospel of Jesus Christ.

A CHILD'S WORLD

Great for the Kids

San Francisco presents opportunities for children that few other places can. The area's moderate climate means that outdoor play is available just about any day of the year: parks and playgrounds dot the landscape, wide beaches offer endless play in the sand, and schools offer extensive extracurricular sports programs. The ethnic diversity of the city means that children will have a culturally stimulating environment in which to grow and learn. And the open friendliness of the city means a generally nurturing environment to those who avail themselves of opportunities presented. Well-behaved children are welcome in most restaurants, and even the most elegant restaurants have booster seats. Theaters, museums, private organizations, and the city's Parks and Recreation Department all have enriching programs for children. And the options for schooling, although seemingly complex and perhaps slightly discouraging at the outset, can offer a well-rounded education. Whatever you want for your child, you will no doubt find it in San Francisco.

Even now, during economic uncertainties, the cost of living in San Francisco is so substantial that the city has fewer children than any other similar metropolitan area in the country. Yet San Francisco is still welcoming and rewarding for children. Check out these resources:

- San Francisco Unified School District (SFUSD), 555 Franklin Street; tel: (415) 241-6000; website: http://www.sfusd.edu. Everything you need to know about schooling your children in San Francisco can be obtained here. This includes the important Educational Placement Center, which is open on weekdays.
- SFUSD Office of Parent Relations, 555 Franklin Street; tel: (415) 241-6185; website: http://www.sfusd.edu. This organization works with parents to ensure the success of their kids in the San Francisco schools, and it encourages parents to become involved in their children's schools and activities. Open weekdays.
- Three free monthly magazines with articles and advertising of interest—about schools, products, recreational activities, and more—to parents. These are found in child-oriented venues and also online. *Bay Area Parent*; website: http://bayareaparent.parenthood.com/; *Parents' Press*; website: http://www.parentspress.com; and *Parent-teen.com* (an online magazine); website: http://www.parent-teen.com
- California Department of Education: Access this comprehensive website to learn about all the aspects of education and current state educational news: http://www.cde.ca.gov/index.asp

Thinking About Schools

Having decided on San Francisco for your family, the next thing you will now think about is schools. Choosing a school in San Francisco, whether elementary, middle, or high school, is not as simple as showing up on the first day of school in your neighborhood and expecting your child to receive a good education. In fact, it is wise to consider the educational opportunities available while you are deciding on the neighborhood where you might want to live. With research and care, you should be able to find a good public school for your child, or you may choose a charter school or even a private school, if tuition fees that may run from US$ 17,000–US$ 25,000 per student are within your budget. Many of the private schools, however, do offer financial assistance. If you can make a trip to San Francisco before your actual move, investigating schools should be among your priorities. Get advice from the Human Resources Department of your company, visit the San Francisco Unified School District and then the schools you are considering, and talk to parents of children in those schools. Then, when you have found the schools appropriate for your children, follow carefully every procedure for application, for the most popular schools draw the most applicants, and acceptance to each of these is not always guaranteed.

There is no easy solution to schooling in the city of San Francisco. Public schools tend to be overcrowded and in the upper grades of some schools the large class size may not be academically rewarding as teachers have to divide their attention among more students and individual attention is reduced. Not all schools are equal in their facilities, programs, educational approach, or results, and budget cutbacks have forced some to cut back in enrichment programs in areas such as art and music. Unfortunately, state and federal funding of schools is often inadequate; California consistently ranks well below the national average in educational expenditure or funding per student. In 2004, for instance, the national average of spending per child was US$ 8,087, while California spent only US$ 7,748.

In addition, California has more students per teacher than almost all other states; the ratio in California 2006-2007 was 20.9 students per teacher, while the overall national average was 15.5. Only three other states rated lower. Fortunately, however, California ranks the highest of all states in teachers' salaries, and teaching quality is quite high.

Yet, the San Francisco public school system is consistently improving its performance. Recently the District met all the student achievement targets set by both State and Federal governments. The Board of Education is working to improve teaching and learning, in order to increase and optimize the achievement and potential of every student. But parents should remember that it also takes active parental participation to educate children in any city. Join parents' groups to understand the strengths and weaknesses of your school. If arts or music programs in your child's school have been cut back, for example, make sure your child attends enrichment programs outside, either in structured public programs or through private lessons. Everything you need to supplement public school education is available in San Francisco; it just takes determination to find it.

Other options also exist. If you have several children to educate, you might want to consider enrolling them in a public elementary school and then perhaps a private high school. Legislation may have lowered the number of students permitted in each class in a public elementary

The Application Process

The key to acceptance in the school you want for your child is the Application Process. SFUSD recommends that applicants follow a step-by-step process for enrollment:

- Learn the deadline for the application and make sure to apply on time.
- Research all the school options available
- Visit the schools that interest you.
- Visit the Education Placement Center (Hours: 8:00 am–5:00 pm weekdays)
- Contact the Parent Relations Office (tel: (415) 241-6184) for information on district resources.
- Obtain and complete the enrollment application forms. These are available at SFUSD headquarters or on its website. Parents are encouraged to ask or opt for seven schools, one of them being the regular school in your attendance zone.
- Return the application form in person and on time to the Educational Placement Center.

After all applications are in, SFUSD then compiles the requests and matches them with the number of slots available in each school. By March, the first round of acceptances is announced and the appeals process begins. (Appeals are based on medical conditions, family hardship, no acceptance into any of the seven schools requested, and some others.) In April, the waiting lists are determined. In June, students who have not been placed are assigned to a school. Occasionally, vacancies occur at the last minute for students on waiting lists, but they should not be counted on, unless the school is in the regular attendance zone.

school, but some public high school classes still tend to be overcrowded. Private high schools generally take a fair number of students from public schools, especially those who have tested well or who were in GATE (Gifted and Talented Education) programs.

Try to start your research before arriving in San Francisco. You might contact School Match, which has detailed statistics on public and private schools across the country (tel: (614) 890-1573; website: http://www.schoolmatch.com). School Match can do a full search for the right school for your child. After you fill out a questionnaire detailing all your priorities, School Match will suggest schools in the area that match your preferences. Prices vary for a full search or a "snapshot."

The Public School System

In San Francisco, some 55,000 children attend the public schools, down from 65,000 about a decade ago. As mentioned, much of the decline is owing to the high cost of living in the city and that many families are finding less costly options in the surrounding areas. It is interesting to note that the highest percentage of public school students are Chinese (32 percent), followed by Latino children (22 percent), and African Americans (13 percent). Happily, what this means is that in this multicultural city, no ethnic or cultural background dominates.

Not all schools are the same, although every school offers a required core curriculum. Yet, schools at all levels offer differing educational themes and teaching approaches; some offer academic programs while others stress technology, and a few have language immersion programs. Some have a Special Education focus or the Gifted and Talented Education Program (GATE); almost 15 percent of the city's students are enrolled in GATE programs. But some have better educational track records than others; for an idea of a school's performance, access the SFUSD Internet site and click on School Accountability Report Card. Also ask for the SFUSD Student and Parent/Guardian Handbook (available in five languages). Or call the Pupil Services Administration and ask to have one sent to you (tel: (415) 695-5543).

The Schools

Every block and every street of the city is assigned to a public school "attendance zone." The sizes of these zones vary according to the number of school-age children living in them. The zones include all children, even those attending private schools. It would be ideal if popular schools were in each neighborhood and if each neighborhood had schools to accommodate all the area's children, but this is not the case. Thus, parents must apply for the public schools they believe would be best for their children. There is no guarantee, however, that they will be accepted. Yet, the application process is crucial, so make sure you know all the current regulations by checking the SFUSD website.

A regular school is one in which children are assigned based on where they live. Most of the city's children go to schools in their attendance zone. Even if you are hoping that your child will be accepted into a different school, apply also to the school in your neighborhood.

An alternative school may offer special curriculum programs or have higher standards for academic programs than a regular school. It may also have a higher degree of parental involvement. Sometimes students from particular zip codes which have had lower average performance results may be given higher priority for acceptance into an alternative school. Otherwise, acceptance is by lottery and based on the application submitted.

> **An Additional Application?**
> Because they are so in demand, two of the top high schools, the application schools, require a special application in addition to the regular form. These are the highly desired Lowell Alternative High School and School of the Arts Alternative High School (SOTA).

For Non-native English Speakers

Several elementary schools offer language immersion programs for children whose native language is not English, and whose ability in the English language would not yet allow them to integrate fully into a regular English-language school. Languages include Japanese, Spanish, Chinese, and Korean. Inquire at SFUSD. In addition, Newcomer High School at 1350 7th Avenue offers a transitional program for newly arrived high school students who lack adequate English language proficiency (tel: (415) 242-2601). The program lasts approximately one year. Upon a successful completion of the program, the student transfers to other high schools.

The newest school is the Cantonese Immersion School, at 1351 Haight Street, which opened in 2009; tel: (415) 241-6310. This magnet school currently stresses biliteracy in Cantonese and English, but new programs are expected to be added as time goes on.

The Assignment Process

Any student may apply to any public school. The most important factors in acceptance are the schools requested and their capacity. But other factors are designed to ensure there is no segregation or discrimination in the school district: the goal is to create classrooms with a healthy diversity of profiles. These are:

- Socioeconomic Status
- Academic Achievement Status
- Mother's Educational Background
- Language Status
- Home Language
- Academic Performance Rank of Sending School (if the child is transferring)

Public School Registration Requirements

A child must have turned five years old before December 2 to enter kindergarten during that year. Proof of birth date is required for entrance into a public school; this might be a birth certificate or passport, for instance. As students must be legal residents of San Francisco, two proofs of current address might include a recent utility bill in the name of the parent/guardian, a valid California driver's license, or a dated lease or property tax statement. Records from other schools the child has attended should also be brought.

Kindergartners and first graders must have a complete physical examination before entering a public school. You will need to produce your child's immunization record. (Records from a foreign country must be reviewed by a local health facility.) DTaP (Diphtheria, Tetanus, Pertussis), MMR (measles, mumps, rubella), Hepatitis B, and polio vaccination records will be reviewed. All children entering school are required to undergo a Tuberculin Skin Test, and if tested positive, will then need a chest x-ray.

Preschools

Preschooling has long been important in San Francisco, a city in which both parents are likely to work outside the home, and to which people migrate without having any family in the area to help take care of the kids. But preschool is important on other grounds; it is widely held that children who have been "socialized" when they attend preschools perform better in their early school years than children who have not.

SFUSD's Child Development Program is for children aged three to five. (The child must be toilet trained.) There are 38 Child Development Centers in the city, offering full-or part-day programs. The highest priority for acceptance is for families with the lowest income per family size. The Child Development Program office is located at 20 Cook Street (tel: (415) 750-8500). Requirements for application are the same as for public schools: official identification, proof of address, your child's birth certificate and immunization records.

When investigating other preschools, consider only those facilities that have been licensed by the State Department of Social Services. Licensing means that the facility has met the state's criteria concerning the physical plant (amount of fenced playground areas, number of toilets per child, safe food preparation area, and so on) and that the staff has met educational and experiential qualifications. But these are minimum criteria: when you visit a school, inquire about its staff-child ratio, its activities and play materials, its teaching approach and its general philosophy for young children. Ask also about parent involvement and the process of feedback and evaluations concerning a child's progress.

Each school is different. No matter how positive a recommendation you receive from someone you know, you should visit the schools you are considering and determine for yourself whether the facility, the teaching methods, and overall environment are suitable for your child. First, you should decide which kind of preschool fits the personality of your child and your budget (and see if those have places available). There are independent, private preschools, and those sponsored by religious agencies. See *Schools: Academic-Preschool & Kindergarten* in the *Yellow Pages*; many private preschools advertise their qualifications and special features on these pages.

You may be surprised by how costly the private preschools may be, despite some being incorporated or classified as non-profit; ask about financial aid, which may be available, depending on need. Cooperative schools, in which the parents are expected to participate regularly, cost less, but you should be prepared to make a commitment to a particular time and activity at your child's school.

- Independent preschools are not affiliated with public or religious agencies. Many are neighborhood schools, serving the ethnic mix of that area. Some have bilingual programs, also depending on the neighborhood. There are dozens of these private, independent schools, so shop around. In addition to the *Yellow Pages*, if you are interested in a particular bilingual program, ask for information at the elementary school in the area you are considering, or of people who share your native language.
- Agency-affiliated preschools are sponsored by an organization such as the Jewish Community Center (JCC) or the Young Men's Christian Association (YMCA). Both have schools throughout the city. Each school sets its own approach; some have a religious component to the program, but others do not.
- Religious preschools are sponsored by a particular church or synagogue, and not by the agencies mentioned above. If you are interested in a religious component to your child's schooling, ask your church or synagogue for recommendations.

- College and university preschools are sponsored by the city's institutions of higher learning, servicing their faculty and students. Inquire of the university.
- Montessori schools are all similar, using the philosophy of Dr. Maria Montessori, who advocated stimulating, non-competitive activities in a structured atmosphere while providing creative freedom for children.

Charter Schools

In certain instances, school funds are contracted out to private concerns that manage the public schools. Technically, charter schools are district schools that receive state funding, but they are independently run and have greater flexibility than municipality-run schools. They have autonomy in management of the schools, in hiring of teachers, and in the development of curricula and enrichment programs. They must, however, adhere to public school norms. In California, for example, they must keep track of the number of minutes of instruction for each age level, keep attendance records, and administer the annual standardized achievement tests. But standards are high; class size is usually reasonable and students receive more individual attention than in many public schools. Students often study longer hours each day and may have a somewhat longer term than a regular public school schedule. Included in the curriculum are enriched art, music, and language programs, which, unfortunately, have been reduced at the city's cash-strapped public schools. Teachers may also be paid somewhat higher salaries. In San Francisco, there are nine charter schools; the SFUSD Internet site has details on the schools. And you can call the schools themselves for enrollment information.

Private Schools

Private schools have distinct advantages, and you may find their education worth paying for. Although each has its own character, basically they all provide a high standard of education, have a smaller class size with a better teacher to student ratio, and give more individual attention to each child. They generally also provide enriching extracurricular activities, all in a safe, nurturing, and stimulating environment. Some 20,000 students attend the city's private schools, and others commute to private schools in nearby towns.

But all these advantages come with a price tag. Tuition and other fees at private schools in the Bay Area are high, but they are generally in line with similar schools around the country. Some schools have financial aid programs and some offer reduced tuition fees if there are siblings in the school.

Some of the schools outside the city (especially in Marin) are extremely popular. And, although they are usually filled to capacity and the application process is stringent, there are many different types to choose from. For general information access the California Department of Education website (http://www.cde.ca.gov).

Regulation/Accreditation

Private schools are generally accredited by one of a number of governing bodies, such as the Accrediting Commission for Schools or the Western Association of Secondary Schools. Religious schools may also (or instead) be accredited by their own religious accrediting body, such as the Western Catholic Education Association or the National Association of Episcopal Schools. Accreditation is a lengthy process during which the school must meet the requirements of the accrediting body, including standards for curriculum, teaching philosophy, etc. For general information, access the Online Guide to Bay Area Private Schools at http://www.baprivateschools.com.

Types of Private Schools

There are several types of private schools and within them, their philosophies, goals, teaching approaches and curricula may differ widely. Some are traditional, others may be innovative in approach. There are boys' schools and girls' schools, but most are co-educational.

Non-profit (or independent) schools are just that, and they are overseen by a Board of Trustees, often with parents on the Board or on committees that advise the Board. Many independent schools are eligible for outside funding and grants, and in order to receive them must meet the requirements of the funding agencies.

Proprietary schools may be a corporation or partnership, incorporated to make a profit, and although they are not necessarily governed by a board, they often have parents' committees that advise the administration, and being entirely dependent on tuition, are responsive to parents' concerns.

Most of the parochial (religious-based) schools in San Francisco are Catholic, although there are Jewish, Episcopal, and Baptist schools as well; inquire of your church or synagogue. Of the Catholic schools some are attached to parishes, some are independent and incorporated not-for-profit, and some are administered by the Archdiocese itself. Most have parent-teacher committees and some have advisory boards. For information, contact the Archdiocese of San Francisco, Department of Catholic Schools, 1 Peter Yorke Way (tel: (415) 614-5660; website: http://www.sfcatholicschools.org).

The Admissions Process

Private schools are usually filled to capacity. Thus, any new slots are filled according to a priority system; first to be considered are children who have other siblings in the school, children who have attended that school's pre-school, or children of the school's alumni or teaching staff. Only after these children have been considered are outside applications taken.

In fact, the application/admission process is quite stringent and is lengthier and more detailed than application into a public school. The process starts earlier, and each school may have a slightly different schedule for applications. Schools generally require an interview with both parents, and a "play" period with the child to evaluate the child's readiness for the program. References from previous schools attended may be required as well. Most schools charge an application fee.

Have all your questions ready. Inquire about the school's teaching philosophy, curriculum, amount of homework, ethnic diversity, after-school programs, expectations for parent participation, and information about all costs, not just tuition. For example, there are often extra costs for after-school "extended care," or for uniforms, if the school requires that they be worn.

After-school Programs

As in any major city, children need to be supervised by an adult in their after-school hours, whether by a parent or in a structured program. Working parents should inquire about after-school "extended care" on the school premises, and whether there are places available and at what cost. The Child Development Program mentioned in the preceding pages offers after-school programs; call for information.

The Recreation and Parks Department sponsors a year-round after-school Latchkey Program for children 6–12 years of age (website: http://www.parks.sfgov.org). Programs are held in more than 30 of the Department's recreation centers around the city. These are structured programs: during the school year leisure and craft activities are encouraged (according to the specialty of the staff at a particular center), homework is supervised and a snack is provided. Summer programs feature arts and crafts, athletics, and field trips. These programs use a priority registration system, and there is a waiting list, especially for the most popular sites. Children in the Latchkey Program sign in upon arrival, sign out upon departure, and are expected to stay on site. Call for a detailed brochure (tel: (415) 715-4065).

Private schools also offer after-school programs for their students, invariably at extra cost. Each school's program is different, so if this is important to you, inquire during the application process.

Child Care

One of the most widespread daycare and preschools is the non-profit Marin Day Schools, based at 100 Shoreline Highway, Mill Valley (tel: (415) 331-7766; website: http://www.marindayschools.org). It has 14 campuses around the Bay Area, including San Francisco.

You might also contact Children's Counsel of San Francisco, at 445 Church Street (tel: (415) 276-2900;

child care info tel: (415) 343-3300; website: http://www.childrenscouncil.org). Among its services, the Council provides workshops and counseling for parents needing childcare, and referrals to licensed child-care providers in San Francisco; it does not screen individual providers, so all interviews and reference gathering are up to the discretion of the parent. Some subsidy funds are available for less well-off parents. Wu Yee Children's Services at 831 Broadway provides much the same services, with bilingual (Chinese) resources (tel: (415) 391-4721; website: http://www.wuyee.org).

Recreation and Parks Department

Get to know The Parks Department, whose headquarters are located in Golden Gate Park at McLaren Lodge, 501 Stanyan Street (tel: (415) 831-2700; website: http://www.sfreconline.org). Latchkey is only one of many programs for children; others include sports lessons, programs, and events. One of the most popular is the affordable Camp Mather, a rustic summer camp in the Stanislaus National Forest that allows families to spend a week together swimming and playing sports, and participating in camp-like activities (info tel: (415) 831-2715). Applications are taken in April and are selected by lottery; San Francisco residents are given priority.

Educational Entertainment

The following is a small but representative sample of the range of opportunities for enriching entertainment for children (and their parents!) in the area. For outdoor activities, make sure to bring a jacket for your child.

- Aquarium of the Bay, Pier 39, Embarcadero at Beach Street; tel: (415) 623-5300; website: http://www.aquariumofthebay.com. Visitors progress on a moving walkway through this wraparound aquarium to see marine life of the Pacific Ocean.
- Bay Area Discovery Museum, 557 McReynolds Road, East Fort Baker, in Sausalito, just over the Golden Gate Bridge; tel: (415) 339-3900; website: http://www.baykidsmuseum.

org/home/. Hands-on multi-building museum for the entire family, focusing on natural sciences, art and multimedia. Opening hours change according to the season.
- California Academy of Sciences is located at 55 Music Concourse Drive in Golden Gate Park, tel: (415) 379-8000; website: http://www.calacademy.org. (*See page 290*.)
- Children's Art Center, Fort Mason Center, Building C; tel: (415) 771-0292; website: http://www.childrensartcenter.org. This conducts art classes for children from age three to twelve. Workshops for parents and children are also available.
- Exploratorium, 3601 Lyon Street, at the Palace of Fine Arts; tel: (415) 347-5673; website: http://www.exploratorium.edu. The Exploratorium is a hands-on and interactive science museum for children of all ages (adults like it, too); it is closed on Mondays. Also check out the new outdoor Exploratorium interactive science exhibits at Fort Mason.
- M.H. De Young Memorial Museum, Hagiwara Tea Garden Drive, Golden Gate Park; tel: (415) 863-3330; website: http://www.famsf.org. The museum provides creative workshops for children, tours, and an "education room" with computer stations, reading areas, and art-appreciation activities. Summer programs for children ages four to sixteen are also available and worth considering.
- Musée Mecanique, Pier 45 at the end of Taylor Street; tel: (415) 346-2000; website: http://www.museemecanique.org. Its large collection of mechanically operated musical instruments and antique arcade machines is sure to fascinate and engross.
- Randall Museum, 199 Museum Way, at Roosevelt; tel: (415) 554-9600; website: http://www.randallmuseum.org. A hands-on nature and history museum of the Parks Department, with a petting zoo, woodworking and ceramics shops. Environmental learning garden, providing an educational platform for children to feed their curiosity and make discoveries of their own. Summer classes are also conducted. Closed Sunday and Monday.

The Golden Gate Bridge

The spectacular, soaring Golden Gate Bridge, spanning the Golden Gate Strait, where the Pacific Ocean meets San Francisco Bay, is beloved by locals and tourists alike. Having taken four years to build, the bridge was completed in 1937, and at the time—with a 4,200 foot suspension—was the longest suspension bridge in the world. (Now it ranks seventh). In today's dollars, it cost US$ 1.2 billion to build. Hundreds of men worked high above the choppy frigid waters, and although a safety net below saved many lives, ten men met their deaths when a scaffold broke and fell through the net. Currently, using modern safety equipment, dozens of ironworkers and painters work fulltime to make sure the bridge is well maintained and that it keeps its beautiful orange glow.

The International Orange color of the bridge, which enhanced visibility for ships, was also chosen to blend with the natural colors of the landmasses on either side and to contrast with the blue sky above and the dark waters below. Beginning in 1965 (a project that took thirty years), the original paint was replaced with modern synthetic materials that would resist rust and corrosion from the high salt content of the ocean winds. Think of the work! Each tower rises 746 feet (227 m) and has 600,000 rivets, and there is more than enough cable to circle the globe several times.

Well more than a billion vehicles have crossed the bridge since its opening, and now some 41 million cross it each year. In 1987, on the 50th anniversary, some 300,000 people crossed the bridge on foot, just 100,000 more than crossed it on its glorious opening day a half-century before. If you would like to be one of the nine million people who visit the bridge annually, take the Number 28 bus. If you are driving, turn right from route 101 at the last San Francisco exit (just before the Toll Plaza). The sign reads "Golden Gate National Recreation Area View Area." After the stop sign, turn left into the southeast parking lot. If you are on a bike, just ride across the bridge and enjoy! But, no matter what, do not forget to bring a warm jacket. On any day of the year.

Children at play in a neighborhood park.

- San Francisco Maritime National Historical Park, Hyde Street Pier: Foot of Hyde Street, near Fisherman's Wharf; tel: (415) 556-3002; website: http://www.maritime.org. Explore 19th century sailing ships, a side-wheel ferry, schooners, and, incongruously, a World War II submarine. Operated by the National Park Service, the museum itself is currently being restored, and scheduled to reopen in 2010.
- San Francisco Zoo, Sloat Boulevard at 45th Avenue; tel: (415) 753-7080; website: http://www.sfzoo.org. This is an extensive zoo with many attractions, including a children's zoo, a lion house, a primate center, and a playground.
- Zeum in the Yerba Buena Gardens, 221 4th Street; tel: (415) 820-3320; website: http://www.zeum.org. Zeum is an art and technology center for a hands-on creative experience in exploring the high-tech and the performing arts.

And Just Plain Fun

There is nothing more to be said about these attractions, which are unique to San Francisco, except that children of all ages love them.

- Rooftop at Yerba Buena Gardens, 4th Street and Mission; tel: (415) 820-3550; website: http://www.yerbabuenagardens.com. An entire city block devoted to children of all ages. An ice skating and bowling complex, carousel, child-care center, landscaped gardens, and a memorial to Martin Luther King, Jr.
- Golden Gate Fortune Cookie Factory, Chinatown at 56 Ross Alley; tel: (415) 781-3956. Watch fortune cookies being made, and then buy some.
- Cartoon Art Museum, 655 Mission Street; tel: (415) 227-8666; website: http://www.cartoonart.org. Original art exhibits of cartoon panels, classic comics, and many more are displayed here.
- Metreon, 4th Street at Mission; tel: (415) 369-6000; website: http://www.metreon.com. In addition to the huge 15-screen cinema complex and the variety of exotic eateries and small shops it is known for, Metreon has a Games Workshop (paint the toys you have bought), a tech-arcade, a Sony store, and a new food market.

Toys and Games

Toys 'R' Us, the internationally known and well-stocked chain of toy stores is situated at 2675 Geary Boulevard; tel: (415) 931-8896. But local toy stores offer a high-quality selection, more personal service, and are known for their educational toys and games.

- **Noe Valley**—The Ark, 3845 24th Street; tel: (415) 821-1257
- **Downtown**—Jeffrey's Toys. 685 Market Street; tel: (415) 546-6551.
- **West Portal/Cow Hollow**—Ambassador Toys, 186 W. Portal Avenue; tel: (415) 759-8697. Also located at 2 Embarcadero Center; tel: (415) 345-8697

Pier 39

Pier 39 may well be the most touristy attraction in the city; you will not find many locals here (website: http://www.pier39.com). Nonetheless, there are attractions at Pier 39 that everyone should see once. And kids love it! The exquisite view from the end of the pier may keep everyone in the family riveted for hours. The city's world-famous sea lions bask on their own pier on the northern side, occasionally barking loudly or swiping at each other, and always a delight to see. (Great photo-ops here!) The Aquarium of the Bay is fun, and children also love the carousel. There are rides, bungee jumps, and dozens of shops, casual eateries and restaurants, all enough to keep the family browsing a half-day. And, this is where to pick up the Blue and Gold Fleet for a cruise on the Bay or to Alcatraz.

THE STUDENT LIFE

Opportunities Galore

The Bay Area has 35 degree-granting universities, colleges, and specialized technical schools, some the finest of their class in the country. Non-degree and certificate courses are also available in a surprising number of fields, traditional or "New Age," and all can further enrich your life—or your lifestyle. Some representative samples of schools are listed below; their names should give an idea of what they are about, their websites should allow you access to more substantive information about them, and their addresses should allow you to contact them.

The major universities in San Francisco are extremely competitive when it comes to admission. Even admissions to small technical schools require application in advance, and you may be asked to provide academic transcripts, references, proof of financial independence, and health insurance.

If you are a foreigner, you will have to apply for a student visa and you will no doubt have to take the Test of English as a Foreign Language (TOEFL) as part of the application procedure. If you want to study in the United States, learn English first. For a listing of language schools you may consider, see page 333.

Getting a Student Visa

Some 480,000 foreigners are studying in the United States, the majority in California. The highest percentage are Asians from Japan, China, and Korea. Universities welcome foreign students, providing their credentials meet the institutions' standards and all immigration criteria are met.

If you are entering the United States as a tourist and are taking a short course of less than 18 hours a week, you probably do not need a student visa. But for educational courses that require more than 18 hours a week, you will need one of two types of visas, either the F-1, or the M-1, which is for nonacademic or vocational studies. In either case, however, even before applying for the visa, you will need a letter of acceptance by the school in which you intend to enroll, and a SEVIS I-901 certificate, which the school provides. The following are some government sites that detail student visas and procedures:

- http://travel.state.gov/visa/temp/types/types_1268.html
- http://educationusa.state.gov/
- http://www.ice.gov/sevis/index.htm

In order to qualify for either of the two visas, you must have been accepted as a full-time student in an educational program that is approved by the government. Unless you are enrolled in English-language courses, you must be proficient in English. You have to prove that you have funds available for your entire course of study, and you must still maintain a residence abroad.

The Visa Process

Once you have been accepted into a school, and it has provided you with a letter of acceptance and the I-20 form, (which shows your eligibility to study at that school), you may apply for the student visa.

First, you will need a personal interview with the American embassy or consulate nearest you. Schedule it well in advance, while you are compiling the documents you need to bring with you. Summer months are busiest, so if you intend to start school in the United States in September, do all your research, gather all your documentation, and set your appointments early. It may take several months for the process to be completed.

Download and complete the following visa application forms from the afore-mentioned governmental sites, or perhaps from the school that has accepted you as their student. If you do not have access to the Internet, inquire of the American embassy.

- DS-156 (non-immigrant visa application form)
- DS-157 (supplemental form for men between ages 16-45)
- DS-158 (contact information and work history form)

Pay the fees and obtain official receipts, as explained by the Embassy or on its Internet site. There are two fees: the Visa Application fee and the SEVIS fee. It is best to download the SEVIS I-901 form and pay the fee online, because you can print the official I-797 receipt immediately (website: http://www.fmjfee.com/index.html). Fees should be paid well in advance of your interview, so the interviewing officer can access the SEVIS site and confirm that the fee has been paid. Your I-20 Form has your SEVIS number on it, for easy reference.

All told, here are the items you will need to bring to the personal interview. All documents must be in English.

- Passport (this must remain valid for at least six months from your arrival date in the United States)
- Acceptance letter from the school and the I-20 form (signed)
- Visa Application Forms: DS-156, DS 157 (if applicable), DS-158

- Two 2x2 inch approved passport photographs: for detailed requirements access http://travel.state.gov/visa/temp/info/info_1287.html
- Receipts for Visa application fee and the SEVIS fee
- Transcripts and diplomas from schools, proof of English proficiency (as appropriate)
- Financial evidence that you can cover your tuition and living expenses
- Proof that your ties to your home community are such that you will return home after finishing your studies.

You are also required to have health insurance. If the health insurance from your home country will not cover you abroad, inquire of your school or see pages 148–149 for health insurance options.

With the Visa

Once you have received your visa, you may enter the United States up to 30 days before the starting date of your I-20, and no later than that date. If, however, you want to enter earlier, you will have to apply for the tourist visa and then apply to change your status. So, it is probably easier (and best) to do your sightseeing during school vacations, once you have started your course of studies.

Follow all legal procedures that allow you to maintain your F-1 status, including reporting address changes. If you drop out of your authorized school, you will be considered an "illegal alien." Generally you may stay in the country for the duration of the course that is specified on the I-20 and on the I-94 entry card (*See page 76.*), plus practical training, if that is appropriate.

Student Housing

If you are in San Francisco to study at one of the English-language schools, it will no doubt have a program for temporary housing. Also, universities have housing offices to help students find housing; some also have on-campus housing.

For temporary and inexpensive accommodations, San Francisco has several youth hostels that offer basic dormitory-style rooms at basic prices. Currently, the price of lodging per night runs to between US$ 23–26, and there is a two-week maximum stay. If you are bringing valuables such as computers or printers, inquire as to their safekeeping; some have provision for safe storage, others do not. Hostelling International membership is required, but may be purchased on-site (website: http://www.hiusa.org). The following three hostels in San Francisco are members of HI (website: http://www.norcalhostels.org), but there are others; see the Yellow Pages under Hostels. Reservations are advisable in all.

- HI Fisherman's Wharf, Fort Mason, Building 240; tel: (415) 771-7277
- HI Downtown, 312 Mason Street; tel: (415) 788-5604
- HI City Center, 685 Ellis Street; tel: (415) 474-5721

Roommates

Sharing apartments is common. Inquire at the housing office at your school and on bulletin boards at churches or at supermarkets such as the Rainbow Grocery. You might also check the website: http://www.roommates.com.

State-wide Education Systems

Four higher education systems are funded by the State of California. The most prestigious and stringent belong to the University of California system: in the Bay Area its major campus is in Berkeley, and its medical and other health-profession schools are in San Francisco, as is one of its law schools. Next come the California State Universities, which in the Bay Area are San Francisco State, Sonoma State, San Jose State, and Cal State Hayward. These are followed by the city and community colleges: San Francisco City College.

University of California

The University of California system offers some of the best education in the country, whether in its undergraduate colleges, graduate programs, or professional schools. The University of California, Berkeley, is one of the country's finest teaching and research universities, as are the Medical Center in San Francisco and its new Mission Bay research complex. Admissions are extremely competitive, and priority is given to California residents. Of some 30,000 applicants, only about 8,000 are accepted. No one ethnic or racial group constitutes a majority, which makes for an eclectic and diverse population.

- University of California, Berkeley, 110 Sproul Hall, Berkeley 94720; tel: (510) 642-6000; website: http://www.berkeley.edu
- UCSF Graduate Medical School, 500 Parnassus; tel: (415) 476-9000; website: http://www.ucsf.edu. Also pharmacy, nursing, and dentistry.
- University of California Hastings College of the Law, 200 McAllister Street; tel: (415) 565-4600; website: http://www.uchastings.edu

California State University

The widespread California State University system is known for educating the bulk of California high school graduates. Although the number and type of high school courses required for admission are almost identical to that of the University of California system, the admissions process is less competitive. The San Francisco State University is located at 1600 Holloway Avenue; tel: (415) 338-1111; website: http://www.sfsu.edu. This 25,000 student "commuter" university offers undergraduate and graduate degrees, a law school, and several certificate and credential programs.

City College

City College of San Francisco, at 50 Phelan Avenue, is a community college that offers associate degrees and certificates, international trade programs, and a small-business institute (tel: (415) 239-3000; website: http://www.ccsf.org. It has ten campuses and more "instructional sites" in the city.

Private Universities

In a class by itself among private universities, the beautiful campus of Stanford University is located on the Peninsula, at Palo Alto, about 35 minutes south of San Francisco. Its address is Stanford University, Stanford CA 94305 (tel: (650) 723-2300; website: http://www.stanford.edu). Its undergraduate application process is extremely competitive;

less than 15 percent of applicants are accepted. Also located in San Francisco are:

- University of San Francisco, 2130 Fulton Street; tel: (415) 422-5555; website: http://www.usfca.edu. A Jesuit university founded 150 years ago, it offers undergraduate and graduate degrees in business, education, law, and many other fields.
- Golden Gate University, 536 Mission Street; tel: (415) 442-7800; website: http://www.ggu.edu. Located in the heart of downtown, Golden Gate offers undergraduate and graduate degrees, and has a law school.
- New College of California, 777 Valencia Street; voicemail only tel: (415) 324-8474; website: http://www.newcollege.edu. Since 1971, this small college fosters "inquiry and critical thinking, and the integration of education with social action." Accredited by the Western Association of Schools and Colleges, NCOC offers BA degrees, weekend BA completion programs, teacher credential programs, a public interest law school, and MBA, MFA, and MA degrees.

Specialized and Technical Schools

Specialized schools may offer full degrees or professional certificates and other credentials in particular fields. This

representative sample should give you an idea of the range of education offered. For cooking programs, see the following.
- Academy of Art University, 79 New Montgomery Street; tel: (800) 544-2787; website: http://www.academyart.edu. A leading arts and design educator, the academy offers courses and degree programs in ten visual arts, including film, computer art, video, graphic design, photography, advertising, and industrial design. It offers Bachelor of Fine Art and Master of Fine Art degrees, and has campuses all around the city.
- Heald Business Colleges, 350 Mission Street; tel: (415) 808-3000; (800) 884-3253; website: http://www.heald.edu. Since 1863, Heald has been an accredited carreer school, in business, technology, healthcare.
- San Francisco Law School, 20 Haight Street; tel: (415) 626-5550; website: http://www.sfls.edu. This is a long-established evening law school.
- American College of Traditional Chinese Medicine, 455 Arkansas Street; tel: (415) 282-7600; website: http://www.actcm.edu
- San Francisco Conservatory of Music, 50 Oak Street; tel: (415) 864-7326; website: http://www.sfcm.edu
- University of the Pacific School of Dentistry, 2155 Webster Street; tel: (415) 929-6400; website: http://dental.pacific.edu
- San Francisco Art Institute, 800 Chestnut Street; tel: (415) 771-7020; website: http://www.sfai.edu. Since 1871, this institute has been educating artists in fine arts, photography, sculpture, and filmmaking.

Extended Education

Extended education courses and workshops may be short in duration but may offer certificates in some professional or technical fields. Others offer lifestyle courses such as "Wine Appreciation," or "Learning the Internet."
- San Francisco State University, College of Extended Learning, 835 Market Street, second floor; tel: (415) 405-7700; website: http://www.cel.sfsu.edu. "State" provides hundreds of classes or courses for professional development and personal enrichment.

- University of California Berkeley Extension; enrollment info tel: (510) 642-4111; website: http://www.unex.berkeley.edu. UC Berkeley has institutions at several downtown locations in San Francisco for continuing education, and it provides a wide variety of courses and certificate programs, from art to business and education to engineering. Enroll at any of the centers listed on the Internet site.
- The Learning Annex, 291 Geary Street; info tel: (415) 788-5500; website: http://www.learningannex.com. Take non-credit courses in a variety of subjects, including computers, Power Point, and the Internet, health and healing, personal development, business and careers, and finance and investing are available. Locations vary. Look for free catalogues in news boxes.

Learning California Cuisine

If you would like to be able to replicate—or at least try to—the meals you have had in some of San Francisco's temples of gastronomy, you can at least learn how. There are cooking schools for all levels of chefs, and the great chefs of San Francisco themselves are willing to give people a look at how they work their kitchens, sharing their expertise.

- California Culinary Academy, 350 Rhode Island Street; tel: (888) 897-3222; website: http://www.baychef.com. This premier culinary training institute trains some of the Bay Area's best chefs. Diners can sample artistically prepared foods in the making and watch them being made. And if you are interested in trying your hand at haute cuisine, enroll in one of the Saturday hands-on Weekend Gourmet cooking classes taught by professional chefs.
- Kuleto's Italian Restaurant, 221 Powell Street; tel: (415) 397-7720. Kuleto's has a "chef for a day" program where you can help and learn in the kitchen, and then get a full Italian meal. Kuleto's proceeds are donated to the San Francisco Food Bank.
- One Market, 1 Market Street; tel: (415) 777-5577; website: http://www.onemarket.com. As part of a prix-fixe meal, reserve to sit at the "Chef's Table" in the kitchen (either for lunch or dinner), get a tour of the kitchen, and watch

the food being prepared. You can wear a chef's jacket and help in doing a little of the prep work yourself.
- Tante Marie's Cooking School, 271 Francisco Street; tel: (415) 788-6699; website: http://www.tantemarie.com. Tane Marie has been around for quite a while. This full-time culinary school also offers the opportunity (three afternoons each week) to watch demonstrations, or on other days and weekends to take a short-term participatory course that also includes a great lunch.

International Student Identity Card

While in the United States, carry your student identification card with you. Also get the International Student Identity Card (ISIC), an internationally recognized document which shows your student status and offers discounts on a variety of services and travel; you will need to prove your registration as a student (website: http://www.isic.org). Cards cost about US$ 20, and travel agents often carry them. It may take several weeks for your card to be processed and delivered to you when you apply via the Internet. Therefore, leave sufficient time before your travel departure date to receive your card.
- STA Travel, 530 Bush Street; tel: (415) 421-3473; website: http://www.statravelgroup.com/; 36 Geary Street; tel: (415) 391-8407
- Adventure Travel, 595 Market Street; tel: (415) 247-1800; website: http://www.atcadventure.com/usa

Part-time Work

Part-time work on campus may exist at some universities, especially for graduate students who may be offered teaching/research assistantships. Although almost all foreign students must have taken the TOEFL test for admission to an American institution, a test of spoken English may also be required for those interested in teaching assistantships. Spouses who enter the country with an F2 visa (dependent of an F-1 holder) may not work but may study full- or part-time as long as they are living with the holder of the F1.

For work and study programs, internships and seasonal work, you may contact the Council on International

Educational Exchange (CIEE) or access their website for extensive information.

- Council on International Educational Exchange (CIEE), 300 Fore Street, 3rd Floor, Portland Maine; tel: (207) 553-4000; website: http://www.ciee.org

Libraries

To obtain a library card that allows book borrowing from any of the city's neighborhood public libraries, bring your driver's license or other picture identification, plus a document that shows your current address. There are libraries in many neighborhoods; those in multilingual districts offer books and periodicals in the languages primarily spoken in that area.

- San Francisco Public Library, 100 Larkin Street, in the Civic Center; tel: (415) 557-4400; website: http://www.sfpl.org. The library has extensive collections, a local history wing, work stations for connection to the Internet, and special-interest sections on history, gay and lesbian studies, art, and music. If you need information that a library would have, you may call the SFPL reference librarian at (415) 557-4400, or access the Internet site given above and send an e-mail.
- Mechanics' Institute Library and Chess Room, 57 Post Street; membership tel: (415) 293-0105; website: http://www.milibrary.org. A long-established private reference and lending library, a wide range of periodicals, video, and audio cassettes are also available for loan. It also hosts and organizes author readings and events, and its Chess Club is open to all members of any skill level. Classes and tournaments are held too. Day and week passes are available for a small fee.

TO YOUR HEALTH!

Medical Care in San Francisco

The quality of medical care in San Francisco is excellent. Practicing physicians who are also researchers at the area's major medical research centers and hospitals bring cutting-edge knowledge and techniques to their patients, assuring them of the best of care. Exceptional health care is provided by the city's qualified and competent healthcare workers. There is a question, however, as to accessibility—how much access any individual has to the best care—and this is most often determined by finances and health insurance.

If You Become Ill

Travelers are not required to have health insurance when in the United States, but as health care is costly, it is strongly advisable to have coverage. If you do not have health insurance in your home country, inquire of your travel agent when booking your ticket; sometimes they sell temporary insurance policies. Even people with health insurance should inquire of their carriers about the documents needed and which receipts to keep in order to be reimbursed for any financial outlay.

All public hospitals have 24-hour emergency rooms, and many of them have bilingual staff (Spanish, Russian, Chinese). All emergencies are treated, regardless of a person's ability to pay; once in stable condition, however, the patient may be transferred to a different facility. Each hospital has its own procedures for payment or insurance reimbursement. If your insurance is American, you should have no trouble sending the itemized bill to your carrier; most hospitals will do that for you. If you are covered by insurance in another country, you may be required to pay in advance and submit the itemized bill to your own carrier.

Emergency Services

In the event of a dire emergency, dial 911 to reach the police, the fire department, or an ambulance; for poison assistance call the 24-hour poison control service (tel: (800) 222-1222) immediately. Response to a 911 call during a medical emergency will be by a Fire Department ambulance. Paramedics will first stabilize the patient during the trip to the hospital. In the case of an accident or a sudden trauma, the hospital to which the patient will be transported to will probably be San Francisco General, known for its trauma services; or for burns, Saint Francis Memorial. In other cases, the ambulance will probably be directed to the nearest hospital, unless that hospital's Intensive Care Unit (ICU) has no beds available, and the ambulance is diverted to another emergency center.

If you have a health-related emergency and go to a hospital's emergency room, you will receive the appropriate prescription to treat your condition and enough medication to last until pharmacies open the next morning. There are pharmacies that have 24-hour prescription departments. For over-the-counter remedies such as cough medicine or aspirin, you can also try 24-hour supermarkets.

Health Insurance

The United States has no national health insurance plan, but there are many options for obtaining insurance, provided you can pay for it. Workers may be covered through their employer's health plan, and some employers offer several to choose among. While discussing health benefits with your future employer, ask what the company's plan covers; many people do not know which health conditions or treatment procedures are covered until they are unexpectedly denied payment for some treatment. But small businesses often do not offer health insurance, and employees must thus find coverage elsewhere, through their spouse or domestic partner, through associations or unions, or through an individual plan, which is more costly.

Even among individual plans there are several types. Under some, the holder is allowed to see any doctor for medical consultation; others specify physicians and clinics under their plans. Most usually have an initial amount that the patient must pay before the insurance company begins to reimburse at the percentage allowed, and these "deductibles" vary. And not all insurance plans provide the exact same coverage, not even within the same company. It is best to compare plans and prices, but not to take too long, for people without insurance are at great financial and health risks.

When choosing your physicians, inquire as to the insurance plans they accept. A few specialists—including some dentists—prefer not to allow insurance companies to dictate how they practice their profession and do not participate in insurance plans. Instead they require payment to be made at the time of treatment and, providing the appropriate treatment forms, ask patients to submit the insurance claims themselves. Invariably, the patient using non-participating doctors receives a lower percentage of reimbursement.

Kaiser Permanente is a major membership Health Maintenance Organization (HMO) throughout the state of California and in other western states. With its several campuses with their own physicians, a membership offers comprehensive health care on all levels (tel: (415) 833-2000; website: http://www.kaiserpermanente.org). A plan is also available for Medicare recipients and disabled persons. Inquire about the dental program.

Veterans of the United States military are entitled to use the services of the Veterans' Administration; contact the San Francisco Veterans' Affairs Medical Center, at 4150 Clement Street; tel: (415) 221-4810; website: http://www.sanfrancisco.va.gov.

The Healthy San Francisco program makes basic and ongoing medical care accessible and affordable to residents who do not have health insurance, and who make up to US$54,000 (website: http://www.healthysanfrancisco.org/visitors/). Availability is regardless of immigration or employment status, or even pre-existing medical conditions. Check the website to find out if you are eligible.

San Francisco Hospitals

The following is a list of hospitals in San Francisco, listed by area, so you can find the one most convenient for you. For emergency rooms, see *Resource Guide* on page 369. Kaiser Permanente members should go to 2425 Geary Boulevard; tel: (415) 833-2200; website: http://www.kaiserpermanente.org.

- **Castro/Hayes Valley**—California Pacific Medical Center/Davies Campus, Castro and Duboce; tel: (415) 565-6000; website: http://www.cmpc.org
- **Haight**—Saint Mary's Medical Center, 450 Stanyan Street; tel: (415) 668-6000; website: http://www.stmarymedicalcenter.org
- **Mission/Bernal Heights**—Saint Luke's Hospital, 3555 Cesar Chavez Street; tel: (415) 647-8600; website: http://www.stlukes-sf.org
- **Mission**—San Francisco General Hospital, 1001 Potrero Avenue; tel: (415) 206-8000; website: http://www.dph.sf.ca.us/chn/SFGH/default.asp. The city's public hospital, San Francisco General Hospital is especially known for its trauma center.
- **Pacific Heights**—California Pacific Medical Center/Pacific Campus, 2333 Buchanan; tel: (415) 600-6000; website: http://www.cmpc.org
- **Polk Gulch/Tenderloin/Van Ness**—Saint Francis Memorial Hospital, 900 Hyde Street; tel: (415) 353-6000; website: http://www.saintfrancismemorial.org. It is known for its treatment of burns and spinal injuries.
- **Presidio Heights/Inner Richmond**—California Pacific Medical Center/California Campus, 3700 California Street; tel: (415) 600-6000; website: http://www.cmpc.org
- **Sunset**—University of California, San Francisco at Parnassus, 505 Parnassus Avenue; tel: (415) 476-1000; website: http://www.ucsfhealth.org. An excellent hospital, it is attached to the university's medical school.

Pharmacies

When you first arrive in San Francisco, have with you enough medications to tide you over until you have found a doctor and pharmacy (usually called drugstores) of your own. Foreigners should understand that many medications that are over-the-counter in other countries might require a doctor's prescription here. Ask your physician to write new prescriptions using both the trade and generic name of the medication. Bring a copy of your eyeglass prescription and an extra pair of glasses as well.

In addition to prescription medications, drugstores carry over-the-counter medications, vitamins, and a wide variety of familiar brands of health- and beauty-related items, plus foods, cold drinks, magazines and stationery, candies, and more. Cosmetic brands are generally well-known, and are less expensive than those found in the department stores. Neighborhood drug stores stay open late, depending on the traffic in their area, sometimes until 8:00 pm or 10:00 pm. The city's chain drugstores are open on Sunday, although small neighborhood pharmacies may not be. The major chains in San Francisco are Walgreens and Rite-Aid. For drugstores that are open 24-hours for prescriptions, see page 370.

In the United States, when you take your prescription to a pharmacy to be filled, it is that same pharmacy that will refill it when you need a new supply. Although in some countries the prescription is returned to you and you can refill it at any pharmacy you choose, this is not the case in America. So, make sure that the drugstore you go to is convenient for you in the future, should your prescriptions need to be refilled. If, however, you use a chain such as Walgreens or Rite-Aid, they should be able to transfer the prescription within the chain.

Women's Health

The Women's Health Resource Center of University of California at San Francisco (UCSF) is situated at 2356 Sutter Street (tel: (415) 353-2668; website: http://www.whrc.ucsf.edu/). Care includes primary care, gynecology services, obstetrics, and breast cancer screening and treatment. The Women's Health Library and Resource Center offers resource materials and classes on women's health, including a Pregnancy Program.

The Women's Program of California Pacific Medical Center at 3698 California Street also consults on and treats all aspects of women's health (tel: (415) 600-6000; website:

http://www.cpmc.org). It has a medical referral service that finds a doctor who is "sensitive to your needs."

Natural Resources, at 1367 Valencia Street, is a pregnancy, childbirth, and parenting center that provides many excellent resources (tel: (415) 550-2611; website: http://www.naturalresources-sf.com). It offers classes and support groups for expectant mothers and for new parents, has referrals listings for birth and child professionals, has a reference library, and sells supplies and clothing, as well as health-care products for mother and baby, at good prices.

Alternative Medicine

San Francisco is one of the foremost cities in the United States in the practice and development of alternative medicine, including Eastern techniques and homeopathic healing. Traditional Western physicians in San Francisco are open-minded, probably to a greater degree than those in other American cities; for the most part they are willing to discuss non-traditional techniques and remedies with their patients, as well as to consider alternative options their patients present to them. Some hospitals also have Eastern-oriented medical clinics, and the major insurance companies accept claims for acupuncture. Licensed acupuncturists work on their own or in conjunction with Western colleagues, and herbalists and homeopaths prescribe natural remedies. Therapeutic massage of varying internationally recognized techniques is available, as are classes for yoga and other relaxation methods. Massage is sometimes covered under health plans if prescribed by a physician or chiropractor.

Chiropractic, considered an alternative medicine in some countries, is considered mainstream in the United States, and chiropractic treatments for muscular and skeletal difficulties are generally covered by health insurance carriers, depending on the condition. There are many licensed Doctors of Chiropractic in the city; it is best to ask among your friends and colleagues for a recommendation.

For an excellent guide to services for natural living, look for the free semiannual publication *Bay Area Naturally* in natural food shops and outlets. It includes descriptions and advertisements for holistic health professionals, "green" products and services, natural food restaurants, and natural food markets. *Open Exchange*, which advertises courses and seminars in healthy living and healing, can be found in news boxes around the city.

- American College of Traditional Chinese Medicine, 450 Connecticut Street; tel: (415) 282-9603. The clinic of this accredited school offers acupuncture and Chinese herb treatments for a variety of maladies: upper-respiratory, gastrointestinal and cardiovascular problems, and more.

Free Clinics

The Community Health Network of San Francisco provides low-cost health care to residents (website: http://www.dph.sf.ca.us/chn). Funded by the city, clinics provide both primary and specialized care for people who have no health insurance and cannot afford traditional health care providers. In most, patients pay on a sliding scale geared to their ability to pay. Many of the clinics are staffed by professional volunteers—physicians, nurses, residents, interns—who donate their expertise to people who could not otherwise afford health care.

Practising *tai chi* in Washington Square.

Fishing from a municipal pier, away from the hustle and bustle of life in the city.

To get medical attention for an immediate health problem, call San Francisco General Hospital, which is a primary care site, also with Women's and Family Health Centers (tel: (415) 206-8000). For more health centers, look in the City Government section of the *White Pages* under the Health Department. The clinics listed here by area are well-known:

- **Haight-Ashbury**—Haight Ashbury Free Clinic; 558 Clayton Street, at Haight; tel: (415) 746-1967. This long-established clinic offers low-cost basic health services to the uninsured, HIV treatment, drug and alcohol detox, etc.
- **Hayes Valley**—Lyon-Martin Women's Health Services; 1748 Market Street, #201; tel: (415) 565-7667. This primary care clinic for women provides treatment for acute and chronic conditions, physical examinations, gynecology, internal medicine, family planning, and preventive health care.
- **Mission**—Castro-Mission Health Center; 3850 17th Street, at Noe; tel: (415) 487-7500
- **The Tenderloin**—Saint Anthony Free Medical Clinic; 121 Golden Gate Avenue; tel: (415) 241-8320. This clinic provides free medical services and a walk-in clinic for uninsured adults and children.

Dentists

Although the quality of dental care in San Francisco is extremely high, finding the right dentist might take some time, depending on your individual needs and preferences. Thus, before moving, have any remaining dental work done, and bring with you current x-rays and copies of your dental records for your new dentist's reference.

Your friends, neighbors, and colleagues may recommend dentists, but as with choosing any professional relationship, you will have to determine whether that person is right for you. This may depend not only on your physical needs, but whether you have dental insurance and whether the dentist you choose accepts it. For a recommendation, you might also call the 24-hour San Francisco Dental Society Referral Service; (tel: (415) 421-1435). Be specific as to the type of dentist you are seeking, the type of dental work you need done, and any financial concerns. The same holds true for another referral service, 1-800-Dentist.

Until you have found a dentist of your own, you might try the clinics of the dental schools in San Francisco. Both schools listed below offer inexpensive dental care by dental students under the supervision of faculty members who have first made the initial evaluation of condition and treatment. In addition to their regular clinics, both provide, on a first-come first-served basis, weekday emergency services for patients, and after-hours emergency assistance as well.

- University of California School of Dentistry, 707 Parnassus Street; tel: (415) 476-1891
- University of the Pacific School of Dentistry, 2155 Webster Street; tel: (415) 929-6501

For 24-hour dental emergencies, you might also try San Francisco General Hospital.

HIV/AIDS

It has now been more than 25 years since the first outbreak of HIV/AIDS. Unfortunately, San Francisco has been hit particularly hard by the epidemic—some 18,000 people have died from it here, and there is still no cure. But fortunately, new medications have extended the life of some HIV/AIDS patients, and San Francisco has extensive public resources for testing and care.

Both San Francisco General and the Davies Campus of California Pacific Medical Center have well-known AIDS clinics. The City Clinic at 356 7th Street tests and treats sexually transmitted diseases at low cost or for free (tel: (415) 487-5500); it is open on weekdays.

- The Gay and Lesbian Medical Association offers referrals to physicians and other medical services in the Bay Area, publishes helpful guides, and offers forums and seminars; call on weekdays; tel: (415) 255-4547.
- San Francisco Department of Public Health: AIDS Health Project; 1930 Market at Laguna; tel: (415) 502-8378. Free anonymous and confidential HIV testing.

- California HIV/AIDS Hot-line; tel: (800) 367-2437. Information on HIV/AIDS, safe sex, and a database of HIV-related services; In English, Spanish, Filipino.
- A New Leaf, 103 Hayes Street; tel: (415) 626-7000; website: http://www.newleafservices.org. A comprehensive mental health, substance abuse, HIV/AIDS, and social support organization specifically established for the LGBT communities.
- AIDS/HIV Nightline; Emotional support hot-line that is open 5:00 pm–5:00 am every night; tel: (415) 434-2437.
- Pharmacare (Stadtlander's) Pharmacy, 445 Castro Street, is a branch of the nationwide pharmacy specializing in HIV/AIDS care; tel: (415) 864-7030; website: http://www.stadtlander.com. Open daily.

UP AND DOWN THE HILLS

In From the San Francisco International Airport (SFO)

First you have to get into the city. There are several options for transportation from SFO, and your choice will depend on your budget and time constraints, how much luggage you are carrying and the degree of inconvenience you are willing to bear. Taxis, of course, are the most expensive; the meter may run as high as US$ 45 plus tip.

> **Flights and more**
>
> For the latest on all flights in and out of San Francisco, as well as ground transportation, and details on shopping, dining, and cultural exhibitions, access San Francisco International Airport's website: http://www.flysfo.com.

Yet taxis are the most convenient, and passengers are dropped off in front of the door; usually the driver is willing to help with suitcases—at least as far as the door. (And do not forget to tip the driver 10–15 percent of the total fare.) Taxi stands are located at each terminal, and signs in the airport clearly indicate where they are to be found. (*Refer also to section on* Taxis, pages 170-171.) Yet, they may not be the fastest option, depending on time of day. At rush hours the freeways (highways) are often jammed, and while the traffic crawls along you will see the meter clicking away merrily. It may take a half-hour to get into the city. Here are some other less expensive and time-consuming options.

- BART (Bay Area Rapid Transit); About a 30-minute ride to downtown San Francisco, this is one of the cheapest and most efficient ways to get into the city, if you do not have a lot of luggage to carry; tel: (510) 989-2278; website: http://www.bart.gov. There is a free airport shuttle bus to the BART station in the International Terminal. Currently the ride costs US$ 5.35 one way.
- Super Shuttle; tel: (415) 558-8500; website: http://www.supershuttle.com. Door-to-door service is convenient. For transportation to the airport, reservations are required. Because the shuttle arranges its stops according to its route, you may not be the first to get off. (And on your way back to the airport you may not be the first to get on. So, allow more time to get to the airport than if you were taking BART or a cab.)
- SamTrans (San Mateo County Transit); Buses run from the airport to the Transbay Terminal at Mission and First Streets; tel: (800) 660-4287; website: http://www.samtrans.com. A trip on board the No. 292 bus costs only US$ 1.75, but the bus takes longer than the KX, which costs US$ 4.50 and makes the ride in about 35 minutes. Check the bus schedules and baggage allowance.

In From Oakland International Airport (OAK)

Again, taxis may be the most convenient way to get into San Francisco, depending on the amount of luggage you have. But they are also the most expensive, perhaps costing up to US$ 50 for the trip into the city.

- BART: BART is the cheapest and most efficient, but you have to take a brief shuttle bus ride from the airport

(terminals one and two) to the station; it may not be easy if you are loaded with baggage for a long stay. Buy your ticket at the airport vending machines. Fares vary according to destination; Currently the ride costs US$ 3.35 from the airport into San Francisco.
- Bayporter Express; tel: (415) 467-1800; website: http://www.bayporter.com. An airport door-to-door shuttle service; Reservations are required. Currently it costs US$ 32 one way for the first person; reduced rates are charged for others in the party and children. With a large group, think about chartering the entire van for US$ 90.

By Car

If you are driving into the city, you will most likely have followed the directions of a road map. The highways are clearly marked, at least until you get into the city, when you should switch to a street map. Here are some recommended routes depending on the direction you are driving in from.

- **From the South:** You will most likely be taking either California Highway 101, or Interstate 280. You might also arrive on the scenic Highway 1, which runs along the ocean, and which moves inland as it crosses the city. Eventually it joins with 101 as it crosses the Golden Gate Bridge going north. Another scenic route is the winding Highway 35, the Skyline Drive, which ends at 19th avenue, joining Highway 1. If you take either of the two major highways, try not to arrive between 7:00 am–9:30 am, or between 4:00 pm–7:00 pm. Traffic is heavily congested during rush hours, but if you have more than one passenger in a car you are entitled to use the "diamond" lanes.
- **From the North:** You will cross the Golden Gate Bridge on that same Highway 101. The toll to enter San Francisco is US$ 5. (Leaving San Francisco across the bridge incurs no charge.) On late Sunday afternoons, when people are returning from weekends in the country, the bridge traffic can delay you by at least a half hour.
- **From the East:** You will be on Interstate Highway 80, crossing the San Francisco-Oakland Bay Bridge, and the

cost to enter San Francisco is US$ 3. (Again, there is no toll as you leave San Francisco to the east.) The eastern span of the Bay Bridge is being reconstructed, and it is due to be finished by 2012. So, over the next few years expect traffic delays from time to time, and do not be surprised if sometime soon the rate hikes up to US$ 5, to match that of the Golden Gate Bridge.

Understanding the City

The city plan of San Francisco should not be difficult to understand. Streets are laid out in a more or less grid-like pattern, except where one of the city's 42 hills intrudes; on either side of a hill the name of a continuing street is most likely different. To understand the city, first take into consideration the role of the diagonal Market Street, which starts at the bay and cuts southwest through much of the city. North of Market, the streets are named; south of Market, the streets are numbered.

North of Market, the street names have no particular order to them; you just have to learn them. South of Market, the north/south streets start with First Street and continue regularly to 30th Street, where Twin Peaks and then Mount Davidson loom above. At Twin Peaks, Market Street changes its name to Portola, and as it winds toward Ocean Avenue, the names and contours of streets follow no system or plan.

This network of numbered streets south of Market should not be confused with what are called "The Avenues." These begin at Arguello (north of Golden Gate Park) and Stanyan (south of the Park). These straight avenues run north/south from Second Avenue (there is no First Avenue) to Forty-Eighth Avenue, at the edge of the sea. And intersecting with them, making orientation easier, are alphabetically consecutive streets (running east/west), starting with Anza and Balboa, and—after jumping the Park—continuing to Wawona.

If none of these make sense at first, take heart; most intersections throughout the city have large green signs above them, indicating the cross street, which is helpful when driving, for street signs may occasionally be missing or hidden by foliage.

Small city maps, found at bookshops, can be carried in a briefcase or purse, but there are no pocket-sized street atlases for San Francisco. Some maps—mostly of the downtown and tourist areas—may be had at the San Francisco Visitors Center. More detailed, indexed street and transit maps are available at newsstands, in bookshops and some gasoline stations, and at the "Triple A" at 150 Van Ness Avenue, if you are a member. A detailed street atlas to keep in your car may be bought at bookstores. The *Yellow Pages* has a few helpful maps of neighborhoods, downtown streets, public transportation routes, and city zip codes.

If you call someone for directions, ask what the cross street is, so that on a long street you can more easily pinpoint your destination. House numbers start with 1 at the beginning of each block. So the first building in the 1700 block of Geary might be 1701, and the first building on the next block, the 1800 block, will be 1801. Across the street will be 1702 and 1802, respectively. Even numbers are on one side of the street, odd numbers on the facing side.

Thinking about Transportation

Transportation is an important issue in San Francisco. The population of this small city almost doubles each workday, when more than 200,000 commuters file into the city—in vehicles, on ferries, on trains. Rush hours may be among the busiest in the country, as vehicle access into the city is limited to two bridges and two major highways coming up from the Peninsula. Traffic problems are further complicated by the millions of tourists who come to the Bay Area every year, many of whom either drive their own cars or rent one to go out into the countryside. Traffic is also a problem on

Transportation Information
Information on every facet of transportation around the Bay Area can be obtained by calling 511 Transit or by accessing its website (tel: 511; website: http://www.511.org). This includes up-to-date traffic conditions, contact information for all the public transportation systems, bicycling, and current traffic conditions, events, and changes relating to transportation.

weekends, as residents themselves head to the country and suburbanites come into the city. Thus, if you decide to live in a suburb and work in the city, you will have to think carefully about commuting strategies. In the city itself, driving and parking in the city center is difficult, depending on time of day and the number of delivery trucks double-parked. There are, however, numerous parking lots, but on a daily basis, they are also costly to use.

Compounding the problem, the city's municipal transit system is continually beset by problems. Mayoral candidates promise during campaigns to fix them, then once elected state that problems are being addressed. Nonetheless, San Franciscans consistently rate public transit—along with unaffordable housing—as the city's worst problems; people who use the system, however, do manage to get to work on time, and the system is more or less reliable. Many people walk or use bicycles to get to work, and banks of parking meters downtown are designated for motorcycles.

Walking

San Francisco, despite its hills, is a walking city, and people walk whenever and wherever they can. In fact, some 30,000 people walk to work each day.

According to California law, all vehicles must stop for a pedestrian in a crosswalk. (Jaywalkers in the middle of a block do not have the right of way, but this does not mean that a driver has the right to hit them.) Surprisingly, for the most part, drivers actually obey the laws. Occasionally an impatient driver will pretend not to see the person crossing, or a tourist in a rented car might be ignorant of the law, so it is still important to pay attention to traffic and cross when it is safe to. Obey the traffic signals and the "Walk" or "Don't Walk" signs. Many of these signs now also blink how many seconds remain until the light changes to red, informing both drivers and pedestrians of how much time they have left to get out of the intersection.

When crossing the street, watch out for cars that are turning right on a red light, which is legal. Be sure to pay attention to cars that dash through the intersection just after the light has turned red. This is a major problem in San Francisco, but it has abated somewhat after serious accidents happened. Do not assume that the instant the light has turned green in your direction, it is safe to cross. Be vigilant. Your safety is your own concern.

Bicycling

San Francisco rates among the top ten urban centers in the country for bicycling. The city encourages bicycling for daily transportation, and more than 35,000 San Franciscans commute regularly to work by bike. There are 45 miles of bicycle lanes on the city's streets, and more are being added. Color-coded signs on bike routes indicate the direction (primary crosstown routes in full color or neighborhood routes in green and white), and odd numbers indicate north-south routes while even numbers are for east-west routes. The routes try to avoid the hills. To aid commuters, bicycle lockers have been installed at several public garages, and some Muni routes are experimenting with bike racks. Always lock your bike to an anchored, solid object with a

U-lock. Bicyclists are expected to obey all the laws pertaining to motorists. For bicycling as a sport, see page 278.

The San Francisco Bicycle Coalition promotes bicycles in everyday life, and has regular meetups and events. Its website keeps cyclists up to date on all aspects of bicycling in the city (website: http://www.sfbike.org).

Public Transportation

The Muni (Municipal Railway), San Francisco's public transportation system, accommodates more than half a million passenger rides each day (info tells: 511 or 311; website: http://www.sfmuni.com). Muni is responsible for the buses (diesel) the trolley buses (electric), the cable cars, historic streetcars, and the city's light rail streetcars known as Muni Metro.

The Fares

For a single trip, exact fare is required; adults currently pay US$ 2.00; children over the age of four, seniors over 65, and students and disabled people with a discount card pay 75 cents. If you plan another trip within 90 minutes, ask for a "transfer" while paying your fare. Transfers, which are free, allow two additional trips within the time limit marked on them, usually about 1½–2 hours, although some drivers are more liberal in where they mark the expiration. These fares refer to all public transportation except the cable car, which costs US$ 5 per ride, with no transfers.

For regular use of Muni, it is best to buy a monthly Fast Pass (US$ 55), that allows unlimited access to any Muni vehicle, including cable cars (and to BART and Caltrain within San Francisco). There is no need for transfers, no need to search for dollar bills or change. Fast Passes are widely available, and prices vary according to category: see the Muni Timetables booklet that is sometimes in a rack at the front of the bus.

Muni is currently testing a new TransLink card, a reusable "smart card" that will work across all transportation networks—Muni, BART and Caltrain (website: http://www.translink.org). You replenish the card as the amount left on it dwindles.

Tourists should inquire about the public transportation Passport, which is sold at the Tourist Office, cable car booths, and a few other places. The Passport is sold in denominations of one day (US$ 11), three days (US$ 18) or seven days (US$ 24), and depending on how often you intend to use public transportation during your visit, it can be a good deal, especially if you intend to take a ride or two on San Francisco's cable cars.

Also investigate the San Francisco City Pass, which is good for seven consecutive days on all Muni lines and also gives discounts to several cultural attractions in the city (*See page 372.*).

The Cable Car

Cable cars are certainly not the major way to get around the city on public transportation, but we start with them here, as they are—since 1964—a registered national landmark and contribute much to the city's charm, for tourists and locals alike. Everyone loves them.

Although an omnibus system of horse-drawn carriages was in operation in the city by 1851, the heavily laden horses could not climb the steep hills, whose summits remained out of reach as residences. Thus, the availability of sturdy, mechanized transportation affected the development of the modern city as much as its geology. In their heyday at the end of the 19th century, some 600 cable cars traversed more than 100 miles (160.9 km) of tracks, transforming the rocky summits—Nob Hill, Russian Hill—into areas of prime real estate. Although the poor had long trudged part way up those and other hills to their small cottages (enjoying the best views in town), the advent of the cable cars opened up the city in a way that nothing else had. The Castro, Diamond Heights, the Mission—all seen as distant from the city's commerce—were suddenly vital neighborhoods of their own. If these working class neighborhoods were not as fashionable as Nob Hill, Pacific Heights, or the then-aristocratic residential Van Ness Boulevard, a century later that is certainly no longer the case.

Today the cable cars continue to clang charmingly up and down the hills on their underground cables at just under 10 miles (16.1 km) per hour. The 40 little cars with their brass and wood fittings run for 12 miles (19.3 km) on three lines—the Powell/Mason and Powell/Hyde lines, which begin at Powell and Market and head toward Fisherman's Wharf, and the California Street line, which begins at Market and California and terminates at Van Ness. The gripman rings the bell to alert pedestrians and traffic of the cable car's arrival, and to signal a stop coming up. (If you are near Union Square in July, perhaps you will hear the gripmen's bell ringing contest!) Stops are at every few corners and may (or may not) be marked with a maroon and white sign on the curb, or by a yellow line between the rails. Wait on the sidewalk, signal the gripman to stop, and board only when the car is fully stopped. Theoretically, automobiles are supposed to stop to allow people to cross to the cable car, but they do not always, so watch carefully when stepping off the sidewalk when the cable car is approaching. During the height of the tourist season it is hard to find a seat inside. Generally it is the tourists who like to sit on the outside in the fog and the wind, while the locals head for the inside seats.

One of San Francisco's beloved cable cars with a stunning view of the glistening surface of the bay and Alcatraz Island in the background.

Historic Streetcars

And there is still more charm. When the freeway that ran along the Embarcadero was demolished in the Nineties, the entire waterfront was refurbished into the beautiful stretch it is today. This allowed the completion of a project already started, the building of a streetcar service using restored antique streetcars from the 1920s. Now some 17 brightly colored streetcars are in service along the F-Market line running from the Castro to the Embarcadero, joining the Wharves line that glides along the Embarcadero to Fisherman's Wharf. The new 3rd Street line passes Mission Bay on its way down to Visitacion Valley. The streetcars run from about 6:00 am to 12:30 am. Along with the cable cars, they make public transportation in San Francisco fun.

The Buses

Buses run from about 5:00 am until 1:00 am; in the early morning hours, the city is serviced by nine Owl lines.

The front of each bus displays the route number/letter and name, destination, and type of service: black/white lettering indicates local buses with many stops, green/white lettering indicates limited stops, and red/white lettering means express service. Buses are numbered with their routes (e.g. 38-Geary), and streetcars are lettered (e.g. J-Church). The bus stops themselves indicate which buses/streetcars stop there and their schedules. Buses stop only at designated bus stops, and not even in the pouring rain is the driver likely to open the door for you one inch away from the bus stop.

Bus routes that go to some of the most popular San Francisco attractions are listed as follows:

- The Castro: 24, 33, 35, 37
- Chinatown: 1, 9X, 12, 15, 30
- Civic Center: 5, 21, 47, 49
- Coit Tower: 39
- Crissy Field: 29
- Ferry Building: 1
- Fisherman's Wharf: 10, 15, 19, 30, 39
- Golden Gate Bridge: 29
- Japantown: 2, 3, 4, 22, 38L 15,30,

Taking BART makes commuting into the city easy.

- North Beach: 15, 30, 45
- San Francisco Zoo: 23
- Union Square: 38

BART

BART (Bay Area Rapid Transit) is a five-line, 72-mile commuter railway that stops at some 39 stations on its route between the East Bay and Colma/Daly City (info tel: (415) 989-2278; website: http://www.bart.gov). Efficiently run, BART accommodates more than 250,000 passenger rides each day. Bus lines are set up throughout the Bay Area to take people directly to the BART. The service starts around 4:00 am (later on weekends) and shuts down around midnight. Check the schedules, for on weekends the service period is somewhat reduced. Informational brochures are available at BART stations.

Paying the Fare

To determine the fare to your destination, check the information charts displayed in each BART station. For regular commuting, buy a multi-trip ticket, which saves you time and money The magnetic ticket is read by the computerized turnstiles at the entrances and exits. If you buy a one-trip ticket, save it in order to exit the station at your destination.

Commuter Transit

Regularly scheduled buses and ferries bring commuters into the Financial District each day from around the Bay Area. Most ferries have differing weekday and weekend schedules, and some also provide service to tourist attractions or to sports events. For information on all aspects of commuter travel, access the 511 Internet site.
- East Bay—AC Transit (Alameda-Contra Costa Transit): bus service to San Francisco, connecting to BART in the East Bay.
- Marin/Sonoma—Golden Gate Transit (GGT): fixed-route bus service from Marin to downtown San Francisco, and ferry service to the Ferry Building from Larkspur and Sausalito. Bus service to and from Marin county locations. Ferries are

wheelchair accessible, and Whistlestop Wheels is GGT's intercounty paratransit service for disabled passengers (tel: (415) 454-0964).

- Marin—Blue & Gold Fleet: Commuter ferries from East Bay and Tiburon to Ferry Building; all-day ferry between Pier 41, Sausalito, and Tiburon, and service to Alcatraz and Angel Island.
- East Bay—Harbor Bay Maritime Ferry: weekday commuter ferry between Harbor Bay Isle and the San Francisco Ferry Building.
- East Bay—Alameda Oakland Ferry: commuter service between Alameda, Oakland, and the city.
- Peninsula—Caltrain: daily train service between San Francisco and San Jose, The terminus is San Francisco's Fourth Street Station, at Townsend.
- Richmond—Red & White Fleet: weekday rush hour commuter service between the Ferry Terminal and Harbor Way.
- San Mateo—SamTrans (San Mateo County Transit District): bus service within San Mateo County and commuter service to the Financial District. Also services SFO and the Colma BART station.

Taxis

Taxis in San Francisco do not cruise the streets regularly as they do in many other major cities. There are taxi stands at the major hotels downtown, but at rush hours, on rainy days, or when there is a major convention in town, there may be no taxis to be hailed, even at the stands. Trying to call one on the telephone can be frustrating at any hour, but if you are out of the direct city center, it is still best to call a cab well in advance of the time you will need it, and then at the appointed time to confirm that it is on its way. Some hospitals, hotels, and apartment complexes have direct lines to the taxi companies, and any restaurant will call a taxi for you when you are ready to leave.

Taxis may be yellow, blue, or red and green, but all have the name and contact number of the cab company in prominent letters and numerals on the sides. The light on the roof of the taxi is illuminated when it is vacant. If an empty cab passes you by even though you are flagging it down, it has probably been called on the radio to go to a particular address. In San Francisco, the meter does not start running until you have entered the cab. Tip between 15–20 percent of the fare.

You can either give the taxi driver the exact street address of your destination, or you can indicate the two cross streets, such as "the corner of Washington and Battery." If you think you know the best route to get there, tell the driver on which streets you want to go. Generally, however, the driver is aware of the traffic conditions at that time and will send you via the shortest and quickest way possible.

Do not take an illegal cab or limousine. Accredited cabs say "San Francisco Taxi Cab" on the side and rear, and they have a small metal identification visible on the dashboard. The driver's identification should be visible from the backseat. The benefits of using legal cabs are that they are insured, they must undergo safety inspections, and their meters are checked regularly.

- DeSoto Cab; tel: (415) 970-1300
- Luxor Cab; tel: (415) 282-4141
- Veterans Cab; tel: (415) 684-4444
- Yellow Cab; tel: (415) 626-2345

Driving In The City

Some 800,000 cars move around this small city each day, so the most important thing about driving in San Francisco is to drive defensively. The congested downtown streets, the few major arteries, and the hills and the sun in drivers' eyes all contribute to the highest rate of traffic accidents in the state (although not involving pedestrians).

Do not let the hills intimidate you. People drive up and down the hills every day, and some major routes go over the steepest of hills. When stopping at a traffic light while driving up a hill, leave at least ten feet between you and the car ahead, in case that car rolls back a little when starting up again. On some steep hills, you may have to downshift to maintain the car's power level, and some streets are marked with the percentage of grade and warnings to trucks not to attempt them. Make sure you have a pair of sunglasses in your car when you drive. If you drive toward the East in the morning or toward the West in the afternoons—especially when maneuvering the hills—the sun can be blinding.

When parking on a hill, "curb your wheels." This means if your car is heading down a hill, turn the front wheels toward the curb, to keep it from rolling. If your car is heading up a hill, turn the back part of the front wheels toward the curb to keep it from rolling back down. If you do not, your car will be ticketed, for curbing your wheels is a San Francisco law. Worse, if your car rolls down a steep street, it could hurt someone.

Streets are narrowest in the downtown area, and it is on these streets, of course, that delivery trucks routinely double park, forcing lanes to merge and causing traffic jams. Try to glance two to three blocks ahead while you are driving, to determine whether your lane is clear. Drivers in San Francisco are not particularly generous in allowing cars to cut into their lanes, so it is best to leave yourself as much time as possible to change lanes.

And a word of caution: on the narrow downtown streets or even on the multi-lane Market Street, do not let yourself get trapped behind a bus or streetcar. They move slowly and stop frequently.

Many of the streets east of Van Ness are one-way; past Arguello, however, most streets are two-way. Two important one-way streets are Bush, which heads east ("Bush to the Bay"), and Pine, which heads west ("Pine to the Pacific"), for their lights are "timed," meaning that if you maintain a certain speed (and if there are no obstacles), you should not meet any red lights once you are in the traffic flow.

Some downtown streets have "diamond lanes," reserved for buses and for cars turning right at the next corner. Cars may turn right on a red light, after having come to a complete stop and all pedestrians in the crosswalk have crossed; some busy intersections, however, have signs saying "No turn on red." Left turn on red from a one-way street and into another one-way street is permitted under the same conditions.

Rush hours in San Francisco are generally 7:00 am–

9:30 am and 4:00 pm–7:00 pm. Streets leading to the bridges or freeways begin to be crowded by 3:30 in the afternoon, and traffic is slow until early evening. Local radio and television stations report traffic conditions every few minutes during rush hours and regularly throughout the day.

Last, all car passengers must wear seat belts, and occasionally a ticket will be given for failure to do so. Babies must be strapped in a car seat in the back of the car, and children under four years of age and under 40 pounds (18.1kg) must wear a child restraint.

Gasoline

Do not be shocked at the price of gasoline (generally called "gas"); Look at gas station signs as you drive, for the price per gallon varies widely from station to station, even when they're just across the street from each other. Be prepared to pump your own gas. "Full service" stations are increasingly rare, except for drivers with a "disabled" placard, who are always entitled to full service.

The Parking Problem

There may be about 800,000 cars moving around in the city each day, but there are only about 400,000 parking spaces, so parking is a major concern of residents. The closer to the bay, the harder it is to find a parking space. Downtown, parking meter spaces are generally reserved until 6:00 pm for commercially licensed vehicles to load and unload merchandise. Other meters may run on a half-hour basis. People who do find a parking space tend to stay there and return periodically to "feed" the meter, which is supposedly illegal; "meter maids" (parking police) regularly mark the tires of cars with chalk to indicate the time they passed by; if the car is still there the next time the "meter maid" passes, it will be ticketed. Do not assume that parking is free on holidays, especially in tourist areas. And do not even think about parking in a bus zone.

Meter maids in their little vehicles are eagle-eyed in spotting offenders. By issuing almost 8,000 tickets a month, they make a lot of money for the city. Do not help them by overparking. Fines double if you do not pay them, and ultimately you will be found.

So, if you drive and intend to park at meters, you will have to keep a stash of quarters with you. (If not, and you go into a shop to ask for change for a dollar, your car may well have been ticketed by the time you come out!) Perhaps this will change, though, for the Municipal Transportation Authority has a pilot program that is testing a prepaid, refillable smart card in some 23,000 meters. Read the city's newspapers to keep current on the status of this program.

Making the problem even worse, some downtown streets prohibit parking during morning or evening rush hours; for infractions, your car will most likely be towed. These streets are usually marked with the hours you may not park, and the indication that it is a "tow-away zone." Most downtown and neighborhood streets are cleaned on certain regular days. So, you may not park there on those days. If you do, or if you forget to move your car, it will not be there the next morning. It will have been towed. (If you see a street on which no one is parked, do not thank your lucky stars that you found a parking space: look to see if this is street cleaning day.)

So, if a sign where you are parking says it is a towaway zone, believe it. Your car will be ticketed and towed. If your car is towed call the DPT TOW Line (tel: (415) 553-1239; auto return tel: (415) 865-8200). Ask why it was impounded (if you do not really know!), how much cash you have to bring to get it released, and where to go. Usually it is at 850 Bryant Street, Room 145 (tel: (415) 558-7411). You will have to bring identification ("picture i.d."), the ticket, any other outstanding tickets (see, they do catch up with you!) and the fee of the car pound.

Pay strict attention to the color of the curb you are parking near. Each color has a different meaning:
- **Red**: No stopping or parking, ever.
- **Yellow**: reserved for commercial vehicles loading and unloading during hours specified;
- **Yellow and black**: for commercial trucks during business hours
- **Green-yellow-black**: taxi zone:

- **Blue**: parking for vehicles with the blue California disabled placard
- **Green**: 10-minute parking
- **White**: passenger dropoff and pickup (usually a hotel or restaurant), generally for five minutes

Parking Garages

Parking garages and outdoor lots help with the problem, but they are crowded and prices vary: it depends on their location, whether they are city-owned or private, whether you are a short- or long-term parker and what time of day you park; early morning entry may allow a flat day rate, and evening parking also may incur a flat fee, paid in advance. In the popular areas around North Beach, Chinatown and Fisherman's Wharf, a US$ 2 charge for 20 minutes is common, pretty expensive if you are planning a leisurely evening out. But if you are staying for only 20 minutes, it might be worth it. The garages mentioned here are reasonable in price; there are others around the city, and fortunately supermarkets and most shopping centers have their own free parking lots.

- Union Square: Sutter/Stockton Garage
- Union Square: Under Union Square, enter on Geary
- Union Square: Ellis/O'Farrell Garage (entrances either on O'Farrell or Ellis)
- Financial District: Saint Mary's Garage, 433 Kearny
- Yerba Buena: Fifth and Mission Garage
- Japantown: Entrances on Post and Geary, off Webster
- Chinatown: Portsmouth Square Garage, enter on Kearny, just past Clay
- Financial District: Saint Mary's Square Garage, enter from Kearny, north of Pine
- Polk Village: Bush and Pine
- Civic Center Garage: Enter on McAllister, between Larkin and Polk
- SoMa: Moscone Center
- North Beach: Vallejo/Stockton Garage, enter from Vallejo
- Richmond: Geary and 16th Avenue, on second floor, above shops.

When you make a reservation at a restaurant, ask about parking; valet parking is often available, but can be expensive, for the price displayed does not include the expected tip to the valet. Some restaurants and cinemas offer validated parking in nearby parking garages; your parking ticket stamped by the restaurant or theater entitles you to a discount on the charge.

Driver's Licenses

Residents of San Francisco—defined as people who are making their home here or who have taken a job here—must apply for a California driver's license within ten days to the DMV (California Department of Motor Vehicles), at 1377 Fell Street (tel: (415) 557-1179; (800) 777-0133; website: http://www.dmv.ca.gov). If your license is from another country, you will have to take the written and practical driving test. And you will have to prove you have a legal presence in the United States.

If you have a valid license from another state, you may not be required to take the driving test; all applicants, however, must take the written "rules of the road" test and a vision test. If you fail, you may take the test twice more. All applicants must give a thumbprint and have a picture taken. DMV offices are located in towns throughout the Bay Area. A driver's license is generally valid for four or five years, and expires on your birthday of that year.

If you are here only on a temporary basis, however, you may drive for one year with a valid license from your home state. This applies also to citizens of Western nations; others must possess a current International Driving License.

Car Share

If you do not drive every day, you may not need to keep a car. Several "car share" companies offer the option to use a car when you need it, charging a low hourly fee that usually includes the mileage, gas, insurance, and parking. You pick up the car when you want it and return when you are finished. Each company has slightly different procedures and rates; check them out.

- City Car Share; 1182 Market Street; tel: (415) 995-8588; website: http://www.citycarshare.com

- Zip Car; 191 2nd Street; tel: (415) 495-7478; website: http://www.zipcar.com

Registering Your Car

If you bring your car with you, you have 20 days after establishing residency in California, to register your out-of-state car. (Residency means paying resident-based tuition at a school, having a job, filing for homeowner's tax exemptions, obtaining any kind of lease or contract, or having any other benefit non-residents do not obtain.) In order to register the vehicle with the DMV, you will need to fill out the application, pay the current fee, and produce the title to the car and a "smog certificate" (available at many full-service gasoline stations). The car must be inspected by the DMV.

If you are staying in California for only a short time, you do not need to register your car and may drive with your own state's license plates. This may pose a problem if you are living in a neighborhood which requires parking permits to park on the street; you cannot get a permit for a car not registered in California. In this case, it is best to rent a space in a garage nearby, or to make sure in advance that your apartment has a garage space.

Automobile Insurance

California state law requires that all drivers be financially responsible for their actions while driving and for the vehicles they own; if you have an accident not covered by your insurance, your driver's license will be suspended. In fact, car dealers do not permit you to take possession of a new car without proof of liability insurance; make sure to arrange for it in advance.

If you are bringing a car with you, you may be able to transfer your insurance if the company does business in California; check in advance with your carrier. Otherwise, some major insurance companies that service California are Allstate, California State Automobile Association (AAA), Farmers, and State Farm. Rates vary considerably. Many companies have discounted rates for drivers with proven safety records, some give discounts for cars with alarm systems, some have discounts for professionals, and some offer towing services.

Triple A

California State Automobile Association (part of the American Automobile Association) at 160 Sutter Street is an excellent resource for anyone driving in California. Any AAA ("Triple A") member may use its services (tel: (415) 773-1900; website: http://www.csaa.com). One of the most important services is their emergency road service. But you can also obtain maps and request for help with trips, and you can get insurance as well. And, as will be described in the next section, you can obtain information on the best pricing when buying an automobile. Check the website for other addresses.

Purchasing a Car

Advertising supplements for new cars appear in each Friday's newspaper. Used cars are advertised in the classified ad section, especially on Sundays. When purchasing a car, it is best to determine the dealer's factory invoice price on the car (not the "sticker price" which is affixed to the window). Several services help buyers get the best deal possible.

AAA members may use its Vehicle Purchasing Service to receive suggested retail prices on new and used vehicles, and to buy a new car from participating dealers at a fair price, without haggling (vehicle pricing tel: (877) 228-3722; website: http://www.csaa.com). When you indicate the make, model, and options of the car you want, Triple A will tell you which dealers in the area have agreed to sell at the pre-arranged price.

Residential Parking

Once you have found your home, and you have registered your car, you will need permanent parking. The large apartment complexes offer parking spaces; these generally cost extra and are not included in the lease. In some residential districts, however, residents may park indefinitely on non-metered streets with a permit issued by the Department of Parking, at 1380 Howard Street (info tel: (415) 255-3900).

You must have proof that the car is registered in California and that you live where you say you do. Street signs indicate the permit needed for that area, and they also specify how long non-permit cars may park during certain hours.

Handicapped Accessibility

San Francisco is basically wheelchair friendly. Buses have operator-assisted ramps for wheelchairs, all BART stations are wheelchair accessible, and curbs throughout the city are cut to a slope for easy access to sidewalks and crosswalks. All streetcar stations are wheelchair accessible, although cable cars are not. Hotels, restaurants, and most public rest rooms have wide stalls that will accommodate wheelchairs. And most taxi companies have cabs that can accommodate wheelchairs.

- The San Francisco Convention & Visitors Bureau offers *Access San Francisco*, which can be downloaded online or picked up at the tourist office (website: http://www.onlyinsanfrancisco.com).
- Access Northern California, a non-profit association that facilitates accessible travel, has information about access in Northern California on its website; website: http://www.accessnca.com
- Golden Gate Transit offers a *Welcome Aboard* brochure that gives details about its accessibility on its buses and ferries; website: http://www.goldengatetransit.org
- The San Francisco Paratransit Broker, a transportation service, has information about accessible travel and arranges reasonably priced taxi transportation for people with physical disabilities; tel: (415) 351-7000; website: http://www.sfparatransit.com
- Muni Accessible Services; tel: (415) 701-4485; website: http:// www.sfmta.com. Disabled persons (and those over age 65) may apply for the Regional Transit Connection Discount Card. You must meet the criteria and then apply at 2630 Geary Street; info tel: (415) 923-6070

Drivers with physical disabilities may apply to the DMV for a permit to park in any of the blue-marked parking spaces reserved for handicapped drivers. Your doctor should have a form that entitles you to such application. When accepted, you will receive a blue placard to hang on the rear-view mirror of your car.

The Call of Nature

It should not be hard to find a clean public bathroom in San Francisco. In addition to rest rooms in the large hotels, department stores, shopping centers, supermarkets and drug stores, there are a few French-style coin-operated sanisettes, standing lavatories with toilet and sink; when you are finished, open the door to exit. As the door closes behind you, the toilet flushes and the entire facility is sterilized.

Fast-food restaurants, bars, and coffee shops may expect you to purchase at least a cup of coffee to use their rest rooms, and some small restaurants on the tourist path have clear signs indicating that rest rooms are for customers only. Rest rooms at service stations may require that you ask the attendant for an access key. In most places, if you ask to use a rest room, you will not be refused.

Shops, restaurants, and a spectacular bay view please the crowds at Pier 39, near Fisherman's Wharf.

SHOPPING AT YOUR DOOR

All Day, Every Day

As small and compact as it is, San Francisco's stores sell everything you need for your home. Nothing is hard to find; consulting the *Yellow Pages* and understanding the commercial character of the different districts should allow you to make your way comfortably onto the shopping scene without trouble—and without much wait, for you can shop seven days a week, if the fancy strikes you.

Almost all stores open by 10:00 am. Department stores may stay open until 9:00 pm and some of the national chains even later. Small shops generally close around dinnertime, although specialty boutiques and bookshops in areas where the evening traffic is lively often stay open late. Supermarkets open early and stay open late every day, and for all-in-one shopping, they often sell some hardware needs, stationery, liquor, and even some underwear. Although service and repair shops generally close on Sunday, all large stores and the superstore chains are open, and in fact, this is a popular shopping day. Opening hours on Sundays, however, may be shorter than on weekdays, so it is best to call ahead to check.

> "This is a user-friendly city. In a way it seems small. You walk around the corner, go to the store, talk to people. It's the combination of the people and the place, that's what I like about it most."
> —Robin Williams

Where to Shop

A description of the city's shopping districts must begin directly on Union Square, where large multi-department stores rule the scene, selling goods from the utilitarian to the upscale and elegant. Macy's is the only true department store, stocking household goods, furniture and linens, as well as clothing and accessories, and it has reliable merchandise at good prices. Saks Fifth Avenue and Neiman Marcus are the most fashionable of the clothing chains. But the streets that surround Union Square house smaller, upmarket shops, and both local boutiques and branches of national chains. Gump's, the most elegant and prestigious of old San Francisco shops, has entrances on both Post and Maiden Lane. Just across Market Street—now an extension of the Union Square area—are the huge vertical City Centre and Westfield City Centre shopping complexes, housing Nordstrom and Bloomingdales, and a multitude of smaller shops—as well as restaurants and cinemas.

It would be your lucky day if you found a parking space around Union Square, so do not count on it. Most parking meters in this area have yellow tops and are reserved during the day for commercial vehicles unloading their wares (so why trucks insist on double parking and blocking the streets remains a mystery). Other meters may allow you to park only for a half-hour and cost as much as 25 cents for five minutes. Fortunately, three city-run parking lots are located in the area (*See pages 174–175.*), and nearby Market Street offers public transportation to many parts of the city on Muni and BART.

Each neighborhood has its commercial character, and you will come to know what type of items and prices you will find on Union Street (high) as opposed to those you will find on Haight (low). On Union, for example, starting at about Gough, you will find unusual and upscale clothing and jewelry boutiques intermingled with crowded trendy restaurants and cafes, bars and nightspots. The same holds true on Chestnut Street and on Upper Fillmore, from about Washington to California, which includes some elegant resale shops. The Sacramento and Presidio intersection has artsy shops of all sorts, but also a large selection of children's items, reflecting its neighborhood's residents (also true of Noe Valley). North Beach has fewer clothing shops than coffeehouses, but Chestnut and Union Streets are only a short drive away, and the four-building Embarcadero Center a short walk.

Check also commercial corridors such as Geary Boulevard, Lombard Street, 9th and 19th Avenues, as well as 24th, Fillmore, and Union Streets. Arteries, such as Geary Boulevard, and their side streets all have stores and local services, and in these areas parking may well be easier. The malls and some large shops and chains, of course, have parking lots for their customers. The Outer Sunset has the huge Stonestown Mall, which has adequate parking for its large number of shops and department stores.

Some areas are known for a particular focus: art galleries downtown and around the Civic Center, antique shops on lower Jackson and on Sacramento near Presidio, modern furniture below Potrero Hill, appliances South of Market or in the Mission. South of Market also sees many outlets of the huge nationwide superstore chains. These superstores are increasingly present in San Francisco. They offer good prices and an extensive selection of merchandise. Because they require so much square footage, the stores are generally in areas where real estate prices are reasonable and parking can be provided. Also, some citizens' groups have fought to exclude these megastores from their districts, trying to preserve both the character of their neighborhoods and the small independent merchant. So, some of the large stores are just outside the city limits, and others are South of Market in areas that have not yet been gentrified. In any case, with both large chain stores and local businesses to choose among, you should have no trouble finding what you want.

Prices and Paying

The few stores and services that will be mentioned later have been selected as representative examples of the types of shops in San Francisco that give good quality for the price—whatever the price. That does not mean that you will not find a bargain elsewhere, for you certainly will. Nor does it mean that a particular superstore will be inexpensive, but it is likely to offer the best prices available for that particular item. People do not bargain on prices, as a rule, but if the merchandise is damaged and you still want to buy it, you may be given a discount.

Except for some small shops, stores accept the major credit cards. A few might still take a personal check on a California bank when you produce photo identification, although fewer do so now that almost everyone has a credit or debit card. It is illegal for a shop to ask that a credit card be used as identification. Stores do not charge extra for using a credit card, but a few will offer a discount for cash.

Ask about the store's refund policy. The large stores and chains generally make refunds with no questions asked if you bring back the merchandise and the receipt within a reasonable length of time—a week or so—and will also exchange ill-fitting goods for a larger or smaller size, or even a different color. Some stores will exchange for other merchandise only. Stores are not required to make refunds, and each store sets its own policy. If there is an unusual policy, such as "all sales final," a notice is often displayed; this sign is also often displayed during a sale. If you have doubts, ask in advance.

The sales tax is added to the price of the item you purchase, not included on the price tag. In San Francisco the sales tax is 8.5 percent. This is not a value added tax, and foreign visitors do not receive a refund upon leaving the United States. There are duty free shops in the Union Square area.

Shopping Centers

Small shopping malls that cater to locals—with markets, repair shops, pharmacies—cluster in the different neighborhoods in San Francisco. The larger malls are generally anchored by a large clothing store such as Macy's, surrounded by dozens of smaller specialty stores. Stonestown Galleria is the largest and most varied shopping mall in the city, rivaling those that sprawl in the suburbs; downtown, at Market and 5th, there are two connected indoor centers, anchored by Nordstrom and Bloomingdale's. Otherwise, for the best range of shops, think about the enormous suburban shopping malls that are close to the city, but which would require you to travel there by car.

In addition to the malls listed below, these tourist destinations—The Cannery, Pier 39, The Anchorage, and Ghirardelli Square—hold some interesting and offbeat shops. And the Canton Bazaar and China Trade Center on the tourist path in Chinatown stock imported goods such as clothing, jewelry, some Oriental furniture, and table linens.

- **Market Street**—San Francisco Centre, 855 Market at 5th Street. A vertical shopping mall of small shops, anchored by the upscale Nordstrom clothing retailer.

- **Market Street**—Westfield San Francisco Centre; new mall connecting to the San Francisco Centre, Westfield offers Bloomingdale's, shops, restaurants, a food court and emporium, and a cinema complex.
- **Financial District**—Crocker Galleria, 50 Sutter Street, near Montgomery. This is a multi-story mall of elegant boutiques and little eateries; its cafe-style tables and chairs under the skylight give the feeling of eating outdoors in any season.
- **Embarcadero**—Embarcadero Center; Battery and Sacramento Streets. A three-level shopping, dining, and cinema complex, shopping spreads across four buildings connected by walkways, and it has a parking garage.
- **Potrero Hill**—Potrero Center; A neighborhood shopping center anchored by a Safeway, with many smaller shops and services, bank, and Radio Shack.
- **Pacific/Presidio Heights**—Laurel Village, 3500 California Street, past Presidio. This is an excellent local mall, with upscale supermarts, wine store, kitchenware store, children's clothing and toy stores, bookstore, cafes, etc; It also has metered parking in front and free parking in the rear.
- **SoMa**—Metreon, 4th and Mission Streets. Basically a Sony cinema complex, there are some high-tech entertainment shops here, and many little eateries.
- **Sunset**—Stonestown Galleria, 19th Avenue at Winston Drive. Almost a city in itself, Stonestown contains a supermarket, dozens of shops, Nordstrom's and Macy's department stores, a multiplex cinema, a medical building, and restaurants.

Setting Up House

After you have secured a home and have turned on the electricity, you can look around to see what the house needs to make you comfortable. Kitchens and bathrooms come fully equipped with appliances and cupboards, but you may need some smaller appliances, lamps, carpets, or housewares. The superstores here offer extremely good prices and an extensive selection, but look at the local merchants such as those listed here, who may offer more personal service both during the purchase and afterwards.

- Bed, Bath & Beyond, 555 9th Street; tel: (415) 252-0490. Brand-names of bed and bath, kitchen and dining room equipment and furnishings, housewares, and gadgets can be found here. Also in Colma, at 19 Colma Boulevard; tel: (415) 992-9689.
- Best Buy, 1717 Harrison Street, tel: (415) 626-9682. Just what it says: excellent prices on appliances and electronics. Also at 2675 Geary Boulevard; tel: (415) 409-4960
- Costco, 450 10th Street; tel: (415) 626-4388. This warehouse carries home supplies, electronics, some appliances, clothing, both fresh and packaged foods, and pharmaceuticals.
- Cost Plus, 2552 Taylor Street; tel: (415) 928-6200. It sells colorful housewares, some furniture, baskets of all shapes and sizes, and has a gourmet food and wine section.
- Discount Builders Supply, 1695 Mission at 13th Street; tel: (415) 621-8511. Appliances, kitchen cabinets, hardware, building materials and supplies can be bought here.
- Home Depot, 2 Colma Boulevard, Colma; tel: (415) 755-9600. Everything that you may need for the home may be found here. Across the street at 91 Colma Boulevard is Home Depot Pro, which focuses on the building trade; tel: (415) 650-9360. Also at 303 East Lake Merced Boulevard, Daly City; tel: (650) 755-0178
- Ikea, 4400 Shellmound Street, Emeryville; tel: (510) 420-4532; website: http://www.ikea.com. Huge international home furnishings store. Call for a catalog or access the Internet site.
- Target, 5001 Junipero Serra Boulevard, Colma; tel: (650) 992-8433. Appliances, bath and bed linens, kitchen items, clothes for adults and kids, pharmacy, packaged foods, and furniture.

And More for the Home

For smaller items, try the specialty stores in each neighborhood, such as Cole Hardware, Cliff's, or Fredricksons, where you will find a good selection and more personal service.

- **Bayshore**—Peer Light, 301 Toland Street, near Cesar Chavez; tel: (415) 206-0689. Electrical and lighting supplies.
- **Castro**—Cliff's Variety, 479 Castro, near 18th Street; tel: (415) 431-5365. Housewares, hardware, gadgets, knickknacks in a large, friendly store.
- **Chinatown**—Ginn Wall Hardware, 1016 Grant Avenue; tel: (415) 982-6307. Large shop selling hardware, plus woks, steam baskets, kitchen implements and everything else you would want for Chinese cooking.
- **Cow Hollow**—Fredericksen's Hardware, 3029 Fillmore Street, near Union; tel: (415) 292-2950. Much more than a hardware store, its well-stocked shelves hold a good selection of kitchen implements and housewares.
- **Mission**—A&M Carpets, 98 12th Street, at South Van Ness; tel: (415) 863-1410. Good prices on carpets, reproductions of Oriental rugs, discontinued smaller rugs, Berbers.
- **Mission**—Cherin's, 727 Valencia Street; tel: (415) 864-2111. Long-established shop selling kitchen equipment, washers and dryers, and built-in appliances at low prices.
- **Presidio Heights**—Forrest Jones, 3274 Sacramento Street, near Presidio; tel: (415) 567-2483. Lamps, housewares, gadgets, baskets—wonderful displays to browse through.
- **Richmond**—Lamps Plus, 4700 Geary Boulevard; tel: (415) 386-0933. Lamps and electrical fixtures, at factory-direct prices.
- **South of Market**—Louie Appliance Center, 1045 Bryant, at 9th Street; tel: (415) 621-7100. Excellent prices on all kinds of appliances.
- **SoMa**—City Lights, 1585 Folsom, at 12th Street; tel: (415) 863-2020. City Lights offers an extensive selection of lighting fixtures, lamps, bulbs, ceiling fans.
- **Sunset**—ABC Appliances, 2048 Taraval, at 31st Avenue; tel: (415) 564-8166. Good prices on large appliances, kitchen and bathroom equipment.
- **Union Square**—Sur La Table, 77 Maiden Lane; tel: (415) 732-7900. Interesting kitchen implements you might not find elsewhere—for people who take cooking seriously. Cookbooks, dishware, little gems of jams, mustards,

etc. Also at the Ferry Building Marketplace; tel: (415) 262-9970.
- **Union Square**—Williams-Sonoma, 2 Embarcadero Center; tel: (415) 421-2033. Expensive, elegant kitchen and diningware, gadgets, and cookbooks. Other addresses.
- **Union Square**—Crate and Barrel, 55 Stockton Street; tel: (415) 982-5200. Inexpensive homeware chain, with dishes, glassware, some furniture and furnishing accessories can be found here.

Furniture

Furniture stores run the gamut from tiny expensive boutiques to large showrooms in nearby suburbs, to discount clearance centers. Some of the smallest shops are the most interesting, and these often advertise in the Sunday Chronicle. Several shops with eclectic collections are focused just below Potrero Hill. Macy's has an extensive furniture showroom. Look also in the *Yellow Pages*.
- Noriega Furniture, 1455 Taraval, at 25th Avenue; tel: (415) 564-4110. Upscale furniture outlet with downscale prices. Excellent designer pieces, lamps, wall decorations. What they do not have can be ordered.
- Limn; 290 Townsend Street, tel: (415) 543-5466. Contemporary and ultra-modern designer furniture.
- The Chair Place, 531 Bryant Street; tel: (415) 278-9640. Back support ergonomic office chairs, so you are comfortable and back-healthy while you work.

If you are confident of your ability to detect imperfections, or if you are willing to take a color or fabric someone else ordered and then returned, or a discontinued style, try a clearance center.
- Sears Outlet Store, 1936 West Avenue 140th, San Leandro; tel: (510) 895-0546. Major appliances and furniture. One of a kind, out of carton, discontinued, used, scratched, and dented merchandise. Call for days and hours when they are open.
- Macy's Furniture Clearance Center, 1208 Whipple Road, Union City, about 1 mile (1.6 km) east of Highway 880;

tel: (510) 441-8833. Enormous depot for canceled orders, floor samples, returned, damaged or slightly soiled merchandise, surplus inventory, etc.

Furniture Rental

If you are staying short-term or renting temporarily, you might try renting furniture. Both the following companies offer high-quality, attractive furniture and appliances that you may need.
- Cort Furniture Rental, 447 Battery Street; tel: (415) 982-1077.
- Brook Furniture Rental, 500 Washington Street, at Sansome; tel: (415) 956-6008.

Computers and Office Supplies

One thing that is not hard to find in this totally wired city, is everything you need for computers and the Internet. Best Buy and Costco have excellent prices on both Apple and PC products, and Apple has several stores in the city, but if you see a small, independent shop in your neighborhood, you should also check it out
- Apple Store, 1 Stockton Street, at Ellis; tel: (415) 392-0202.
- Office Max, 1750 Harrison Street; tel: (415) 252-7611; 3700 Geary Boulevard; tel: (415) 831-1080.
- Office Depot, 2300 16th Street; tel: (415) 252-8280; 33 Third Street; tel: (415) 777-1728; 2675 Geary Boulevard; tel: (415) 441-3044.
- Staples, 1700 Van Ness Avenue; tel: (415) 771-7030; 300 California Street; tel: (415) 394-6648
- Radio Shack; website: http://www.radioshack.com; Check website for store nearest to you.
- Circuit City, 1200 Van Ness; tel: (415) 441-1300.

Filling Your Bookcase

The superstore Borders has outlets throughout the Bay Area, four in San Francisco alone. It's easiest to park at the Stonestown mall, but for Union Square convenience, there's a store at 400 Post Street; tel: (415) 391-1633. In addition to an enormous number of books, they stock audio and video cassettes, book-related merchandise, and a café. Parking is easier at the King Street location. Parking is also good at Barnes and Noble, an outlet of another large chain at 2550 Taylor Street (tel: (415) 292-6762). Both chains have excellent travel sections.

The selection at these chains may be broader, but do not neglect the independent bookshops in your neighborhood—Browser Books on Fillmore, Booksmith in the Haight, or Red Hill Books on Cortland Avenue, for example—as they are no doubt striving to survive in a market increasingly infiltrated by the chains. Several well-known bookshops have been forced to close their doors, even though their prices were competitive and service more personal. Patronize also the specialty shops and those that sell used books, offering bargains and some great finds. Independent bookshops can order the books you want, if they are not in stock.

- **Castro**—A Different Light Bookstore, 489 Castro Street; tel: (415) 431-0891. Center for gay and lesbian books and periodicals.
- **Civic Center**—McDonald's Bookshop, 48 Turk Street, at Market; tel: (415) 673-2235. Large shop selling used books and periodicals—in all categories and languages.
- **Downtown**—Alexander Book Co, 50 2nd Street; tel: (415) 495-2992. Excellent collection on three levels.
- **Embarcadero**—Book Passage, Ferry Plaza; tel: (415) 835-1020. An outpost of the major store in Corte Madera.
- **Inner Richmond**—Green Apple Books, 506 Clement Street; tel: (415) 387-2272. One of the best for used books, plus an annex on the same street.
- **Japantown**—Marcus Book Store, 1712 Fillmore Street; tel: (415) 346-4222. Marcus offers books of interest to the African American community.
- **Hayes Valley**—Get Lost Travel Books, 1825 Market Street; tel: (415) 437-0529. Travel books, maps, and gear.
- **Mission**—Modern Times, 888 Valencia, at 20th Street; tel: (415) 282-9246. This is a progressive bookshop, with titles on politics, globalization, gender and sexuality, and focusing on Latino writers. Titles in Spanish, and multicultural books for children are available as well.

- **North Beach**—City Lights, 261 Columbus Avenue, at Broadway; tel: (415) 362-8193; Owned by Lawrence Ferlinghetti, poet laureate of San Francisco.
- **Opera Plaza**—Books Inc, 601 Van Ness Avenue, at Turk; tel: (415) 776-1111. A well-known independent bookstore with a good selection and authors' events. Branches throughout the Bay Area.

Foreign Language Bookstores
- **Chinese**—Eastwind Books & Arts, 1435 Stockton Street; tel: (415) 772-5888. Extensive selection for adults and children. English-language section upstairs.
- **Chinese**—New China Books, 642 Pacific Avenue; tel: (415) 956-0752. A general store and cultural center with current periodicals, books, videos, etc.
- **European**—European Book Company, 925 Larkin Street, near Geary; tel: (415) 474-0626. French, German and Spanish books. Current foreign newspapers and magazines.
- **Japanese**—Kinokuniya Bookstore, 1581 Webster Street, in the Japan Center; tel: (415) 567-7625. Major Japanese bookshop, with some books in English.
- **Spanish**—Casa del Libro, 973 Valencia, at 20th Street; tel: (415) 285-1399.
- **Spanish**—Iaconi Books, 970 Tennessee Street; tel: (415) 821-1216. Books for children and adults.

Music
The Lower Haight is known for some great shops stocking vinyl as well as CDs, These shops are great for browsing. So, in addition to looking at superstores such as Best Buy and Costco, check out the shops both in your own neighborhood and beyond.
- **Haight**—Amoeba Records, 1855 Haight Street; tel: (415) 831-1200
- **Lower Haight**—Jack's Record Cellar, 254 Scott Street; tel: (415) 431-3047
- **Japantown**— Mikado Music, 1737 Post Street; tel: (415) 431-3047

House Plantings and Flowers

Flower stands dot the street corners of the city in every season of the year, and flowers and plants can be purchased at supermarkets and even some hardware stores. Large garden stores can be found in towns throughout the Bay Area. Also visit the bustling Flower Market at Sixth and Brannan Streets; some of the wholesalers sell their plants and flowers to retail customers, plus accessories and holiday decorations. One of the most well-established florists in the city is Hoogasian Flowers located at 615, 7th Street (tel: (415) 229-2732).

And for sending flowers call any of the florists that advertise in the *Yellow Pages* that they are FTD (tel: (800) 736-3383; website: http://www.ftd.com) or Blooms Today (tel: (800) 359-5309; website: http://www.bloomstoday.com) For an excellent selection of plants, try:

- Plant Warehouse, 1461 Pine Street, near Polk; tel: (415) 885-1515.
- Plant'It Earth, 661 Divisadero Street ; tel: (415) 626-5082.
- Sloat Garden Center, 2700 Sloat Street; tel: (415) 566-4415.

Clothing

Shops throughout the city offer clothing of all styles, quality, and prices. Those near Union Square may sport designer labels and the highest prices, but even the outlying districts sell interesting clothes at prices that match the quality and design. Shopping is almost a game for many San Franciscans who, however, tend to brag about how little they paid for an item of clothing or an accessory. That one can shop adequately and inexpensively is not only owing to the frequent sales of those department stores and boutiques, but to the presence in the city and the entire Bay Area of a wide selection of designer discount shops, factory outlet malls, and nationwide discount clothing chains. These offer out-of-season clothes, discontinued styles, and overstocks. It is not likely that you would find any damaged or inferior merchandise, but of course the quality reflects each manufacturer's approach.

Sales assistance in the smaller shops may be more personal than in the larger stores, but customer service is generally good no matter where you go. And, although many shops have been in their locations for years, stores do come and go. Call in advance to be certain the shop is still there and to ascertain its hours.

Most shops have storewide sales now and then, and many have sale items all year round. And there are some shops somewhat like the superstores above, that offer low prices on their merchandise because they buy in large volume and have many outlets. The shops listed on the next page, which are well-established, are just a few examples of the range of merchandise available. For well-priced appliances, furniture, and household items, see section on *Setting up House* on pages 185–188.

- Clothing—Nordstrom Rack, 555 9th Street; tel: (415) 934-1211. Save up to 50 percent on clothes and shoes from Nordstrom Stores.
- Clothing—H&M, 150 Powell Street; tel: (415) 986-4215; and 150 Post; tel: (415) 986-0156. This is a successful Swedish clothing chain of low priced clothing for the entire family.
- Clothing—Burlington Coat Factory, 899 Howard Street; tel: (415) 495-7234. Not just coats—although there is a huge selection of all kinds of outerwear—there is clothing for the entire family.
- Wilkes Bashford, 375 Sutter Street; tel: (415) 986-4380. Seven floors of upscale clothing for men and women, an excellent sportswear department, and all are pricey.
- Men's shirts—Van Heusen Factory Store, 601 Mission Street; tel: (415) 243-0750. Van Heusen shirts for men, casual sportswear for men and women.
- Women's clothing—Georgiou Factory Outlet, 925 Bryant Street; tel: (415) 554-0150. Past season's designs and overstocks from this well-known chain of contemporary women's clothes.
- Women's clothing—Loehmann's, 222 Sutter Street; tel: (415) 982-3215. Outpost of New York store selling designer clothes at excellent prices.

- Women's clothing—Ross Dress for Less; There are three locations for this well-known national chain of inexpensive clothing stores: 5200 Geary Boulevard (tel: (415) 386-7677); 2300 16th Street (tel: (415) 554-1901); 1545 Sloat (tel: (415) 661-0481)
- Bedclothes—Warm Things, 3063 Fillmore Street, near Union; tel: (415) 931-1660. Factory-direct prices on goose down comforters, shams, covers, robes, slippers, and down vests.
- Jewelry—Cresalia Jewelers, 111 Sutter Street; tel: (415) 781-7371. Excellent prices on jewelry and watches, silver, and table accessories.

Shoes

The department stores carry many different brands of ladies and men's shoes. Nordstrom has an especially wide and varied collection, one of the largest in the city. Athletic shoe stores dot the city, and the sporting clothes and gear shops listed below should also have a selection of running, walking, and tennis shoes.

- **Union Square**—DSW, 111 Powell Street; tel: (415) 445-9511. The Designer Shoe Warehouse has three levels of shoes and accessories, much of it heavily discounted.
- **Hayes Valley**—Gimme Shoes, 415 Hayes Street, at Gough; tel: : (415) 864-0691. Gimme carries European imports and high-end shoes, and can be found at two other locations: 2358 Fillmore Street; tel: (415) 441-3040; 416 Hayes Street; tel: (415) 864-0691.

Until you find the shoemaker in your own neighborhood, try Anthony's Shoe Service at 30 Geary Street (tel: (415) 781-1338).

Children's Clothing and Furnishings

Department stores and small shops carry good quality children's clothing, shoes, and equipment, and the Gap Kids chain has several outlets. Target also has a large children's clothes department. Small shops tend to be clustered in family neighborhoods, especially in Presidio Heights and

Noe Valley. For advertisements for children's shops and services (as well as articles of interest and schedules of child-oriented events), pick up *Bay Area Parent* or access its Internet site.

- **Noe Valley**—Small Frys, 4066 24th Street; tel: (415) 648-3954. This has comfortable, affordable clothing (newborn to size 7) for children and carries famous brands.
- **Presidio Heights**—Jonathan Kaye Baby, 3615 Sacramento Street; tel: (415) 563-0773. An interesting shop for children's furniture, clothes, knickknacks, wooden, unfinished furniture, cribs, and changing units.
- **Presidio Heights**—Kindersport, 3566 Sacramento Street; tel: (415) 563-7778. Junior ski and sports outfitters. Good selection.
- **Presidio Heights**—Dottie Dolittle, 3680 Sacramento Street; tel: (415) 563-3244. Upscale, classic children's clothing for play or dress from infants to girls size 14.
- **Laurel Village**—Junior Boot Shop, 3555 California Street; tel: (415) 751-5444. This is a longtime children's shoe shop.
- **Presidio Heights**—Brooks Shoes for Kids, 3307 Sacramento Street; tel: (415) 440-7599. Brooks is a chain of kids' shoe stores, with both domestic and European brands.

Sports Clothing and Gear

Most of the pro shops at sports clubs have clothing items and equipment, but these may be more expensive than the large chain stores or small shops dedicated to the sport you are interested in. Here's a list of where and what you can buy.

- Big 5, Lakeshore Plaza, 1533 Sloat Boulevard; tel: (415) 681-4593. Sporting equipment and clothing chain can be obtained here.
- **Marina**—MetroSport, 2198 Filbert Street, at Fillmore; tel: (415) 923-6453. Dedicated to the runner, this sells footware, apparel, and running accessories.
- **Presidio**—Sports Basement, 610 Old Mason Street; tel: (415) 437-0100. Sports gear at outlet prices. Camping & hiking, snow sports, fitness, and gear for children. Also at 1590 Bryant Street; tel: (415) 575-3000.

- **Russian Hill**—Lombardi Sports, 1600 Jackson Street, at Polk; tel: (415) 771-0600. Huge sporting goods shop selling equipment and clothes at good prices.
- **SoMa**—REI Coop, 840 Brannan Street; tel: (415) 934-1938. Famous for its outdoor gear and clothing. Bikes, tents, canoes, outdoor clothing for the family, and rugged footwear.
- **SoMa**—Soma Ski & Sports, 689 3rd Street, at Townsend; tel: (415) 777-2165. Everything for the skier, as well as for other sports.
- **Union Square**—Copeland's Sports, 901 Market Street; tel: (415) 495-0928; golf tel: (415) 512-7272. Large store with sporting equipment, athletic shoes, active wear, and a large golf selection at good prices.
- **Union Square**—North Face, 180 Post Street; tel: (415) 433-3223. Outdoor gear, clothing, and footwear.

Cosmetics

Department stores carry the famous international brands of skincare and makeup products, but drug stores, and supermarkets carry cosmetics, as well as—moisturizers, sunscreens, makeup, hair products, wrinkle removers—

anything you need. And, your hair salon will carry the products it uses in the salon. Try also these two dedicated cosmetic and skincare shops. Both have several addresses
- Kiehl's, 2360 Fillmore Street; tel: (415) 359-9260; Known for its century-old apothecary updated for the most modern of skin and hair products.
- Sephora, 33 Powell Street; tel: (415) 362-9360; An international chain carrying a selection of known brand-name cosmetics and skin-care products.

And...Beyond the City

Depending on where you live, these shopping malls that are near to San Francisco might be convenient for you. Daly City, with several large shopping areas, is contiguous with the southern districts of Lake Merced, Visitacion Valley, and Ingleside. And Colma, again with a number of superstores clustered together, is only five minutes beyond. In any case, these are all easily accessible to Highways 101 and 280. Many others are situated in the East Bay.
- Corte Madera: Town and Country and The Village
- Daly City: Serramonte Center and Westlake Shopping Center
- Palo Alto: Stanford Shopping Center
- San Bruno: Tanforan Park
- San Mateo: Hillsdale Shopping Center

Factory outlet malls offer good prices because the stores are run by the companies themselves, thereby bypassing the wholesaler and retailer whose prices must reflect their own profits. Several outlet malls are located within an hour's drive of the city in all directions (except West, of course). Famous designers have stores in these malls offering out of season clothes and overstocks, and sometimes returns from other shops; clothing is generally of the same quality as found in retail stores.

Some of the malls have so many stores and are so spread out they have free shuttle buses. All are open on Sunday and have ample parking space but are especially crowded on weekends and before holidays.

- **Napa County**—Napa Premium Outlets; At Highway 29 and First Street in Napa.
- **Napa County**—St. Helena Premium Outlets; On Highway 29, just north of St. Helena.
- **Sonoma County**—Petaluma Village Outlets; Take 101 north; exit at old Redwood Highway.
- **South**—Outlets at Gilroy; Take Highway 101 south to the Leavesley exit. Shuttle bus between three different areas of shops.
- **South**—Great Mall of the Bay Area; At Milpitas, off Highways 680 and 880, at the Montague Expressway and Capitol Avenue.
- **Northeast**—Factory Stores at Vacaville; 321 Nut Tree Road, Vacaville.

FOOD LOVERS' HAVEN

CHAPTER 6

'You can't have a bad meal in this town.'
—Emeril Lagasse

GASTRONOMIC SUPERLATIVES

San Francisco—The Best?

San Franciscans believe their city to be the gastronomic capital of America. Residents of a few other American cities may dispute this claim, of course. But the seemingly endless numbers of tourists who patiently await their tables at the city's crowded restaurants and the repeated rankings by national magazines tend to confirm that San Francisco's offerings rise to the top. But how has this come to pass? The answer is itself a stew, combining the city's particular geography, climate, history—and attitude.

Begin with the ingredients: the area's moderate climate and the city's proximity to rich, fertile, agricultural lands, to the Pacific Ocean, and to the country's top wine-producing region. See the fishing boats coming in early each morning to the piers off Jefferson Street, and you will never doubt that

> **Bon Appetit!**
> Of the more than 4000 eating establishments in this gastronomic heaven called San Francisco, only about 200 could be mentioned or described in these several chapters devoted to nectar and ambrosia. Alas, there was not enough room. So, think of the pleasurable exploration you have in store, and enjoy the process! Bon appetit!

the fish is fresh, year-round. Drive south or east, passing the rich vegetable fields and flourishing orchards that supply the city's restaurants directly, and you can tell what is in season and what will be on the menu at that time. Or pass the miles of grape-laden vines as you head up to warm, sunny Napa or Sonoma—just an hour north of the city—and then do not be surprised to find outstanding wines produced by those vineyards in restaurants all over town.

Now stir in a bit of history. The city's unusual approach to food combinations has grown from its own cultural diversity. From its earliest days, San Francisco was a town where people ate out. It started with the Gold Rush, when thousands of miners with money—or gold nuggets—in their pockets, came down from the hills for a taste of "civilization" and "home cooking." Restaurants of all types flourished. Even at that time, the cooks were immigrants—Italians, Hungarians, French, and Chinese—melding their own cooking traditions with the ingredients on hand. After the flurries of the Gold Rush and the Silver Rush died down, eating establishments remained.

Since then, each wave of immigrants has added to the tastes and aromas of the city: Italian food with Oriental overtones, Vietnamese food presented in the style of the French, and pan-Asian or pan-Latin cuisines. Although you might hear such appellations as eclectic or international, or the slightly passé term "fusion" for this bringing together of traditions and tastes, recent categorizations keep up the practice: "East Meets West," "Mediterranean/Italian," "contemporary American with world accents," or even "contemporary French," as opposed to the traditional cuisine one tends to think of as French. What matters, no matter the category, is that each flavor contributes to the overall dish served, but is identifiable in itself. But this type of fusion and melding is not new in San Francisco, and in fact, fusion of cultures, cuisines, and traditions—with each contributing but still identifiable in itself—is what has always defined the city itself.

Food in San Francisco can also be high art. What is known as California Cuisine—which originated at Berkeley's Chez Panisse and which has now been adopted around the globe—epitomizes this trend. Emphasizing regional, in-season ingredients, California Cuisine presents a beautiful yet simple-seeming and healthy effect (sometimes with a touch of humor) although the exotic combinations of ingredients and presentation may not be simple at all. Yet even with California Cuisine, distinctions blur. Some restaurants known for California Cuisine also use Asian flavors and approach; others might borrow from the Italian or French. But they all use seasonal and local ingredients, and if the word "fusion" is less used, the idea of combining and fusing is not.

Attitude of San Franciscans

Adding spice to the answer of why San Francisco's restaurants are so exceptional is that San Franciscans demand they be so. San Franciscans love to eat out—at restaurants of all levels—and with a mean household income of about US$ 60,000, residents spend about US$ 2,700 per household per year eating out. Thus, no one needs to settle for just a "good dinner." Although it is not true that San Francisco has more restaurants than people, with some 4,000 eating and drinking establishments, it may well have more restaurants per capita than other cities. Thus, diners get a wide choice, and they set the tone. In fact, the city works on the premise that the entire experience of eating should be fun. San Franciscans consider eating out to be one of their major cultural—albeit playful—experiences, and they demand, and get, the best.

"The best" does not necessarily mean the most expensive restaurant or those that are lavishly reviewed. A Thai restaurant out in the Avenues might have the best lemongrass soup, and an otherwise undistinguished Italian restaurant might well have the best calamari, at least to some diners' tastes. Other places may tickle diners' fancy with their imaginative decor, and many now are offering entertainment of one sort of another along with the dining experience.

Also, particularity rules. It is clear that the days when Italian food meant spaghetti with tomato sauce are long gone; now San Franciscans may select among their favorite Ligurian- or Roman-style restaurants, or choose a place just for one particular dish. Or a particular way of preparing, for example, one type of fish or steak. And long gone are the days when Chinese food meant Chicken Fried Rice; now San Franciscans pick carefully among Hunan, Chiu Chow, or Cantonese cuisines, and they know which restaurants serve the best dim sum. San Franciscan restaurants demonstrate a strong sense of place.

But even the cuisines do not tell the entire story. San Franciscans also demand that restaurants, no matter the style of cuisine, mirror their lifestyles. The restaurants themselves should be attractive. The food they eat should be healthy and look good, whether it is a luxurious dinner in an elegant restaurant, a hearty meal in a neighborhood pub, or—the current trend—a meal of "small plates" to share, eating less (perhaps), but very well. What San Franciscans want, in short, is everything all at once: delicious and healthful food imaginatively prepared, a splendid view, an attractive space, and friendly service. If San Franciscans, as some people claim, "want everything now," at least in terms of dining out, they seem to be able to get it.

Resources

It is a passion of San Franciscans to seek out the best in whatever it is they want at the moment—and then to keep seeking, even if perhaps they had thought they found it before. Weekdays find people out early eating hearty breakfasts or, on weekends, a delicately prepared brunch. Weekday lunchtime sees crowds in most of the downtown business-style restaurants, workers still looking not just to eat but for a culinary experience. (It is wise to reserve for lunch, just as much as for dinner.) And dinner is a constant process of happy exploration in any neighborhood, sometimes the more offbeat, the better. Currently, expanding out of the tried and true districts (North Beach, Union Street, Pacific Heights), San Franciscans are seeking out the restaurants and bars on the Valencia Corridor, the Inner Sunset nexus around 9th Avenue, and the continually appearing new offerings in SoMa and near the AT&T baseball park. (Just do not try to find a parking space when there is a game on.)

It would be impossible to describe all the city's excellent restaurants here. There are so many international cuisines and traditions that these chapters can give only representative samples of the diverse culinary experiences the city offers. To aid in your pleasant search, buy one of the guides dedicated entirely to eating out in the Bay Area. The best, which covers both restaurants and food markets, is Patricia Unterman's *San Francisco Food Lover's Guide*, by a local food writer who knows San Francisco's restaurants better than anyone else. Loosely arranged by district and within district by category, her book makes it easy to find anything you want to know about food in the area. The famous *Zagat's* rates restaurants according to diners' choices; most recently, Gary Danko, Boulevard, Slanted Door, Aqua, and Delfina have been rated by diners as the five favorite restaurants, with Zuni, Farallon, Michael Mina, and Jardinière close behind.

Look also at the daily newspapers, weekly tabloids and city magazines, which review and rate restaurants and often conduct readers' polls, which accounts for the myriad restaurants that boast that their specialty (sushi, hamburger, pizza, barbeque, salsa, etc) has been judged the best in the city. They probably all have, by one contest or another. The media also regularly publish surveys of the "best" in dozens of categories, always interesting, always with a surprise. Beauty of the establishment is often rated, and many are imaginative in their décor. If noise bothers you, pay attention to the decibel ratings in restaurant reviews, as the current trend for a lively atmosphere has resulted in large open spaces with high ceilings, which greatly increases the noise. Those dining in groups, however, often do not care about noise (or creating it), so long as they are having a good time.

Reserving a Table

Most but not all restaurants take reservations. The currently fashionable restaurants require reservations to be made one month in advance, and if you do not call exactly when specified, you might not get a table; sometimes, however, tables are available at off-hours, such as 5:45 pm or 10:00 pm. As a general rule, the better the restaurant, the longer in advance you should book. This also holds true for the restaurants that play live music, or those with a view. To find out about table availability and making a reservation on the Internet, try Open Table (*see next page*) or SFGate.

On the other hand, there is no harm in calling to see whether there has been a cancellation. Ask whether the restaurant serves dinner at the bar to walk-in customers, for bar food is of the same quality as in the rest of the restaurant. (Some restaurants have open kitchens, and sitting at the counter/bar allows you to watch the chefs perform their culinary magic.) Sitting at the bar is an attractive option for solo diners, although San Franciscan restaurants are welcoming to people dining alone.

But most restaurants can accommodate you if you make a reservation the day before or even on the morning of the day you intend to dine, and in some, if you do not reserve in advance, you can wait for a table to be vacated. Restaurants generally figure 90 minutes for a couple to remain at a table and two hours for a party of four. The maître d'hôtel (maitre d') will be as honest as possible—given the unpredictable time a party may linger—in assessing the waiting time, or indeed, if there is a chance to get a table. If you have to wait, the maître d' will almost always offer a seat at the bar.

Not all restaurants take reservations. Some of the fish restaurants do not or will take reservations only for parties of more than six people; this also holds true for the Asian eateries and many small, neighborhood establishments. In popular places where there is a line, there will usually be a waiting list; seating is first come, first served, according to the tables available and the number of people in the party.

Do not forget that tourists love San Francisco restaurants. When a large convention is in town, it can be impossible to get a table at a restaurant that might have been reviewed in a guidebook or that was recommended by the convention planners. Make your reservation as far in advance as you can and call if you must cancel (they appreciate this); don't just not show up. Some restaurants require confirmation of the reservation the day before, and a few ask for your telephone number, explaining that you will be charged a fee if you do not show up. If you have reserved online at Open Table (www.opentable.com), your reservation will be confirmed by e-mail the day before.

And San Franciscans love to eat outside; some restaurants have patios sheltered from the wind by glass screens, their gas heaters suspended under an overhanging roof. These popular establishments are likely to be crowded on warm spring or autumn nights (and always for brunch on weekends), so make sure you reserve in advance, and mention that you would like a table on the patio or one with a view. The reservations taker usually says, "we'll see what we can do," meaning that you will probably get a table you want, given the traffic flow at the time.

Dress is generally casual, and it is rare to find a man wearing a suit, except for holidays or special occasions. In the most fashionable restaurants, a man might wear a sports jacket, with or without a tie, and women either a dress or slacks and a fashionable top. In any case, it is always good to dress appropriately to the establishment and the occasion. In most neighborhood restaurants and smaller cafes, casual dress is the rule; even blue jeans and sneakers are acceptable. One casual Berkeley establishment humorously advertised, "food so good, you might want to wear your nice jeans."

Web-based Reservations

Www.opentable.com is a nationwide Internet reservation service that has proved extremely successful. Choose your locale, the restaurant you are interested in, and the day and time you want. You will find out immediately whether there are any tables available and, if not, when the next one will be. Having provided your e-mail address, a reminder or confirmation will appear in your inbox the day before the reservation you made. Some restaurants prefer reservations made through Open Table, and some do not use the service at all.

The same holds true for www.sfgate.com, the extensive and helpful Internet site of the *San Francisco Chronicle*.

Opening Times

San Francisco is an "early town." Because the Pacific Time

Zone is three hours behind New York's financial markets, financial workers start working before dawn and eat lunch and dinner early. Because they most often dine before performances, not after, do not expect to get into popular restaurants around the Union Square theater district or near the Civic Center music venues in the early evening (or on days when there are matinees) unless you reserve well in advance. On the other hand, you can generally get a table if you are willing to eat a little later, after a performance has started.

Restaurants start to serve breakfast around 6:30 am and begin lunch at 11:30 am. Those that do not stay open all day may start dinner service at 5:30 pm, taking their last orders around 10:00 pm. Some restaurants in the Financial District close by 9:00 pm, and a few are open weekdays only.

The hours of neighborhood restaurants generally reflect the habits of the locals. Asian restaurants usually serve all day, as do the coffeehouses. Fashionable restaurants may take their last orders around 10:30, but neighborhood eateries are generally closed by then.

A few restaurants fill the void in late-night dining: Yuet Lee and Sam Wo in Chinatown; Sparky's, The Grubstake, and Mel's for burgers into the wee hours, and Katanya for a ramen fix; Denny's for breakfast any time of the day; Oola, Cosmopolitan and the trendy Mexican Tres Agaves in SoMa; Brazen Head in Cow Hollow; and the Absinthe brasserie in the Civic Center area always appeal.

Most of the large restaurants serve dinner every day, but serve lunch only on weekdays. Most of the Asian restaurants are open daily as well, although any small family-run establishment may close one day a week. Days of closure vary, but generally it is either Sunday or Monday.

The Menu

The menu depends on the season. Some restaurants print their menus daily, and in others servers recite the list of that day's special dishes. These invariably reflect the fishermen's catch and the produce that is then most plentiful in the markets. Pay attention to the specials, for they generally offer the best value for the money. Do not hesitate to ask how a dish is prepared, and in the case of an oral recitation of the specials, to ask the price, if the server omits it. (This includes asking the price of the wine if you just say "a glass of the house Chardonnay, please." It is best not to be surprised.)

If you have dietary restrictions, specify your needs to the server in advance, so that you can be assured of ordering a meal that you can eat. The server will ask the chef what is in the dish you are considering, and then you can decide. In general, you send back a meal only if it is not cooked properly or if it is different from its description on the menu.

Order only as much as you want. Currently the "small plates" and tapas restaurants are popular, allowing tastes of several different dishes in manageable portions. But restaurants are used to people ordering two appetizers, to splitting appetizers and main courses between two diners, or serving just an appetizer and a dessert. And every establishment, from the grungiest dive to the most fashionable temple of gastronomy, will cheerfully wrap your unfinished meal to take home. If you have not finished the bottle of wine you have ordered, you can take that, too, providing the cork is still on the table. Sometimes a waiter whisks the cork away, so be vigilant if you think you might not finish the bottle. On the other hand, you do not have to order an entire bottle. Order a glass or a half bottle if that suits your need.

Coffee may be served at any time during the meal and generally with the dessert, not after; all restaurants offer decaffeinated coffee and most now offer espresso and cappuccino. Tea drinking is becoming trendy, and most restaurants offer a selection of teas, including decaffeinated versions and herbal infusions.

What Will It Cost?

Chinese and other Asian restaurants may offer an appetizing lunchtime special of soup, a hearty main course with plenty of rice, plus tea for about US$ 6.00. Dinner specials may be slightly, but not much, higher in price. The same holds true in the Latino eateries, although not in the more upscale restaurants. An excellent meal in one of the city's top restaurants, however, may cost up to US$ 100 per person. Yet the average per-person dinner tab is currently US$ 40, on a par with New York and for that price you will get a high quality meal with the freshest of ingredients, no doubt well-prepared and nicely presented. What matters to San Francisco diners is value for the money, and in general, eating out in San Francisco is an affordable and delectable pastime.

In fact, because the best restaurants are crowded year-round, and the inexpensive restaurants are affordable at any time, few have "early bird specials," for people arriving (and leaving) before normal dining hours. Occasionally restaurants offer specials with a coupon from the newspapers.

Paying the Bill

All the major restaurants accept credit cards. In the United States the tip (gratuity) is generally not included in the bill, although some restaurants will add 15 percent for a party of at least six people. The standard tip is 15–20 percent, depending on level of service; 20 percent is becoming more common for good service. In San Francisco, the sales tax is 8.5 percent, and when figuring the tip it's convenient just to double the tax that appears on the bill. This assumes the service was good; if not, point it out to the manager or tip accordingly.

It is best not to assume that the small Asian eateries accept credit cards. Even some of the popular neighborhood restaurants do not, so call ahead or carry enough cash. In some Asian establishments you may not understand the bill because it is written in Chinese on a small slip of paper only somewhat resembling a bill. On the other hand, the amount may be so cheap—under US$ 20 for two people—that a rarely-made mistake of a few cents does not matter much.

Hotel Dining

If you are here for just a short time and think of dining in your hotel as a last resort, think again. Some of the city's best chefs are now using hotel dining rooms to show off their innovative talents, turning the tried and true into a San

Francisco experience. Those in the following list are in elegant hotels in the Union Square-SoMa-Financial District areas. If most of them are pricey, they all outstanding in their various cuisines and are good value for the money.

- Westin Saint Francis, 335 Powell Street—Restaurant Michael Mina; tel: (415) 397-9222. Rated as one of the city's top restaurants, Mina provides the ultimate in New American cuisine with a multi-course tasting menu and wines to match.
- Clift Hotel, 495 Geary Street—Asia de Cuba; tel: (415) 929-2300. Toothsome Asian/Latino combinations in a nightclub-like atmosphere.
- Campton Place Hotel, 340 Stockton Street—Campton Place; tel: (866) 332-1670. One of the most formal of the city's restaurants, Campton Place Hotel offers graceful French/Mediterranean cuisine.
- Mandarin Oriental Hotel, 222 Sansome Street—Silks; tel: (415) 986-2020. In one of the city's most luxurious hotels, the elegant Silks entices with impeccable California/Asian fusion cuisine.
- Kabuki Hotel at 1625 Post Street—O Izakaya; tel: (415) 614-5040). If you're near Japantown, don't miss this contemporary Asian lounge, serving 20 blends of sake, a tasting menu, and even an Asia-inspired burger.
- Nikko Hotel, 222 Mason Street—Anzu; tel: (415) 394-1100. Only superlatives could describe the sushi and steaks here, in a hotel that caters to Japanese travellers who expect no less.
- Savoy Hotel, 580 Geary Street—Millennium; tel: (415) 345-3900. Consistently rated as one of the best vegetarian restaurants in the city, Millennium serves stylish combinations of vegan, organic, low-fat foods ... and luscious desserts.
- Serrano Hotel, 401 Taylor Street—Ponzu; tel: (415) 775-7979. East meets West here, with both imaginative small plates and larger portions.
- Vitale Hotel, the Embarcadero and Mission Street—Americano; tel: (415) 278-3777. Enjoy modern California/Italian cuisine that emphasizes local produce and a panoramic view of the bay.

- St. Regis Hotel at 689 Mission Street—Ame; tel: (415) 284-4040. Asian-American cuisines and decors are flawlessly woven in this elegant restaurant near Moscone Center.

Going Green

San Francisco has long favored organic foods—those grown with no artificial fertilizers, antibiotics, or growth hormones. Now the "sustainable" food movement is adding the goal of preserving regional cuisines and the ecosystems that produce them. This includes reawakening palates to natural foods, and stressing local producers and ethical packaging and marketplaces.

In San Francisco restaurants, menus use seasonal ingredients, and they also often mention from which regions their offerings come, or even how the food is raised—such as "grass-fed beef." And chefs are adhering to the sustainable and "slow food" movements. Many rely on the Monterey Bay Aquarium's Seafood Watch list to know whether a particular fish is endangered, over-fished, or even illegally caught: http://www.montereybayaquarium.org/cr.aspx. And some also belong to the Clean Fish Alliance: http://www.cleanfish.com. Check out these websites for your own purchases.

The City is also doing its best. In 2008 it banned plastic bags in supermarkets, and it is now intensifying its recycling programs, working to meet its goal of no waste to landfills by the year 2020. Residents are required to recycle: the black bin is for trash, the blue for recyclables, and the green bin is for wet waste, which is ground for compost. Currently, the city composts 400 tons of food scraps daily, most of which is used to enrich the soil of the vineyards in the Wine Country.

Eating By the Sea…

Their city being on the sea, San Franciscans tend to be partial to fish. The city boasts its own local specialties, always in demand. Expect all restaurants to serve fish, and for it to be fresh. Restaurants that do not print their menus every day generally announce fish dishes as specials of the day. Often they will give the origin of the fish. If they do not, you can ask where the fish was caught.

The season (November–May) for the sweet, meaty Dungeness crab is eagerly awaited, and people keep track of the weather, for stormy weather makes for a bad catch. Cracked crab, served cold with a cocktail or butter sauce, or the beloved Crab Louie, a crab salad with a Thousand Island-type dressing, are always popular. Outside crab season, the

> ### Fisherman's Wharf
> It's been a long time since Fisherman's Wharf (the first wharf in the city) was commanded by fishing boats and their captains. Yet, amid the souvenir shops and touristy eateries you can still find glimpses of old San Francisco and some pretty good fish restaurants: Scoma's, Alioto's and the Boudin bakery with its original sourdough bread. And, although most commercial fishing is done elsewhere, fishing boats do still come in to Fisherman's Alley, across from Jefferson Street—bringing in Chinook salmon, herring, and Dungeness crab. Nearby is the Fisherman's and Seaman's Chapel, memorializing those who have made their living on the sea. A few streets away, the red brick 19th century Ghiradelli Square may now have contemporary shops and restaurants, but since 1859 it has also had the Ghiradelli Chocolate Factory, where for a luscious ice cream concoction, you still can't go wrong.

crab is likely to have been frozen or imported. (You can then order a Shrimp Louie.) Asian restaurants serve well-sauced crab dishes, and the two family-run establishments below offer Euro/Asian menus and are often seen as the citywide best for roast crab. And pay attention in February for the annual Crab Festival when Dungeness crab dishes are highlighted in restaurants all around the city.

- Polk Gulch—Crustacean, 1475 Polk Street; tel: (415) 776-2722
- Outer Richmond—Thanh Long, 4101 Judah Street; tel: (415) 665-1146

If every fishing port has its favorite seafood soups, San Francisco's is cioppino, a fish stew based loosely on the Ligurian ciuppin. It also resembles the French bouillabaisse and the Spanish zarzuela. Basically, cioppino features locally-caught crab in season, other fresh shellfish and fish, all stewed in a spicy tomato broth. Note that squid, a favorite seafood in San Francisco, is called by its Italian name calamari, even in some Asian restaurants. Eat the stew with San Francisco's favourite sourdough bread (*see* Bakeries *on page 251*).

- Alioto's, 8 Fisherman's Wharf, at Taylor; tel: (415) 673-0183. Despite the tourist atmosphere, this is one of the best cioppinos in the city. Also serves the Dungeness crab, in season, and Sicilian specialties.
- Rose Pistola, 532 Columbus Avenue in North Beach; tel: (415) 399-0499. Outstanding cioppino and other Ligurian dishes are enjoyed here.

Although there are many admirable fish restaurants, two of the oldest fish houses in the city are still going strong and should not be missed. If their ambiance is staid, their food is not.

- Sam's Grill, 374 Bush Street, near Kearny; tel: (415) 421-0594. For almost 150 years, Sam's has served delicious fish, all wild, all fresh. Try the rex sole. It is crowded especially at lunch, and closes early at dinner. Sam's is closed over the weekends.
- Tadich Grill, 240 California Street; tel: (415) 391-1849. Perennially popular, Tadich's has been serving seafood in San Francisco since 1849, making it the oldest in the city. Try the Hangtown Fry, which dates back to the Gold Rush and the Forty-Niners who wanted a dish that could be cooked in one pan. It is made with fried breaded oysters and fried bacon, folded into an egg omelette. This fish house is always crowded; be prepared to wait or eat at the bar, if there is space.

A serving of fish is generally about $5^{1}/_{2}$ or 6 ounces (156 or 170 g). Do not neglect the fish dishes in Asian restaurants: although the portion of fish may be smaller, the flavors meld together with the vegetables and sauces of each region's culinary traditions.

The stylish Aqua and Farallon are esteemed for their beautifully prepared fish creations and graceful ambience, but there will no doubt be a fish restaurant that you will like in your own neighborhood. Try also these below, and see the following chapter for Asian restaurants.

- **Castro**—Catch, 2362 Market Street; tel: (415) 431-5000. A casual atmosphere and affordable well-prepared fresh seafood with a Mediterranean attitude. It also boasts of a heated patio looking out at Market Street, a terrific bar, jazz nightly, and a distinctly appreciative crowd.

- **Hayes Valley**—Hayes Street Grill, 320 Hayes Street; tel: (415) 863-5545. Modern grill menu that changes daily in a place that never loses its appeal. Tell the staff if you have a performance to make in the Civic Center, and service will be speedy. Splendid French fries are to be enjoyed here too.
- **Mission**—Weird Fish: 2193 Mission Street: tel: (415) 863-4744. Sustainable fish, local farms, vegan opportunities. This tiny eatery does good and does it well.
- **Polk Corridor**—Swan Oyster Depot, 1517 Polk Street; tel: (415) 673-1101. Lunch only at the counter of this wonderful almost century-old fish market. Watch the oysters being shucked, and order a bowl of the outstanding chowder or one of its various seafood salads.
- **Polk/Broadway**—Yabbies Coastal Kitchen, 2237 Polk Street; tel: (415) 474-4088. Oysters are a hit here, as well as toothsome Asian/Mediterranean combinations highlighting locally caught fish.
- **Nopa**—Bar Crudo, 655 Divisadero Street; tel: (415) 409-0679. Raw bar at its best, with oysters, shellfish

and combinations deliciously imagined, hot dishes, and seafood chowder that's a more than satisfying meal in itself.
- **Western Addition**—Alamo Square, a Seafood Grill, 803 Fillmore Street, at Fulton; tel: (415) 440-2828. Fish any way you like it at this popular French seafood bistro. Dinners daily; Sunday brunch.

...And with A View

This is San Francisco after all, and many restaurants highlight their breathtaking views of ocean, city, or bay along with their gastronomy. Some of the examples below might ordinarily fit into other categories (bars, vegetarian or Asian food, etc.) but in San Francisco, as you have no doubt noticed by now, nothing is ordinary, and that includes dining with a view. Herewith just a hint of what you can find, for in a city with water on three sides and hills that soar, there is a view wherever you go.

Two recently-opened destinations have captured Bayside adventurers: Epic Roasthouse at 369 the Embarcadero near Folsom; which has excellent meat dishes and a good-weather patio; tel: (415) 369-9955. For a lunchtime special, try the "burger, beer, and brownie." The adjacent Waterbar at 399 the Embarcadero; tel: (415) 284-9922, completes the picture with sustainable seafood, also with a terrace for those sunny days; tel: (415) 284-9922.

- **Bayside**—Waterfront Restaurant, Pier 7, the Embarcadero at Broadway; tel: (415) 391-2696. California fish restaurant with two outdoor patios right by the bay, letting you watch the boats coming into the piers. Try the Crab Louie in season, or just about any of the fish-of-the-day specials that the waiter announces.
- **Bayside**—Greens, Building A, Fort Mason, neat the Marina Green; tel: (415) 771-6222. The king of vegetarian restaurants—crowded, upscale, with its big windows almost in the bay. The delicate vegetarian creations all have a "Zen" flavor. Reservations a must.
- **Bayside**—Pier 23 Café, North Embarcadero at Pier 23; tel: (415) 362-5125. Right on the water, this bar is a must all

day long. Tables outside, live music in the evenings, and a popular weekend brunch. On sunny, warm days head for Pier 23.

- **Bayside**—The Ramp, 885 China Basin Street at Mariposa; tel: (415) 621-2378. At the city's working port (as opposed to the tourist part of the bay to the north), this more than casual eatery is a treat on rare sunny days. Burgers, salads, sandwiches. Enjoy performances by a live band on weekend afternoons, and outdoor barbeques in the summer.
- **Seaside**—Beach Chalet, 1000 Great Ocean Highway; tel: (415) 386-8439. This micro-brewery at the western edge of Golden Gate Park serves casual New American food, and is a an outstanding daytime experience. First look at the beautiful murals on the ground floor that were painted during the 1930s. Pick up some San Francisco brochures from the Visitor Center, and then go up to the restaurant for a breathtaking view of the ocean, of the surfers navigating the waves, of ships heading toward the Golden Gate, and on a sunny day, of perhaps, a glimpse of the Farallon Islands. Order a sampler of the homemade brews with your meal.
- **Seaside**—The Cliff House at 1090 Point Lobos Avenue, at the end of Geary Boulevard, has two restaurants, Sutro's or the non-reservation Cliff House Bistro: tel: (415) 386-2220. Both tourists and locals appreciate the outstanding panorama. After your meal, check the seaside rocks for cormorants, and look through the camera obscura.

California/American Cuisine

As mentioned earlier, California Cuisine is a modern American style of cooking that emphasizes fresh, regional ingredients in creative combinations and presentations. Chez Panisse at 1517 Shattuck Avenue, Berkeley, is still the high temple of California Cuisine (tel: (510) 548-5525; café tel: (510) 548-5049). Beautiful ingredients in magically pure combinations look deceptively simple on the plate yet are addictive to the palate. Make reservations for the restaurant (downstairs) a month in advance and expect a lovely culinary experience during an expensive price-fixed meal. In the cafe (upstairs) reserve the same day and expect a delicious, imaginative selection at more moderate prices.

Nowadays California Cuisine seems to be morphing into other appellations such as New American, American bistro, Modern American, or even Contemporary American with French overtones. Whatever the moniker, you will get seasonal ingredients artfully prepared, often with a touch of whimsy.

- **Embarcadero**—Boulevard, 1 Mission Street; tel: (415) 543-6084. Along with Gary Danko listed next, this is San Francisco at its ultimate. "New American" cuisine that rates only superlatives, and a splendid wine list.
- **Fisherman's Wharf**—Gary Danko, 800 North Point Street; tel: (415) 749-2060. Hard to get in, for this is rated—in every current ranking—as the city's most popular restaurant. New American Cuisine. The first time you go, you might try the tasting menu. Although there are no pretensions in the restaurant, it is still more casual at the bar.
- **Market Street**—Zuni Café, 1658 Market Street; tel: (415) 552-2522. Perhaps the widest selection of oysters in town, a highly prized roast chicken for two, and a hamburger people think rates three stars. Whatever your taste, Zuni has survived all the trends. There may be French and Italian reminders, but it is undoubtedly California at the core.
- **Noe Valley**—Firefly, 4288 24th Street; tel: (415) 821-7652. American seasonal "comfort food," in a popular neighborhood eatery. Local organic produce and meat from Marin County's Niman Ranch are used here.
- **SoMa**—Delancey Street Restaurant, Embarcadero at Brannan; tel: (415) 512-5179. Upscale "ethnic American bistro" on the Embarcadero, staffed by people who have "hit bottom" and are now being rehabilitated. Patio with a view of the bay, and a friendly atmosphere.
- **SoMa**—MoMo's, 760 2nd Street ; tel: (415) 227-8660. American bistro food, across from the ballpark, which during games makes it difficult to park (except with the

valet parker). Both light dishes and hearty comfort food, such as its not-to-be-missed American meat loaf and mashed potatoes. Outdoor dining, and a lively bar.

Small Plates/Tapas

The current craze in San Francisco is for "small plates" or the Spanish "tapas," and why not? Why not experiment with a variety of flavours and textures, sharing them with your friends, and without eating too much? Fitness and fun can go together, and with small plates, they do. Order as many or as few as you wish. They come in any number of the city's multi-cultural cuisines. Herewith a sampling:

- **Financial District**—Bocadillos, 710 Montgomery Street; tel: (415) 982-2622. Classic Spanish tapas bar, with Basque and Spanish wines.
- **Marina**—Isa, 3324 Steiner Street; tel: (415) 567-9588. Contemporary French restaurant with a covered and heated patio.
- **Marina**—Lüx, 2263 Chestnut Street; tel: (415) 567-2998. Small plates with a French/Asian attitude. Try any dish you like; you will not go wrong.
- **Pacific Heights**—Chez Nous, 1911 Fillmore Street; tel: (415) 441-8044. The Mediterranean/French small plates are appealing to the denizens of increasingly gentrified Fillmore Street.
- **Upper Market**—Destino, 1815 Market Street; tel: (415) 552-4451. Latin American influences, terrific South American cocktails (try the mojitos!), and a festive ambience can be enjoyed here.

Vegetarian Cuisine

In a city where fitness and health are on people's minds, it is not surprising that vegetarians can eat as well and interestingly as their stubbornly carnivore friends. In fact, catering to a healthy, fitness-oriented crowd, even the city's best restaurants offer well-presented vegetarian selections. Italian restaurants offer meatless dishes and the ubiquitous Asian restaurants do, too. And have you ever tried Portobello mushroom sushi? Japanese restaurants can suit vegetarians, too. For everything up-to-date, access http://www.bayareaveg.org

- **Chinatown**—Lucky Creation, 854 Washington Street, near Stockton; tel: (415) 989-0818. Popular vegetarian eatery in the heart of Chinatown. Try the tofu roll with mushrooms.
- **Civic Center**—Ananda Fuara, 1298 Market, at 9th Street; tel: (415) 621-1994. Hearty breakfasts, curries, pizza, salads, and sandwiches are offered here; vegetarian and vegan.
- **Cow Hollow**—Alive! Raw Restaurant, 1972 Lombard Street; tel: (415) 923-1052. Raw vegetarian dishes, using no wheat, dairy or honey. Healthful delicacies include a scallion paté, a lasagne of zucchini, mushrooms and nut cheese, and a quiche with a flax seed crust. Greet desserts as well.
- **Mission**—Herbivore, 983 Valencia Street at 21st; tel: (415) 826-5657. Small multi-cultural animal-free café, with vegan dishes from the Middle East, Italy, and India, etc. Also at 531 Divisadero; tel: (415) 885-7133.
- **Mission**—Cha-Ya Vegetarian Japanese: 762 Valencia; tel: (415) 252-7825. This small restaurant satisfies the vegan taste for no-fish sushi and other Japanese favorites, plus a delicious vegan chocolate dessert.
- **Inner Sunset**—Enjoy Vegetarian Restaurant: 754 Kirkham; tel: (415) 682-0826. No meat or fish, no garlic or onion, no eggs or dairy products. But don't be fooled, Enjoy is so popular it has opened a branch in the Financial District at 839 Kearny Street (tel: 415) 956-7868.

American Through and Through

To the rest of the world American food means steaks, roast beef, barbeque, fried chicken, burgers and fries, and San Francisco does not disappoint. But here—although you can find McDonalds and other international burger chains—even the purveyors of down-home ribs and burgers do so with their own San Francisco twist.

Note, too, that the sausage is making a comeback, from spicy Cajun hot links, Italian or Polish sausage or knockwurst, to corn dogs and even the just plain hot dog, which in San Francisco style, of course, is not plain at all. Look for the particular approach in each place; they're sure to please the palate.

- Big Nate's Barbecue, 1665 Folsom, near 12th Street; tel: (415) 861-4242. Ribs, chicken and sausage links in this takeout storefront owned by Nate Thurmond, the famous basketball player. A few tables for eat-in.
- Bill's Place, 2315 Clement Street; tel: (415) 221-5262. For more than 30 years, consistently rated among the best for burgers and crispy fries.
- Brother-in-law's Barbeque #2, 705 Divisadero Street; tel: (415) 931-7427 Mouth-watering brisket and "short-end ribs," plus greens, beans, spaghetti, and corn bread. Take out, for there are only two small tables in front for eating-in.
- Let's Be Frank: 3318 Steiner St, in the Marina (tel: (415) 675-6755). True to San Francisco, these grass-fed beef sausages contain no nitrites or nitrates. Plus all the fixin's and sides they usually go with.
- Memphis Minnie's Bar-B-Que Joint, 576 Haight Street; tel: (415) 864-7675. Finger-licking smokehouse ribs, brisket, Andouille sausage, pulled pork, and a good selection of sides.
- Mo's, 1322 Grant Avenue; tel: (415) 788-3779. Among the best burgers in town. Also at Yerba Buena Gardens on the second level of the bowling alley-ice skating rink.
- Miller's East Coast Deli: 1725 Polk Street, at Clay; tel: (415) 563-3542. Authentic New York-style deli, where "every bite tastes like more." Good matzoh brei and smoked fish platters.
- Harris' Restaurant, 2100 Van Ness Avenue; tel: (415) 673-1888. Tasty steaks that are often rated among the city's best. Traditional décor.
- House of Prime Rib, 1906 Van Ness Avenue; tel: (415) 885-4605. Succulent prime rib is carved at your table.

Foreign Cuisines

Because Asian restaurants are found on just about every commercial street, the next section is devoted only to *Eating Out in Asia*.

But as to other cuisines, for a city that prides itself in being multicultural, it is difficult to mention only a few. (Nontheless, we will try.) Since Latin and Italian cooking form so much a part of the city's essence, their cuisines are listed separately in the next categories below.

- **French**—Cassis: 2101 Sutter Street; tel: (415) 440-4500. Unlike the refined Fleur de Lys and La Folie, which remain traditional favorites, Cassis serves modern Southern French cuisine with Italian nuances, and Niçoise specialties in a local restaurant just west of Japantown. The preparations are also classic and well presented, but the atmosphere is more like a true French bistro, open and friendly. Also, Café de la Presse, 352 Grant Avenue; tel: (415) 398-2680. This is a classic French bistro with foreign newspapers and magazines, so you can come and stay for a while, to get that feeling of Paris.
- **German**—Hearty and good, and always with a beer or two. Schnitzelhaus, 294 9th Street; tel: (415) 864-4038. Authentic, rustic Austrian/German eatery in the Tenderloin, serving schnitzels, sauerbraten, rabbit. Also try Suppenküche; 601 Hayes Street; tel: (415) 252-9289. German pub and wursthaus serving a fine pea soup, sausages, sauerkraut, and a selection of German beers.
- **Greek**—Kokkari Estiatorio, 200 Jackson Street; tel: (415) 981-0983. An upmarket Mediterranean/Greek restaurant with impressive lamb grills, fish dishes, and a "taverna menu." Reserve well in advance, although it is fun to sit at the bar—if you can find a space.
- **Middle Eastern**—Helmand Palace, 2424 Van Ness Boulevard. If you have never thought of Afghanistan as a country for good food, The Helmand will change your mind. Inexpensive but impressive, its Kabul cuisine offers hints of aromas from India and the Middle East.

Latin American

With a large and vibrant Latino community, San Francisco offers more than just "Mexican food." It is true that taquerias abound—there are more than 150 in the city—but here the ingredients are often regionally based, using good-quality meats and fish, relying on fresh vegetables and fruit, and with rice and beans as tasty side dishes. Some places advertise, for the healthy set, that they use no lard. Spicy salsas are often competitively rated, and some restaurants will boast that they were judged to have the "best salsa in S.F." by some panel at some time. What this means is that the tomato salsa is made with fresh ingredients, but the degree of chunkiness and fire varies from place to place. The Mission, as one would expect, is home to the most Mexican establishments, plus Peruvian, Salvadoran and Nicaraguan restaurants, which have slightly different aromas and traditions. Combinations of cuisines are coming to be known as nuevo Latino.

- **Cuban/Puerto Rican**—El Nuevo Frutilandia; tel: (415) 648-2958. There are only ten tables in this eatery that serves Caribbean cuisine: Cuban pork sandwiches, plantains, and refreshing fresh-fruit smoothies.
- **Mexican**—Maya, 303 2nd Street; tel: (415) 543-2928. Elegant Mexican seafood dishes in SoMa, beautifully prepared and presented.
- **Mexican**—Tres Agaves (Mexican Kitchen and Tequila Lounge), 130 Townsend Street; tel: (415) 227-0500. This is a place that is trendy, noisy, hip, and terrific, with the finest (no-salt!) margaritas you will ever taste. Enjoy cuisine from the Jalisco region of Mexico that uses fresh ingredients from local farms. Open late, a treat for brunch any day. Just be sure not to plan to park on a night when the Giants are playing at the AT&T ballpark nearby.
- **Nicaraguan**—Nicaragua Restaurant, 3015 Mission Street, near Cezar Chavez; tel: (415) 826-3672. Locals have been coming here for more than 20 years for the unmatched Central American regional dishes.
- **Nuevo Peruvian**—Fresca, 2114 Fillmore Street; tel: (415) 447-2668. Small storefront in Pacific heights serves perfectly constructed ceviche (marinated raw fish), seafood specialties with just the right amount of tangy spices, and other Nuevo Peruvian combinations.

- **Nuevo Peruvian**—Limón, 524 Valencia Street; tel: (415) 252-0918. Limón serves imaginative cuisine with influences both from Asia and the Andes. There are several different ceviches to choose among, and a menu focusing on seafood, although the lomo saltado (sirloin, onions, tomato and potatoes) can't be beat.
- **Salvadoran**—El Zócalo, 3230 Mission, near 29th Street; tel: (415) 282-2572. Pupusas (like a filled tortilla). Fish soup and other well-prepared fish and shrimp dishes, fried plantains, etc.

Italian

One hundred years ago, Italian workers coming to North Beach could eat a full meal for fifty cents. Wine, later during Prohibition, was made secretly in the basement and served in coffee cups. Now, North Beach is still the focus for Italian restaurants—although prices are slightly higher, to say the least. Yet there are dozens of interesting Italian restaurants in all corners of the city, offering regional specialties. And excellent Italian wines are served in glasses, to be sure.

Although traditional southern Italian cuisine—pasta, tomato sauce, and garlic—can still be found in just about any Italian restaurant, in San Francisco even this basic combination is becoming increasingly refined and imaginative. Some restaurants now feature the buttery, rich cuisine from the north, fish dishes from the coasts, the simple yet flavorful dishes of Rome, or even the specialized hearty cuisine of a small area past Trieste that is now part of Croatia. And, of course, each restaurant features its region's wines. (*For pizza, see next section on* Pizza *on page 224.*)

- **Embarcadero**—Il Fornaio, 1265 Battery Street, at Levi's Plaza; tel: (415) 986-0100. Monthly specials feature the differing regions of Italy; the standard menu always reliable. Outdoor dining.
- **Hunter's Point**—Dago Mary's, East on Evans, off 3rd Street, the Hunter's Point Shipyard; tel: (415) 822-2633. Since 1931, this old-world, basic Italian and fish restaurant has thrived in an unlikely location.
- **Marina**—A 16, 2355 Chestnut Street; tel: (415) 771-

2216. This is a Marina hotspot serving rustic Campania fare, crispy-crust pizza, meatball specials on Mondays, and Italian wines to wash it all down. It is named after a Campania highway.
- **Mission**—Delfin, 3621 18th Street; tel: (415) 552-4055. Small, reasonably priced, and friendly restaurant serving simple yet elegant Tuscan specialties.
- **North Beach**—Albona, 545 Francisco Street, in North Beach; tel: (415) 441-1040. Unusual spices from the Istrian region on the Adriatic make the Croatian/Italian combinations interesting and alluring. Closed Sunday and Monday.
- **North Beach**—Ideale, 1315 Grant Avenue; tel: (415) 391-4129. Roman specialties, lightly sauced fresh pasta dishes, and roast meats.
- **Pacific Heights**—Quince, 1701 Octavia, at Bush; tel: (415) 775-8500. Using organic produce and cheeses from Northern California farms, this modern rather pricey restaurant offers lovely Italian/French dishes, especially the pastas.
- **Polk/Van Ness**—Acquerello, 1722 Sacramento Street, off Polk; tel: (415) 567-5432. Luxurious restaurant, with north Italian specialties, homemade pastas, and delicious antipasti.

Pizza

Although a few restaurants serve the individual Italian-style, thin-crust pizza (afore-mentioned Il Fornaio and Pazzia at 337 3rd Street come to mind), most pizzas are American, in that they come in a number of sizes suitable for sharing, and the toppings are denser. Most of these neighborhood favorites also serve pasta and other Italian dishes. And note that Pizza Orgasmica boasts, "We never fake it," serving its satisfying pizzas at several locations,
- **Cow Hollow**—Amici's East Coast Pizzeria, 2200 Lombard Street; tel: (415) 885-4500. Also at the ballpark at 216 King Street at 3rd Street; tel: (415) 546-6666. Eastern-style pizzas, crispy crusts, even a pizza for vegans with a soy mozzarella topping are available.

- **Lower Broadway**—Tommaso's, 1042 Kearny Street; tel: (415) 398-9696. The city's oldest pizzeria, and some say still the best. Dinner only; closed Monday. Parking is almost impossible.
- **Mission**—Pauline's, 260 Valencia Street, near 14th; tel: (415) 552-2050. For many decades, a San Francisco insider's favorite. Try the pesto pizza. Only dinner.
- **North Beach**—North Beach Pizza, 1499 Grant Avenue at Union; tel: (415) 433-2444; Always crowded, it serves a wide variety of pizza toppings, plus Italian entrees.
- **Pacific Heights**—Extreme Pizza, 1730 Fillmore Street; tel: (415) 929-9900; and also at 1980 Union Street; tel: (415) 929-8234. This makes some of the city's best pizzas. It has many other addresses too.
- **Potrero Hill**—Goat Hill Pizza, 300 Connecticut, at 18th Street; tel: (415) 641-1440. Crunchy sourdough crust pizzas, and all you can eat on Monday nights. Also in SoMa, at 715 Harrison Street; tel: (415) 974-1303
- **The Richmond**—Pizzetta 211, 211 23rd Avenue; tel: (415) 379-9880. Only a few tables, so think about take-out. The pizzas have some unusual (in season) toppings as well as the standbys, and the crispy crust makes all of them worth sampling.

Grabbing a Bite

Although McDonalds and other chains exist in San Francisco, eating fast here does not necessarily mean "fast food," as you will soon see. (*Refer to box on* The Burrito *on page 227*.) And good quickly-obtained food is a plus in San Francisco, where people love to eat lunch outdoors—on benches, in parks, on the edge of fountains—anywhere they can.

Some office, shopping, and entertainment complexes (Rincon Annex, Metreon, and Crocker Galleria, for example), have food courts, with stalls lining a central set of tables for fast eating, and the four-building Embarcadero Center abounds with quick-eating solutions, including a row of take-out storefronts on the south side of Embarcardero Four. Supermarkets and bakeries usually have sandwiches to go. And chains such as Jamba Juice offer smoothies and salads.

> Once you become a true san Francisco "foodie," subscribe (free) to the weekly online e-column "tablehopper," at http://www.tablehopper.com. Keep up with all that's new in the city's innovative selections of nectar an ambrosia, and learn of the fairs and markets and tastings coming up. Subscribe for yourself and be "in the know."

Yet take-out hearty lunches can be had, as well, if that is what you are after.

- **Citywide**—Noah's Bagels: Extensive chain selling bagel sandwiches featuring smoked salmon and cheese spreads making for an inexpensive and hearty lunch. Hot bagels to take out.
- **Civic Center**—Saigon Sandwiches, 560 Larkin Street, at Eddy; tel: (415) 474-5698. Vietnamese sandwiches (banh mi) of meatballs, roast chicken, or pork, plus vegetables, spices, melded with a hot and sour sauce.
- **Laurel Heights**—California Street Delicatessen and Café, 3200 California Street, in the Jewish Community Center; tel: (415) 922-3354. A good Jewish deli, serving corned beef and pastrami sandwiches, brisket, and other authentic New York deli fare.
- **Civic Center**—Morty's Deli: 280 Golden Gate Avenue, at Hyde; tel: (415) 567-3354. Saying it has "East Coast soul and West Coast style," Morty's has tasty Reuben and meatball sandwiches, among many others. Order online at http://www.mortysdeli.com, and your food will be ready for you to pick up. Closed weekends.
- **Market Street**—Grain d'Or Bakery and Café, 665 Market Street; tel: (415) 512-8160. This serves sandwiches made on crusty sourdough bread, good desserts.
- **North Beach**—Golden Boy Pizza, 542 Green Street; tel: (415) 982-9738. A local staple of North Beach for decades, offering doughy squares of utterly delicious Sicilian pizza. No atmosphere and no amenities. Do not miss it.
- **Yerba Buena**—Beard Papa's, 99 Yerba Buena Lane; tel: (415) 978-9972. If you like cream puffs, this is the place for you. Crispy choux pastry filled with the lightest, creamiest filling.

Weekend Breakfast

When one door closes, another opens. If many of the better restaurants are closed for Saturday lunch, others

The Burrito

Certainly there are fast food chains, sandwich shops and cafés throughout the city where you can grab a quick bite to eat. But in San Francisco, the "fast food" of choice is often the burrito, an all-in-one Mexican sandwich that you can eat on the run and feel satisfied—for quite a few hours afterwards. And fortunately, with more than 150 taquerias—fast food emporia that take orders at the counter and either do or do not have tables for eating in—there is no lack of places to search out your favorite burrito. Do not expect fancy service or a charming atmosphere. That is not what taquerias are about; they are about good food and the price—cheap. Just be happy if you get two napkins. You may need both.

So, what is a burrito? It is a large flour tortilla stuffed with a number of ingredients, heated, and then folded over so you can eat it (you hope) without it bursting and spilling everything down your shirt. Burritos that do not come open are highly sought after, but there is a knack to eating them, which you have to figure out for yourself. But it's the ingredients that count, of course. And you can choose which among them you want.

Start with cheese that melts in the tortilla and—again, one hopes—holds the other ingredients in. And then there's the meat, rice and beans, guacamole or avocado slices, tomato, sour cream, cilantro, and, of course, the salsa. (Many burrito purists disdain the shredded lettuce.) Within these categories, you can choose among different types of cheese and meats, and without doubt, the salsa: red salsa, green salsa, picadillo, or mild. And if you are a vegetarian, you can get a delicious burrito without any meat or cheese at all.

It is hard to find a truly bad burrito. But there are some taquerias that burrito aficionados rate above the rest. Most of the places are plain and basic--what Americans call "dives"—and others are more upscale.

(Continued on next page.)

> ### The Burrito
>
> *(Continued from previous page)*
> What counts in any place, however, is the burrito itself.
> - Taqueria San Francisco, 2794 24th Street
> - Papalote, 3409 24th Street; also at 1777 Fulton Street
> - La Taqueria, 2880 Mission Street
> - Taqueria El Castillito, 136 Church Street; also at 2095 Mission Street
> - El Burrito Express, 1812 Divisadero Boulevard
> - Taqueria Can-cun, 2288 Mission Street; and 3211 Mission Street
> - Los Hermanos, 2026 Chestnut Street
> - Andalé, 845 Market Street, Westfield Center

offer imaginative weekend breakfasts and especially the lingering brunch. Many outdo themselves in their inventive eggy combinations for this popular repast (and also their breakfast-type cocktails). Popular also is a hearty weekday breakfast—pancakes, red flannel hash, French toast and omelettes. Both types of breakfast are true San Francisco social occasions, so be prepared to add your name to the list and to wait. Some of the cafés open only for breakfast and lunch and may be closed Monday, after the Sunday crush. A few take cash only.

- **Downtown**—Dottie's True Blue Cafe, 522 Jones Street; tel: (415) 885-2767
- **Haight**—Pork Store Café, 1451 Haight Street, near Ashbury; tel: (415) 864-6981; also at 3122 16th Street in the Mission; tel: (415) 626-5523
- **Hayes Valley/Castro**—It's Tops, 1801 Market Street; tel: (415) 431-6395
- **Lower Haight**—Kate's Kitchen, 471 Haight Street, near Fillmore; tel: (415) 626-3984
- **Pacific Heights**—Ella's, 500 Presidio; tel: (415) 441-5669
- **Potrero Hill**—Just For You Cafe; 732 22nd Street; tel: (415) 647-3033

The Crepevine (three locations) serves crepes with inventive fillings, omelettes, pancakes, and light meals of sandwiches, salads, and pastas. These are packed for weekend brunch and The Crepevine opens daily for breakfast.
- Inner Sunset, 624 Irving; tel: (415) 681-5858
- Noe Valley, 216 Church; tel: (415) 431-4646
- Pacific Heights, 2301 Fillmore; tel: (415) 922-0102

Tea and Coffee Houses

Cafes in each neighborhood reflect the character of their clientele, but North Beach seems driven by the mystique of coffee. Once, North Beach's coffeehouses comforted Italian workers coming back from the docks, and now they welcome anyone who wants to sit for a while and relax. Many of the most famous of the North Beach coffeehouses—Caffè Greco, Caffè Puccini, Steps of Rome Caffè Roma—line a few short blocks of Columbus, between Broadway and Union. Another, the most famous Beatnik Caffè Trieste, is nearby at 601 Vallejo.

Of the 100 coffeehouses in the city, most offer some kind of pastry selection to go with the coffees, teas, or Italian sodas, and some also serve light meals and salads. (And quite a few offer free wireless Internet access.) What is important is that in any coffeehouse, you may order something refreshing and then sit as long as you like. Even in the most undistinguished-looking establishment, the quality of the coffee (and selection of aromatic teas) may be very good. As with everything else, San Franciscans are espresso snobs, knowing just which cafe serves the type of coffee they like. (Often it is Illy). Some people rail at the ubiquitous Starbucks intruding into neighborhood businesses; others like the chain's coffee and reliable atmosphere. For Irish coffee, try the ever-popular Buena Vista Café at 2765 Hyde, near Ghirardelli Square (tel: (415) 474-5044). (*See page 256 for coffee roasters.*)

- **Cow Hollow/Marina**—Emporio Rulli Gran Caffè & Ristorante, 2300 Chestnut Street; tel: (415) 923-6464. Light and airy modern Italian café, easy for lingering over a morning coffee, partaking of a a panino for lunch, or joining the crowd for the weekend brunch.

- **Castro**—Samovar Tea Lounge, 498 Sanchez Street; tel: (415) 626-4700. Lots to choose from, breakfast fare and some dishes with an Asian influence. Tea tastings on Tuesday evenings. Other addresses,
- **Ferry Building**—Imperial Tea Court; Stall No. 27; tel: (415) 544-9830). Traditional and unusual teas to purchase or enjoy in this well-known Chinese tea shop.
- **Financial District**—Torrefazione Italia, 295 California; tel: (415) 395-9667. Deep leather couches and a friendly atmosphere in which to enjoy the good Italian coffees.
- **Hayes Valley**—Modern Tea, 602 Hayes Street; tel: (415) 626-5406. Stylish tearoom, offering a variety exotic teas and sweets, good soups based on seasonal produce, and light foods.
- **Lower Haight**—Bean There, 201 Steiner; tel: (415) 255-8855. Modern, airy coffeehouse, with pleasant decor and welcoming ambience.
- **Noe Valley**—Lovejoy's, 1351 Church Street; tel: (415) 648-5895. This is probably the most charming tea room in the city, with antiques and a cosy English atmosphere.
- **Outer Sunset**—Java Beach Cafe, 1396 La Playa Boulevard, at Judah; tel: (415) 665-5282. Enjoy a rejuvenating beach environment, good coffee, and a relaxed atmosphere here.

Ice Cream

In addition to the imaginative flavor combinations found in supermarkets freezers and in the San Francisco restaurants, you should try the neighborhood ice cream parlors, most of which create their own offbeat, exotic flavor combinations. Double Rainbow, the famous Ghirardelli Ice Cream and Chocolate Shop in Ghiradelli Square, and Swensen's are San Francisco institutions.

- **Bernal Heights**—Maggie Mudd Ice Cream Parlor & Internet Café; 903 Cortland Street; tel: (415) 641-5291
- **Inner Richmond**—Toy Boat Dessert Cafe, Clement at 5th

Avenue; tel: (415) 751-7505. Welcoming, traditional ice-cream parlor on inner Clement.
- **Mission**—Mitchell's Ice Cream, 688 San Jose, near 29th Street and Guerrero; tel: (415) 648-2300. Light but tasty concoctions, often rated the best in the city.
- **Mission**—Bombay Ice Creamery, 552 Valencia Street; tel: (415) 861-3995. Flavored with Indian herbs and spices.
- **Mission**—Saint Francis Fountain, 2801 24th Street, at York Street; tel: (415) 826-4200; Go for its delicious hot fudge sundaes, tempting banana splits, and the classic grilled cheese sandwich and burgers.
- **Outer Sunset**—Marco Polo Italian Ice Cream, 1447 Taraval Street; tel: (415) 731-2833. Exotic Asian flavors, plus well-made traditional combinations.
- **Potrero Hill**—The Scoop, 1415 18th Street; tel: (415) 642-0165. Friendly, neighborhood ice cream parlor.
- **Richmond**—Joe's Ice Cream, 5351 Geary, near 18th Avenue; tel: (415) 751-1950. Great flavors since 1959, always popular.
- **Russian Hill**—Swensen's, 1999 Hyde Street; tel: (415) 775-6818. The city's own, always with a line out the door. Take the cable car, for there is almost never a place to park on Russian Hill.
- **Sunset**—Polly Ann Ice Cream, 3142 Noriega, near 38th Avenue; tel: (415) 664-2472. More than 400 tasty and exotic flavors in a tiny, cheerful shop.
- **Union Square**—Cold Stone Creamery, 119 Ellis Street; tel: (415) 986-0086. Freshly made daily, choose your own toppings, and watch them being folded directly into the mixture on a chilled granite stone.

EATING OUT IN ASIA

An Asian Town

If it is all just Chinese food to you, it will not be after you have lived in San Francisco a while. Differing aromas from the hundreds of Chinese, Vietnamese, Thai, Korean, and Japanese restaurants permeate the city, satisfying an Asian population that numbers upwards of 200,000 and enticing the rest of the city as well. Each neighborhood has its Asian restaurants, and some areas cater to particular nationalities: Japantown and Chinatown of course, but also Larkin Street for Vietnamese restaurants and provisions, Clement Street for a lively mix of Asian establishments, and Irving Street in the Outer Sunset for its own eclectic mix from the Far East. Geary Boulevard on both sides is lined with Asian restaurants of all kinds and prices.

But do not think that Asian food means only a simple eatery, a dish with some rice and fish on it that you finish in a half hour, and a bill of US$ 10. Some of this eclectic city's true haute cuisine is Asian. And, as you might expect in a city where differing cultures meet head on, the trend now is for Asian restaurants to meld and fuse their own cuisines with others, providing beautifully constructed meals of all inventions and imaginations. In addition to these following stylish—oh, so San Francisco!—examples, look again at the Japanese restaurants Anzu and Silks, both described on page 210.

- **Asian/French**—Azie, 826 Folsom Street; tel: (415) 538-0918. East-meets West cuisine in this red-draped exotic and fashionable family-style restaurant. Sister to the Provençal cuisine restaurant Lulu, next door.

- **Asian fusion**—AsiaSF, 201 9th Street, at Howard; tel: (415) 255-2742. In a class by itself, actually. Crowded, noisy, and good-natured, this restaurant/cabaret catering to both straights and gays offers good Asian fusion small plates served by a crossdressing staff, and a "gender illusion" show on the catwalk.
- **California/Asian**—Butterfly Embarcadero, Pier 33; tel: (415) 787-4784. California Asian cuisine with one of those exquisite views the city is famous for. It plays good jazz too.
- **California/Asian**—Namu, 439 Balboa at 6th Avenue; tel: (415) 666-3553). Three Korean-American brothers present small plates of imaginatively conceived Asian-inspired California Cuisine. Bring friends and order lots of plates to share.
- **Indochinese/French**—Ana Mandara, 891 Beach Street; tel: (415) 771-6800. It may seem as though you are remembering old Vietnam (when it was a colony of France), but the delicate sweet-spicy blendings here, although authentic, are thoroughly contemporary and stylishly presented. Seafood appetizers, caramelized claypot fish, and an exquisite Molten Lava Cake—warm with a liquid chocolate center.
- **Japanese**—Ozumo, 161 Steuart; tel: (415) 882-1333. Ultra-modern Japanese restaurant spread across several different dining areas. Sake bar with dozens of sakes (or teas, if you are so inclined) a robata room for grilling (with another bar), and a main dining room and sushi bar for fabulous chef-inspired creations. There is also a view of the bay for you to enjoy.
- **Pan-Asian**—Betelnut, 2030 Union Street; tel: (415) 929-8855. Crowded and fun, serving Pan-Asian cuisine with flavors of China, Indonesia, and Vietnam. Small plates are good for grazing. Tropical drinks. Walk-in traffic eats at the bar.
- **Vietnamese**—Slanted Door, Ferry Building, the Embarcadero; tel: (415) 861-8032. One of the long-lasting culinary hotspots in the city, so take whatever reservation you can get, or "walk-in" at 5:30 pm.

Modernized Vietnamese cuisine that make you think about coming back even while you are eating. Spicy short ribs are not to be missed.

And now, the Chinese!

Chinese restaurants are in the majority in San Francisco. Both complex and subtle, Chinese food is almost always economical; a hearty lunch in a neighborhood Chinese restaurant may cost about US$ 7.00, and a dinner not much more. In a society not rich enough to offer a slab of meat or a quarter-chicken to each person, Chinese cooks learned to base their dishes on the inexpensive rice or noodles, topped with the region's vegetables and a flavored sauce. To this might be added a few ounces of meat or poultry, or along the coast, fish. For thousands of years this method of cooking has provided a nutritious diet of carbohydrates, vegetables, and an adequate amount of protein.

Yet, the cuisines of China differ widely, owing to differences in regional ingredients, soil and climatic conditions, and of course, ancient traditions. Here, although the ingredients come from this one fertile area, many Chinese restaurants focus on one region's cuisine, and often this can be identified by their names, such as The Hunan, the House of Nanking or Parc Hong Kong. Even these, however, may include in their repertoire special dishes from other regions—Cantonese dishes in a Hakka restaurant, or Shanghai dishes in one that says it is Cantonese.

The restaurants differ in style, quality, popularity, and price, as do all others. In Chinatown especially, you cannot judge the quality of the food by how the place looks. Some unpretentious, basic-looking dives serve the best food in their class (although you might hesitate to take an out-of-town colleague there) and some of the most reputable-looking places may not be as good. With Chinese food, price does not determine quality. You probably cannot go too far wrong when you are in Chinatown if you pick a place that is crowded with Chinese eaters; if you cannot read the menu, look around at what people are eating and point at what appeals to you.

Chinese chefs, like others in the city, cater to San Franciscan tastes by cooking with low or no oil and some, such as Brandy Ho and The Hunan, without monosodium glutamate (MSG). Hearty and healthy Chinese breakfasts are popular, especially the thick rice porridge known as congee (or *juk/jook*) from the south of China; it can come with meatballs, fish—even jellyfish. Or from northern China, try the dough dishes such as "Chinese donuts" and warm bowls of soybean milk, either salty or sweet.

Fortunately for San Francisco's discerning diners, there are simply too many Asian restaurants to describe here, so just a few representative samples are given, along with a description of their culinary approach. Become a true San Franciscan and make your own list of favorites.

Differing Cuisines

It was Cantonese immigrants who originally brought their cuisine to these shores during the mid-19th century. Canton specializes in a delicate cuisine, lightly flavored and sauced, thus preserving the character of the ingredients, especially the mild fish and chicken pieces that are added to the fresh vegetables. This also holds true of the cuisine from Hong Kong.

Slightly more piquant, with highly flavored, sometimes sweetened sauces are the seafood dishes from the city of Chiu Chow, which sits just at the northern edge of Guangzhou (Canton). Even farther north, on the Pacific coast by the mouth of the Yangtze River, Shanghai developed a heavy and hearty cuisine, with strongly flavored dishes braised in dark soy sauces.

- Shanghai 1930, 133 Steuart Street; tel: (415) 896-5600. Classic Shanghai offerings, updated for a San Francisco clientele. Fine dining, an extensive wine list.
- Oriental Pearl, 760 Clay Street, near Kearny; tel: (415) 433-1817. Cantonese and Chiu Chow seafood cuisine. Dim sum at lunch. Though more expensive than others in the area, the menu is also more imaginative. Chiu Chow duck is a specialty.
- Bow Hon, 850 Grant Avenue; tel: (415) 362-0601. This inexpensive Cantonese eatery specializes in clay pot

dishes, in which flavors of the various ingredients—meat or fish, dumplings, vegetables are retained, while contributing to the whole. The broccoli in garlic sauce should not be missed.

- Hing Lung, 674 Broadway; tel: (415) 398-8838. Congee (hot porridge), flavored with herbs and spices, meatballs, finely sliced fish or shrimp, or chicken. Later in the day, try the rice noodles, also enhanced by meats and vegetables, plus sauces that tie the flavors together.
- House of Nanking, 919 Kearny Street; tel: (415) 421-1429. Always crowded, this cheap little café is original in its approach: vegetable dumplings unlike others you might have tried, and a chicken dish in a beer sauce, are just two. Also try Nanking's new Fang Restaurant at 660 Howard Street, that features Nanking's signature dishes and others that are new; tel: (415) 777-8568
- R&G Lounge, 631 Kearny Street; tel: (415) 982-7877. Multi-level Hong-Kong eatery, where crowds come especially for the fried salt-and-pepper crab.

In the north, where rice does not grow plentifully, dough dishes provide the major starch. Noodles served with a variety of sauces and toppings, dough-wrapped dumplings, and dishes made with pancakes are standard. Because Peking (now Beijing) was the capital of the empire, some particularly delicate dishes were created for the Mandarins who ruled. Peking/Mandarin cuisine also offers some of China's more imaginative dishes.

- San Tung, 1031 Irving; tel: (415) 242-0828. Neighborhood restaurant in the Sunset, featuring excellent dumplings and noodles. Always crowded; be prepared to wait.
- Firecracker, 1007 Valencia Street; tel: (415) 642-3470. Popular and noisy spot for imaginative Beijing cuisine, offering low oil and lots of garlic.

In the hot southern portion of China, Hunan has always been a poor district. Its cuisine was developed to keep people cool and to preserve perishable meats. Hot and spicy food, the Chinese believe, keeps people cool internally, so Hunan food especially is very salty and extremely spicy. Chilies and salt also encourage people to eat more rice and drink more tea, so that they eat only a little meat. Smoking preserves meats, and smoked hams and ducks and heavy, spicy sauces characterize this cuisine, which is very much appreciated in San Francisco.

- Hunan Homes: 622 Jackson Street; tel: (415) 982-2844. Excellent Hunan food, serving extremely spicy dishes (that can be modified to your taste).

Hakka means "guest." The Hakka were wanderers, nomads who adapted their own cuisine to the regions where they stopped, incorporating those regions' cuisines into their own. Try the creative dumplings, the hearty clay pot dishes, and the salt-baked chicken, all traditional Hakka favorites.

- Ton Kiang, 5821 Geary Boulevard, near 22nd Avenue; tel: (415) 221-2121. Salt-cooked chicken, clay pot dishes, fermented, wine-flavored dishes, seafood, and some of the city's best dim sum, any time of day.
- Mon Kiang, 683 Broadway; tel: (415) 421-2015. Hakka/Hong Kong eatery in Chinatown with a good rice-paper wrapped chicken roasted in sea salt, and seafood soup.
- Dragon River, 5045 Geary, at 14th Avenue; tel: (415) 387-6698. Flavorful Hakka and Cantonese dishes in a neighborhood restaurant in the Richmond are served here, along with salt baked dishes,

Muslim Chinese cuisine dates from the seventh century, when Arab and Persian merchants first came regularly to China. There are no pork dishes in Muslim Chinese cooking; the specialty is the Mongolian fire pot, in which you cook your own meal in boiling broth from fresh raw ingredients you have chosen.

- Old Mandarin Islamic, 3132 Vicente; tel: (415) 564-3481. This is a popular halal restaurant in the Sunset. The choices of ingredients for the warm pot are wide, from tofu to meats, innards such as liver and kidneys, fresh vegetables, and to top it all off, a delicious dipping sauce. There is also a full menu featuring an interesting range of dishes, with dumplings and fried flour balls, and then dessert. Whichever you order, also sometime try the Peking beef pie and onion pancakes.

Dim Sum

Dim sum ("small bites") is popular for lunch and brunch. In dim sum restaurants, carts with stacks of little bamboo baskets containing steamed or fried dumplings (filled with seafood, chicken, pork, vegetables—or tasty combinations thereof) are wheeled by the tables for the diners to choose among. Bow (large steamed rolls with barbequed pork), siu mai (pork dumplings), ha gow (steamed shrimp dumplings), egg rolls, and pot stickers (fried dumplings) are standards. On the table are small carafes of soy sauce, vinegar, and hot sauce, to mix and use as you choose.

Dim sum is usually served at midday, and a traditional dim sum house will usually open at about 10:00 am and close mid-afternoon. In San Francisco, however, these restaurants may also serve a regular menu at midday and stay open with their regular menu in the evenings.

In some restaurants the little dishes and baskets left on the tables are counted in order to determine the bill; in others, the waiter marks on the bill how many items have been chosen.

In the smaller eateries in Chinatown, the waiters may not speak English, so just point to dishes that look appealing. Dim sum is not expensive; if you do not like what you have chosen, you are not risking much. Of course, if you see chicken feet you will know right away what they are.

There are many dim sum restaurants in town, but these two often have a wait, as does the above-mentioned Ton Kiang.

- **SoMa**—Yank Sing, 49 Stevenson Street; tel: 541-4949; also at Rincon Center; tel: (415) 957-9300.
- **Chinatown**—Gold Mountain, 644 Broadway; tel: (415) 296-7733

Japanese Cuisine

Japanese food emphasizes harmony, and dishes are

arranged to be as pleasing to the eye as to the palate. Japanese cuisine is delicate, featuring low-fat fish, gently sauced dishes, braised meats, tofu, fresh vegetables, several types of flavorful noodles, and, of course, the increasingly sought-after sushi. The lightly battered and fried tempura fish and vegetables are popular, as is sukiyaki, a meat and vegetable casserole. The many varieties of sake—a clear rice wine—may be consumed hot or cold; experiment with different sakes at some of the new sake bars that are opening up, both on their own or in conjunction with regular wine bars and in Japanese restaurants.

Authentic and varied Japanese restaurants are clustered in and around the Japan Center but most neighborhoods have their own favorites, both for cooked dishes and for sushi, which is one of San Franciscans' favorite foods. Because sushi is so much in demand, it is fortunate that neighborhood residents think the sushi bar in their own district is the best. This means delicious sushi is available throughout the city any day of the year. And in the most popular restaurants, if you have not reserved in advance, expect a long wait.

If you are a beginner at sushi, consider Isobune at 1737 Post Street in the Japan Center (tel: (415) 563-1030). Little boats carrying freshly made sushi dishes sail along an oval canal, displaying the preparations as they move along. Choose those that look appealing. Prices are reasonable, so as with dim sum, if you select a dish you do not care for, you have not risked very much. Isobune is a friendly place: sushi lovers sitting next to you will be happy to advise you on selections if you are not sure.

- **Cow Hollow**—Ace Wasabi's Rock 'n' Roll Sushi, 3339 Steiner Street, at Chestnut; tel: (415) 567-4903. Great sushi in a loud, trendy, typical San Francisco atmosphere. Open only for dinner, and is always crowded.
- **Inner Sunset**—Ebisu, 1283 9th Avenue; tel: (415) 566-1770. Popular eatery with first-rate sushi and other dishes.
- **Inner Sunset**—Hotei, 1290 9th Avenue; tel: (415) 753-6045. Japanese noodle cuisine in this ramen bar; a charming setting.

- **Japan Center**—Mifune, 1737 Post Street; tel: (415) 922-0337. Soba and udon noodles with a variety of add-ins, to make a delicious, inexpensive soupy meal.
- **Japan Center**—Maki, 1825 Post Street; tel: (415) 921-5215. Small country-style home-cooking restaurant, serving bamboo containers with rice and a variety of toppings. Sushi and vegetarian options, and a good selection of sakes.
- **Marina/Cow Hollow**—Zushi Puzzle, 1910 Lombard Street; tel: (415) 931-9319. Sushi fused with art: imaginative original rolls and admirable concoctions.
- **Mission**—Blowfish Sushi to Die For, 2170 Bryant Street; tel: (415) 285-3848. Some of the city's best sushi, plus an imaginative and well-created menu. Hectic, noisy, and lots of fun, with TV animations visible and (very) audible anywhere you sit.
- **Mission**—Minako Organic Japanese, 2154 Mission Street; tel: (415) 864-1888. Sushi, teriyaki grilled chicken, vegetarian specialties, all organic and in Mission-sized portions.
- **Mission**–Nombe: 2491 Mission Street; tel: (415) 681-7150. Following the Japanese Izakaya tradition of small plates to share and lots of sake, Nombe (the name means "hearty drinker") uses seasonal and sustainable ingredients from regional producers, and boasts some 75 brands of sake.
- **Richmond**—Kabuto Sushi, 5116 Geary Boulevard; tel: (415) 752-5652. Kabuto offers a full Japanese menu, exceptional sushi, and friendly service.

Southeast Asian Cuisines

Of course, in San Francisco there is always more to try, and dozens of Southeast Asian restaurants show off their differing cultural and historical traditions. Many use rice or noodles as a base, and most specialize in seafood dishes. Because the climate of these countries is generally hot, the food can be quite spicy; you can order "medium spicy" or "not spicy" if you think the fiery peppers will not suit your palate.

Burmese
A fusing of Thai, Chinese and Indian spices and approaches, culminating in a delicious melange of Asian textures sand flavors. Samosas, fish cakes, curries, and noodle dishes.
- Mandalay, 4348 California Street, in the inner Richmond; tel: (415) 386-3895.
- Burma Super Star, 309 Clement Street, in the inner Richmond; tel: (415) 387-2147.

Cambodian
Tropical Asian flavors using coconut milks and lemongrass, often with an overtone of Colonial France.
- Angkor Wat, 4217 Geary Boulevard; tel: (415) 221-7887.

Indian
So many restaurants from the subcontinent—Indian and Pakistani—from dives to elegant, and too little room here to describe their mouth-watering flavors. Curries of all types and heat, tandoori, vegetarian offerings. Dosa on Fillmore at 1700 Fillmore uses sustainable ingredients from South Indian regions; "home-style cuisine," in dosas—Indian-style wraps—come with a variety of fillings. (tel: (415) 441-3672).
- Maharani, 1122 Post Street; tel: (415) 775-1988
- India Garden, 1261 Folsom Street, south of Market; tel: (415) 626-2798.
- Indian Oven, 233 Fillmore Street, in the Lower Haight; tel: (415) 626-1628.

Korean
The highlight of Korean restaurants in San Francisco is to grill your own marinated meats at the table on a charcoal brazier, accompanied by rice, pickles and salads. If you are brave, try the fiery kimchee, a cabbage condiment often put on the table.
- Seoul Garden, 22 Peace Plaza in Japantown; tel: (415) 563-7664
- Brother's Restaurant, 4128 Geary Boulevard; tel: (415) 387-7991. Also in the next block east at 4014 Geary; tel: (415) 668-2028.

Singaporean

One well-established restaurant serving Pacific seafood cuisines, Indian curries, other exotic dishes and melanges of Pacific cuisines, some of the dishes set out attractively on banana leaves.

- Straits Cafe, 845 Market Street in the Westfield Center; tel: (415) 668-1783

Thai

Thai restaurants abound, most serving sweet and spicy seafood dishes and soups, curries with coconut, and lots of aromatic lemongrass. The first one listed is often rated as the "best" in the city, but the others are examples of inexpensive neighborhood places that locals love. Find your own where you live.

- Thep Phanom, 400 Waller Street in the Haight; tel: (415) 431-2526
- Lemongrass, 2348 Polk Street, near Union Street; tel: (415) 346-1818
- Neecha, 2100 Sutter Street, just north of Japantown; tel: (415) 922-9419

Vietnamese

This cuisine has its own characteristics, but it also often incorporates nuances from the French, from when Vietnam was a colony of France, and from China to the north. Three of the city's most well known Vietnamese restaurants have already been mentioned: Crustacean and Thanh Long (*Refer to page 212*) and The Slanted Door. But of course there are others, many more than the two below:

- La Vie, 5830 Geary, in the Richmond; tel: (415) 668-8080
- Golden Flower, 667 Jackson Street, in Chinatown; tel: (415) 433-6469

GOURMET DINING AT HOME: THE MARKETS

If you are at all concerned about your budget or your waistline, you will not dine out every day of the year. Fortunately, you can eat almost as well at home in San

Francisco as in a restaurant, whether you want to cook or not. (Well, almost.) So, knowing how and where to shop for food will be on your mind as you begin to settle in. Wide-ranging options include buying fresh ingredients and starting from scratch or moving up to the artistically prepared meats from the butcher that are ready to cook, adding potatoes and vegetables already cleaned. You can also buy delicious entire freshly-cooked meals from supermarkets or specialty groceries, or even high-quality frozen meals.

Farmers Markets

Outdoor markets, often called "farmers markets," are held on particular days in different districts of the city, and along with selling the region's freshest seasonal produce, they are often—as you might expect—social occasions. Some may offer opportunities for tasting or actually eating a prepared meal, and others might have live music, but all of them offer produce that is usually of better quality and often at lower cost than that of standard supermarkets. In addition to these year-round markets in the city, there are farmers markets in most of the towns of the Bay Area, including one that is exceptionally varied at the Marin Civic Center in San Rafael on Thursday and Sunday.

Look for produce that is certified "organic," meaning that it was not treated with chemical pesticides or fertilizers and that the soil is rotated according to healthful standards. Organic meats come from animals raised without growth hormones or antibiotics, and without pesticide-treated feed. Organic foods tend to cost slightly more. Note that markets are not open on Monday. These are year-round:

- Tuesday & Saturday: Ferry Building, foot of Market Street
- Wednesday & Sunday: Market Street at United Nations Plaza. "Heart of the City" market is large and inexpensive, with many stalls for Asian produce. Flowers, fish, herbs, etc.
- Saturday: Fillmore Plaza: Fillmore Street and O'Farrell. Lively new market, good produce, music, lots of fun.
- Saturday: Alemany Boulevard at Crescent, near Highway

280. Enormous international market open from dawn to dusk. Go early before the crowds arrive, or late when some produce is reduced in price.
- Sunday: Stonestown Mall: Fairly new to the scene and already successful, the most extensive market in the area.

A new market concept is at the entertainment complex Metreon, at 101 4th Street. Buy your produce at the market, get a claim check, and pick up your packages when you're ready; perhaps after a movie or a meal.

The Ferry Building Marketplace

The Ferry Building at the foot of Market Street and directly on the Bay, was built in 1896, one of the few buildings in the city that withstood the 1906 earthquake and fire. After the freeway was built along the Embarcadero, separating the waterside building and its clock tower from the daily life of the city, it unfortunately languished. But after the "big one" (earthquake) in 1989 damaged the freeway and it was demolished, the Ferry Building—and the Embarcadero itself—was beautifully restored. Happily, it is now one of the vibrant hotspots of the city. It is a haven for small artisan food shops of all sorts, for wine and tea lovers, and even for "chocaholics." (Two of the Bay Area's best chocolate makers are here.) There is a bookstore and a shop for upscale cooking gadgetry, numerous cafés, and two major restaurants, one of them the highly popular Slanted Door.

If you want to have a one-stop market experience—finding the highest quality cheese, marvelous fish and meats, the freshest produce, and the most refined wine, chocolates, and teas—the Ferry Building Marketplace is for you. Pick up your ingredients, an already-prepared (and ready to reheat) dinner for the evening, or have a bowl of chowder at the Hog Island Oyster Bar. Find them all here lining a long central corridor. Then stop at Peets for a cup of coffee and pick up a book at Book Passage. And, of course you can always watch—or catch—one of the ferries leaving the port.

The outdoor market almost surrounds the Ferry Building

on Tuesday and Saturday. On Thursdays, there is a night market from 4:00 pm to 8:00 pm in the central passageway. There are tables for eating and conversation, live music, and a convivial atmosphere. Currently, these are among the providers:

- Acme Bread
- Boulette's Larder
- Cowgirl Creamer's Artisan Cheese Shop
- Far West Fungi
- Farm Fresh to You
- Ferry Plaza Seafood
- Ferry Plaza Wine Merchant
- Golden Gate Meat Company
- Hog Island Oyster Company
- Imperial Tea Court
- Kingdom of Herbs
- Noe Valley Bakery
- Peet's Coffee and Teas
- Prather Ranch Meat Company
- Recchiuti Confections
- San Francisco Fish Company
- ScharffenBerger Chocolates
- Stonehouse California Olive Oil
- Village Market

The Supermarkets

The Safeway and Cala Foods chains have stores throughout the city. They are open daily—including Sunday—at least until 9:00 pm and usually for some portion of the day on holidays. In addition to their freshly cut meats, fish, produce, and staple goods, supermarkets carry alcoholic beverages, magazines, and over-the-counter medications. Some have prescription-filling pharmacies, either within or next door. All the large supermarkets accept major credit cards and bank debit cards. Many also have ATM machines on the premises if you need cash.

The merchandise at San Francisco supermarkets is usually guaranteed, so if there is something wrong with a product you have bought, most will take back the item provided you have a receipt. On perishable items, look on the package to make sure that the expiration date has not passed; if it has, supermarkets will generally exchange the item. (Foreigners should note that in the United States, dates are written with the month, day, and year, in that order.)

Several supermarkets stand out for their particularly fine selections. Many offer only organic or chemical-free foods and other products, and you might also find some brochures and books on natural living in the Bay Area. Others just have the highest quality of whatever products they stock. With these, of course, the prices match the quality.

Trader Joe's, extremely popular, has an extensive selection of packaged and frozen goods, dairy products, snack foods, bakery items, and spirits. Currently there are four stores in the city. Although there is parking at all four, you can expect a line of cars waiting to get into the lots. Laurel Heights—3 Masonic Ave (tel: (415) 346-9964); South of Market—555 9th Street (tel: (415) 863-1292); North Point—401 Bay Street (tel: (415) 351-1013); and in the Stonestown Mall, where parking is easiest.

- **Inner Mission**—Rainbow Grocery, 1745 Folsom Street; tel: (415) 863-0620. Cooperative, worker-owned health food market, with a well-rounded selection at good prices. Some parking is available as well.
- **Mission**—Bi-Rite Market, 3639 18th Street; tel: (415) 241-9760. High quality and organic dairy products, fruits and vegetables, good prepared foods to take out. Fresh salads, sandwiches, etc. Mediterranean and Middle-eastern delicacies are a highlight here. The Bi-Rite Creamery across the street, has artisan ice creams and other confections.
- **Pacific Heights**—Mollie Stone's, 2435 California Street, near Fillmore; tel: (415) 567-4902. Upscale market with ample fresh and smoked fish counters, well-cut meats, beautifully prepared meals to take out, cheeses, organic produce. A small cafe. Parking is available.
- **Polk/Broadway**—Real Foods, 2140 Polk Street; tel: (415) 673-7420. Fresh seasonal produce, healthy packaged

foods, vitamins, in the interests of "environmentally sensitive consumerism." Also at 3060 Fillmore Street (tel: (415) 567-7385).

- **Presidio Heights**—Cal-Mart, 3585 California Street, in Laurel Village; tel: (415) 751-3516. Fashionable, well-maintained supermarket. It has an interesting deli section and independently run meat and fish department, and it sells fresh breads and a wide variety of produce.
- **SoMa**—Harvest Urban Market, 191 8th Street, at Howard; tel: (415) 621-1000. Vegetarian/vegan food products, organic produce, and environmental household supplies can all be purchased here; There is also a modern café with a fresh salad bar, sandwiches, and vegetarian and vegan soups; The bakery here also sells vegan baked goods.
- **Sunset**—Andronico's, 1200 Irving Street, at Funston; tel: (415) 661-3220. Upscale supermarket with a superior takeout department (hot and cold), a salad bar, and seating nearby. Extensive meat and fish departments, a table just for different olives, a wealth of cheeses and fresh breads, interesting produce.
- **Van Ness/California**—Whole Foods Market, 1765 California Street; tel: (415) 674-0500. Elegant health food supermarket, with an extensive takeout section of prepared foods, artistically prepared meats to take home and cook, outstanding fresh fish, bakery. Generally expensive, but of extremely high quality. Also at 399 4th Street; tel: (415) 618-0066.

Discount Superstores

Discount stores may not carry all the particular brands you like, but those that do are generally good value for the money—cheap. Occasionally you have to buy by the case.

- Smart & Final; Three locations. Packaged foods, cleaning items, and janitorial supplies.
- Foods Co; Two locations. A warehouse supermarket with a well-rounded selection at good prices, it also offers ample parking space.

- Costco, 450 10th Street; tel: (415) 626-4388. This is a huge warehouse selling all sorts of items, mostly in bulk. You can purchase packaged and fresh foods, frozen items, alcoholic beverages, and much more from here. A small membership fee is charged.

Shopping in Asia

Shopping in Chinatown can be an otherworld experience, especially on Saturday and Sunday. Crowds of people carrying overflowing bags bump into each other as they push their way down Stockton, Powell, or the side streets. They, however, will no doubt have found good prices for fresh fish and poultry, and produce of all sorts. Both produce and packaged goods are displayed outside the shops in boxes or on shelves, contributing to the traffic jam.

Because signs are in Chinese and not all personnel speak English, shopping is sometimes a challenge. Nonetheless, Chinatown is a great place to shop if you are not faint of heart. Parking is impossible, and parking lots on the periphery can cost up to US$ 2.50 for 15 minutes. Either hoof it or take public transportation. No matter how you get there, do not miss Chinatown on market days, for it embodies what is quintessentially San Franciscan. But remember that

Asian shops are located throughout the city. The specialty markets—fish markets and butchers—are listed within their categories below.

- **Chinatown**—Lien Hing Supermarket, 1112 Stockton Street; tel: (415) 986-8488. If you can find your way along the chaotically stocked and crowded aisles—you will eventually find what you want at prices so low that despite the chaos, you will keep coming back. Pork, chicken, and beef are well-cut. A smaller easier-to-maneuver branch is located down the street at 1401 Stockton; tel: (415) 397-2668.
- **Japantown**—Uoki Market, 1656 Post Street, between Buchanan and Laguna; tel: (415) 921-0514. A busy Japanese grocery selling fish freshly prepared, a range of fresh produce, as well as canned goods.
- **Japantown**—Super Mira, 1790 Sutter Street; tel: (415) 921-6529. Modern Japanese grocery. Fresh ingredients for sushi, sukiyaki, soups, and most Japanese meals can be bought here. Also available are exellent fresh tofu and a good bakery. Fish and meat are freshly cut, and the produce is of good quality.
- **Mission**—Bombay Bazar, 548 Valencia, near 16th Street; tel: (415) 621-1717. Indian goods, spices, and herbs. Next door is Bombay's chaat (snacks) café, with exotic ice cream flavors.
- **Outer Sunset**—Twenty-Second and Irving Market, 2101 Irving Street; tel: (415) 681-5212. This is a multicultural market with a little of everything from everywhere. With its rich variety of produce, Asians, Russians, and Arabs come to find what they need here.
- **Richmond**—New May Wah Supermarket, 547 Clement Street; tel: (415) 668-2583. Largest of the Richmond's Asian supermarkets, it is well-stocked with Asian and other international products, fresh produce, meats, and fish.

International Shops

In addition to the ubiquitous Asian shops, do not miss the small ethnic delicatessens with their international selections. Most have packaged goods as well as deli counters for fresh-made specialties, and ready-cooked dishes to take home. Of course the Mission will have more Latin American shops, Chinatown and Japantown their own shops, Outer Geary the Russian stores, and North Beach the Italian. Here are just a few.

- **British**—You Say Tomato: 1526 California Street (tel: (415) 921-2828. Get your Marmite and Bisto at this small shop in Polk Gulch that stocks your favorite foods, packaged, fresh and frozen.
- **Caviar**—Tsar Nicoulai Caviar, 60 Dorman Avenue, just south of the Mission; tel: (415) 543-3007. This is where you will find just caviar: American, Iranian, Chinese. Also a café at the Ferry Building Marketplace (tel: (415) 288-8630).
- **Italian**—Lucca Ravioli Company, 1100 Valencia Street at 22nd Street; tel: (415) 647-5581. This is an old-time deli offering ready-to-cook pasta dishes, pizza, sausages, sauces, wines, cheeses, etc.
- **Italian**—Lucca Delicatessen, 2120 Chestnut Street in the Marina; tel: (415) 921-7873. Exceptional Italian delicatessen selling pastas, sauces, cheese, frittatas, focaccia, salads, and imported packaged products.
- **Italian**—Molinari, 373 Columbus Avenue, at Vallejo; tel: (415) 421-2337. Freshly cut sandwiches, smoked meats, buffalo milk mozzarella, sausages; a selection of everything Italian. Closed on Sunday.
- **Latin American**—Casa Lucas, 2934 24th Street; tel: (415) 826-4334. Fresh produce, herbs, Mexican sausages and cheeses. Everything for Latin American cooking.
- **Mexican**—La Palma Mexicatessen, 2884 24th Street; tel: (415) 647-1500. This is where you find tortillas, of course, fixings for Mexican dishes, and freshly made chips.
- **Middle Eastern**—Haig's Delicacies, 642 Clement, near 8th Avenue; tel: (415) 752-6283. Haig's famous hummus and baba ganoush can be found in supermarkets, which is fortunate, for parking near Clement Street can be difficult. Packaged goods; there are also tables to eat in.
- **Middle Eastern**—Samiramis Imports, 2990 Mission Street; tel: (415) 824-6555. Couscous, olive oils, spices and grains, Persian-style yoghurt, hummus and tahini, and different

kinds of feta are available here.
- **Polish**—Seakor, 5957 Geary Boulevard; tel: (415) 387-8660. This venerable European deli and sausage factory specializes in homemade Polish sausages. The aroma upon entering makes you want to buy them all.
- **Russian**—Gastronom Deli & Bakery, 5801 Geary Boulevard; tel: (415) 387-4211. Smoked meats and fish, Russian salads, and packaged goods are available here. Also at 2801 Judah Street (tel: (415) 664-1835).

Bakeries

San Francisco is proud of its sourdough bread, crusty and flavorful, with a vaguely sour and slightly chewy interior. It originated here during the Gold Rush, when French baker Isadore Boudin melded sourdough yeast into a French baguette. Today, it is standard for restaurants to bring sourdough loaves or rolls to the table, and San Franciscans expect nothing less. Supermarkets sell it sliced, as classic baguettes, and even as sourdough English muffins.

Boudin, with outlets around the city, still sells its breads after 150 years of baking. The bakery is at 160 Jefferson Street (tel: (415) 928-1849). Tour the bakery and learn about sourdough bread, and sample the warm, freshly baked sourdough. Then go upstairs to Bistro Boudin, with its waterfront views, and munch on "Wharf Cuisine" crab cakes, Crab Louie, sourdough crust pizzas, and Boudin's own Sourdough Bread Bowl, filled with a delicious clam chowder.

Bakeries serve their neighborhood's ethnic populations: North Beach is known for its Italian pastry shops, the Mission along 24th Street for a wide selection of Mexican baked goods. Supermarkets stock locally baked breads, bagels, and pastries. Acme Bread with its one outlet in the Ferry Building can be found in some shops, and Just Desserts is renowned for its delicious cakes. Below are a few of the city's fine bakeries—ones you might miss if you do not know that neighborhood.
- **Bayview**—Wendy's Cheesecake Bakery, 4942 3rd Street; tel: (415) 822-4959. Cheesecake, sweet potato pie, pecan pies, etc. Barbeques. Closed on Sunday.

- **Chinatown**—Eastern Bakery, 720 Grant Avenue; tel: (415) 982-5157. One of Chinatown's oldest and most extensive bakeries, offering prepared pork buns and pot stickers, other baked goods, plus mooncakes—a sweetened pastry with a variety of fillings and egg yolk, which serves as a representation of the full moon.
- **Hayes Valley**—Citizen Cake, 399 Grove Street at Gough; tel: (415) 861-2228. Delicious breads, and pastries, gelato. Café open all day, but on concert matinees and evenings in the Civic Center, it can be crowded.
- **Noe Valley**—Noe Valley Bakery, 4073 24th Street; tel: (415) 550-1405. Independent neighborhood bakery, offering cakes, breads and rolls. Challah, and fresh frozen dough using the bakery's own recipes, so you bake your own at home.
- **North Beach**—Liguria, 1700 Stockton Street; tel: (415) 421-3786. Just Italian focaccia bread: plain, tomato, onion, raisin. And just mouth-watering. Sometimes there are discounted loaves in the freezer. Go early, for when they sell out, the shop closes.
- **North Beach**—Italian French Baking Company, 1501 Grant Avenue; tel: (415) 421-3796. A rich variety of homemade breads, rolls, and pastries.
- **North Beach**—Victoria Pastry Co, 1362 Stockton; tel: (415) 781-2015. For more than 90 years, the ever-popular Victoria has been selling Italian pastries, cakes, pies, etc.
- **Pacific Heights**—Bay Bread, 2325 Pine Street; tel: (415) 440-0356. Hearth-baked artisan breads, made with organic flour, from the retail store of this restaurant supplier. Olive bread, herbed fougasse, brioche, and others.
- **Pacific Heights**—Pâtisserie Delanghe, 1890 Fillmore Street, at Bush; tel: (415) 923-0711. French pastries such as sweet rolls filled with fresh fruit and custard, eclairs, cream puffs.
- **Richmond**—Moscow and Tblisi Bakery; 5540 Geary Boulevard; tel: (415) 668-6959. Wonderful and always

crowded, this is a bakery that sells well-selected fresh rye breads, filled piroshkis, and Russian pastries.
- **Sunset**—John Campbell's Irish Bakery; 5625 Geary Boulevard, tel: (415) 387-1536. Authentically Irish soda bread, Celtic almond bread, pasties, Shepards' pies, and more—including soups and tarts.
- **Sunset**—Zanze's Cheesecake; 2405 Ocean Avenue; tel: (415) 334-2264. The most sought-after in the city. Unusually—and always—light and delicate with seasonal toppings, plus the traditional.

Cheese

Cheese in the United States tends to be pasteurized, so until recently there may have been fewer of the delicate flavors and varieties found in other countries. But now even supermarkets are stocking high-quality, freshly-cut cheeses, and some of the better stores mentioned above (Andronico's, Whole Foods, etc) have superior selections. A few dedicated cheese shops carry an extensive stock, and most also carry interesting gourmet items and some wines.

But, if you are someone who loves cheese, make a point of finding a cheese store, and to learn about locally-produced cheeses. Also, the farmers markets usually have cheese stands with locally produced products. And, do not forget the Cowgirl Creamery Artisan Cheese Shop in the Ferry Building.

- **Cole Valley**—Say Cheese, 856 Cole Street; tel: (415) 665-5020
- **Polk/Broadway**—Cheese Plus, 2001 Polk Street; tel: (415) 921-2001
- **Twin Peaks**—Creighton's Cheese and Fine Foods, 673 Portola; tel: (415) 753-0750
- **Glen Park**—Cheese Boutique, 666 Chenery; tel: (415) 333-3390; also at 1298 12th Avenue; tel: (415) 566-3155
- **Mission**—24th Street Cheese Company, 3893 24th Street; tel: (415) 821-6658
- **Haight**—Country Cheese, 415 Divisadero Street; tel: (415) 621-8130. Closed on Sunday.

Fish

Living so close to the sea, there is no reason to settle for less than the freshest of seafood. Domestic fish is available according to the season, and with refrigeration standards so high, fish from other regions is also excellent. During Dungeness Crab season, feast on the luscious crab, both in restaurants at home: supermarkets and fish markets sell crab already cooked and cleaned.

Supermarkets carry seafood already cut and packaged, and not relying on local weather conditions, may stock Atlantic salmon or other non-local fish. Whole Foods, Andronico's and other superior supermarkets, however, tend to use local suppliers; a few have sushi chefs cutting fresh sushi. Dedicated fish markets throughout the city also use local suppliers.

Although many of the old fishing piers have been taken over by tourist attractions, the fishing fleet still docks at "Fish Alley," on the Jefferson Street promenade, between Taylor and Jones. If you do not mind cleaning your own fish, try buying whole fish direct from the fishermen on Saturday morning; go early to have a better selection. And, there are two fish markets in the Ferry Building.

Asian fish stores are generally of high quality. Look especially around the Japan Center, where groceries specialize in sliced fish for sushi.

In Chinatown, you basically have to know your fish, because few people speak English, and the vendors and staff are so busy handling crowds they would not have time to explain, in any case.

- **Chinatown**—New Sang Sang Market, 1143 Stockton Street; tel: (415) 433-0403. One of the best fish stores in Chinatown. Wide and fresh selection, good prices.
- **Chinatown**—Luen Sing, 1207 Stockton Street; tel: (415) 399-8788, Live crabs, frogs, shellfish, ready for you to take home to prepare. What can be fresher than that?!
- **Inner Richmond**—Wing Hing Seafood Market, 633 Clement Street; tel: (415) 668-1666. Freshly cut and live fish to choose among in this authentic Asian fish mart.

- **Inner Richmond**—Seafood Center, 831 Clement, near 10th Avenue; tel: (415) 752-3496. Extremely wide, high-quality selection.
- **Mission**—Mission Market Fish and Poultry, 2590 Mission, at 22nd Street; tel: (415) 282-3331. Fresh fish and seafood in a center that also houses the Mission Market Meat
- **Outer Sunset**—Irving Seafood Market, 2130 Irving Street; tel: (415) 681-3282. Small but well-rounded fish selection.
- **Polk/Van Ness**—Swan Oyster Depot, 1517 Polk Street, near California; tel: (415) 673-1101. A San Francisco tradition for more than 75 years. Fresh fish to take out, but regulars sit at the counter for delicious oysters, Crab Louie, chowder. Closes 5:30 pm. Closed on Sunday.

Meats and Poultry

The better supermarkets listed above have selections of ready-cut meats and some specially prepared items ready to take home and cook, such as kabobs and marinated or stuffed meats. The offerings at Whole Foods are especially impressive. Look also for the exceptional 4505 Meat products at meat counters throughout the city, and check out its stall—and sample its weekly servings—on Thursdays at the Ferry Building outdoor market.

- **Bayshore**—Polarica, 107 Quint Street, near Third and Cesar Chavez; tel: (415) 647-1300. Game and game birds, excellent chicken, imported lamb, wild mushrooms, berries, and smokehouse products.
- **Chinatown**—New On Sang Poultry Co, 1114 Grant Avenue; tel: (415) 982-8887. Fresh fish and poultry, nicely displayed, plus prepared dishes to take out.
- **Laurel Village**—Bryan's Quality Meats, 3473 California Street; tel: (415) 752-3430. Respected grocer and butcher of exceptional quality. Fresh fish, artfully cut meats, prepared foods, salads. Parking in back. Closed on Sunday.
- **Mission**—Mission Market Meat, 2590 Mission, at 22nd Street; tel: (415) 282-1030. Meat market in a Latino market building that also houses the Mission Market Fish and Poultry.

- **Mission**—Lucky Pork Market, 2659 Mission, near 22nd Street; tel: (415) 285-3611. A Chinese pork butcher popular with the Latino community and others in the Mission district. All cuts, plus beef and goat, are available.
- **North Beach**—Little City, 1400 Stockton, at Vallejo; tel: (415) 986-2601. North Beach's premier butcher, with a good variety of high-quality, well-cut products.
- **Van Ness**—Harris' Restaurant, 2100 Van Ness; tel: (415) 673-1888. Fine steak house that sells prime, aged meat at a retail counter during the hours when the restaurant is open.

Coffee and Tea

Those same people who know exactly what kind of coffee they want in the coffeehouses also know exactly what kind of bean they want to grind at home or have the coffee roasters blend for them. Many supermarkets have their own selection of coffee beans and grinders, and Peet's Coffee and Tea has several locations in the city.

The upscale supermarkets also have a wide selection of exotic teas, as do the tearooms described on page 230. The tea stores also carry teaware for best results in brewing your own tea. And, the coffee roasters may carry a selection of teas.

- **Chinatown**—Red Blossom Tea Co, 831 Grant Avenue; tel: (415) 395-0868. At least 100 different teas, some of them quite rare, are available, and instructions on brewing them to their best advantage are provided (tel: (415) 395-0868).
- **Chinatown**—Ten Ren Tea Co, 949 Grant Avenue; tel: (415) 362-0565. Like the above-mentioned, also with some rare and exotic teas.
- **Cole Valley**—Bean There, 201 Steiner Street; tel: (415) 255-8855. Sip in or take out coffee and teas. Coffee is ground to order for your cup of coffee. Light meals can also be had.
- **Cow Hollow**—Union Street Coffee Roastery, 2191 Union Street; tel: (415) 922-9559. Enjoy pleasant coffee from this small roastery at the corner of Steiner Street.

- **North Beach**—Graffeo Coffee Roasting Co, 735 Columbus Avenue; tel: (415) 986-2420. Since 1935, it has been roasting dark and light Arabica beans.
- **North Beach**—Caffé Roma Coffee Roasting Company, 526 Columbus Street; tel: (415) 296-7942. A famous café and roaster. Also at 895 Bryant Street; tel: (415) 431-8555.
- **North Beach**—Caffe Trieste, 609 Vallejo; tel: (415) 982-2605. Next to the famous North Beach coffeehouse, this is a long-established coffee roaster, with its rich aromas wafting down the street.
- **Outer Sunset**—House of Coffee, 1618 Noriega Street; tel: (415) 681-9363. A Middle Eastern shop with good ground beans for Turkish coffee.

Chocolate

People all over the world swear by Belgian or French chocolates, and sometimes they overlook the confections prepared close to home. This would be a mistake in San Francisco, where there are some extremely good artisan chocolate makers. The well-known Reccchiuti and Scharffen Berger are both in the Ferry Building Marketplace. In addition, when you are in these neighborhoods listed here, go out of your way to taste their chocolates, and you will be even more convinced that San Francisco is not a city that disappoints.

- **Cow Hollow**—CocoaBella, 2102 Union Street; tel: (415) 931-6213
- **Inner Mission**—Joseph Schmidt, 3489 16th Street; tel: (415) 861-8682
- **Union Square**—Richart, 393 Sutter Street; tel: (415) 291-9600

Eating Out at Home

After all this, do you still not feel either like cooking or even picking up something on the way home? Then pick up a catalogue at street-side boxes from Waiters on Wheels (tel: (415) 452-6600; website: http://www.waitersonwheels.com) and order a delicious restaurant meal to be delivered. Look at the facsimiles of their menus on the Internet and then order. It is as simple as that. Pay a small surcharge and tip the driver, and you can have hot, ready-cooked meals from restaurants you love.

WATERING HOLES

The Attitude

San Franciscans like to drink. This does not mean that they are drunk. It only means that they approach enjoying good wine, interesting brews, and the most recent cocktail craze with the same intensity that they do everything else. Wine and beer tastings are always popular, and cocktail manias move on quickly—from the martini to the cosmopolitan to the mojito to the margarita—and then back to start all over again. "Happy hour" (a few hours after work, on weekdays) in restaurants and bars are happy occasions indeed.

And San Franciscans expect high quality food in the bars they frequent—although happy hour provides some snacks in keeping with the cultural approach of the locale—and they often get it. Some brew pubs serve tapas, some bars serve excellent fusion food, and some of the most popular bars are actually fine restaurants whose bars stay well-populated into the wee hours.

As with just about everything else in San Francisco, distinctions blur, which means you will probably find what you are looking for somewhere and that you will be content during the search. Pay attention to the local newspapers and magazines that regularly rank the "best" bars and lounges, the "best" for singles, the "best" for martinis, the "best" sports bars, or the "best" of whatever it is they have in mind at that time.

First, the Fruit of the Vine

California produces more than 90 percent of the wine produced in the United States. There is nothing to say about California wines except that many of them are spectacular and if you are a wine drinker, you are going to enjoy yourself here. And if not—at least not yet—you have a treat in store. The longer you are in California, the more you can appreciate its wines. The more you learn about them, the more you will be able to distinguish each nuance and overtone in their wide range of tastes, colors, and textures.

The reasons why wine has captured the world's imagination are many—and only part of this is the taste. It is basically because the entire understanding of wine is complex, unlike any other libation that you might very well enjoy. Understanding wines, of course, starts with the soil and climate of each different grape-growing region in the world—its particular ancient geology and current geography. This is most evident. But if you are going to value particular wines, you will have to take into account the social history, traditions, tastes, and attitudes of the populace of the region, for these all go into understanding why certain wines are valued more than others. No other beverage has such complexity built in, even before you take a sip. And this is all worth knowing, for once you have tasted an extraordinary wine, complementing a perfect meal—well, there is no turning back.

To begin, consider one of the wine appreciation seminars at the continuing education establishments in San Francisco mentioned in Chapter Five, haunt the wine shops that have tastings on weekends, and make periodic ventures to the Wine Country. Look in the newspapers for tours, special wine-related outings, and wine festivals, and check the Internet (website: http://www.localwineevents.com).

Do not forget, though, that the whole point of drinking wine is to enjoy it. No matter the current popularity of certain wines, the superior attitude of wine snobs, and even the authoritative stance of shop proprietors—everybody has different tastes, so if you do not like wine, it is not for you.

Ordering Wines

In restaurants, wine is sold by the glass, by the half-bottle, and by the bottle (generally 750 ml). Depending on how much you drink, it can make economic sense to order a bottle of wine for two people, as there are four 6 oz. servings in a bottle, and the cost is perhaps 20 percent less than four single glasses.

Waiters in just about any restaurant are knowledgeable about the wines of that restaurant and will be glad to discuss the wine appropriate for your meal and for your taste. Some restaurants will allow you a small taste of a wine before you order a glass, and most will also allow you to exchange it for another if you do not like it. Wines are occasionally "corked," (when it tastes like the cork), but it is very rare for a wine to be sent back because it has "turned" and is no longer good. Many restaurants have a "house wine," and these are often produced from famous wineries but labeled with the name of the restaurant.

The price of a bottle of wine in a restaurant is increasing, as establishments try to turn a larger profit any way they can. Generally, the price should be about double what the establishment paid for the bottle, but some restaurants charge triple. Once you have learned about wines and their prices, you can determine which varietals and vintages are worth the price.

Wine Bars

Many bars hold special tastings from particular wineries (*as do the wine shops mentioned on pages 261–262*). Some offer "flights," which are samplings of similar wines, often in half-glass sizes. Hotel lounges offer their own ambience and cocktails, and don't overlook the popular wine bars, which serve food, from snacks to full meals.

- **Ferry Building**—Ferry Plaza Wine Merchant; tel: (415) 391-9400
- **Embarcadero Center**—Wine, 2 Embarcadero Center; tel: (415) 391-0758
- **Hayes Valley**—Hotel Biron, 45 Rose Street; tel: (415) 703-0403
- **Russian Hill**—Bacchus Wine and Sake Bar, 1954 Hyde Street; tel: (415) 928-2633
- **Union Square**—First Crush, 101 Cyril Magnin; tel: (415) 982-7874
- **Union Square**—Enoteca Viansa, 334 Grant Street; tel: (415) 391-0207
- **Union Square**—The Hidden Vine, Cosmo Place; tel: (415) 674-3567
- **Upper Market**—Cav, 1666 Market Street; tel: (415) 437-1770

Purchasing Wine

Wine prices run the gamut from the very cheap to the astronomical. The type of wine, the vineyard, the number of bottles produced, and the particular year the grapes were harvested all contribute to how a wine is priced. California wines have become popular worldwide and some recent harvests have been small, so the price of the better wines has increased. In general—but not always—the better the wine, the higher the cost. But good wines at reasonable prices are available, often at under US$ 10 per bottle, so it is not necessary to spend a fortune on wine. It all just takes know-how: knowing what you like, where and when to shop for special offers, reading advertisements for sales, buying enough to create a cellar of wines to drink at future dates, and paying attention not only to the offerings of major wineries, but experimenting with "boutique" wineries that produce small amounts of good wines.

All shops have promotional sales from time to time on particular items, and when they do, think about stocking your cellar. Discount shops such as Trader Joe's sell well-known labels at reasonable prices, plus interesting imported wines, not just from France or Italy, but from Chile and Australia as well. Supermarkets sell a variety of wines, but these are not necessarily the best buys, and there may not be anyone knowledgeable to help in your selection. Many of the wine shops have tastings of the wines they are currently featuring, and these wines are usually good value for the money.

- **Bayshore/Avenues**—Beverages & More, 201 Bayshore Boulevard; tel: (415) 648-1233. Offering a large selection of wines and spirits, this chain has both domestic and imported, at good prices. Also at 3445 Geary Boulevard; tel: (415) 933-8494; and at 1301 Van Ness Avenue; tel: (415) 447-8483.
- **Cow Hollow**—PlumpJack Wines, 3201 Fillmore Street, near Union; tel: (415) 346-9870. Popular neighborhood shop, offering more than one hundred California and Italian wines at reasonable prices, and liqueurs, sake, and microbrews. Also at 4011 24th Street in Noe Valley;

tel: (415) 282-3841.
- **Cow Hollow**—California Wine Merchant, 2113 Chestnut Street; tel: (415) 567-0646. Appreciated for 25 years as a wine bar and purveyor of California wines.
- **Mission**—Ruby Wine, 1419 18th Street; tel: (415) 401-7708). Specializing in both old- and new-world small producers. Wine club and wine tasting.
- **Embarcadero Center**—Wine, 2 Embarcadero Center; tel: (415) 391-0758. Wine bar and shop; open until midnight on weekends.
- **Hayes Valley**—True Sake, 560 Hayes; tel: (415) 355-9555. The new craze for sake is well represented here: sake of all flavors, tastes...and prices. A knowledgeable proprietor can help you with your choices.
- **North Beach**—Coit Liquor, 585 Columbus Avenue; tel: (415) 986-4036. This is a small shop, but it has an extensive selection of domestic, French and Italian wines. The prices are good and the place can boast of its knowledgeable personnel.
- **Polk/Van Ness**—The Jug Shop, 1590 Pacific Street; tel: (415) 885-2922. This is a large liquor shop with excellent prices and an extensive collection of wines and beers.
- **Potrero Hill**—Wine House Limited, 129 Carolina Street; tel: (415) 355-9463. In business for 30 years near Potrero Hill, this place has friendly, knowledgeable staff and tastings.
- **SoMa**—Wine Club, 953 Harrison Street; tel: (415) 512-9086. The Wine Club offers excellent prices on a large selection of domestic and imported wines; tastings, books, and accessories.
- **Theater District**—Napa Valley Winery Exchange, 415 Taylor Street; tel: (800) 653-9463. Learn everything you ever wanted to know about Napa Valley wines, and the opportunity to purchase them.

The Wine Label

Labels say it all, front and back. The front carries specific information that is required by the U.S. Bureau of Alcohol, Tobacco and Firearms. The brand name of the wine is often most prominent, as wineries strive for customer recognition and loyalty. For small companies this may be the name of the winery itself; large companies may have several brand names. The type of wine is generally specified by the variety of grape, and if labeled as such, it is a "varietal," and must contain at least 75 percent of the named grape. Some lesser wines may use a semi-generic name such as Burgundy or even an overall name such as "red table wine," and some blends may bear the name Meritage. Nearby will be the "appellation of origin," indicating where the grapes were grown. Appellation is increasingly noticed by consumers, focusing on the soil and the site as much as the winemaker.

At the bottom, the name of the winery that bottled the wine usually appears. Although the winery may be in Napa, it does not mean the grapes are from there (that is the appellation of origin): if the label says "produced by," it means that at least 75 percent of the wine was made by the bottler; if it says "cellared by," or "vinted by," the wine was probably purchased from a different winery. The percentage of alcohol appears on the front label along with the date, known as the "vintage year." The "vintage year" refers to the year in which the grapes were picked.

The back of the label often describes the wine in detail, and sometimes says which food it best accompanies. It also contains the required warnings about alcohol and health.

Bars and Lounges

Bars come in many shapes and forms: the romantic lounge with a spectacular view atop a tall hotel, the loud sports bar with television screens in every corner, the neighborhood lounge and restaurant where you can spend a comfortable evening dining and chatting with your friends. Or the funky bar that you love but might not take your mother to.

Even the best restaurants have a bar in front, and these can seat people waiting for their table, diners without a reservation, or those who just find the bar a congenial place to hang out, having a cocktail or two along with a delicious bite to eat from specialties offered at the bar. Two of these are Rincon Center's Cosmopolitan Restaurant (delectable New American cuisine) and the bar at Hotel W on Third Street, which also houses the Asian-influenced favorite XYZ—with another bar within. And for the best margarita ever, people flock to the bar at the chic Mexican restaurant Tres Agaves (*See page 222.*) Levende at Mission and Duboce—the current lounge of choice for the young and trendy—is another example of a chic lounge that serves an excellent small plate, eclectic menu.

Some bars open by lunchtime, some in the late afternoon, and restaurant bars are generally open during the restaurant's business hours. Some bars hold theme nights, many have live jazz or a DJ (disk jockey); some are known for their particularly delicious concoction, for experimentation is what San Francisco is about.

As mentioned, restaurant and other bars usually offer inexpensive cocktails, beers, and snacks in the early evening, during an often loosely defined "happy hour," to a regular clientele that gathers after work. No bar may serve alcoholic beverages between 2:00 am and 6:00 am, and most take their last call around 1:45 am. And pay serious attention to advice about not drinking and driving. (*Refer to page 265.*)

Rooftop bars at The Carnelian Room, Top of the Mark in the Mark Hopkins Hotel, Harry Denton's Starlight Room at the Sir Francis Drake, Cityscape at the Hilton, or The Equinox at the top of the Grand Hyatt have spectacular panoramas and are fun to go to from time to time but are often crowded with tourists and may be pricier than you want. Others also have great views and are directly on the waterfront, and have outdoor tables during good weather. Otherwise—with apologies to all the bars that could have been mentioned had there been more room—here are few of the classic and current greats:

- **Financial District**—Bubble Lounge, 714 Montgomery Street; tel: (415) 434-4204. This plush lounge focuses on the bubbly: Champagne and other sparkling wines, caviar and paté appetizers, music. It appeals to the Pacific Rim executives who work nearby and anyone who wants to sip in style.
- **Embarcadero**—Bix, 56 Gold Street, between Sansome and Montgomery; tel: (415) 433-6300. Always rated among the best of everything, this vibrant

> **Drinking and Driving**
>
> The drinking age is 21 in California, and it is enforced. You may be asked for your identification in any place you try to purchase alcohol (called "being carded"), even if you are well over the minimum age. Just take it as a compliment. Do not drive even if you have had only a couple of drinks. DUI (Driving Under the Influence) laws are strict, and San Francisco policemen are not lenient with offenders. It is illegal to drive with a blood alcohol level of 0.08 or more; you will not know your blood alcohol levels, but the police will. And they will test you on the spot. So, for a night on the town, it is best to ask someone in your group to be the "designated driver" and not drink. If you are the designated driver, try Northern California's delicious Calistoga Water or a non-alcoholic beer, which all bars serve. If you are stopped for "driving under the influence," never try to bribe a police officer. You will only make matters much worse than they already are. If you are convicted of DUI, you might go to jail for up to six months, you will no doubt pay a fine, your license may be restricted or suspended, and you might have to successfully complete a treatment program—all depending on the circumstances. So, be prudent. Do not drink and drive.

supper-club offers an Art Deco bar and martinis that are simply splendid. Known for its excellent jazz.

- **Hayes Valley**—Jade Bar, 650 Gough Street; tel: (415) 869-1900. Now this is pure San Francisco: three levels, three bars; a waterfall, a fishpond, an inexpensive happy hour, and good small plates, Asian-style.
- **Mission**—Blondie's Bar and No Grill, 540 Valencia Street; tel: (415) 864-2419. No ambience, no grill, nothing but what some people say are the best drinks in town, especially the over-sized, delicious martini.
- **Mission**—Dalva, 3121 16th Street, at Albion; tel: (415) 252-7740. A DJ spins music for a lively crowd in this bar that is rated among the best in the city.
- **Noe Valley**—Bliss Bar, 4026 24th Street; tel: (415) 826-6200. An aptly named sophisticated bar for a stylish Noe Valley clientele, it provides music, a cosy fireplace, and good food, upscale wines and cocktails.

- **Noe Valley**—Lime, 2247 Market Street; tel: (415) 621-5256. Boasting bi-level modernity, Lime has mini-TVs here and there, interesting appetizers for grazing, and its own mix of cocktails.
- **North Beach**—Tosca, 242 Columbus Avenue, near Broadway; tel: (415) 986-9651. Almost a landmark for everyone who comes to San Francisco, Tosca has a loyal clientele of locals and is famous for its brandy-laced cappuccino. The jukebox plays only opera.
- **North Beach**—Spec's, William Saroyan Place, off Columbus near Broadway; tel: (415) 421-4112. This standby gets funkier by the year, and San Franciscans have loved it and imbibed here for decades.
- **Union Square**—Red Room, 827 Sutter, in the Commodore Hotel; tel: (415) 346-7666. Also a city favorite (or at least of people who like the color red), this bar is glamorous in its all-red decor and is crowded with fashionable red-lovers.
- **Union Square**—The Redwood Room, Clift Hotel, 495 Geary; tel: (415) 775-4700. Not to be confused with the Red Room, this is one of the city's classiest bars, good for a drink before or after the theater.

Gay And Lesbian Watering Holes

Make no mistake. Gays and lesbians are welcome in any bar and in any club in any neighborhood of the city. San Francisco is a gay- and lesbian-friendly town. But many bars and clubs throughout the city are known as catering to the LGBT communities. And, if a description locates a bar or club in "The Castro" or on "Upper Market," whether it is officially a gay hangout or restaurant or not, it is most likely that the ambience and clientele mirror that of the residents nearby. Last, especially if a place has recently opened, it is likely to be quickly explored by the various gay communities, which are like any San Franciscan group: always on the lookout for the hot new scene.

The clubs—classic or new—tend to have it all: dancing, games, exotic cocktails, patios. Some are good for cruising, others for conversation, and all are good for hanging out. To find out which clubs and bars are currently "in," refer to Internet sites listed on page 375–376. Herewith a representative sample of what you can find, without even looking too hard:

- Cherry Bar and Lounge, 917 Folsom Street at Fifth; tel: (415) 974-1585. Dancing for the women, seven days a week.
- The Café, 2367 Market Street; tel: (415) 861-3846. Sometimes voted the best gay club in the city, women tend to hang out here in the afternoons, especially on Sunday. And the patio is mobbed on a sunny afternoon. There are two bars, computer games, and an always-animated dance floor.
- Café Flore, 2298 Market; tel: (415) 621-8597. This could be the best café in the Castro, if the sheer number of customers are any indication. Right on Market at Noe in a former gas station, with a terrific outdoor space, the requisite good cocktails and wines, an excellent cappuccino as well, and a mixed clientele to enjoy it all.
- The Lexington Club, 3464 19th Street between Mission and Valencia; tel: (415) 863-2052. A perennially popular Lesbian-owned bar, this is sometimes rated as the "best lesbian hangout."
- Mecca, 2029 Market Street; tel: (415) 621-7000. This is actually a restaurant serving fine New American cuisine, but much of the fashionable gay and straight clientele comes to belly up to the circular bar for its vodka martinis, other exotic cocktails.
- Pendulum, 4146 18th Street at Collingwood; tel: (415) 863-4441. Mostly Latino and African American men hang out here. There are a dance floor, drag shows, and cantina nights. And a patio, of course.
- El Rio, 3158 Mission Street; tel: (415) 282-3325. A mixed clientele here dances to live music with a distinctly Latin rhythm.
- The Stud, 399 9th Street at Harrison; tel: (415) 863-6623. This old bar has been around for several decades but is regularly voted among the top gay clubs in the city. Mostly men, but not always. Dancing, special events, and Trannyshack on Tuesdays.

- Trax, 1437 Haight Street; tel: (415) 786-4213). Both gays and straights hang out in this comfortable, typically Haight bar.
- Twin Peaks, 401 Castro Street; tel: (415) 864-9470. One of the classics, a small quiet tavern in the heart of everything—for conversation, good drinks. Another bar with full-length windows to see and be seen.
- Wild Side West, 424 Cortland Avenue, in Bernal Heights; tel: (415) 647-3099. One of the oldest lesbian bars, this friendly and open place has a patio, and plays live music.

Brew Pubs

Do not think that San Francisco's beverage scene is just about wine, for the city has recently been voted—in yet another magazine ranking—as one of the top cities in the country for microbrewery and brewpub beers. (Would you expect anything less?). Brewpubs—saloons that handcraft their own recipes for beers and ales on the premises—offer the most innovative selections of brews. Some offer standard pub fare, some are elegant restaurants in themselves, and all provide a convivial atmosphere. And thus, beer appreciation is quite high among San Franciscans. In addition to their own craft beers, pubs also offer bottled domestic beers, plus imported beers and ales. Taking on the character of the neighborhood they serve, pubs offer various kinds of entertainment, including large television screens for sports viewing.

Actually, the microbrewery trend may well have started here in San Francisco, when in 1965 the decision was made to preserve the bankrupt Anchor Brewing Company, at 1705 Mariposa Street (tel: (415) 863-8350). Now it is San Francisco's local pride, brewing the famous Anchor Steam Beer; the factory does not have a pub, but does give tours and tastings.

To know more about the beers available in the city, visit City Beer at 1168 Folsom; tel: (415) 503-1033. Mix and match among the 300 brands of beer available, or sit down for a cool one, with small plates for snacking.

- **Embarcadero (South)**—Gordon Biersch, 2 Harrison Street, at the Embarcadero; tel: (415) 243-8246. German beers, extensive menu, plus pizza and snacks. Crowds often spill out onto the street.
- **Haight**—Magnolia,1398 Haight Street, at Masonic; tel: (415) 864-7468. A brew pub in the heart of the Haight, serving lunch, dinner until late in the evening, and weekend brunch.
- **North Beach**—San Francisco Brewing Company, 155 Columbus Avenue, at Pacific; tel: (415) 434-3344. Domestic and imported beers, plus those brewed on the premises. Enjoy tastings, good food, and live music provided most evenings.
- **Ocean Beach**—Beach Chalet, 1000 The Great Highway at John F. Kennedy Drive; tel: (415) 386-8439. Fabulous views of the beach, a fashionable menu, plus a sampler of beers brewed on the premises.
- **SoMa**—Thirsty Bear, 661 Howard Street; tel: (415) 974-0905. A microbrewery and restaurant serving tapas, paella, and other Spanish offerings, it also has pooltables and darts for its customers' entertainment.
- **SoMa**—21st Amendment Brewery Cafe, 563-2nd Street; tel: (415) 369-0900. A brewpub with its own brews and others as well. It also offers good food.

Also do not miss Toronado at 547 Haight Street, which offers an enormous variety of microbrews, advertising it has "48 kickass beers on tap" (tel: (415) 863-2276). Actually there are more than that, what with another 100 bottled beers offered. If you are hungry (or even if you are not), do not miss the opportunity to bring in and munch on a delicious sausage from the Rosamunde Sausage Grill next door. A typical Lower Haight experience.

A Taste of the Irish

And in terms of pubs, well, they are all over the city—hundreds of them, in every neighborhood and with every kind of ambience. Many have large-screen televisions for sports viewing and others have darts, but they all have beer and more beer, appreciated by a steady clientele. There are more than one hundred Irish pubs, and this is important for on Saint Patrick's Day on March 17th, the city turns green. Irish or not, people wear green, they sport shamrocks, and, without doubt, they drink. Irish lager, stout (Guinness, most likely), ale, whiskies, and ciders rule the day and into the wee hours. Celebrations, block parties, Irish meals, and entertainment round out the festivities, and the annual Market Street parade culminates it all.

The Buena Vista Café at 2765 Hyde Street is not technically a pub, but it is the home of the first Irish Coffee in the United States—a cup of cream-frothed coffee happily laced with whiskey—and the celebrations there of Saint Patrick's day seemingly do not ever stop (tel: (415) 474-5044).

- **The Avenues**—The Abbey Tavern, 4100 Geary Boulevard, at 5th Avenue
- **The Avenues**—Ireland's 32, 3920 Geary Boulevard, at 4th Avenue
- **Financial District**—Harrington's Bar and Grill, 245 Front Street
- **Financial District**—The Irish Bank, 10 Mark Lane, Bush Street near Kearny
- **North Beach**—O'Reilly's, 622 Green Street, near Columbus
- **The Richmond**—The Plough and Stars, 116 Clement Street, at 2nd Street
- **SoMa**—The Chieftan Irish Pub, 198 5th Street, at Howard Street

ENJOYING THE GOOD LIFE

CHAPTER 7

'When you get tired of walking around San Francisco,
you can always lean against it.'
—Unknown Wit

THE SPORTING SCENE

All Year 'Round

The Bay Area's moderate climate allows outdoor activity on just about any day of the year, from sailing on the Bay, to jogging along its shores, to bicycling on hilly trails, to playing tennis and rollerblading—almost anything that can be done outdoors. Access to outdoor sports, in fact, is a main draw for people moving to the Bay Area. San Francisco itself has more than 120 parks (many with miles of hiking trails), over 70 playgrounds, five golf courses, 100 tennis courts, nine swimming pools, almost six miles of ocean beach, several lakes, fishing piers, fly-casting pools, and a marina with a small craft harbor. Private facilities throughout the city offer gyms with aerobics and strength training programs, yoga, pilates, and martial arts. The Bay Area also has famous national baseball and football teams to root for. What more could one want?

Spectator Sports

San Franciscans are avid sports spectators. Seats for the major games are often sold out long in advance, but the city's sports bars provide large-screen TVs for viewing of just about any match shown by cable or satellite. Tickets for all sporting events are available from the team's box office or from ticket agencies.

Baseball

The San Francisco team, The San Francisco Giants, belongs to the National League (ticket office tel: (415) 972-2000; website: http://www.sfgiants.com). After many years of torturing fans at windy, cold Candlestick Park, the team plays in the AT&T Park, in warm, sunny, China Basin. (In just its last ten years, the park has had three names: Pac Bell Park, SBC Park, and now AT&T Park. And is this the end?) Seating 41,000 people, the ballpark may be reached by public transportation: bus, train, streetcar, and ferry. You can also drive and try and park in public parking or at a private garage nearby, if you want to spend US$ 20 for the event. The team has several stores in San Francisco where you can get information on the schedule, and buy tickets and souvenirs.

AT&T Park is interesting in itself. Walk around the stadium and see the statues to former Giants greats: Willy McCovey who hit 521 home runs in his time; the beloved outfielder Willy Mays; and spectacular pitcher Juan Marichal. Fans will be more than happy to regale you with stories about their sports heroes.

The Oakland team, The Oakland Athletics (The A's), belongs to the American League (ticket office tel: (800) 724-3377; website: http://www.oaklandathletics.com). It plays at the McAfee Coliseum, at Interstate 880 and Hegenberger Road. The BART Colosseum Station is close by.

Football

Overlapping the summer baseball season, the football season begins in late August. The San Francisco 49ers ("The Niners") are the home team (ticket office tel: (415) 656-4900; website: http://www.sf49ers.com). And in Oakland, the team is The Oakland Raiders (tel: (510) 864-5000; website: http://www.raiders.com). Both are among the top teams in their respective "conferences"; the rivalry between them (and their fans) is fierce, and fans are as partial to their football teams as they are to their baseball teams.

The Raiders play in the Coliseum, and the Niners play at Monster Park (formerly named Candlestick Park and still sometimes called The Stick by fans). Season ticket-holders account for most of the Niners seats, but tickets to the Raiders can sometimes be had.

Ice Hockey
The Bay Area professional ice hockey team, The San Jose Sharks, plays at HP Stadium in San Jose (HP ticket office tel: (408) 287-7070; website: http://www.sjsharks.com).

Basketball
The Bay Area team is the Golden State Warriors, which generally plays in the Oracle Arena; website: http://www.nba.com/warriors. The season runs from November through April. Tickets are available at the box office or from Ticketmaster.

Horse Racing
The two racetracks in the Bay Area alternate their schedules, so that racing takes place almost the entire year. Golden Gate Fields is in Albany, on E. Shore Highway, off Interstate 80; tel: (510) 559-7300; website: http://www.goldengatefields.com. Bay Meadows in San Mateo, off US 101, Hillsdale Exit has thoroughbred and quarter horse tracks; tel: (650) 574-7223; website: http://www.baymeadows.com.

Outdoors and free
Everyone walks. There is little to say about walking in San Francisco except that everyone does it. Walking is a favorite exercise, and here in this moderate climate, many people walk 365 days a year. People walk to work whenever they can, wearing business suits and walking shoes (to be changed to dress shoes at work). For exercise, people walk up and down the hills, slowly or quickly, singly or in groups, along the Embarcadero, in the parks, at Crissy Field, along the $3^1/_2$-mile Golden Gate Promenade, across the Golden Gate Bridge. The best walking is where the views are breathtaking: the trails in the Presidio and Golden Gate Park certainly qualify, and Strybing Arboretum in Golden Gate Park is exceptional. And if you are hardy, so is Ocean Beach, even when the fog and wind are fierce. Run anywhere you want in San Francisco,

on city streets, up and down the hills, in the parks, along the waterfront. Joggers of all speeds run through the city streets before work and at lunchtime, and drivers are used to weaving around them. On weekends, runners prefer jogging where there is one of the city's famous views—all the afore-mentioned places. In the parks, women should stay on well-traveled paths, run during daylight hours, and consider running with a group. If you are a serious runner—or even a not-so-serious runner—check the calendar of events on pages 304–309 and enter one of the numerous races San Francisco puts on during the year.

Hiking

You can appreciate the beautiful natural resources of the area in dozens of locations within the city, but the entire Bay Area is a wealth of opportunities that can take many pleasant years to explore. In the city itself, though, and in addition to the two major parks described below, McLaren Park, Glen Canyon Park, Bernal Park, and others have hiking trails. Consider especially Crissy Field, Ocean Beach, or the Ridge Trail, which stretches from Lake Merced to Golden Gate Park, and which will eventually circle the entire bay.

Sierra Club, an environmental association, puts on a year-round schedule of hikes, backpacking trips, and other activities, plus social events. Contact the Bay Chapter office at 2530 San Pablo Avenue, Berkeley; tel: (510) 848-0800; website: http://www.sierraclub.org. For trail guides and environmental information, visit the Sierra Club Bookstore at 85 2nd Street; tel: (415) 977-5500.

Golden Gate Park

Golden Gate Park, dating from about 1865, is one of the country's major urban parks. Reclaimed from sand dunes and landscaped over about 25 years, the park now comprises some 1,017 diverse acres (411.6 ha), offering respite and outdoor activities to hundreds of thousands of people each year. With rolling hills, fragrant forests, and seemingly endless variety, the park continues for some three miles out to the sandy beaches at the edge of the continent. Within its confines there is an arboretum and botanical garden, a conservatory of flowers, a lake where you can rent a boat and another where you can sail a model. There is a Japanese Tea Garden next to the world class De Young Museum—just rebuilt and as spectacular outside as well as within. (The science museum, aquarium, and planetarium will soon return to the park, once their rebuilding is complete.) And every weekend there is an event, a concert, or a happening. This is Golden Gate Park.

The park begins at the Panhandle, between Oak and Fell Streets, which is lined by some of the oldest trees in the city. East of the 19th Avenue bisect, the park is the most civilized. Here are tennis courts, playgrounds, museums, and the exquisite Strybing Arboretum and Botanical Gardens, as well as Stow Lake, the largest in the park. The De Young Museum on Tea Garden Drive sits next to the tranquil Japanese Tea Gardens, and the California Academy of Sciences, should reopen in 2008.

West of 19th Avenue, where the fog may hover for days, are the activities that take more space: golf, doggie runs and training, horseback riding, soccer, polo, fly-casting, and model boat sailing. Especially beloved are the bison in the large paddock on John F. Kennedy Drive, at about 39th

The Embarcadero

The Embarcadero has stretched its arc along the Bay for 150 years, but for decades in the 20th century no one could enjoy it, with a double-decker freeway obscuring the view. In 1989, however, the Loma Prieta Earthquake damaged the highway, and San Franciscans demanded it be torn down. Now, after refurbishment, the Embarcadero promenades are glorious. Start by exploring the Ferry Building, a landmark that survived the 1906 earthquake and fire, and—after a US$ 100 million renovation—is a vibrant community resource, with an outdoor market and indoor stalls, trendy restaurants and shops, along with the adjacent ferry terminal itself. To the north, Piers 1–5 are being restored and Pier 7 is already a lovely expanse. The north promenade takes you to Pier 39 and Fisherman's Wharf. To the south you will see sculptures dotting the waterside, and eventually you will come to the AT&T Baseball Park, where you might take in a game (if you have tickets). And, adding to the "only in San Francisco" charm, in either direction as you walk on, you will be passed by the colorful antique streetcars as they glide along the tracks between rows of stately palms. San Franciscans can love their waterfront once again.

Avenue. Throughout the park there are hiking trails and bicycle paths, forested groves, and lawns and meadows for picnics or games of Frisbee.

If you are around in February and March, look for the exquisitely blooming Queen Wilhelmina Tulip Garden, adjacent to the Dutch Windmill at the western end of the park (and then go for a beer at the Beach Chalet and enjoy the ocean view). And, at the eastern beginning of the park is the National AIDS Memorial Grove, planted with thousands of new trees, native species, pants and shrubs, to memorialize those who struggled against AIDS.

On weekends, some roads are closed to traffic. People stroll, visit the museums, listen to a concert, jog, rollerblade, or just hang out. There is not one foggy or rainy day of the year that the park is not appreciated and enjoyed.

GGNRA

The Golden Gate National Recreation Area (GGNRA) spans more than 75,000 acres (30,352 ha) and 115 miles (185.1 km) over a three-county area and is the largest urban national park in the world. It protects 1000 historic structures, 27 rare and endangered species, and islands whose habitats are threatened. Some 20 million people visit the GGNRA each year. It includes parts of San Francisco itself as well as the wilder reaches outside the city. In the city it includes The Presidio and Crissy Field, and the beaches mentioned below, Fort Mason, and even sites that might surprise you: The Cliff House, and Alcatraz Island. Among the most popular attractions outside the city are the Marin Headlands directly across the Golden Gate Bridge, and Muir Woods.

Larger than Golden Gate Park (almost twice as large as New York's Central Park), the Presidio's 1,410 acres (570.6 ha), sometimes called "the jewel of the Pacific," are part of the Golden Gate National Recreation Area, an urban national park. The fragrant forests, unspoiled beaches, and coastal bluffs are open to the public, including many miles of paved roads and hiking trails, plus a golf course, bowling alley, and tennis courts for more structured recreation. For a fuller description, see pages 29–30.

Crissy Field is one of the gems of San Francisco. Transformed from 100 acres (40.5 ha) of asphalt to an exquisite shoreline national park, it now encompasses a shoreline promenade for jogging or strolling (part of the 400-mile (643.7-km) Bay Trail), paths for bicycling, 28 acres (11.3 ha) of grass fields and picnic areas, 20 acres of tidal marshes welcoming to native wildlife, and access to the bay for boardsailing.

The Beaches

Yes, San Francisco is on the ocean, but swimming in the cold waters off the city's beaches can not only be chilling, it can definitely be risky; some of the most inviting-looking beaches have dangerous undertows and rip tides, so swimming, and wading—even in waters that appear calm—may be unsafe. And occasionally there are sharks. So, it is best to sun yourself, jog, or walk along the beaches to enjoy the view, but to reserve your swimming for the city's pools.

The best swimming beach in the city is China Beach at 28th Avenue off El Camino del Mar. Down a steep trail, the beach is protected from the tides. Sometimes a lifeguard is on duty. Or, take a drive up to Stinson Beach, about 45 minutes north on the Panoramic Highway. The beach—despite the cold water, has pleasant amenities and is very popular.

Bicycling

For sports cycling, the entire Bay Area has excellent trails on an extremely varied terrain, from mountainous to flat, and often with outstanding views. In the city, bikers head for Golden Gate Park, along the Great Highway, the Golden Gate Promenade, and around Lake Merced. There's a bicycle path on the Golden Gate Bridge, leading to some of Marin's most outstanding trails. For a complete resource, buy one of the guides to bicycling in the Bay Area; most rate the rides from gentle to challenging.

Find out about Critical Mass, the gathering of cyclists on the last Friday evening of each month, when up to 2000 riders pedal happily (and loudly) around the city, somewhat like the rollerblade evening described below. For information about this and cycling in general, check out the San Francisco Bicycle Coalition (website: http://www.sfbike.org).

For day rental in Golden Gate Park and nearby, try the stand at Stow Lake or one of the bike shops on Stanyan Street.

- **Cow Hollow**—City Cycle, 3001 Steiner Street; tel: (415) 346-2242. Bicycles for the serious cyclist.
- **Fisherman's Wharf**—Blazing Saddles has six locations near Fisherman's Wharf; check its website to determine which location suits you, and whether you want a guided or unguided tour; tel: (415) 202-8888; website:http://www.blazingsaddles.com.
- **Fisherman's Wharf**—Bike and Roll: three addresses, so check the website or call to determine the most convenient; tel: (415) 229-2000; website: http://www.adventurebike.com
- **Golden Gate Park**—Surrey Bikes & Blades, Stow Lake; tel: (415) 668-6699. Closed on Wednesdays and in inclement weather.
- **Golden Gate Park**—Golden Gate Park Bike and Skate, 3038 Fulton, at 6th Avenue; tel: (415) 668-1117. Bikes and inline skates for rent.
- **Haight**—Avenue Cyclery, 756 Stanyan Street; tel: (415) 387-3155. Sales of upscale bicycling equipment, plus rentals for those who want to pedal in the park. Excellent repair shop.
- **Haight**—American Cyclery, 510 Frederick Street; tel: (415) 876-4545. Oldest independent bicycle shop in San Francisco.
- **Mission**—Valencia Cyclery, 1077 Valencia, at 22nd Street; tel: (415) 550-6600; repair and parts shop tel: (415) 550-6601. Large selection of equipment and accessories.

Inline Skating

For roller or inline skating, many people take their skates to Golden Gate Park, where a rollerblade hockey game can often be found near the tennis courts. The Marina Green or the Embarcadero are also popular, but basically people skate just about anyplace they want. Rent skates at Golden Gate Park Bike & Skate (address: 3038 Fulton Street;

tel: (415) 668-1117 and in various other locations around the city; see Skates in the *Yellow Pages*.

On Friday evenings, join the Midnight Rollers, and with hundreds of other skaters follow a serpentine course through the north part of the city and back to the starting point at the Ferry Building. Starts about 9:15pm; tel: (415) 752-1967; website: http://web.cora.org/friday.html.

Multi-sport Fitness Clubs

Urban San Francisco offers several private multi-sport fitness clubs, almost country clubs within the city. In addition to their standard facilities, most offer scheduled athletic events, tournaments, and social gatherings.

- **City-wide**—Embarcadero YMCA, 169 Steuart Street, near Mission; tel: (415) 957-9622. The YMCAs are popular, offering aerobics, yoga, and dance classes, swimming pools, and racquetball courts. Several addresses: In the Presidio, at Lincoln and Funston Streets, (tel: (415) 447-9622); Check website for other addresses: http://www.ymcasf.org.
- **Embarcadero**—Golden Gateway Tennis and Swim Club, 370 Drumm Street; tel: (415) 616-8800. It has two outdoor swimming pools, nine tennis courts, and a fitness center, and conducts aerobics classes and holds tournaments.
- **Masonic**—Koret Health & Recreation Center, 2130 Fulton Street; tel: (415) 422-6821. Part of the University of San Francisco, this facility with swimming pool, gym, and classes is open to the public. Pay by the session or buy a pass for 15 sessions.
- **Mission Bay/India Basin**—UCSF Bakar Fitness & Recreation Center, 1675 Owens Street; tel: (415) 514-4545. Extensive multi-sport and fitness club, with two pools, weights, classes, outdoor activities, and children's programs.
- **SoMa**—San Francisco Tennis Club, 645 5th Street; tel: (415) 777-9000. An upscale club including indoor and outdoor tennis courts, a fitness facility, aerobics classes, sauna and hot tub, restaurant. In addition to the monthly dues, there is a court fee for using the indoor courts.

- **Telegraph Hill**—San Francisco Bay Club, 150 Greenwich Street; tel: (415) 433-2200. Tennis, racquetball, and squash, aerobics, sun deck, swimming pool, and special events.

Gyms

In addition to the more extensive multi-sport clubs mentioned above, every neighborhood has its storefront gym, some just with workout machines, some more extensively equipped, offering aerobics classes, jacuzzi, and steam baths. You will see these small clubs as you walk around your neighborhood; monthly dues are generally reasonable, and some clubs allow per-use payment. The downtown district has several chains of fitness clubs—Crunch, Curves (for women), 24-hour Fitness, and Club One. Most of the clubs open early and stay open late, and these, obviously, are most crowded before and after work, and at lunchtime. Facilities at these clubs vary; some have swimming pools and some do not, but they are all generally well-equipped for the activities they offer. These usually have short-term as well as regular membership, and if you belong to one, you may use the others in the chain.

- **Castro**—Gold's Gym, 2301 Market Street, in the Castro; tel: (415) 626-4488. Full gym with co-ed classes, various yoga disciplines, cardio workouts, tai-chi, pilates, and kick boxing. Also, South of Market, 1001 Brannan Street; tel: (415) 552-4653.
- **Potrero Hill**—World Gym, 290 De Haro Street; tel: (415) 703-9650. Personal training and classes of all sorts—boxing, spin, yoga, etc—complete cardio facilities, special events, nutrition.

Tennis

More than 130 free public tennis courts dot the city's parks, and they are "first-come first-served." For the Guide to Public Tennis Courts ask at the San Francisco Recreation and Parks Department at McLaren Lodge, Fell and Stanyan Streets, in Golden Gate Park, or call the Tennis Department (tel: (415) 831-6302). Golden Gate Park has 21 courts, which must be reserved in advance, and which cost a small fee (tel: (415) 753-7131). The city also offers an extensive program of free tennis lessons. Below are some popular public courts; see also afore-mentioned Multi-sport Fitness Clubs.

- **Noe Valley**—Mission Dolores Park, 18th Street and Dolores; Six courts. Daytime only.
- **Marina**—Moscone Recreation Center, Chestnut and Buchanan Streets; Four lighted courts.
- **Excelsior**—McLaren Park, Mansell Drive, near University Street; Six courts.
- **North Beach**—North Beach Playground, Lombard and Mason Streets; Three lighted courts.

Swimming

Since ocean swimming is not reliable, try a pool. The multi-sport fitness clubs listed above have swimming pools, and "Park and Rec" maintains eight municipal public pools. Prices are reasonable, especially if you buy a series. Swim lessons are also available.

- **Japantown**—Hamilton Recreational Center, Geary at Steiner; tel: (415) 292-2001
- **Mission**—Garfield Pool, Harrison and 26th Streets; tel: (415) 695-5001
- **Mission**—Mission Pool, 19th Street at Linda; tel: : (415) 641-2841
- **North Beach**—North Beach Pool, Lombard Street at Mason; tel: (415) 274-0200
- **Inner Richmond**—Rossi Pool, Arguello Boulevard at Anza; tel: (415) 666-7014
- **Parkside**—Sava Pool, 19th Avenue and Wawona; tel: (415) 661-6327
- **Sunset**—Balboa Park, San Jose Avenue and Hsavelock; tel: (415) 337-4701
- **Visitacion Valley**—Coffman Pool; Visitacion Avenue at Hahn; tel: (415) 337-4702

Other Water Sports

- Sailing: The opportunity to go sailing just about any time of the year is a distinct benefit of the San Francisco life. Opening Day on the bay in May can be an awesome sight, and during events over the bay such as fireworks or the aerial displays of the Blue Angels, thousands of boats perch in the water waiting for the show. For people without boats, it is sometimes possible to sign on as crew. Try the Saint Francis Yacht Club (tel: (415) 563-6363), or the Golden Gate Yacht Club (tel: (415) 346-2628), both membership clubs located in The Marina.

- Surfing: Surfing in wet suits is popular, but despite the surfers who brave the currents, remember that the undertows off Ocean Beach are dangerous. Beginners often surf at Pacifica's Linda Mar Beach, and experts go down to Half Moon Bay. Windsurfers tend to use Lake Merced and the more challenging area at Crissy Field.
- Rowing— Dolphin Swimming and Boating Club, a group of hardy folk who swim in the Bay year round and row on the Bay and on Lake Merced. The clubhouse is at 502 Jefferson Street, at the foot of Hyde Street; tel: (415) 441-9329. Try also the South End Rowing Club, next door at 500 Jefferson; tel: (415) 776-7372. See above also for swimming and sailing. Lake Merced Boathouse: Rent a rowboat, canoe, or pedal boat, at Harding Road and Skyline Boulevard. Stow Lake Boathouse—Rent a rowboat or pedal boat in Golden Gate Park. Picnic on the island of Strawberry Hill.
- Fishing—The city's municipal piers—at the end of Van Ness or at the end of Broadway—permit fishing in the heart of the city, and people occasionally reel in flounder, sand dabs, cod, bass, perch, or crabs. Unfortunately, cleanup programs to eliminate toxic substances and other contaminants in the Bay have been only partially successful. The California Office of Environmental Hazard Assessment suggests that adults should eat sport fish (excluding salmon) no more than twice each month, and that striped bass more than 35 inches long not be consumed.

Fortunately, people also fish from the banks or a boat on the 350 acre Lake Merced, which has been stocked with trout, rock cod, catfish and bass. Golden Gate Park has several fly-casting pools by the Anglers Lodge, just west of the Polo Fields.

- Kayaking—City Kayak, Pier 38; tel: (415) 357-1010. Tour San Francisco on the water in a kayak. Start by the Bay Bridge, see the skyline of the city, Alcatraz, the Golden Gate Bridge, etc.

Golf

It may be surprising that there are five golf courses in a city as small as San Francisco; some are nine holes only, but full of twists and turns. Golf is a year-round sport, despite the winter rains and the summer fog, but San Franciscans are hardy, and swathed in sweaters and jackets, they wait patiently for their tee. There are a few private membership clubs in the city, and many clubs around the Bay Area are open to the public. In the East Bay, Tilden Park Golf Course in Berkeley is particularly popular (tel: (510) 848-7373), as is the Chuck Corica Golf Complex in Alameda (tel: (510) 747-7800).

- Gleneagle's Golf Course, in McLaren Park, at Sunnydale Avenue and Hahn Street; tel: (415) 587-2425. A hilly nine-hole course, with wonderful views.
- Golden Gate Park Golf Course, 47th Avenue between Fulton and John F. Kennedy Drive; tel: (415) 751-8987. Compact nine-hole course.
- Harding Golf Course, Harding Park, at 99 Harding Road near Skyline Boulevard; tel: (415) 664-4690. An 18-hole challenge in a forested setting. Fleming Park course is nine-hole.
- Presidio Golf Course, 300 Finley Road, at Arguello, in the Presidio; tel: (415) 561-4661. Eighteen holes, practice center.
- Lincoln Park Golf Course, 34th Avenue and Clement Street; tel: (415) 221-9911. Eighteen difficult holes on beautiful terrain with spectaclar views. Practice area, putting green, etc.

Skiing

Some of the best skiing in the country takes place on the ski slopes of the Sierra Nevada, only three hours from San Francisco. In the winter, daily weather updates report the snow level and depth of snow pack of the major ski areas of the region: Lake Tahoe, Incline, Alpine Meadows, Yosemite, and Bear Valley. Be prepared to carry tire chains in your car and from time to time to be stuck in the mountains until the roads are cleared of snow. Sunday night traffic off the mountains can be slow. For highway conditions, call the California Department of Transportation's 24-hour automated information line; you will need to enter the number of the highway you are inquiring about (tel: (800) 427-7623).

Sporting goods shops sell ski wear and gear; some shops rent it, and most have information on ski areas. (*See section* Shopping, *pages 195–196.*)

Other Sports

- Basketball—You can probably pick up a basketball game in the Golden Gate panhandle, Dolores Park, at some of the city's playgrounds, the Moscone Recreation Center in the Marina, or the Potrero Hill Recreation Center.
- Bowling—Presidio Bowling, Building 93, between Moraga and Montgomery Streets; tel: (415) 561-2695. Yerba Buena Bowling Center; 750 Folsom Street; tel: (415) 820-3540.
- Dance—Academy of Ballet, 2121 Market Street; tel: (415) 552-1166. For all ages. Classes for toning and stretching, through classical ballet moves. Renaissance Ballroom; 285 Ellis Street; tel: (415) 474-0920. Learn the cha cha or the waltz; most social dances are taught here. Recreation and Parks Department Dance; 50 Scott Street in the Harvey Milk Center; tel: (415) 554-9523. Dance lessons in a variety of steps: square dancing, jazz, tap, etc.
- Horseback riding—Golden Gate Park Stables, John F. Kennedy Jr. Drive and 36th Avenue; tel: (415) 668-7360. Guided rides through the park and along the oceanfront, plus pony rides for children. Instruction available.
- Ice-skating—Yerba Buena Gardens at 750 Folsom Street sports a year-round, covered ice-skating rink; tel: (415) 820-3532. Justin Herman Plaza, at California Street and the Embarcadero, erects a small rink in the winter.
- Martial Arts and Yoga—As would be expected, San Francisco has many Asian exercise establishments. For any one of a dozen types of martial arts dojos, see

the *Yellow Pages* under Martial Arts Instruction. Health clubs offer yoga classes for all levels of ability, and there are small studios in just about every neighborhood that specialize in a particular yoga technique. Both Funky Door Yoga and Yoga Tree have three locations. And the Yoga Society at 2827 Folsom Street has information on yoga and practices Hatha Yoga; tel: (415) 285-5537.

- Pilates—The same is true for pilates. Gyms offer both mat and reformer classes , and if you search "pilates San Francisco" on the Internet, you'll find some neighborhood studios.
- Rock Climbing—Mission Cliffs Climbing and Fitness Center, 2295 Harrison, at 19th Street; tel: (415) 550-0515. Indoor rock climbing on about 14,000 square feet (1,300.6 sq m) of terrain, yoga, cardio workouts, and weights.

Spas

What could be better after a long week at work than a relaxing couple of hours at a spa? Most health clubs have sauna and steam baths, and some offer massage. There is some overlap these days, since hair salons are also giving massages, wraps, and other healthful treatments, so see page 113, for more than those listed here.

Locals are particularly fond of the Kabuki Hot Springs in the Japan Center, at 1750 Geary Boulevard, at Fillmore (info tel: (415) 922-6000). Kabuki offers a full range of shiatsu massages, body treatments and Japanese baths. And, Jin Healing for Women, at 999 Powell Street, features female therapists offering healing massages, acupressure, reflexology and other treatments; tel: (415) 986-1111.

- **Mission**—Osento Baths, 955 Valencia Street; tel: (415) 282-6333. A gathering place for women. Osento is a peaceful bath house, with saunas and an outdoor deck, and it provides massages as well.
- **Noe Valley**—Elisa's Beauty and Health Spa, 4028 24th Street; tel: (415) 821-6727. Outdoor/indoor hot tubs, steam baths, and sauna. Massage, skin peels, herbal body wraps.

- **Presidio**—SenSpa, 1161 Gorgas Avenue; tel: (415) 441-1777. Large, elegant spa and wellness center. Non-invasive Chinese medical techniques practiced by master healers, promoting a balance of mind body and spirit. To unleash the wellness within.
- **Union Square**—Nourish Spa by Chakra, San Francisco Hilton, 333 O'Farrell Street; tel (415) 923-5014. Urban retreat and fitness meet at this state-of-the-art club.
- **Van Ness**—The Hot Tubs, 2200 Van Ness Avenue; tel: (415) 441-8827. Hot tubs and saunas, shiatsu and Swedish massage.
- **ReFresh Day Spa**, 1130 Post Street; tel: (415) 563-2316. Body and skin treatments, hands and feet, massage therapists, body wraps.

And Last... About Dogs

Brisk dog-walking is good exercise and an excellent way to meet neighbors. While dogs are not allowed in most parks (signs are generally posted at entrances), some parks have areas designated "off leash" where dogs may run freely, and some neighborhood parks have dog runs. Golden Gate Park has several off-leash areas and Ocean Beach is off-leash until Stairway 21. Dolores Park between the Mission and Noe Valley is a dog and owner gathering place, as is Bernal Park. Call the Parks Department for information on dog running areas in the city parks.

CULTURE—HIGH AND LOW!

From world-class opera, ballet, and symphony, to live theater, to American and international films, to rock concerts that draw thousands, and to cabaret, dance and comedy clubs, San Francisco has something for everyone. Restaurants offer jazz, jazz clubs serve food, art galleries and museums serve wine and canapés at their exhibit openings, bookstores host readings by famous authors, and in general, you can find something interesting to do just about any time of day—and night.

Each district reflects the mood of the area. The Civic Center is the hub of culture—opera, classical music concerts, and ballet. Just off Union Square is the Theater District. North

Beach is known for its coffeehouses and topless bars, Nob Hill for its plush piano bars. SoMa—down to China Basin—has its art center but also trendy eating places and offbeat offbeat nightspots and dance clubs. The Castro, of course, is known for its gay hangouts, although gay-friendly entertainment can be found throughout the city. And the Mission, while remaining distinctly Latino, is definitely reflecting an expanded popularity in all regards, with something new cropping up on almost every block.

For outdoor events, pay attention to the weather of the particular area. Sunday afternoon concerts at Stern Grove, for example, may be foggy and windy, even as eastern portions of the city are still basking in the sun. The same holds true for the annual outdoor Shakespeare Festival. Be prepared to bring a jacket to any outdoor event, plus groundsheets for the damp grass.

San Francisco is often interactive in its offerings: the sing-along Handel's Messiah, for example, is a favorite annual event, as is the Sound of Music sing-a-long at the Castro Theater. Also, to get the most out of cultural activities, you might attend "preview" seminars and lectures that focus on current performances and exhibits—the San Francisco Opera's lectures, for example, take place 55 minutes before each performance.

And last, if you are thinking of an evening out and want everything all at once, remember that some of the best restaurants serve jazz with their food, and even the skuzziest-looking bars serve pretty decent food with their jazz. At the movies you can buy food for snacking while you watch (and not just popcorn), and at the popular Foreign Cinema restaurant, you can watch a film while you eat. As to weekend brunch—or even a weekday lunch—there is often music while you munch.

Infinite Resources

The San Francisco Chronicle and *The Examiner* list each day's events and those that are in the wind. On Friday, along with weekend listings, most of the new films and other events are reviewed; opera and concert reviews generally appear a day or two after the opening. And on Sunday, *Chronicle* publishes its Datebook, listing the events for the week to come. The free weekly tabloids, *The Bay Guardian* (website: http://www.sfbg.com) and *SF Weekly* (website: http://www.sfweekly.com), announce all the major events as well, and also more of the small offbeat and eclectic happenings. Advertisements for events project well into the future, sometimes several months. Some of the publications mentioned on page 114 also offer reviews and listings of events.

The San Francisco Convention and Tourist Bureau has a recorded-message hotline for current events: tel: (415) 391-2001. And there are many online sites:

- http://www.sfgate.com
- http://www.sfbg.com
- http://www.sf.weekly.com
- http://www.laughingsquid.com
- http://www.sfstation.com
- http://www.sanfranmag.com
- http://www.bayinsider.com

The Museums

With 65 museums of one sort of another in San Francisco, they cannot all be listed here. So, herewith a sampling of the most important or interesting or new—to give an idea of the diversity you can find, if you look. As for the rest, access the city's own Internet site at http://www.sfgov.org for links to museums, read the tabloids for special exhibitions and news of openings, and be ready to enjoy yourself and be edified for years to come. (*Also refer to the activities for children on pages 132–136.*) The first four are the city's public museums. Some museums offer one free day, usually the first Tuesday or Wednesday of each month.

- The de Young museum, Golden Gate Park, 50 Hagiwara Tea Garden Drive; tel: (415) 863-3330. The pride of San Francisco, the De Young is open again after having been spectacularly rebuilt. Three interconnected, parallel space form a series of interior courtyards, and special areas showcase the museum's major collections: American

paintings, sculptures, 19th century furniture, and objects from Latin America, Africa, and Oceania.
- Asian Art Museum, 200 Larkin Street at Civic Center Plaza; tel: (415) 581-3500. More than 15,000 artwork spanning 6,000 years of history in this museum opened in 2003 that is devoted exclusively to Asian Art.
- California Academy of Sciences: 55 Music Concourse Drive, Golden Gate Park ; tel: (415) 379-8000. Ten years in the planning, the Academy has been stunningly rebuilt, with an aquarium, all-digital planetarium, natural history museum, a naturalist center, a 2.5 acre living roof, and a 4-story rain forest. Even the café with its multicultural menu, and the fine-dining Moss Room with its California/Mediterranean cuisine are already drawing San Francisco crowds.
- The Contemporary Jewish Museum: 736 Mission Street; tel: (415) 685-7800. New, expanded quarters for this interesting collection that offers contemporary Jewish art, music, films, and special exhibits and programs. Visit the café for "kosher-sytle" food.
- Museum of Craft and Folk Art: 51, Yerba Buena Lane; tel: (415) 227-4888; website: http://www.mocfa.org. The only folk art museum in Northern California features exhibitions of folk art and craft from the around the world.
- California Palace of the Legion of Honor, Lincoln Park at 34th and Clement; tel: (415) 750-3600. Outside, the imposing museum overlooks the Golden Gate Bridge. Inside, there is a stunning collection of European art—El Greco, Rembrandt, Monet, Picasso. A good representation of prints and drawings, sculpture and period furniture.
- San Francisco Museum of Modern Art (MOMA), 151 3rd Street; tel: (415) 357-4000. Opened in 1995, this four-story dramatically modern museum displays the best of European and American artists, including many American abstracts, an outstanding photography collection, works by Diego Rivera and Frida Kahlo, and usually an interesting traveling exhibits.
- Museum of Gay, Lesbian, Bisexual, Transgender History, 657 Mission Street; tel: (415) 777-5455. The archives

contain primary source material on GLBT history: works of artists and writers, documents from leaders of the movements, posters flyers—from the Gold Rush to today. Exhibits and programs.
- Precita Eyes Mural Arts Center, 2981 24th Street; tel: (415) 285-2287. A different kind of "museum," in that it offers guided tours of the more than 200 murals in the Mission district. Some are by famous Mexican artists, others are in the style of Rivera or José Orozco. The murals depict the life and achievements of Mexicans in the Mission and elsewhere.
- The Museum of the African Diaspora (MOAD), 685 Mission Street; tel: (415) 358-7200. Exhibitions, presentations, and appreciation of the impact of people of African descent on contemporary life.
- Mission Dolores, 3321 16th Street; tel: (415) 621-8203. The oldest structure in San Francisco, completed in 1791, the four-foot thick adobe walls, tiled roof and façade are typically "Mission style." The chapel contains original redwood beams, and the Mexican altarpieces date from the early 1800s. See also the adjacent basilica with its stained glass windows showing the life of Saint Francis of Assisi, the missions of California, the old cemetery, and the life-size sculpture of Father Junipero Serra.
- San Francisco Maritime Museum National Historical Park; Hyde Street Pier; park tel: (415) 447-5000. A museum, a park, a pier with old sailing ships and even a World War II submarine—this National Park has everything for lovers of sea history. The Balclutha built in 1886 to carry grain to Europe is only one of the old sailing ships on display. The San Francisco Maritime Museum (currently closed for remodeling) reveals the country's maritime history, with models, photographs, miniatures, and interactive exhibits. The submarine Pampanito sank enemy ships throughout World War II, and—like the other ships on display—has been totally restored.
- The Walt Disney Family Museum: 104 Montgomery Street in the Presidio; tel: (415) 345-6800; website: http://www.waltdisney.org. Opened at the end of 2009, ten galleries

here exhibit both the life of Walt Disney through photos, home movies and personal letters, and the development of his craft through early drawings of Mickey Mouse, storyboards, and exhibitions and interactive displays of Disney's technical achievements that allowed his animations to continue to captivate generations of fans.

Events—Getting Tickets

Tickets to the most popular events—classical concerts, theater, rock concerts, and sporting events—are snapped up quickly, so order as far in advance as you can. It is cheaper to buy directly from the box office, either by phone or online. But sometimes it is easier to buy them through a ticket agency, despite the service charge. Phone and online orders are accepted with a credit card number, and tickets can be delivered, mailed, or held at "will-call" at the box office.

For the theater, try Tix Bay Area, a small booth nestled on the sidewalk on the east side of Union Square, along Stockton Street; tel: (415) 433-7827; website: http://www.tixbayarea.com. It offers half-price tickets for day-of-performance theater and musical events.

Ticketweb sells only on the Internet: website: http://www.ticketweb.com. And tickets turn up on Craig's List (website: http://www.craigslist.com) from time to time and on E-Bay (website: http://www.ebay.com).

- City Box Office; tel: (415) 392-4400; website: http://www.cityboxoffice.com
- Mr. Ticket; tel: (415) 775-3031; website: http://www.mrticket.com
- Ticketmaster; tel: (415) 512-7770; website: http://www.ticketmaster.com

In addition to reduced price tickets at Tix, there are other opportunities for reduced-price or even free tickets. If you volunteer to usher at a theater, for example, you can see the show for free. Students with valid identification can often get reduced-price tickets. And some smaller theaters may offer reduced-price tickets an hour before a performance starts.

Theater

As you would imagine, San Francisco's theater scene is wildly diverse, from Shakespeare in the Park to experimental efforts in tiny, offbeat venues, and to Broadway musicals that stay around for years. Some theaters offer readings of new works, which of course vary in style and quality. Look for *Theatre Bay Area* magazine which covers all aspects of theater, or access its Internet site; website: http://www.theatrebayarea.org.

Generally, live theater is performed Tuesday–Sunday, and Mondays are "dark." On Sundays, there are matinees at the important theaters, except at "Berkeley Rep," described below. Some touring companies come through with short runs, and their schedules may be different. Note that most theaters use volunteers in some capacity or other, often as ushers. If this interests you, call the theaters directly for information.

One day in October, on National Theater Day, theaters throughout the Bay Area open their doors for free. Check the local papers just before October 16th.

Three downtown theaters—the Curran, Golden Gate, and the Orpheum—are known for "best of Broadway" plays and musicals that have either played in New York or are heading there. They also host some local performances. (info tel: (415) 551-2000; telephone orders tel: (415) 512-7770). Marines Memorial Theater at 609 Sutter Street also hosts local productions and some Broadway-type shows (tel: (415) 771-6900).

- ACT (American Conservatory Theater), at 415 Geary Street, is the city's premier local theater company; box office tel: (415) 749-2228. Pronounced "ay-cee-tee," not "act," ACT offers both classics and new works, and features visiting artists along with the local cast. Subscriptions and single performance tickets are available.
- Berkeley Repertory Theatre, at 2025 Addison Street, near the Berkeley BART station, is the East Bay's premier theater company, and many San Franciscans subscribe as well as to ACT; box office tel: (510) 647-2949. "Berkeley Rep" performs both classic and contemporary

works. The season is fall to spring, with special summer performances.
- Magic Theatre at Fort Mason, the former military installation turned cultural center, presents innovative drama by both newcomers and established playwrights; tel: (415) 441-8822.
- Yerba Buena Center for the Arts, 701 Mission Street; tel: (415) 978-2787. The Yerba Buena Center for the Arts is a great space for a variety of performances and performers, including theater, concerts and dance. Art galleries, video art, and more. Do not miss the summer Yerba Buena Gardens Festival, a series of outdoor performances by multicultural artists.

But of course San Francisco abounds in not-so-traditional theater, as it does with everything else. Herewith just a few:
- Audium, 1616 Bush Street; tel: (415) 771-1616; website: http://www.audium.org. A 75-minute exploration of space through music, as "sound sculptures" move past, over and under the audience.
- Theatre Rhinoceros, 2926 16th Street; website: http://www.therhino.org; tel: (415) 861-5079. Popular LGBT theater company, whose offerings run from the established to the experimental, and from the serious to the raunchy.
- Exit Theatre, 156 Eddy Street; tel: (415) 673-3847; website: http://www.sffringe.org. Experimental theater with four stages in the Tenderloin. In September, Exit hosts the San Francisco Fringe Festival: 12 days of just about anything dramatic you can imagine—classical, comedy, and cabaret—by all types and levels of talent (tel: (415) 931-1094). Other venues as well.
- Marsh, 1062 Valencia Street in the Mission; info tel: (415) 826-5750; website: http://www.themarsh.org. A "breeding ground for new performance," Marsh presents new works of all sorts, and some that open here in previews, getting ready to move on to the big time. Another venue in Berkeley at 2120 Allston Way, near Shattuck.

- Lamplighters Music Theater, 469 Bryant Street, Yerba Buena; tel: (415) 227-4797; website: http://www.lamplighters.org). If you like Gilbert & Sullivan, this is the place for you. Even if not, there are other musicals—both classic and new—and light opera. Limited season.

Classical Music

The San Francisco Symphony holds its concerts at Louise M. Davies Symphony Hall, at Van Ness Avenue, at Grove (ticket office tel: (415) 864-6000). The regular season runs from September to June, with special events year-round. Long-time subscribers retain the best seats from year to year, but as the building dates only from 1982 (upgraded in 1992), the acoustics throughout the hall are very good. Occasionally tickets become available at the last minute, and some inexpensive Center Terrace seats (to the rear of the stage) are sold two hours before performances. The Symphony issues an annual schedule that details all ticket options, including prices and dates for their Open Rehearsals, which take place about once a month.

San Francisco Opera draws international stars for its lavish productions, which are staged at the War Memorial Opera House: 301 Van Ness Avenue (tel: (415) 864-3330). The season usually begins in mid-September. Subscribers renew their seats from year to year, but single tickets can be had, and occasionally people stand outside at performance time trying to sell single tickets for that evening's performance or others in the future. Although opera is always expensive, cheaper alternatives exist and standing room is available—if you are willing to stand for three or four hours, that is.

San Francisco Ballet, the oldest ballet company in America, performs new works and classical ballet. Its regular season takes place at the Opera House, after the opera season closes, generally from February until June (tel: (415) 865-2000). Special events include the ballet's annual performances of Tchaikovsky's Nutcracker Suite at Christmas. Although tickets go quickly, sometimes there are single tickets available, and students with identification may buy discounted tickets on the afternoon of the performance.

San Francisco Performances is a major presenter of chamber music, giving more than 150 concerts each year (tel: (415) 398-6449). It performs primarily at the Herbst Theater at 401 Van Ness, but also at Yerba Buena Center for the Arts, and other locations.

And Classical For Everyone

- **Summer**—Stern Grove Midsummer Music Festival, 19th Street and Sloat Street at the Stern Grove Amphitheater; tel: (415) 252-6252. Ten free outdoor concerts in a lovely eucalyptus stand at Stern Grove, off 19th Avenue and Sloat. Popular with all San Franciscans—from the counter-culture to the highly cultured. Offerings range from classical to blues, from ballet to jazz.
- **All Year**—The San Francisco Conservatory of Music, 50 Oak Street; tel: (415) 864-7326. Hundreds of performances a year by students of the conservatory. Affordable prices and many free.
- **All Year**—Noe Valley Ministry, 1021 Sanchez Street; tel: (415) 454-5238. Music of all sorts—classical and folk, jazz, and world music, all in this 100-year-old church.
- **Summer**—Sunday Concerts in the Park; Every Sunday afternoon from mid-April through October, the Golden Gate Park Band gives a free concert at 1:00 pm. Great for a picnic.

San Francisco's Own

Do not miss performances by the city's own Kronos Quartet (website: http//www.kronosquartet.org), or the San Francisco Contemporary Music Players, (website: http://www.sfcmp.org), both of which perform mostly at Yerba Buena, but also at other venues. The acappella group Chanticleer sings at various locations (website: http://www.chanticleer.org). And the Pocket Opera puts on opera as farce (website: http://www.pocketopera.com).

Look also for performances of the modern dance troupe ODC (website://www.odcdance.org), and the Smuin ballet, which puts ballet to popular music (website: http://www.smuinballet.org).

- **Summer**—Midsummer Mozart Festival; Annual Mozart festival; tel: (415) 627-9145. Famous artists perform Mozart with a San Francisco orchestra at the Herbst Theater and other towns around the Bay Area.
- **All year**—Old First Concerts; Old First Church, 1751 Sacramento Street; tel: (415) 474-1608. Friday evening and Sunday afternoon concerts are held in the church sanctuary.
- **All-year**—Noontime Concerts; International touring musicians play half-hour classical music programs on Tuesday at 12:30 pm at Old Saint Mary's Cathedral at 600 California Street; Wednesdays at Saint Patrick's, at 756 Church Street.
- **Autumn**—Opera in the Park; in September, around the opening of opera season, stars of the San Francisco opera and its orchestra perform at Sharon Meadow in Golden Gate Park.

Rock Concerts

It has been a long time since the Grateful Dead played in San Francisco, but the birthday of the late Jerry Garcia is still celebrated by loyal Deadheads on August 6th. It's also been a long time since Jello Biafra of the Dead Kennedys ran for mayor of San Francisco (1979) coming in fourth (in a field of ten). But you will not have to wait any time at all for a touring rock group to turn up somewhere in the Bay. When they do, they perform at the large concert halls and arenas listed below. Events are publicized well in advance and tickets sell out almost immediately, so check ticket agencies as soon as you see the ad for a concert that appeals to you. For info on the Internet, check the concert halls themselves or try http://www.sfbayconcerts.com, or the Squid List at http://www.laughingsquid.com/squidlist.

- The Fillmore, 1805 Geary Boulevard; website: http://www.thefillmore.com
- Bill Graham Civic Auditorium, 99 Grove Street; website: http://www.billgrahamcivic.com
- The Warfield, 982 Market Street; website: http://www.livenation.com

- Great American Music Hall, 859 O'Farrell Street; website: http://www.musichallsf.com

Most arena concerts around the Bay Area are accessible by public transportation, and most have extensive parking facilities for those who come.
- Chronicle Pavilion, 2000 Kirker Pass Road, Concord; website: http://www.chroniclepavilion.com
- Oakland Coliseum, 7000 Coliseum Way, Oakland; website: http://www.coliseum.com
- Cow Palace, Geneva Avenue and Santos Street, San Francisco; website: http://www.cowpalace.com
- Shoreline Amphitheater, 1 Amphitheater Parkway, Mountain View; website: http://www.shorlineamp.com
- Zellerbach Hall, University of California, Berkeley; website: http://www.calperfs.berkeley.edu
- Greek Theater, University of California, Berkeley; website: http://www.calperfs.berkeley.edu

Until the Wee Hours

To hear visiting artists at the clubs in the city, check the listings above. New venues open all the time, and fortunately, the tried and true stick around. Think about the East Bay, too: Yoshi's in Jack London Square serves the hottest jazz and coolest sushi, and the sophisticated dinner club Kimball's East in Emeryville serves up a great mix of music or comedy with its multi-cultural cuisine. For any of the clubs, make sure to call ahead, for they are not all open early in the week. Ask also if there is a cover charge or a minimum purchase on drinks.
- Paradise Lounge, 1501 Folsom Street; tel: (415) 621-1911. Recently remodeled, this decades old rock'n'roll club has a good dance floor, and an upstairs lounge, and is drawing the crowds again.
- Slim's, 333 11th Street; tel: (415) 255-0333. Rock, hip-hop, reggae, and whoever comes to play at this always popular, well-established music venue—where despite the 500 seats, there often seem to be people standing.
- Bimbo's, 1025 Columbus; tel: (415) 474-0365. Since the 1950s, Bimbo's hosts touring groups, DJs, and a crowd of loyals.

- Bottom of the Hill, 1233 17th Street; tel: (415) 621-4455. At the bottom of Potrero Hill, this small club has long hosted touring rock groups and local bands.
- Biscuits and Blues, 401 Mason Street, at Geary; tel: (415) 292-2583. Blues club serving Southern food—biscuits, shrimp, catfish, chicken, and corn fritters—and live blues.
- Rasselas, 1534 Fillmore Street; tel: (415) 346-8696. Jazz, blues, R&B, and Latin American bands, served up with interesting Ethiopian food. Not just for the neighbors in the Western Addition, although they keep the place going late.
- Jazz at Pearl's, 256 Columbus; tel: (415) 291-8255. Small jazz house serving Spanish-French food along with its great music. On the brink of extinction just a few years ago, Pearl's was bought and rejuvenated. Young North Beachers breathed a sigh of relief.
- Hotel Utah, 500 4th Street; tel: (415) 546-6300. Not much ambience in this century-old saloon, to say the least, but great rock 'n' roll and blues. Open mike on Mondays.
- Yoshi's on Fillmore: 1330 Fillmore Street; tel: (415) 655-5600. Continuing the Yoshi's tradition, only the best jazz and Japanese food, including an excellent sushi bar.

Not So Classical For Everyone
- **March**—Jewish Music Festival: Klezmer, Yidddish, jazz, sacred, and world music, in various venues in the Bay Area
- **March–June**—SF Jazz Spring Season: Various venues
- **June**—San Francisco Accordion Festival: The city' official instrument plays at the Cannery.
- **July**—North Beach Jazz Festival
- **July**—Fillmore Street Jazz Festival
- **September**—San Francisco Blues Festival on the Great Meadow at Fort Mason
- **October**—Hardly Strictly Bluegrass festival in Golden Gate Park
- **Mid-October to Mid-November**—San Francisco Jazz Festival: Two weeks of jazz, in venues around the city.

Wanna Dance?

From salsa to swing, you can find dance opportunities in dozens of venues around the city, whether live to a band, with a disc jockey, or in places where there is just a jukebox and an empty space in front of it. When you check out dance clubs, find out the hours of opening and the cover charges.

And do you want to dance the Nutcracker, yourself? Well, you can—along with professionals giving a real performance—at the annual Dance-Along-Nutcracker, put on by the San Francisco Lesbian/Gay Freedom Band. You do not have to be gay, of course, for anyone who is ever had a yen to dance comes and does so. Check the tabloids for the date each year, or access the band's Internet site (website: http://www.sflgfb.org).

- Harry Denton's Starlight Room at Sir Francis Drake Hotel; tel: (415) 395-8595. A great view from the hotel top, mellow music and dancing in a more formal setting.
- Ruby Skye, 420 Mason Street; tel: (415) 693-0777. An old Victorian theater remodeled into a modern two-level club, with a large dance floor, and good music spun by entertaining DJ's,
- Ten 15 Club, 1015 Folsom; tel: (415) 431-1200. Three floors of loud techno music, lots of space for dancing until early in the morning.
- DNA Lounge, 375 11th Street; tel: (415) 626-1409. Trendy locale, cutting-edge live music with a good sound system, one of the best for dancing.
- Metronome Dance Center, 1830 17th Street; tel: (415) 252-9000. Dance lessons and general dancing in a real ballroom below Potrero Hill. Do not expect to drink or snack; dancing is serious fun here.
- Roccapulco, 3140 Mission Street, near Cesar Chavez; tel: (415) 648-6611. Salsa is the beat in this large two-story club, performed by visiting international groups.

FILMS

Films play a major part in the entertainment life of San Franciscans. If you are looking for a film, you will have lots of choices: first-run American movies, major foreign films in their original language (with subtitles in English), independent art films, and revivals of some of those that have been overlooked or almost forgotten. Almost all the newly released films can be found in different venues at different times, making it convenient to see one where and when you want.

The major movie theaters are multi-screen. The largest (so far) is the Sony Metreon at Mission and 4th Street, with 15 screens, the largest IMAX screen in the country, restaurants, theme and game areas, and retail shops. AMC Van Ness has 14 screens; the AMC Sundance has eight. In a very few (Opera Plaza) some of the screening rooms (and screens) are quite small, so there, too, if you think a film will be popular and the theater will be crowded, go early to get a seat. And, despite the number of theaters, lines can be long for the most popular films, so be prepared to go early and to wait. Often there are two lines: the "ticket holders" line for people who have already bought their tickets, and the line for those waiting to purchase them.

New films open on Friday. Film schedules are printed in every daily newspaper, and on Friday there are film reviews. The free tabloids—*The Examiner*, *The Bay Guardian* and *SF Weekly*—also review films, as do the gay newspapers, *The Bay Area Reporter* and the *Bay Times*.

New People at 1746 Post Street in Japantown; cinema tel: (415) 525-8600, is a new state-of-the-art entertainment and shopping complex, with an underground cinema showing both Japanese and Western classics, documentaries, and animations. Another floor showcases the trendiest Japanese brands, an art gallery, and the New People outlet. Various eating opportunities make this a one-stop destination.

Interesting and Unusual

Some cinemas are known for their particular mix. The Castro hosts revivals and many of the film festivals during the year. The Landmark Chain—with their five theaters—are heavy on international films. And at Opera Plaza, you can often find films that were already shown at other theaters; catch them here before they disappear altogether. Some small "cult" cinemas show unusual foreign films, "art" films, and other independent films that might not be commercial enough to hit the bigger houses.

Films are also sometimes screened at museums, and experimental avant garde films of the San Francisco Cinematheque are shown in several venues around the city. Do check also the film schedules of the various foreign language institutes: Goethe Institute (German), Alliance Française (French), and the Istituto Italiano di Cultura (Italian).

Prices and Bargains

Most theaters offer a "bargain matinee" for the first performance of the day. The Landmark chain offers a multi-ticket discount coupon, and AMC theaters have a card that offers a free film after 20 visits. A regular adult ticket currently costs around US$ 10. Seniors are allowed discounts at any showing, and theaters differ in the age they consider a person a senior—anywhere between 55 and 65.

You can buy tickets in advance for major shows. AMC theaters have a ticket machine in the lobbies. Otherwise, you can go either to the box office and purchase your ticket for a screening later that day or you can call Moviefone and get information on films, and theaters, and order tickets by phone (tel: (415) 777-3456). Most cinemas accept credit cards.

Film Festivals

There are film festivals almost every month, some lasting a few days, or one week or even two weeks. Some draw the entire city to major movie houses, some are revivals shown in smaller venues. Look for festivals that celebrate local film and video makers, of which there are many. Films to be shown have their dates and venues announced well in advance, and often they are screened in more than one theater around the Bay Area.

Film festivals are eagerly awaited, and although there are many of them, they are often sold out, so buy your tickets well in advance. Look in the papers also for film festivals in Berkeley, Oakland, and in Marin.

- January—Berlin and Beyond: German-language festival at the Castro Theater
- January—Noir City 4: Film noir festival, with films, books, arts and music, at the Balboa Theater and Palace of fine arts.
- February—San Francisco Independent Film Festival: Roxie and Castro Theaters: Best of independent local and other films and videos.
- Mid-March—Asian-American Film Festival, at the Kabuki and Castro theatres
- Mid-April—San Francisco International Film Festival: Two weeks of films, held mainly at the Castro and Kabuki, and other venues
- Sometime in April—Italian Film Festival: Various venues around the city.
- Mid-May—San Francisco Documentary Film Festival: Sometimes lighthearted, more often serious. At the Roxie.
- June—San Francisco Black Film Festival: Celebrating African American films and the African cultural diaspora. At the Delancey Street Theater and elsewhere.
- Late in June—International GLBT Film Festival, coinciding with Gay Pride celebration. Generally at the Castro, Victoria and Roxie theatres.
- Mid-July—Silent Film Festival: Silent films as art and history, accompanied by live music. At the Castro.
- Sometime in July—San Francisco Jewish Film Festival: International films with a Jewish theme, generally at the Castro, in Berkeley, and in Mill Valley.
- Sometime in September—Festival Cine Latino, held at the University of San Francisco.
- Late September—Arab Film Festival. Documentaries and other films, from the Arab cinema.
- Mid-November—American Indian Film Festival, held at the Palace of Fine Arts Theater.
- Sometime in November—The Film Arts Festival of Independent Cinema shows works from Bay Area filmmakers. At several venues, including the Castro and the Roxie, plus the Main Library and Asian Art Museum.

> For street fairs, see page 45.
> For film festivals, see previous page.
> For classical music events and festivals, see page 296–297.
> For jazz and blues festivals, see page 299.

And Last, for a Laugh

Not all culture is serious, and not everything serious is culture, either. Laughter rules! Each comedian tries to be more innovative than the other, and those who get the most laughs stay around the longest. Most comedians often poke fun—serious or not—at local and national politicians, and the audience eats it up.

If you are around on October 1st, it is Comedy Celebration Day at Sharon Meadow in Golden Gate Park; you are sure to have a laugh. And, from July to September, the San Francisco Mime Troupe puts on performances in public parks around the Bay Area. Not exactly silent, to say the least, the performances contain outright mimicry, farce, satire, and relevant political jabs. Hugely entertaining. (tel: (415) 285-1717).

- Beach Blanket Babylon, 678 Beach Blanket Babylon Boulevard, Green Street; tel: (415) 421-4222. A totally zany musical spoof of pop culture (and local celebrities) which has been running for 30 years, changing its content to fit the times.
- Teatro Zinzanni, Pier 29 on the Embarcadero; tel: 438-2668. A European night-club setting, a cabaret, circus performers, "divas and madmen," and a madcap spectacle, all while eating a five course dinner.
- Cobb's Comedy Club, 915 Columbus Avenue; tel: (415) 928-4320. Attractive new digs for this old club with new comedians and some musicians.
- The Punchline, 444 Battery Street, at Washington; tel: (415) 397-7573. Punchline hosts nationally-known comics as well as local hopefuls.

NATIONAL HOLIDAYS AND LOCAL EVENTS

An international city, San Francisco celebrates the festivals of many other countries as well as its own.

The 1894 Japanese Tea Garden in Golden Gate Park, known for its koi-filled pools, streams, bridges, and charming tea house, is popular with locals and tourists alike.

The Museum of Modern Art in the trendy SoMa—South of Market—district, opened in 1995. Its collections offer works by both modern masters and younger, less-established artists.

One of San Francisco's eclectic districts is the Haight Ashbury, known for the hippie 1967 "Summer of Love." Still a haven for the current counter-culture, the area is known as the Upper Haight to locals.

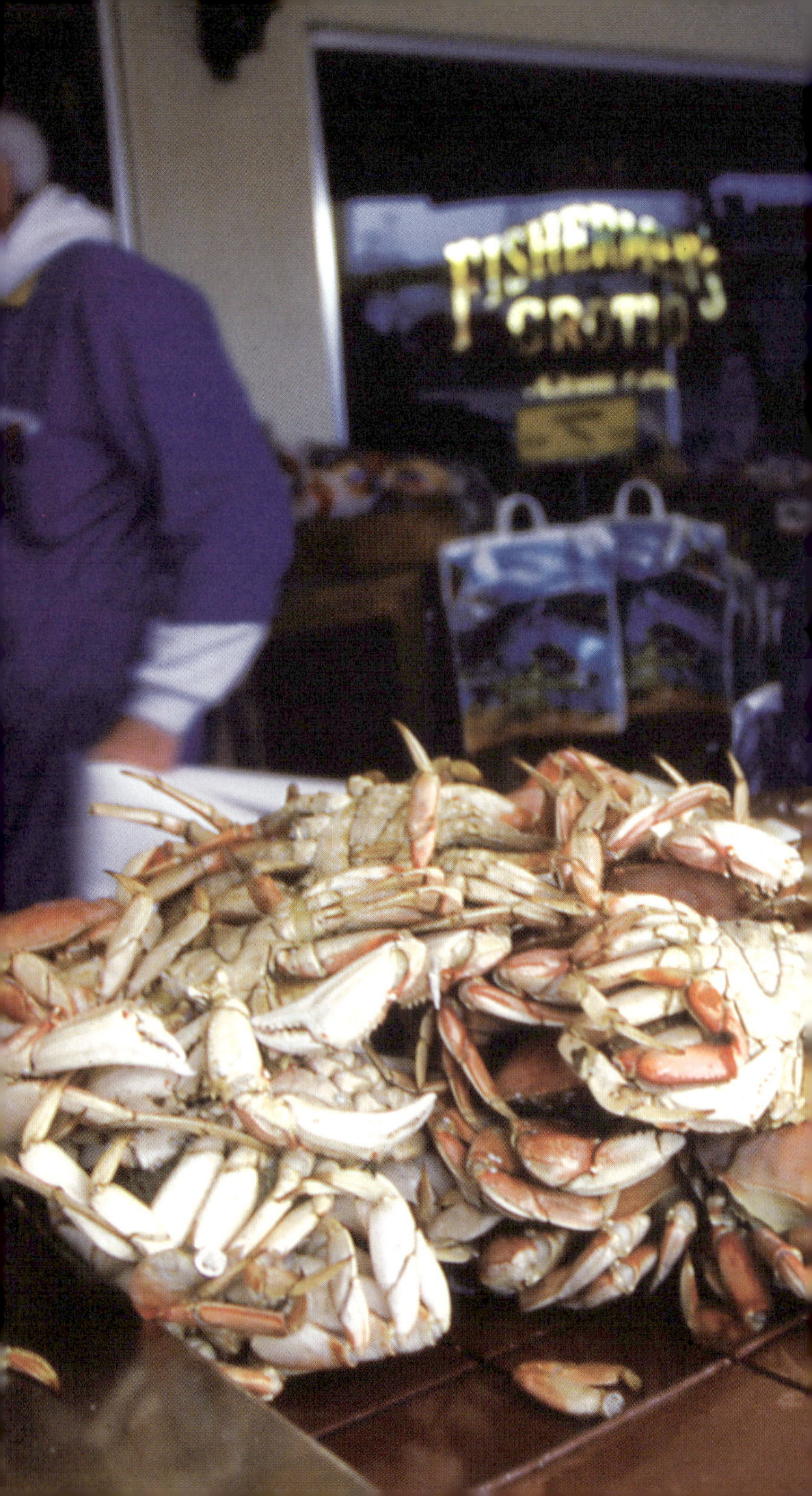

Dungerness crab is a popular delicacy served at San Francisco's Fisherman's Wharf. Watching the chefs prepare the dish is a tourist attraction in itself.

There are many recreational options in San Francisco; you can take a rowboat or pedal boat out on Stow Lake in Golden Gate Park (above) or cycle around and explore the city (below).

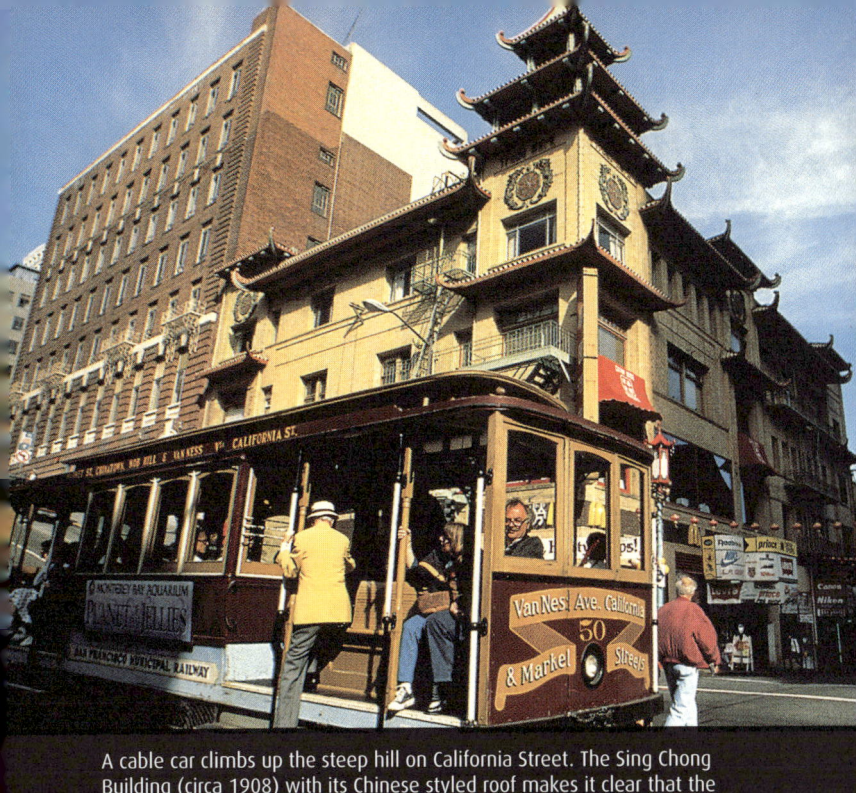

A cable car climbs up the steep hill on California Street. The Sing Chong Building (circa 1908) with its Chinese styled roof makes it clear that the attractions of Chinatown await.
Below: Tourists and locals shop in the largest Chinatown outside of Asia, and the oldest in the United States.

San Francisco is a constant surprise, as tourists quickly understand. Don't forget to bring your camera.

Festival dates may vary from year to year, often depending on the day of the week on which the event falls, and many national holidays are celebrated on Monday, no matter the actual date they commemorate, giving workers a long weekend break. On national holidays, all government offices are closed, including the Post Office; except for Christmas and Easter, the largest stores and supermarkets may be open for at least part of the day. Banks are closed on national holidays but by law may not be closed more than three days in a row, and on any day cash can be had from the ubiquitous ATM machines.

As for the purely local events, do not forget that San Franciscans love to party. When there is nothing official to celebrate and no occurrence to remember, San Francisco creates its own. You can find a parade, fair, race, or walk in honor of a charitable cause almost every weekend of the year.

It would be impossible to list all the events here. Keep current by checking the *Sunday San Francisco Chronicle*, or the weekly *The Bay Guardian* and *SF Weekly*. These will also print updates and announcements on the festivals and fairs in towns throughout the Bay Area, especially the county fairs in summer. And, you can get cultural event information from the Visitors' Information Center on the lower level of Hallidie Plaza, at Market Street and Powell, on the Internet, and also on a recorded telephone message (tel: (415) 391-2000; 24-hour recorded info tel: (415) 391-2001; website: http://www.onlyinsanfrancisco.com).

The following list is a calendar of the most widely known public events in San Francisco:

January

- 1: New Year's Day (National Holiday)
- All month: Dine-About-Town: More than 100 fine restaurants offer lunches and dinners at special prices.
- Third Monday: Martin King Jr Day (National Holiday). In honor of the civil rights leader slain in 1968.
- Late month/early February: Tet Festival. Held near the Civic Center. A multicultural event, with Asian, Latino and African American groups celebrating Vietnamese New Year.

- Zinfandel Festival: Some 300 wineries participate in this mega-tasting of California's own grape.

February
- All month: San Francisco Crab Festival: Restaurants offer Dungeness Crab dishes according to their particular recipes. Mexican, Italian, French, etc.
- Third Monday: President's Day (National Holiday)
- Dates vary: Chinese New Year. A long parade, marching bands, dragons, and lots of firecrackers.
- San Francisco Ballet season begins.

March
- Sunday closest to March 17: Saint Patrick's Day Parade. All the Irish bars celebrate well into the night.
- Late month: Tulip Festival at Pier 39.

April
- 1: Saint Stupid's Day Parade on April Fool's Day: Costume parade starts at Justin Herman Plaza and goes up Market Street.
- Mid-month: Cherry Blossom Festival at the Japan Center. Parade, arts and crafts, tea ceremonies, performances, all held on two successive weekends.
- Baseball season begins: Opening games for San Francisco Giants and Oakland A's.
- End of April: Opening day on the Bay. Sailing season starts with a boat parade and a blessing of the fleet.

May
- 5: Cinco de Mayo: Latin American festival and parade at the Civic Center and at Parque de Niños, 23rd and Folsom.
- Third Sunday: Bay to Breakers Race. 7.5 mile (12.07 km) race, from the Bay to the ocean. A San Francisco "happening," drawing 100,000 runners, would-be runners, people in outrageous costumes, some in no costumes at all.
- Third Sunday: AIDS Candlelight Memorial March and Vigil; Castro and Market Streets; Annual candlelight procession from the Castro to the Main Library.

- Opening day on the Bay: Official sailing season begins.
- Odd-numbered years only: Black and White Ball. The whole city comes to this charity benefit held in various venues. Wear only black or white, dance, and listen to the music.
- Last Monday: Memorial Day (National Holiday)
- Memorial Day Weekend: Carnaval. Large and lively multi-cultural festival and parade in the Mission district.

June
- Early month: Escape from Alcatraz. Triathlon contest: 1.5 mile (2.4 km) swim to Alcatraz, 18-mile (29-km) bike ride and 8-mile run, finishing at the Marina Green.
- Mid-Month: Fiesta Filipina: Philippine Independence Day, celebrated with a great fair, entertainment and pageants.
- Fourth Sunday: SF LGBT Pride Celebration. Week-long festivities and an enormous parade drawing a million people from around the world. Second largest annual event in the State (after the Rose Bowl Parade), with 200 floats, people strolling alone or as couples, celebration on until all hours. This includes the Saturday night Dyke March.
- Dates vary: San Francisco Ethnic Dance Festival. Dozens of ethnic dance troupes and soloists perform at the Palace of Fine Arts.

July
- 4: Independence Day (Known as the Fourth of July). (National Holiday)
- Waterfront Festival: Near Fisherman's Wharf and Pier 39. Entertainment, food stalls, fireworks.
- Midmonth: San Francisco Marathon. Twenty-six mile (41.8-km) course from Golden Gate Park to the Civic Center.
- Books by the Bay: Yerba Buena Gardens; booksellers' booths, discussions of books, authors' events and book signings.

August
- Date varies: Football season begins. San Francisco 49ers pre-opening game.

- Early month: Jerry Day. Concert and fun, celebrating the birthday of Jerry Garcia, the late leader of the Grateful Dead.
- Late in month: Obon Festival and Bon Dance. Buddhist "Festival of the Souls," includes taiko drumming, traditional music, chldren's activities and the evening Bon Dance.

September
- First Monday: Labor Day. (National Holiday)
- Labor Day Weekend: A La Carte, à la Park—Sharon Meadow, Golden Gate Park. Food fair, with offerings from some of San Francisco's popular restaurants. Tastings of California's best wines, as well.
- Latino Summer Fiesta: 24th Street and Mission; formerly celebrating Mexican Independence Day, it is now a general patriotic Latino festival. Crafts, booths, food, entertainment.
- September–October: San Francisco Free Shakespeare in the Park. Plays performed outdoors at the Main Post Lawn in the Presidio.
- San Francisco Opera and Symphony season begins; also a free afternoon of opera in Golden Gate Park on the first Sunday of the season.

October
- Early in month: Blessing of the Animals at Saint Boniface Church, near the Civic Center. On the Feast Day of Saint Francis of Assisi, the patron saint of animals, this is the annual pet-blessing event.
- Early in month: Immigrant Pride Day. Since 1995, a threefold event celebrating Immigrant Pride Day, Dia de la Raza, and Indigenous People's Day, at 24th Street, from Mission Street to Bryant.
- Early month: Litquake. Literary festival showcasing Bay Area writers. Readings, films, discussions at various venues.
- Second Monday: Columbus Day. Columbus Day parade elebrates the Italian heritage in San Francisco. Festivities, in North Beach and at Fisherman's Wharf, including a blessing of the fishing fleet.

- Around Columbus Day, Fleet Week: The U.S. Navy comes to town, and the Blue Angels, precision Navy flyers, take to the skies over San Francisco.
- Closest to full moon: Chinese Moon Festival, annual harvest event in Chinatown.
- Mid-month: Open Studios. Artists all over town open their studios to the public.
- Toward the end of the month. San Francisco Book Festival. San Francisco Bay Area Book Council sponsors a major independent bookseller event at Fort Mason.
- 31: Halloween. Celebrated around the Civic Center, but especially in the Castro, with wonderfully outrageous costumes. One of the major events of the year.
- Exotic Erotic Ball: A weekend blast of entertainment and dancers, the more outrageous the costume, the better. At the Cow palace. For adults only.

November
- 2: Dia de los Muertos. Mexican honoring of the dead, with a fiesta, exhibits, and parade, lighting of candles at a specially-contructed altar. In the Mission.
- 11: Veterans Day. Parade along Market Street to the Ferry Building.
- Fourth Thursday: Thanksgiving Day (National Holiday)
- Late in month: Run to the Far Side. Walk or run, dressed in a costume depicting your favorite cartoon character from Gary Larson's Far Side cartoons. Benefit for the California Academy of Sciences.

December
- Dates vary: Christmas Tree and Chanukah Menorah lighting in various venues around the city: Union Square, Ghirardelli Square, Fisherman's Wharf.
- Mid-month: Sing-it-yourself-Messiah, at Louise M. Davies Symphony Hall. The San Francisco Conservatory of Music gives people the chance to sing Handel's Messiah.
- All month: Nutcracker Suite performed by San Francisco Ballet.
- 25: Christmas Day (National Holiday)

AND MORE AROUND THE BAY: THE WINE COUNTRY
Paradise Awaits!

California grows grapes and produces wine in large portions of the state, starting in the south near Santa Barbara, stretching north to Mendocino, and thriving through the central San Joaquin Valley and as far to the east as the Sierra foothills up into the Gold Country. But, the two best-known and revered valleys—which are known as the Wine Country—are Napa and Sonoma. And fortunately these are within an hour's drive of San Francisco, by car or on a tour. If you have had enough of fog and cool winds for a day or so, there is nothing like the Wine Country to warm your soul.

The Wine Country deserves a book of its own (and several have been written), but even this necessarily brief overview can say the one important thing: Go! No matter how short your time, no matter if you are someone who prefers a martini to the fruit of the vine, the Wine Country is not to be missed. There is wine tasting in hundreds of wineries to be sure, but there are also dazzling views, splendid parks, spas that offer hot volcanic mud baths, a petrified forest and a geyser, hot-air balloon rides, charming towns to stroll, golf courses galore, and numerous restaurants that serve the local bounty and the counties' own wines. So, it is best to spend a few days, if you can. But since these two spectacular valleys are so close to San Francisco, even if you can spare only one day from your exploration of The City, you can still get an idea of what the Wine Country has to offer. Then, without doubt you will begin your planning to come back for more. Nine million visitors come to these valleys each year, and many of them are locals who come back time and time again.

Resources

For detailed information about the Wine Country (more than you could possibly use on a short visit), visit the Valleys' tourist offices, or before you go, access their information online. Information about tours can be had at The San Francisco Visitors Center.

Napa Valley Visitors Bureau, 1310 Napa Town Center, off First Street, Napa; tel: (707) 226-7459; website: http://www.napavalley.com.

Sonoma Valley Visitors Bureau, 453 First Street East, Sonoma; tel: (707) 996-1090; website: http://www.sonomavalley.com. Or try accessing these:
- The Wine Country; website: http://www.winecountry.com
- Napa Valley Wineries; website: http://www.napavintners.com/index.asp
- Sonoma Valley Wineries; website: http://www.sonomavalleywine.com/

By Car from The City

By car, take Highway 101 north over the Golden Gate Bridge. About 20 minutes north, just beyond the turnoff for Nicasio is the exit for Highway 37, clearly marked for Napa/Sonoma. Continue on 37 for about 5 miles (8.05 km), until you see signs for route 121.
- For Sonoma, take the left turnoff on route 121.
- For Glen Ellen, take the 121 turnoff; at the 4-way traffic light, continue straight on Arnold Drive. Or go into Sonoma itself and follow the signs to Route 12.
- For all towns in Napa, keep going on 37 until you get to route 29. Turn north.

Route 29, the main north-south route in Napa, has the most famous wineries and restaurants and is fairly commercial. If you have time, though, take the Silverado Trail from Napa up to Calistoga. You can still visit the wineries, many of which are located between the two roads, but the Trail is less traffic-clogged and the atmosphere is more relaxed.

The Climate

So, now you are in the sun and the air is probably gloriously clear. In fact, it is the climate and the soil that make these valleys produce the exquisite wines they do. Both valleys have the moderate climates one associates with Mediterranean countries; warm dry summers and fairly mild, wet winters. Yet both areas experience several microclimates: areas closer to the coast are affected by the Pacific fog and winds and have cooler days, while inland valleys, protected by the surrounding hills, are warmer. When the winter damp season ends and the hills turn from lush green to golden yellow, when the days are warm and the nights cool, the grapes ripen slowly and evenly. Wine aficionados pay attention to the climate and whether there is even a drop of rain, for these affect whether the harvest will be good, fine, or—as one always hopes—exceptional.

And Now The Wines...

First, the Grapes

Make no mistake: some of the wineries you visit may be charming and small, homey and folksy, but wine is big business here, and nothing less. Ninety percent of all American wine is made in California. The wine Country (including also Mendocino County to the north) produces more than US$ 1 billion each year, and Napa's contribution to this is more than US$ 500 million, with Sonoma next with just under that amount. In 2007, the average price for cabernet grapes was a whopping US$ 4,137 per ton.

To give an idea of the scope of the planting in these two valleys: in the Sonoma Valley alone, some 16,000 acres (6,475 ha) are planted with Chardonnay grapes for white wine, and 12,000 acres (4,856 ha) of Cabernet Sauvignon for red. The Pinot Noir grape accounts for 10,000 acres (4,047 ha) and Merlot another 7,500 (3,035 ha). Of course there are others, including 5,000 acres (2,023 ha) of California's own special grape, Zinfandel, which is found primarily in Napa, just east of the Mayacamas ridge.

Although there are many different grapes grown in the valley—including chenin blanc, pinot grigio, san giovese, syrah, gewürtstraminer—those listed here command the most acreage in the valleys. If a wine highlights the grape on the label, it is a "varietal," meaning that 75 percent of the wine is made from that grape alone. Others used for blending make up 25 per cent or less.

- **Cabernet Sauvignon**: This grape—called the "king of

reds"—makes some of the most popular red wines in the United States. It is the most widely planted red grape in California. Complex and fairly tannic, the flavors among the different "Cabs" vary, as the grape sometimes takes on various subtle reminiscences of black currents, bell peppers, olives, or even mint. This depends on just where the vines are located and their aspect. Cabernets are best when they have been aged at least three or four years.

- **Chardonnay**: Chardonnay is the state's number one grape. To give an idea of the numbers, up to 500,000 tons of the chardonnay grape may be crushed in one year. A wide-ranging wine, Chardonnays can vary according to the vintner, varying from buttery and soft, or fresh and crisp, to rich and multi-layered. They are often aged in oak, but lately the lighter, fruitier Chardonnays have become popular, with less oak aging. The popular Chablis is also made from the Chardonnay grape.
- **Merlot**: It used to be that Merlot was used primarily for blending wines—to soften the more tannic Cabernet, for example—but since the Nineties, it has become popular on its own. The grapes are softer than Cabernets, owing to a smaller percentage of tannin, and many can be drunk young. The longer they age, however, the more complex they become.
- **Pinot Noir**: Pinot Noir is lighter in its redness and less tannic than either Cabernet or Merlot. Now that the craze for Merlot is somewhat abating, the Pinot Noir is regaining its rightful popularity. Pinot Noir is also important for sparkling wines.
- **Sauvignon Blanc**: This grape makes two kinds of wine, the varied Sauvignon Blanc and the full-bodied Fumé Blanc. Sauvignon Blanc is a versatile grape, producing a rather zesty wine, sometimes with a grassy overtone. The more complex, deeper wines often have a strong fruity taste.
- **Zinfandel**: Although related to the Italian Primitivo, Zinfandel is known as California's own red grape, thriving in warm coastal valleys. The red "Zins" are

generally tannic and rich, especially those of the late harvest, which may have peppery hints. The white "blush" Zinfandels are lighter, less complex, and somewhat sweeter than the reds.

Sparkling Wines

The term Champagne may be applied only to sparkling wines that are produced in the Champagne region of France. Thus, even though the wonderful bubblies of the Wine Country employ the traditional *methode champenoise*, they still are designated as "sparkling wines."

Generally, sparkling wines are made from blends of Pinot Noir and Chardonnay grapes. If the wine is pinkish, then the red skins of the Pinot Noir have been left longer, in order to create the tint. Although some are vintage dated, many are not, since the wines also contain a small blending from the previous year. Sparkling wines are labeled according to their sweetness:

- Extra Brut: Totally dry
- Brut: dry
- Extra Dry: Medium dry
- Sec: Slightly sweet
- Demi-sec: Pretty sweet
- Doux: Sweet

There are several excellent producers of bubblies in the Wine Country. Most assess a charge for the tastings, as do many of the other wineries in the valleys.

- **Sonoma**—Gloria Ferrer, 23555 Carneros Highway, 95476 is one of the premier producers of bubblies in the United States; tel: (707) 996-7256; website: http://www.gloriaferrer.com. Sip Carneros sparkling or still wines, and sit on the terrace and enjoy the view while you sip.
- **Napa**—Domaine Chandon, One California Drive, Highway 29 at Yountville; tel: (707) 944-2280; website: http://www.chandon.com. This is the most elegant of the sparkling wine houses, founded more than thirty years ago by the French Champagne producer Moët et Chandon. The winery is landscaped beautifully, the

restaurant is elegant (more formal at dinnertime), and some half-dozen sparkling wines are featured. Reserve well in advance for the restaurant (and for the terrace), which is open daily for lunch and dinner.
- **Napa**—Schramsberg; 1400 Schramsberg Road, just west of Calistoga; tel (I): (707) 942-2414; tel (II): (800) 877-3623; website: http://www.schramsberg.com. This winery has been here since 1862, and it now specializes in sparkling wines. There are eight different bubblies to choose among. Tours and tasting are by appointment only.

The Wineries

In the Napa and Sonoma valleys there are hundreds of wineries—some offering many wines and different brands, and "boutiques" that make just a few types of wine under one brand name. Napa alone has some 400 wineries, many of which flank the bisecting Highway 29. Almost all have tasting rooms, with opportunities not just to taste the wines, but to learn about the grapes, the winemaking process, and the differences that give the wines their own particular essence. Some of the wineries also have picnic tables and gift shops, and some offer full meals to show off the range of their wines. The tourist offices have information about wineries in their areas, and the Internet sites of the winery associations have detailed information on all aspects of wine.

Although the wineries produce several different kinds of wine, many are known for particular types of wine. If you are a true wine aficionado and intend to taste the wines of just one or two types of grapes, do your research in advance to maximize your time. And do not forget to try the various Zinfandels in the wineries of both valleys. "Zin" is a California experience not to be missed.

In Between Tastings...

Balloon Rides

Colorful hot-air balloons soar high above the Wine Country, giving their passengers a sublime overview of the valleys below. It is hard to want to come down after floating serenely in almost silent wonder across the beautiful Northern California sky, looking down at the lush landscape, the small towns, and the thousands of vines below. (How fortunate, though, that taking in the countryside from the ground is almost equally sublime.) The ride over the Sonoma valley shows different sights than that of Napa, of course, and so you might want to do both!

Balloon rides start shortly after sunrise, when the breezes are mild and the air is fairly stable. They do not take off if the winds are too strong. The rides last up to about two hours, more or less. The balloons float between 500–2,000 feet (152.4–609.6 m) above the valley floor, and the baskets hold 2–4 people, some up to 8–10. Prices generally are toward US$ 200 per person. Pilots are FAA-certified, and although the flights are safe, most companies require passengers to read the safety rules and affirm in writing that they have read them.

Most of the companies offer personalized rides, one way or another, allowing for more or fewer passengers, wedding celebrations, or whatever suits your fancy Most offer a brunch afterwards. And some offer shuttle service from San Francisco hotels.

- **Napa**—Balloons Above the Valley, 603 California Boulevard, Nap 94559; tels: (800) 464-6824; (707) 253-2222; website: http://www.balloonrides.com

- **Napa**—Napa Valley Aloft offers several different opportunities for ballooning; check its website: http://www.nvaloft.com.
- **Napa**—Napa Valley Balloons, P.O. Box 2860, Yountville 94599; tels: (800) 253-2224; (707) 944-0228; website: http://www.napavalleyballoons.com
- **Sonoma**—Wine Country Balloons, 2508 Burnside Road, Sebastopol 95472; tels: (707) 538-7359; (888) 238-6359; website: http://www.balloontours.com). When you reserve, ask for directions to the meeting place, 3 miles (4.83 km) north of Santa Rosa.
- **Sonoma**—Up & Away Ballooning, P.O. Box 68, Windsor 95492; tels: (707) 836-0171; (800) 711-2998; website: http://www.up-away.com

Petrified Forest

The Petrified Forest at 4100 Petrified Forest Road Calistoga 94515 is what remains of an ancient redwood forest that was buried millions of years ago during a massive and long-lasting volcanic eruption (tel: (707) 942-6667; website: http://www.petrifiedforest.org). Hot ash mixed with rains over thousands of years buried the toppled trees. Then, organic matter, silicon, and oxygen, piled high during millions of years, slowly petrified and turned to stone. Hidden until erosion and the upward movement of the earth finally exposed some of the tips of this Pliocene forest, excavations about 150 years ago found an astounding forest of massive redwoods, completely made of stone.

Although privately owned, the Petrified Forest is a California Historical Landmark. It is open every day, closing slightly earlier in winter. You will find it between Santa Rosa and Calistoga on the Mark West Spring Road, at Calistoga Road.

Jack London State Historic Park

Jack London State Historic Park is in Glen Ellen, off Arnold Drive on London Ranch Road (tel: (707) 938-5216; website: http://www.jacklondonpark.com). Named after Jack London (1876–1916) a famous and prolific San Francisco-born writer, whose most celebrated book was *Call of the Wild*, the Park was originally London's 1400-acre (566.6-ha) ranch. Now visitors can see the buildings that remain, including the ruins of Wolf House, which London designed and built, but which burned down in 1913, just weeks before he and his wife were to move in. The furniture that he designed is also on view. After London's death in 1916, his widow built The House of Happy Walls, which is now the Park's museum and visitor center. A memorial to London, there are photographs and exhibits about his life, and a gift shop that sells his books.

But there is much more to the park. Evidence of previous occupants—from early natives to miners and their old homesteads—can be seen as you walk along the hiking and nature trails. (Do stay on trails, avoiding the poison oak and occasional rattlesnakes.) Not far away—about 0.5 mile—is a lake with a dam and bathhouse built by London, and there are wonderful views of the Valley of the Moon. You can walk up to the summit of Sonoma Mountain, or you can ride a bike or horseback along the several ridges (reservations tel: (707) 933-1600). In addition to self-guided tours there are some that are docent-led. In Spring, there are interesting Wildflower Walks.

Picnic Provisions

If you have spent the morning wandering in the parks, or if you are heading to one of the wineries that has picnic tables, you are going to want a delicious picnic. You have come to the right place.

- **Sonoma**—Sonoma Cheese Factory, 2 Spain Street; tel: (707) 966-1931. This really is a cheese factory, the home of all the varieties of Sonoma Jack. The deli offers local breads and meats—all the fixin's for a picnic. Look around, for there is a lot to choose from in this extensive deli.
- **Napa**—Oakville Grocery, 7856 Saint Helena Highway, Oakville; tel: (707) 944-8802. An oldtime country store with the most modern of artisan cheeses, meats, smoked fish, local produce, and California wines. Bakery offers fresh pastries and good coffee, plus unforgettable homemade cookies.

Mud Baths

Yes, mud baths. Calistoga is the home of a dozen spas, most of which feature a relaxing bath—covered up to your neck—in hot volcanic ash, mixed with peat and hot mineral water. It is not nearly as weird as it sounds. As you float almost supine in the tub of hot mud, the minerals and heat draw out the toxins from your body, and you emerge—after having been scraped off, of course—relaxed and ready for the next healthful rounds: often a bath in hot mineral water, a steam, and then a massage. By the time you're done, you do not remember that you ever had a care in the world.

Since the late 1800s when the railroad made the area easily accessible, visitors have flocked by the thousands to "take the waters" at Calistoga's many spas. Deep in the earth, an underground river flows over magma—molten rock—and it is this naturally hot mineral water that provides the waters for the town's spas, as well as the Calistoga Water that is served in so many restaurants. Today there are spas with lodgings, day spas, and even spas for couples, as most mineral baths are not co-ed. Mud baths are popular, so make sure to reserve in advance. Herewith a few:

- Dr. Wilkinson's Hot Springs Resort, 1507 Lincoln Avenue; tel: (707) 942-4102; website: http://www.drwilkinson.com.
- Golden Haven Hot Springs, 1713 Lake Street; tel: (707) 942-8000; website: http://www.goldenhaven.com
- The Spa: 1202 Pine Street; tel: (707) 942-4056; website: www.thespacalistoga.com

Old Faithful Geyser

It is no accident that with those underground waters heated by the deep pockets of magma, there is a geyser right in the middle of Calistoga. Take the time to visit Old Faithful Geyser, at 1299 Tubbs Lane (tel: (707) 942-6463; website: http://www.oldfaithfulgeyser.com). There are three "Old Faithful" geysers in the world: the most famous for Americans is in Yellowstone National Park, another is in New Zealand, and the third is here in Calistoga, California.

"Old Faithful" is less a name than a category, referring to a geyser that erupts on a regular, periodic basis. As the water boils deep underground, it expands and moves into empty spaces, shooting upwards in a cloud of steam and scalding water. Calistoga's Old Faithful erupts every 45 minutes or so, its boiling water and steam shooting 60 feet up into the sky. It is truly amazing. The exhibit on geysers and earthquakes explains how these phenomena occur and that there may well be a correlation between deviations in the eruptions of the geyser and the appearance of earthquakes.

OVER LAND AND ON THE SEA
A Wealth of Choice!

Northern California is so varied and beautiful—with wild bluffs, forests, mountains and ridges, fertile valleys, charming towns, and even a 14,000-foot (4,267.2-m) volcano (Mount Shasta) a bit farther north—that it is hard to suggest just a few outings for those who are here only a short time. There is also more to relish within just a few hours of the City by the Bay in any of the four directions—yes, even to the west on the ocean itself—that there will certainly be something to appeal to your imagination, time, and budget. It should be no surprise that many of the attractions have to do with the appreciation of the natural beauty of the area, and after all, it is California that you are here to see. You can see it all, but you can get an idea of what the area has to offer and immediately start thinking about coming back.

This list puts together some sights that must not be missed in themselves and others that may easily combined into a one-day outing, which should maximize your understanding of why Northern California inspires such awe—adding to the sensation that there will always be more to see and do, no matter how often you come back. In fact, some of the tour companies do combine different excursions into one, such as a one-day tour of Alcatraz, Sausalito, and Muir Woods, for example. Herewith a few that offer a varied selection of tours, some outside the immediate Bay Area, up to Point Reyes and even as far away as Yosemite National Park.

- Blue and Gold Fleet; tel: (415) 705-8200; website: http://www.blueandgoldfleet.com
- Golden Gate Jeep Tours; tel: (415) 567-4400; website: http://www.goldengatejeeptours.com
- Red and White; tel: (415) 673-2900; website: http://www.redandwhite.com
- Super Sightseeing Tours; tel (I): (415) 353-5310; tel (II): (888) 868-7788; website: http://www.supersightseeing.com

Alcatraz and Angel Islands, and Tiburon as well.

In the middle of San Francisco Bay are two large islands, Alcatraz and Angel Island. (The smaller Yerba Buena Island is the mainstay of the Bay Bridge.) For a trip just to Alcatraz, expect to spend about three hours, including the ferry trip and the audio-guided tour. And, since the ferry leaves from Pier 41, it is easy to start first with a morning visit to the tourist shops at Pier 39, to have a coffee while admiring the view, and to glide along the moving footpath through the Aquarium of the Bay. Then get on the ferry at the time you reserved and head out onto the Bay.

Alcatraz (a Spanish name for the gannet bird), the former maximum security prison isolated on a wind-swept rock in the middle of the bay, is now a museum, part of the Golden Gate National Recreation Area (GGNRA) and administered by the National Park Service. Over its 250-year history, the island has served as a military post and a rather inconvenient prison, as all supplies including fresh water had to be brought in by boat. This, plus the fact that several prisoners managed to disappear in 1963 (escaped or drowned) from this rocky crag that was supposed to be escape-proof, determined the closure of the prison in the 1960s. In 1969 it was occupied for about two years by a group of Native Americans, who claimed it as their right. After some 18 months, the island became part of the GGNRA. Now, the factual and anecdotal tours, given by park rangers, describe prison life and some of the infamous inmates once incarcerated here. Walk around the island and see the birds and the life in the tide pools. Or, think perhaps

Alcatraz Island commands a 360-degree view of San Francisco Bay.

of taking the evening tour that displays the entire Bay Area sparkling with lights. It is spectacular.

Angel Island is a state park and wildlife refuge. It is the largest of the islands in the Bay, and it is popular for picnics, hiking, and biking. The views are splendid. The trails are well kept, but for non-hikers there is also a guided tram tour that gives a good overview of the island and its long and varied history. The native Miwoks were here for centuries before the Spaniards displaced them, to explore and settle the surrounding shores. The American government used Angel Island as a military base and then for 100 years as an infamous quarantine station for immigrants, like Ellis Island of New York. Some of the buildings from that era still stand. But now it is preserved for recreation and for wildlife and is popular with tourists and locals alike.

Depending on your starting point and if you are not on a tour, you might check the schedule of the Angel Island-Tiburon Ferry (weekends in winter, and daily in summer). If so, you could go on to Tiburon for a late lunch on a sunny restaurant terrace on the bayside edge of one of the most beautiful of the Marin towns; website: http://www.angelislandferry.com. Admire the spectacular view of the bay and its city across the water, and stroll for a few minutes on the promenade or looking at the shops. The ferry will take you back to San Francisco when you are ready. All in all, a pretty good day.

Ah, Sausalito!

Here are some adjectives to describe Sausalito: quaint, picturesque, romantic, heavenly, Mediterranean, eclectic, adorable. On your way to experiencing them all, start by heading to the historic Ferry Building at the foot of Market Street, one of the few buildings to survive the 1906 earthquake; now beautifully restored, it is worth an hour or more itself. Browse the indoor market stalls and shops or make a tour around the building if it is one of the market days. Then stop a moment at the statue of Gandhi as you approach the Golden Gate Ferry to take you across the bay. Sausalito awaits! Here you will step off the boat into yet another beautiful Bay Area world. Bridgeway is the bayfront promenade, where as you browse the shops you might see San Francisco gleaming in the sun or, as is quite likely, socked in by a blanket of beautifully-white fog. The next street in is Caledonia, also with shops and restaurants to explore. That is all there is here: exquisite beauty, sunshine, and fun. So enjoy your afternoon. Some people call Sausalito paradise. See if you agree.

If you decide to drive, crossing the Golden Gate Bridge—with the bay to your right and the ocean on your left—stay in the right lane and turn off at the first opportunity, into the scenic overlook point. As you gaze at the panorama (if the weather cooperates), think of the Native Americans who lived here for a thousand years, think of the Spaniards who "discovered" the bay, after Sir Francis Drake passed it by (probably on one of those foggy days when he could not see a thing!) and marvel in the beauty as they also must have done. Then get back on the road for the next turnoff winding down into dreamy Sausalito, which actually is quite Northern-California real.

And, if you are driving, this might be the opportunity to continue up Highway 101, to take in Tiburon, or even better, Muir Woods.

Muir Woods and Mount Tamalpais

Some tour companies offer combined excursions to Sausalito and Muir Woods. But no matter how you plan your time, Muir Woods alone is an opportunity to walk among some of the tallest and oldest trees in the world; tel: (415) 338-7059; website: http://www.nps.gov/muwo.

Only 12 miles (19.3 km) north of the Golden Gate Bridge at Mill Valley, up and down steep roads and finally down into an isolated valley, you will find an ancient coastal redwood forest, Muir Woods National Monument. Here you can walk among awe-inspiring 1,000-year old giant trees reaching 260 feet (79.25 m) up into the sky. You can see tall Douglas fir, big-leaf maples, tanbark oak, and bay laurels nestling under their even taller, majestic neighbors. This is the way Northern California might still look if it had not been for loggers, and these beauties too might have been cut in the 1800s if the valley had been more accessible. And thanks to a declaration in 1908 by President Theodore Roosevelt, the *sequoia sempervirens*—that grows only along the Pacific coast and reach no farther than 20 miles (32.2 km) inland—has been protected and preserved. (Note that the famous, massive *sequoia sequoiadendron giganteum* grows only in California's Sierra Nevada Mountains, and can be seen in Yosemite National Park.) Except for Big Basin State Park, an even larger stand of redwoods, and which is about 55 miles (88.5 km) south of San Francisco, this is the only place you will see these original growth lovelies. It is worth a trip.

Route 66 is a shuttle bus to Muir Woods operated by Golden Gate Transit. It leaves from Marin City every half hour on spring and summer weekends; tel: 511; website: http://www.nps.gov/muwo.

Above Muir Woods is Mount Tamalpais, the highest mountain the region, reaching up 2571 feet. On sunny days it has great views, it has nice trails for hiking, and it is a favorite with the locals for a day's escape from city life.

Point Reyes National Seashore

Now, this is nature. Some 30 miles (48.3 km) north of San Francisco on California Highway 1, there is a spectacularly wild peninsula that juts 10 miles out into the ocean, its bluffs overlooking the not-so pacific crashing waves. This is Point Reyes National Seashore, and there is nothing else like it; (tel: (415) 464-5100; website: http://www.nps.gov/pore. Here are vantage points to view the migration routes of the grey whales (seen especially from Chimney Rock and the Point Reyes Lighthouse (Lighthouse tel: (415) 669-1534), as well as sea lions, harbor seals, and even the seemingly indolent elephant seals on the beaches below. Shore- and seabirds abound. Tide pools teem with life. Off the 147 miles (236.6 km) of trails that traverse the area of 85,000 acres (34,398.9 ha), you might also get a glimpse of the rare Tule elk (at the north end), or some of the 30 other species of land mammals that have found a welcoming—and since 1962 federally protected—habitat. About 20 percent of all California's flowering plant species are represented here so something is no doubt blooming at any time of the year. And, this is definitely earthquake territory, for the peninsula sits atop the northern end of the San Andreas Fault. Along the trails you will see evidence of the earth having moved violently, but you will not notice that it is always moving slightly north, even as you stand admiring the view.

Start at the Bear Valley Visitor Center, which has information about the park, current exhibits and the flora and fauna to be seen, plus historical artifacts. And, when you can bear to tear yourself away, stop for a while at one of the charming coastal towns—Inverness, Point Reyes Station, and Olema—that have refused the encroachment of development. And, if you have time, do not miss Drake's Estero, a saltwater lagoon famed for oysters—about 25 percent of the state's production. A visit to Drake's Oyster Farm (a few miles west of Inverness) allows you to watch the process of oyster farming as well as eating the freshest oysters you can imagine and other local shellfish as well (tel: (415) 669-1149).

East to the Sun: Oakland and Berkeley

Why not spend a day in the East Bay sunshine, when tourists back in San Francisco are braving the fog and wind? Both Oakland, with its population of about 400,000, and the town of Berkeley, have attractions not to miss, if you have time. If you are going to do both in one day, rent a car and drive over the Oakland-San Francisco Bay Bridge, completed in 1936, just before its more famous neighbor, the Golden Gate Bridge. Otherwise you can take BART, which is simple and cheap, but which may require more time getting from site to site than you may want.

Oakland is humming these days, having well recovered and moved on from its decades of decline. Stroll around Lake Merritt, the tidal lagoon that is so popular with locals, and plan to spend some fun time at Jack London Square, a waterfront destination in itself. There is always something going on at Jack London Square: the liveliest farmer's market in the East Bay, restaurants, shops, recreation, and even hotels. And then there is Yoshi's, a jazz club that sees international performers and large Oakland crowds. In fact, if you want just to visit Jack London Square, add to the fun by taking the Alameda-East Bay ferry across the bay directly from the Ferry Building to the Square; tel: (510) 749-5972; website: http://www.eastbayferry.com. The views are wonderful, of course, as they would be.

Oakland has several good museums to take in. The Oakland Museum of California, is the only museum to focus on California—its art, history, geography, and natural sciences. Do not miss the permanent exhibit of photographs by Ansel Adams (tel: (510) 238-2200; website: http://www.museumca.org). And the African American Museum and Library is devoted to African Americans in California; tel: (510) 637-0200; website: http://www.oaklandlibrary.org/AAMLO.

Just north of Oakland, Berkeley is primarily known as being one of the radical, hippy branches of the University of California, but some 20 Nobel Prize winners have done their research here, and the school is famed for its academic excellence. The major strolling street near the university is Telegraph Avenue, and it teems with coffee houses, bookshops, and artisan stalls that sell handmade this—and that's. For two good museums, take in the Lawrence Hall of Science (tel: (510) 642-5132; website: http://www.lawrencehallofscience.org) that is an interactive science museum, or the Berkeley Art Museum and Pacific Film Archive on the university campus. (tel: (510) 642-0808; website: http://www.bampfa.berkeley.edu).

But Berkeley, of course, also has its nature to see: do not miss the lovely 2077-acre (840.53 ha) Tilden Park with its botanical garden of California plants, its many picnic areas and camping facilities, Lake Anza for fishing and swimming (in season), and the 18-hole golf course (website: http://www.ebparks.org). The terraced Rose Garden has some 3000 rose bushes and 270 varieties of roses (info tel: (510) 981-5150). And the University of California Botanical Garden is on campus, displaying succulents, redwoods, and greenery of all sorts; tel: (510) 643-2755; website: http://www.botanicalgarden.berkeley.edu.

A Day on the Pacific Ocean

Bring your warm jacket, hat and gloves and take a trip out onto the ocean. Some 27 miles (43.45 km) off the shore of San Francisco is the Gulf of the Farallon Islands National Marine Sanctuary, craggy islands that are a federally-protected food-rich marine ecosystem encouraging to whales, dolphins, seals and seabirds as they feed and breed. The Farallon Islands National Wildlife Refuge itself is one of the country's largest seabird rookeries (nesting season is from March through August), and its beaches welcome sea turtles, seals, and even the large, endangered Stellar's sea lions that are on the Endangered Species List. Only researchers are allowed on the wild, foggy, windswept islands, but boat tours circle the area to view whatever wildlife happens to be there at the time. Naturalist guides also help you spot whichever whales are then on their seasonal migrations, and some summer cruises even take you farther out to the edge of the Continental Shelf itself.

Some 25 species of marine mammals (18 species of whales and dolphins) can be found here, but seasonal migrations and breeding schedules differ, so the wildlife you see will depend on when you come. Sometimes you do not see whales at all, if they happen not to be there that day; nonetheless, there is so much to see and learn from the naturalists on these cruises that it will still be a day well spent. And although cruises usually go ahead as scheduled, rain or shine, occasionally they are canceled, depending on the state of the sea. And it is no joke: make sure you have protection from the weather. You are almost 30 miles (48.28 km) out into the Pacific Ocean, after all.

Whale migration seasons:
- Blue whales (June through October)
- Humpback whales (June through November)
- Pacific White Sided Dolphin (June through November)
- Great White Shark (August through November)
- Grey Whales: (December through May)
- Sperm Whales (November through April, although rarely seen)

Several companies offer whale-watching tours. Currently the costs are around US$ 80–90 per person, varying with the day and for seniors and children. Check the Internet sites for current schedules.
- The Oceanic Society; Fort Mason Center 94123; tel (I): (415) 474-3385; tel (II): (800) 326-7491; website: http://www.oceanic-society.org). Non-profit San Francisco organization. For recorded information on current whale sightings, dial (415) 474-0488.
- San Francisco Bay Whale Watching; Departure point is 10 Marina Boulevard, adjacent to Fort Mason and across from Safeway; tel: (415) 331-6267; website: http://www.sfbaywhalewatching.com.

To the South

The best attractions to the south of San Francisco cannot really be said to be in the Bay Area, but if you are ready for longer ride or a two-day excursion, consider heading south toward the Monterey Peninsula. To begin with, think of taking the slower scenic and curvy ocean road (California

Highway 1) rather than the multi-lane inland highways that get you where you are going faster, but without the charm. Highway 1 will take you eventually to Monterey (and its modern aquarium or famous Cannery Row), the craggy cliffs of wild Big Sur, or the charming town of Carmel-by-the-Sea, and you will have a lovely ride. You will pass small beachside towns—often socked in by fog or buffeted by wind, but which sometimes sparkle gloriously in the sun. And the vast ocean on your right and the mountains on your left, as you curve around the coastal road, will take your breath away.

- Monterey; http://www.monterey.org/
- Monterey Bay Aquarium; http://www.mbayaq.org/
- Monterey Cannery Row; http://www.canneryrow.com/
- Carmel-by-the-Sea; http://www.carmel-california.com/
- Big Sur; http://www.bigsurcalifornia.org/

And there are some impressive places to visit on the way. if you are going to go as even as far as Santa Cruz, about 75 miles south of San Francisco, take time for two important parks. About 55 miles (88.5 km) south of San Francisco and 27 miles (43.5 km) of the town of Half Moon Bay is Año Nuevo State Reserve, and it is amazing. (tel: (650) 879-0227; reservations tel: (800) 444-4445; website: http://www.parks.ca.gov/?page_id = 523). It is on the windy beaches here that the enormous elephant seals come to breed; they rest, they mate, and then they give birth in the sandy dunes. First the males battle to see who is going to get the best gals, and then the females just lie around until it is time to give birth in the dunes. Breeding season is December-March, and guided walks allow people to come fairly close to these huge animals (who are usually doing nothing to the human eye). But not too close, for these are wild animals, despite how peaceful they look, and not only is it dangerous to get too close, it is a federal offense to bother them. After the births, the adults leave their pups, who grow for a month or so before heading out into the ocean, themselves. Eventually they come back to molt and then to start the process once again. Reservations are taken starting around October 20th.

Like Muir Woods to the north, Big Basin State Park, sixty-five miles south of San Francisco at Boulder Creek, is home to some 18,000 acres of old growth (and recovering) coastal redwoods; tel: (831) 338-8860; website: http://www.bigbasin.org. Big Basin is the state's oldest State Park (established 1902). There are some 80 miles (128.8 km)of trails, numerous waterfalls, and abundant wildlife, including egrets, herons, and California woodpeckers. Sometimes you can see deer, raccoons, bobcats, and once in a rare while, even a mountain lion or two.

The Peninsula is also home to that unmapped area designated as "Silicon Valley," which refers to where so many of the innovations of the Information Age took place. Towns include Los Altos, Los Gatos Palo Alto, Saratoga, and the most interesting for visitors, San Jose. This bustling city has an excellent Children's Discovery Museum (website: http://www.cdm.org), and the San Jose Museum of Art (website: http://sjmusart.org), plus an enormous 930-square foot Monopoly outdoor game in a park (website: http://www.monopolyinthepark.com).

Between San Francisco and San Jose, though, is Palo Alto, the ineffable center of Silicon Valley, home to the lovely Stanford University and its Art Museum, the Hoover Institution, and the Stanford Linear Accelerator Center. And if you just want a pleasant lunch and an afternoon of shopping, visit the upscale Stanford Shopping Center, where everything is there for you to find.

LEARNING THE LANGUAGE

CHAPTER 8

'Drawing on my fine command of the English Language,
I said nothing.'
—Robert Benchley

ENGLISH IN THE CITY

San Francisco, as you will see for yourself, is a multilingual city. Corporations that trade around the Pacific Rim are used to doing business in several Asian languages; staff in tourist shops can speak with just about any of their international clients; and the city-wide ethnic groceries and restaurants use the languages of their clienteles. You will hear more Mandarin and other Chinese dialects than English in Chinatown and along parts of Clement Street, and more Spanish than English in the Mission—all with regional variations or dialects. But there are also communities of Russians and Koreans out along Geary, Vietnamese in the outer Tenderloin, and Japanese both around the Japan Center and in the Sunset. Pockets of other ethnic communities are multilingual as well.

In statistical terms, more than 35 percent of San Francisco residents speak and comprehend a native language other than English. These are the most widely heard, measured in number of speakers: Chinese (130,000), Spanish (82,000), Tagalog (20,000), Russian (18,000), Vietnamese (10,000).

Nonetheless, English is the language of America and the official language of California. So, you should make every effort to learn—or improve—your English as quickly as possible. If you do not speak English well, you will certainly be at a disadvantage in business or in school. Despite the plethora of multilingual publications, if you do not read English well, you will not know as much as your neighbors as to the happenings in the city at any given time or even what opportunities are available for you. There are many registered English language schools in the Bay Area; choose one that suits your schedule and budget. For people who wish to apply for further study in the United States, the schools all offer TOEFL (Test of English as a Foreign Language) preparation.

City College of San Francisco offers free English classes for adults at its John Adams Campus, 1860 Hayes Street at Masonic; tel: (415) 561-1954; website: http://www.ccsf.edu/Departments/ESL/jad.html. Courses at all levels are available and held daytimes, evenings, or Saturday mornings.

The private schools listed below are all accredited, but they all differ somewhat in their offerings and prices. Generally, they have programs for students of all levels of linguistic skills and abilities. They have preparation courses for TOEFL and other exams, and they offer business English for professionals as well. Some conduct evening classes and social programs too. They should also assist with F-1 student visas, the I-20 SEVIS form, and temporary accommodations, if you need them. Some also have teacher-training programs. (*For student visa requirements, see pages 137–139.*)

- American Academy of English, 530 Golden Gate Avenue; tel: (415) 567-0189; website: http://www.aae.edu
- Brandon College, 25 Kearny Street, 2nd Floor; tel: (415) 391-5711; fax: (415) 391-3918; website: http://www.brandoncollege.com

Tongue Twisters

Americans love "tongue twisters." Can you say these without making a mistake or getting tongue tied?
- She sells seashells by the seashore.
- How much wood would a woodchuck chuck if a woodchuck could chuck wood?
- Peter Piper picked a peck of pickled peppers. A peck of pickled peppers Peter Piper picked. If Peter Piper picked a peck of pickled peppers, how many pickled peppers did Peter Piper pick?

- Intrax Cultural Exchange, 551 Sutter Street California 94102; tel: (415) 835-9766; website: http://www.intraxinstitute.edu
- Saint Giles Language Teaching Center, 785 Market Street, Suite 300; tel: (415) 788-3552; fax: (415) 788-1923; website: http://www.stgiles-usa.com

Conversing in San Francisco

The spoken language is basically a codification of sounds and speech patterns. In the United States, most Americans speak what is called General American (also referred to as Standard Midwestern). As you meet Americans from various regions of the country, though, you will hear different accents and occasionally a few different words from their region. But if you listen hard and adapt your ear, you will find that Americans actually speak the same language, no matter their place of origin. Even Americans can hear the differences in accents and sometimes must make an effort to comprehend—people from New Jersey often have a distinct accent, different from that of the Deep South. As you study English in a school in San Francisco, though, you will be learning the accent and pronunciation that are standard across America.

Relaxed Speech

By and by, you will also notice and pick up how Americans really speak. In normal casual conversation, for example, Americans use a "relaxed form" of certain verbs. You should learn these, too. It is important to note though, that they are used only in conversation, never in writing. This is what you will hear:

I'm going to	I'm gonna
I don't know	I dunno
I want to	I wanna
I could have	I coulda
I didn't	I didn
I have to/he has to	I hafta/he hasta
Did you	Didja
I've got to	I've gotta

BUSINESS AND EMPLOYMENT

CHAPTER 9

'The extreme geniality of San Francisco's economic,
intellectual and political climate makes it the most varied
and challenging city in the United States.'
—James Michener

WORK AND BUSINESS ON THE PACIFIC RIM

From its earliest days, San Francisco has been a city of opportunities seen and grasped. Even today, whether you are coming to find a job or to start your own business, you will find that San Francisco opens its doors to those who are qualified—and who understand how the city works. But be wise. In uncertain economic conditions, it is especially important to understand what is happening worldwide, and in all of California, before you start your research just on the Bay Area. California has been hit hard economically, but if the Bay Area is a little bit shaky, opportunities still exist.

If the Bay Area were an independent country, it would rank among the top 25 economies in the world. San Francisco plays a crucial part in the economy and trade of the vast Pacific Rim, and with some of the world's largest financial corporations based here, it is sometimes called the "Wall Street of the West." Located here are the headquarters for Wells Fargo Bank, the Pacific Stock Exchange, Charles Schwab & Co, a U.S. Mint, the Federal Home Loan Bank, and the Federal Reserve Bank of San Francisco. The Bay Area also has the highest concentration of venture capital firms in the world, further enhancing its importance as one of the most bustling financial hubs in the United States.

With the city's long-standing ties to Asia, finance and commerce along the Rim have become the most important parts of the economy of the city and the region. The second-largest exporting region in the country, foreign trade generates in the vicinity of US$ 130 billion for the city. Of San Francisco's export partners, Asia itself accounts for more than half the activity, 25 percent goes to Europe, and 16 percent goes to Canada and Mexico.

You should consider the entire Bay Area as your resource, especially that geographically intangible—yet very real—concept called Silicon Valley, which stretches from San Francisco down to San Jose. Companies throughout the Bay Area are world leaders in high-tech innovation, manufacturing, and trade. Think of Apple Computers, Oracle, Cisco Systems, Hewlett-Packard, and Intel as being headquartered in the Bay Area, and you will understand the importance of this area to the Information Age. Silicon Valley has some 4,100 high-tech firms, employing more than 200,000 people of various skills.

The Bay Area is also innovative in life sciences and biotechnology. The Bay Area hosts 820 life-sciences companies, employing 85,000 people. (In all of California, there are 2,600 biomedical companies.) One of the largest in the field is the University of California San Francisco (UCSF), which introduced gene-splicing techniques two decades ago, and which is now completing a new 43-acre (17.4-ha) biotech and life sciences research campus in Mission Bay.

Among the largest corporations with headquarters in San Francisco are Bechtel and Levi Strauss. The largest employers are the City and County of San Francisco, the University of California San Francisco, Wells Fargo, the School District, and the State of California. Yet small, innovative companies are also welcomed in San Francisco and new ones—when appropriately funded and established—tend to succeed.

STARTING A BUSINESS

Many people come to San Francisco hoping to start their own small retail business. In fact, despite the invasion of nationwide chain stores and franchises, locally owned businesses continue to characterize San Francisco, from tourist-oriented kiosks and locally owned restaurants of all quality and prices to the funkiest or most elegant fashion boutiques. Some businesses are successful, yet many fail, certainly owing to economic variables, but also often owing to an incomplete understanding of how the city works. Much will depend on the amount of knowledge you have at the outset—including that all-important aspect of location—and how organized you are in your approach.

First, learn about the activities of The San Francisco Chamber of Commerce, at 235 Montgomery Street, a non-profit membership association of more than 2,000 local businesses of all sizes; tel: (415) 392-4520; fax: (415) 392-0485; website: http://www.sfchamber.com. Working to attract and support businesses in the Bay Area, the Chamber sponsors luncheons, networking socials, and committee meetings, and organizes special events for members and non-members. The Small Business Advisory Council is an important resource for the small business owner. The Women in Business Roundtable supports women in business with regular meetings and interesting speakers (tel: (415) 352-8803). The Job Forum is offered as a free community service designed to aid jobseekers. Not an employment agency, the Job Forum offers brainstorming and problem-solving opportunities.

The Better Business Bureau that services San Francisco is based in Oakland; tel: (510) 844-2000 or (866) 411-2221; website: http://www.oakland.bbb.org. It provides information on companies, including lists of those with good records. You may file complaints here, as well.

> "In all my travels, I have never seen the hospitality of San Francisco equaled anywhere in the world."
> —Conrad Hilton

Tourism Businesses

Businesses that depend on tourism are always a draw. Tourism is big business in San Francisco and is its largest revenue-generating industry, sustaining more than 66,000 of the city's jobs. Often rated by travel magazines as the nation's most popular vacation spot, San Francisco is visited by some 16 million visitors who spend more than US$ 7 billion in the city each year. Other than vacationers, the city is also a draw for some 200 trade shows, conventions, and business meetings. International visitors account for just under half of all hotel guests, and these explore the city every day, spending their money at tourist attractions, in the downtown and outer shopping districts, and especially at the city's restaurants.

Business Setup Advice

Before you do anything else, make sure you understand the legal and financial implications of opening a business and the risks involved. Start with the U.S. Small Business Administration (SBA), located on the sixth floor of 455 Market Street. This is an agency of the federal government that helps anyone who wants to open a small business; tel: (415) 744-6820; website: http://www.sba.gov.

The SBA is also the largest source of long-term small business financing in the nation. Loans are made to qualified applicants by private lending institutions that participate in the SBA program. Inquire of your banker or at the SBA about its help for small business.

Women and minorities should inquire at the SBA about the Women's and Minorities Pre-Qualification Loan Program, in which loan requests may be reviewed and approved by the SBA before application to the lending institution.

The following organizations and resources might be of help as you equip for business:

- The Renaissance Entrepreneurship Center, 275 Fifth Street; tel: (415) 541-8580; website: http://www.rencenter.org; Non-profit entrepreneurial training organization that works in conjunction with SBA and some private businesses, offering training and help for people who want to start their own businesses.
- Mission Economic Development Association (MEDA), 3505, 20th Street; tel: (415) 282-3334; fax: (415) 415-282-3320; website: http://www.medasf.org. This bilingual (Spanish and English) association in the heart of the Mission provides counseling, technical assistance, and loan packaging services (through the SBA and small lenders) to people wishing to set up a new business or improve an existing business.

- Women's Initiative, 1398 Valencia Street at 25th Street; tel: (415) 641-3460; fax: (415) 826-1885; website: http://www.womensinitiative.org. Women's Initiative provides specific training to equip women in various aspects of business and to help them start or expand their own. Sessions in English or Spanish target low-income women, to help overcome economic and social barriers.
- The San Francisco Small Business Network, 2261 Market Street, Suite 288; tel: (415) 281-8412; website: http://www.sfsbn.org. This group promotes and lobbies for small business and education programs and aims to strengthen and unify the voices of small business owners.
- The San Francisco Main Library, 100 Larkin Street; Allows any card holder access to its Business, Science, and Technology Center's services and database; tel: (415) 557-4400; website: http://sfpl.lib.ca.us.
- San Francisco Business Times, 275 Battery Street, Suite 940; tel: (415) 989-2522; fax: (415) 398-2494; website: http://www.bizjournals.com/sanfrancisco; An excellent ongoing resource for current business information and business-related reports.

Networking

San Franciscans are friendly and open, both socially and professionally, so you should have little trouble meeting people and—once settled into your professional life—becoming an active member of the business community. For business networking, consider joining the following groups:
- San Francisco Chamber of Commerce, 465 California Street, 9th Floor; tel: (415) 392-4520; fax: (415) 392-0485; website: http://www.sfchamber.com
- The San Francisco African American Chamber of Commerce, 1485 Bayshore Boulevard; tel: (415) 468-4600; website http://www.sfaacc.org. Helps to connect African American business owners to the global market.
- Asian Business League of San Francisco, 564 Market Street, Suite 404; tel: (415) 788-4664; website: http://www.ablsf.org. This is a membership organization for Asians in business, providing seminars, workshops, networking events.

- The City Club of San Francisco, 155 Sansome Street, 10th Floor; tel: (415) 362-2480; website: http://www.cityclubsf.com. A multi-purpose professional and social club that hosts breakfast speakers, conducts networking forums, and organizes special events.
- The Commonwealth Club of California, 595 Market Street; tel: (415) 597-6700; website: http://www.commonwealthclub.org. A prestigious public affairs group, it invites well-known and interesting people to speak at meal-centered meetings (breakfast, lunch, dinner, receptions). Also organized are special and social events geared to current issues; outings to cultural and sports events.
- Golden Gate Business Association, 1800 Market Street; tel: (415) 865-5545; website: http://www.ggba.com. San Francisco's oldest gay and lesbian business organization, GGBA includes professionals, business owners, and artists, and it conducts networking events and a variety of business-related programs.
- National Association of Women Business Owners—San Francisco, 2325 3rd Street; tel: (415) 333-2130; website: http://www.nawbo-sf.org. This association holds monthly dinner meetings and also provides networking, business, and social contacts. It also has links with women's business groups worldwide.
- Rotary Club of San Francisco, 300 Montgomery Street; tel: (415) 546-0181; website: http://www.sfrotary.com. Call this international community service organization for meeting and luncheon sites.
- World Affairs Council of Northern California, World Affairs Center, 312 Sutter Street, Suite 200; tel: (415) 293-4600; fax: (415) 982-5028; website: http://www.itsyourworld.org. The council holds programs on important foreign policy issues, organizes conferences and dinners with international guests, lectures from government officials, forums on current issues, and special and social events.

Temporary/Shared Office Space

If you do not need a full-time office or need space while looking for permanent quarters, consider shared office space, which provides full services without a long-term financial commitment. You may rent a conference room for a meeting, or rent offices by the day, week, or month. See Office and Desk Space Rental Service in the *Yellow Pages*.

- HQ Global Workplaces; Several locations in San Francisco; tel: (800) 956-9543; website: http://www.hq.com
- Office General Executive Business Centers, 580 California Street, 5th and 16th Floors; tel: (415) 283-3200; website: http://www.officegeneral.com

THE JOB SEARCH

San Francisco has long been home to plentiful jobs—in international trade and especially in tourism, where the turnover is high. During the "dot.com" years, the economy of the region shifted to Information Technology: computer programming, telecommunications, data processing. Now, however, although these fields are still thriving, employment is increasing more in the leisure and hospitality fields, and scientific and business services. With the new research center at Mission Bay, those who have attained education in the life sciences—biotechnology and scientific research—are in demand. The multimedia industry has also taken hold in the Bay Area, and both new jobs and new types of jobs are being created.

Yet if there are jobs, they are easily filled, and the unemployment rate in San Francisco hovers only between six and seven percent, lower than the May 2009 California average of nine percent. Thus, you should ensure that your résumé is well organized and presented. If you have varied experience and several distinct skills, for example, prepare different résumés with different emphases, depending on the job you are applying for. Be prepared also to network with any professional contact you may have and to make "cold calls" to the Human Resources departments of companies, rather than relying solely on your résumé and cover letter. Competition is fierce, and you must use every channel at your disposal. Remember that many people possess similar skills, so the cover letter is important in conveying who you are.

Average wages in San Francisco rose 30 percent in the last decade, compared to 18 percent in the rest of the country. But think carefully about salary and your lifestyle, for the Bay Area has the highest cost of living in the state, and its concomitant higher salaries may not stretch as far as you think. And if San Francisco's highly educated workforce (67 percent of residents have college or other post-secondary degrees) currently earns around US$ 72,000 each, it may still matter little when the median price of a single-family home is now more than US$ 700,000.

In order to apply for a job, you might be asked to prove that you are legally permitted to work in the United States; foreigners may be asked to take an English-language test. In addition, some companies will test you on the skills you claim to have, in addition to checking samples of your work and references.

If you are coming to the city without a job, start your search before arrival by looking at the websites of employment agencies and the San Francisco Chronicle (website: http://www.sfgate.com). The Sunday issue has an extensive career section containing articles, advertisements for career development, and a major section of classified ads for job openings. Some free tabloid magazines can be found at news boxes on street corners.

- *Open Exchange Magazine* is a learning resource directory, detailing thousands of opportunities for professional and skills development, personal growth, and to effect positive social change. Among its coaching programs are many that aim to help enhance one's interpersonal communication and relational skills and ability to live a holistic life; website; http://www.openexchange.org.
- Jobs and Careers is an Internet portal that lists hundreds of jobs and positions that are open, announces career fairs, and facilitates the search process of both employers and jobseekers; website: http://www.jobscareers.com.
- *Bay Area Business Woman* connects women in commerce, community, and the arts, with articles, testimonies, and advertisements, plus a calendar of events; website: http://www.babwnews.com.

Career Help

In addition to listing yourself with the employment agencies, try to take advantage of the organizations that help people to develop their capabilities, to present themselves well, and to understand the San Francisco job market:

- Experience Unlimited, 801 Turk Street, tel: (415) 771-1776; website: http://www.edd.ca.gov/jsrep/jseuloc.htm. A free service of the California Employment Development Department, Experience Unlimited provides workshops on job-searching techniques, cover letter and résumé writing, ways to handle interviews with confidence, career-planning, and so on. Check the website for other offices.
- Jewish Vocational Service and Career Counseling (JVS), 225 Bush Street, Suite 400; tel: (415) 391-3600; fax: (415) 391-3617; website: http://www.jvs.org. This long established non-sectarian non-profit job counseling and employment agency organizes workshops, provides opportunities for networking, and conducts skills training programs, with the objective of "bringing people and work together."
- Media Alliance, 1904 Franklin Street in Oakland; tel: (510) 832-9000; website: http://www.media-alliance.org. A non-profit association for communications and general media professionals. Job listings are free for professional members. Membership can also be earned by volunteering hours and service at the center.

Employment Agencies

The hundreds of employment agencies in the city offer temporary and permanent jobs. If you are willing to work outside San Francisco, inquire whether the agencies service the entire Bay Area. Under Employment Agencies in the *Yellow Pages*, there are extensive advertisements and listings of agencies that specialize in fields such as the dental, insurance, or legal professions. Firms may also help in writing resumés and in training of job skills. The San Francisco Chamber of Commerce sells an Employment Guide that lists agencies and services for job seekers' easy reference. Herewith a few, just to give you an idea of how specialized the agencies are:

An aerial view of San Francisco's Financial District at night and the Bay Bridge in the background.

- Accountants Inc, By appointment only; tel: (415) 434-1411; fax: (415) 434-1124; email: sanfran@accountantsinc.com; website:http://www.accountantsinc.com; For accountants and professionals in the financial industry.
- ABA Staff; tel: (415) 434-4222; website: http://www.abastaff.com; For attorneys and paralegals.
- ProGayJobs, 1800 Market Street; website: http://www.progayjobs.com; Specializing in jobs for the GLBT community, with a wide range of full-time and temporary positions.
- Jackson Personnel Agency, 116 New Montgomery Street, Suite 916; tel: (415) 546-4500; fax: (415) 546-0926; website: http://www.jacksonpersonnel.com; From clerical through management.
- The Job Shop, 163 2nd Street; tel: (415) 227-8610; website: http://www.jobshopsf.com; Temporary and permanent positions in advertising, sales, marketing, financial services, fashion, accounting, real estate, and more.
- Kelly Services Inc, 55 2nd Street; tel: (415) 284-2800; website: http://www.kellyservices.com; Matches jobseekers to temporary positions in several fields, including clerical and accounting.
- Manpower, Three Embarcadero Center, No. 540; tel: (415) 781-7171; website: http://www.manpower.com; Specializes in recruitment, training, selection of job candidates, and listings of jobs.

Jobs For Youth

The United Way of the Bay Area at 221 Main Street (Suite 300) has a Jobs for Youth program that provides entry-level work experience to qualified young people; tel: (415) 861-5627; website: http://www.jobsforyouth.net. All applicants are pre-screened and qualified for the jobs that are listed.

SAN FRANCISCO AT A GLANCE

CHAPTER 10

'It is an odd thing, but every one who disappears is said to be seen at San Francisco.'
—Oscar Wilde

Official Name
City and County of San Francisco

Flag
A gold border on a white background with the crest of a phoenix rising from the fire in the center of the flag. The crest sits on top of the motto, Oro en Paz, Fierro en Guerra (Gold in Peace, Iron in War).

Time
Greenwich Mean Time minus eight hours (GMT -0800) during Standard Time and minus seven hours (GMT -0700) during Daylight Savings Time. San Francisco is on Pacific Standard/Daylight Savings Time. Three hours behind Eastern Time Zone (New York).

Telephone: Country and Area Codes
Country Code for USA: 1
Area Code for San Francisco and most of Marin: 415
Area Code for Berkeley, Oakland, and much of East Bay: 510
Area Code for South Bay: 650

Area
Land area: 46.7 square miles (121 sq km); tip of peninsula between Pacific Ocean and San Francisco Bay
Including ocean and bay portions within city/county limits: 128 square miles (332 sq km)

Climate

Predominantly cool weather owing to ocean currents and winds sweeping through the Golden Gate. Winters tend to be rainy and cool. Summers can be foggy and windy, especially in the mornings. Warmest temperatures are generally in Spring and Fall. Average yearly rainfall: 20 inches (51 cm).

San Francisco Climate			
Month	Average. High Temperature	Average Low Temperature	Average Rainfall
January	55°F	41°F	4.4 inches
February	58°F	45°F	3.2 inches
March	60°F	45°F	3.1 inches
April	64°F	47°F	1.4 inches
May	66°F	48°F	0.2 inches
June	70°F	52°F	0.1 inches
July	71°F	54°F	0 inches
August	72°F	55°F	0.1 inches
September	74°F	55°F	0.2 inches
October	70°F	51°F	1.2 inches
November	62°F	47°F	2.9 inches
December	56°F	42°F	3.1 inches

Population
845,000 (August, 2009)

Government Structure
The City and County of San Francisco is a metropolitan municipality with a consolidated government: a mayor and board of supervisors, elected by the populace.

Ethnic Groups
White (49.7 percent), Asian (30.8 percent), Latino (14.1 percent), African-Americans (7.8 percent). Largest Asian population in America outside Hawaii. Largest center of gays and lesbians in the United States.

Official Language
English is the "common and unifying language" of the United States. It is the official language of California. In San Francisco, much city information and election ballots are in English, Spanish, and Chinese.

Voltage Rating
The standard current in the United States is 110–115 volts (60 Hz). Wall outlets take plugs with two flat prongs and a round ground pin above. Newer foreign electronics should convert voltage automatically; if so, the appliance will need only an adapter. If not, it will need a transformer or converter.

Currency
U.S. dollar (USD or US$)

Gross Domestic Product (GDP)
US$ 1.7 trillion (2007)
San Francisco: US$ 82 billion (2007, est.)

Industries
Manufacturing, banking and finance, tourism, biotechnology, and electronics

San Francisco at A Glance 351

Famous Earthquakes:
April 18,1906: magnitude 8.25 on the Richter scale; 28,000 buildings were destroyed; more than 3,000 people died.
October 17th, 1989: magnitude 6.9 on the Richter scale

Airports
One international airport: San Francisco International Airport (SFO); 14 miles (22 km) south of San Francisco; website: http://www.san-francisco-sfo.com

City Attractions
Highest Point: Mount Davidson (282 m / 925.2 ft)
Lowest Point: Sea level
Shoreline: 29 miles (46.7 km)
Hills: 43
Steepest Streets, with 31.5 percent of grade: Filbert Street, between Leavenworth and Hyde; 22nd Street between Church and Vicksburg
Longest Street: Mission Street (7.29 miles / 11.7 km)
Oldest Street: Grant Avenue (Originally Dupont)
Oldest Square: Portsmouth Square
Oldest Building: Mission Dolores, completed in 1791

Tallest Building: Transamerica Pyramid (853 feet)
Victorian Houses: 14,000
Golden Gate Park: Established 1870, city's largest park at 1,013 acres (410 ha).

Main Districts

Union Square, Financial District, and Nob Hill; Chinatown, North Beach, Telegraph Hill, and Russian Hill; Pacific Heights, the Marina, Cow Hollow, and the Presidio; Japantown, Western Addition, and the Haight; SoMa, The Mission, The Castro, Noe Valley, and Bernal Heights; The Sunset, The Richmond, and OMI.

SOME WELL-KNOWN AMERICANS

George Washington (1732–1799)

"The Father of Our Country." General who led the American armies to victory over the British in the Revolutionary War, and beloved first President of the United States. Official celebration of his birthday: President's Day, the third Monday in February.

Meriwether Lewis (1774–1809)
Asked by President Thomas Jefferson (1743–1826) to lead an expedition to the unexplored Western frontier. Lewis and his friend Will Clark left Illinois on May 14th, 1804. Over 1.5 years, they navigated the Missouri River, crossed the Rockies and followed the Columbia River to the Pacific Ocean. They returned to America in 1806, reaching Saint Louis on September 23rd.

Abraham Lincoln (1809–1865)
One of America's greatest presidents. Lincoln preserved the Union during the Civil War and abolished slavery, but was assassinated for his efforts. Official celebration of his birthday: President's Day, the third Monday in February.

Susan B. Anthony (1820–1906)
Civil rights leader, working for abolition of slavery and then for women's suffrage. Called "the Napoleon of the Women's Rights Movement."

Geronimo (1829–1909)
An Apache born Chiricahua Goyaałé and later nicknamed Geronimo. Fought against the United States to preserve the indpendence of Native Americans and their tribal lands. Brave and determined as he was, he could not succeed.

Louisa May Alcott (1832–1888)
Prominent woman writer, whose most enduring novels are *Little Women* (1868–1869) and *Little Men* (1871).

Mark Twain (1835–1910)
Revered humorist and writer of adventure stories, including *Life on the Mississippi*, *The Adventures of Tom Sawyer*, and *The Adventures of Huckleberry Finn*. Credited with saying, "The coldest winter I ever spent was summer in San Francisco."

Alexander Graham Bell (1847–1922)
Inventor of the telephone and the "photophone," which transmitted sound over a beam of light, the forerunner of the wireless, laser, and fiber optics technology of today.

Jack London (1876–1916)
San Francisco-born writer, whose most famous book is *Call of the Wild*. Some of his vigorous stories of surviving hardships and travail were based on his own life.

John Steinbeck (1902–1968)
California-born novelist, whose writings emphasized the hard lives of poor workers during the Great Depression. His most lasting works are *Of Mice and Men* and *The Grapes of Wrath*. Much of his work takes place in the Salinas Valley-Monterey area of California. Steinbeck won the Nobel Prize for Literature in 1962.

Francis Albert Sinatra (1915–1998)
One of America's first "teenage heartthrobs," Frank Sinatra's singing career as a pop vocalist kept his name always at the top of the charts. Among his 250 million records, his recordings of *My Way*, *Strangers in the Night*, *New York, New York*, and *It Was a Very Good Year*, remain perennial favorites. As an actor, his movie credits included *From Here to Eternity*, for which he won an Academy Award, and *Guys and Dolls*.

John F. Kennedy (1917–1963)
America's 35th President. Young, charming and energetic, Kennedy's presidency brought a refreshed idealism and energy to the United States. Assassinated in 1963, he did not live to see his programs for justice and civil rights put into effect.

Lawrence Ferlinghetti (1919–)
A proponent of the movement called "The Beat Generation," which rejected the traditional values of the 1950s. An influential poet, Ferlinghetti has for 50 years been a powerful challenge to entrenched artistic and literary interests. His City Lights Bookstore in San Francisco is a well-known center for intellectuals and poets. Named first San Francisco Poet Laureate in 1998.

César Chávez (1927–1993)
Founder of the United Farm Workers, he organized a 5-year strike of California grape pickers. Remembered as a powerful

force for the rights of migrant workers. His birthday, March 31, is a California state holiday, the only one honoring a Mexican-American in the United States.

Martin Luther King (1929–1968)
Pivotal and inspirational figure in the American Civil Rights movement, Martin Luther King was awarded the 1964 Nobel Peace Prize. Official celebration of his birthday: Martin Luther King Day, January 15th.

Muhammad Ali (1942–)
Born Cassius Clay, but in embracing Islam (now a Sunni Muslim) refused to retain his "slave name." A boxer and heavyweight Champion of the World, Ali was named Sportsman of the Century in 1999. Ali is respected both for his athleticism and for being outspoken for his beliefs. He received the Presidential Medal of Freedom in 2005.

Barbara Boxer (1940–) and Dianne Feinstein (1933–)
Senators from the State of California, the only state with two women as senators. Both are Democrats and outspoken leaders for justice and equality.

Jerry Garcia (1942–1995)
San Francisco-born, lead guitarist of the psychedlic rock group The Grateful Dead. Epitomized the freedom-loving attitude of the times, Garcia was seen as a guru by legions of devoted fans, called "deadheads."

Arnold Schwarzenegger (1947–)
Body builder and star of The Terminator movies, currently Governor of California.

Gavin Newsom (1967–)
42nd Mayor of San Francisco, elected 2003. A fourth-generation San Franciscan, he served three terms on the Board of Supervisors, before being elected mayor. He is committed to preserving and improving the quality of life in San Francisco for all its diverse residents.

ABBREVIATIONS, ACRONYMS…AND SLANG

San Franciscans often personalize names when speaking, making them shorter or cuter, or just more efficient. Although sometimes you will see the slang in writing, generally it is used only in coversation. Acronyms are pronounced as though they were words.

- American Conservatory Theater: A-C-T
- As soon as possible: A-S-A-P
- California Department of Transportation: Caltrans
- Disk Jockey: D-J
- El Camino Real (Road leading to the South Bay): The Camino
- Fisherman's Wharf: The Wharf
- Freeway 101: One Oh One
- Freeway 280: Two Eighty
- Golden Gate Bridge: The Bridge
- Golden Gate Park: The Park
- Golden Gate Recreation Area: G-G-N-R-A
- Haight Ashbury district: The Haight
- Lesbian, Gay, Bisexual, Transgender: L-G-B-T (sometimes G-L-B-T)
- Mark Hopkins Hotel: The Mark
- Museum of Modern Art: Moma (acronym)
- Pacific Bell: Pac Bell
- Pacific Gas and Electric (PG&E): P-G-'n-E
- Sacramento: Sacto (The state capital)
- San Francisco Chronicle: The Chronicle
- San Francisco: The City
- San Francisco Forty Niners (football team): The Niners
- San Francisco Giants (baseball team): The Giants
- San Francisco Municipal Railway: Muni
- San Francisco International Airport: The Airport, or S-F-O
- San Francisco-Oakland Bay Bridge: The Bay Bridge
- San Mateo County Transit: SamTrans
- South of Market: SoMa (acronym)
- Streets west of Arguello: The Avenues
- Thank God it's Friday: T-G-I-F

CULTURE QUIZ

SITUATION ONE

Your new colleagues have set up a Saturday night dinner at a trendy new restaurant in the Mission. It's a going-away party for the department head. On Saturday, when you're thinking about what to wear, you realize you have no idea how dressy you should look. And you don't have the home telephone numbers of anyone who will be there. What do you wear?

- **A** You don't want to take a chance on dressing too casually for this important occasion, and you want to impress your new colleagues. So you wear what you would wear to the office—a sports jacket and tie for a man, a suit and silk blouse for a woman.
- **B** This is San Francisco and the dinner is in the trendy, young Mission District, so you don't think you have to get dressed up at all. You put on some casual clothes—decently pressed slacks and a sweater—and know you look "put together," but not overly dressed.
- **C** It's the weekend and you've previously noticed people wearing jeans, even in the trendiest of restaurants. You put on your clean jeans and a good shirt and make sure you look put together and trendy, yourself. You want to fit in with your new friends, and this is probably what they will wear.

Comments

The answer is ❸. Unless you're sure it's a dressy occasion in an upscale (expensive) restaurant, you don't need to wear business clothes for an evening out. So, wear something casual and comfortable, but make sure you look good or presentable. San Franciscans—even those who would have chosen answer ❸ and wear jeans—make sure that no matter how casual their dress, they show they care about their appearance. In a city where people spend a lot of time keeping fit, it's not surprising that they would want to flaunt the results of their efforts.

SITUATION TWO

You are an older person who has decided to retire to San Francisco. When you are settling into your new home, you call PG&E to have your electricity hooked up. The telephone representative asks your name and then immediately calls you by your first name. You are surprised by such familiarity from someone you've never met; you come from a culture that respects both age and formality, and where strangers are addressed by their last name, prefaced by Mr. or Ms. You don't like it that someone you don't even know, and who hasn't even told you her own name, seems to show you no respect. How do you handle this?

- ❶ You just say politely, "Excuse me, but I'd prefer you to call me by my last name."
- ❷ You try to be friendly and respond, "If you're going to call me by my first name, at least tell me yours."
- ❸ You don't bother to say anything. This is just a rude person who has no manners, and you probably won't be put in the same situation again.

Comments

If it's important to you to be called by your last name, then say so. In that case, the answer is ❶. The telephone representative on the phone shouldn't be insulted and the situation will have resolved itself. Answer ❷ is somewhat acceptable, but since this is a business telephone call, there's no point in adding a second artificial and insincere friendliness to that of the first.

Answer **C** is the best option, but understand that the person isn't being rude. Americans generally call people by their first names, often upon first meeting. This has now extended itself to business calls, and although you might take such behavior as undue familiarity (even some Americans do), here it's often seen as friendliness, trying to put the customer at ease. So, you might as well get used to it, or on days when you decide more formality is required, resort to answer **A**.

SITUATION THREE

You have finally moved into the new apartment you've purchased in Pacific Heights. It's just the apartment you've been looking for, in the district you wanted, and with all the amenities you hoped for. You're excited, and you tell the good news to a colleague at work. You say what street the apartment is on and all the things you like about the place. You are surprised when your friend asks you how much the apartment cost. You are not used to talking about money and think the price of the apartment is no one's business but your own. What do you say?

- **A** You just laugh and say, "Wow, much more than I thought it would," and then change the subject to a general one of how expensive housing in San Francisco is.
- **B** You say how much it cost you.
- **C** You explain that in your culture people don't talk openly about money the way people do in the United States, and that it isn't something that you can do.

Comments

People in the United States are often more open about discussing the specifics of money than in other countries. Sometimes they crow about how little they've spent on something and other times they remark on how expensive something was. The answer here is **A**. You never have to say what something cost you, so **B** is wrong. As for **C**, comparing your country's cultural ethos with those of the United States would be a fun conversation over a drink sometime, but not in this conversation, where it would seem that you're reproving your colleague, who is, after all, only following American norms.

SITUATION FOUR

You're patiently standing in line at the cinema to buy your ticket to a popular new film, when a guy sneaks past you and the others and inserts himself toward the front of the line. He clearly hasn't come to join friends who are waiting for him. No, he's just a line jumper. You don't like this, because you've been patient, and the others in line have been, too. What do you do?

- **Ⓐ** Nothing. You're new here and you shouldn't be the one to make a fuss. Let the San Franciscans handle it. Besides, if it's so important for him to get in sooner, let him. It's a big theater with a lot of seats, and the film will start at the same time for everyone.
- **Ⓑ** Be polite. Say kindly, "Excuse me, but the line is back there." Hope he takes the hint and goes back where he belongs. If he doesn't, just shrug and let other people take the next step.
- **Ⓒ** React firmly, and make sure he hears you. Yell loudly, "Hey, buddy, the line's back there!" and gesture behind you to the end of the line where people are waiting.

Comments

Actually, any of the above answers are acceptable, although **Ⓑ** might be most effective, if making him do what's fair is important to you. It just depends on your mood of the moment. San Franciscans are tolerant of aberrant behavior—on most days and in most situations—but if they feel like saying that something bothers them, they do. So, gauge the situation and see what suits you. If you choose **Ⓒ**, however, be prepared for a response in the same tone and manner you've used.

SITUATION FIVE

You've just moved here from abroad and are settling in. One day, you're sitting on the bus with your eight-year-old daughter. Two young men board and take seats close by. After a few minutes, one leans over and kisses the other on the mouth. Your daughter asks, "Why are those men kissing?" What do you say?

- **A** You don't know what to say, so you just say, "Beats me, I haven't the slightest idea," and then try to distract her by pointing to something out the window.
- **B** You laugh and say, "We always knew San Francisco was different, didn't we?"
- **C** You say, "They're just showing affection toward each other. Usually it's between a man and a woman, but occasionally a man will love another man, or a woman will love another woman. That's their choice."
- **D** You tell her your opinion of homosexuality (or of public displays of affection) and that it is against your principles. She's old enough to understand.

Comments

Public affection may not be common in your culture, but it is common in San Francisco, not matter the sexual orientation. So, it's best to tell your daughter the truth, one way or the other. The best answer is **C**, for San Francisco teaches tolerance and expects it in return. But if you're adamant in your opposition either to openly-expressed affection or homosexuality, you'll no doubt already have begun at home to explain clearly your carefully-considered views on life. But, even if your answer is **D**, don't be loudly judgmental in front of the affectionate couple.

SITUATION SIX

You are driving home late at night, after a business dinner during which you've shared a couple of bottles of wine. You're not drunk, just tired. Just as you get to the traffic light you see it is about to turn red. Nobody is coming in either direction so you speed up and get through the instant it becomes red. But a police car parked to the side turns on his flashing lights and directs you to pull over to the side. He asks you to step out of the car. You know that you've been drinking and driving. You also know you shouldn't have dashed through the traffic light as it was turning red. How do you handle the situation?

Ⓐ You have an early meeting in the morning. You act friendly with the police officer and explain that you had a late business dinner and are concerned about your important meeting in the morning. Take out your wallet and ask the police officer how much the fine will be, so you can pay him directly and go home

Ⓑ You're tired and just want to go home and go to bed. You're not drunk, and lots of people dash through the light at the last minute. You take out your wallet and fold a US$ 50 bill around it, and smile as you hand it to the police officer.

Ⓒ You know this will be a stain on your record and that you will have to go to the police station and perhaps have your license suspended. Admit to the officer that you were wrong, accept the penalties as they unfold according to the particular situation, and vow to yourself that you will never do either again. And don't.

Comments

Clearly, the answer here is **Ⓒ**. Never (never!) attempt to bribe or even pay a fine to a police officer, for that too could be seen as bribery. If you have no defense to your actions, apologize and follow the instructions of the officer; the penalties will be severe—even more so if this is not your first offense. They could involve license suspension or restriction, a course in safe driving, a fine, or even real jail time. If you are taken to the police station by the officer, call your lawyer, or ask for one if you don't know one. You might also contact your embassy or consulate for a lawyer, although it is not the embassy's responsibility to get you out of jail. The answer **Ⓒ** is obvious, but the question was put in to remind you never to drink and drive, never to offer money to a police officer, and never to run a red light, which is not only illegal but also dangerous. San Francisco is tolerant of unusual behavior, but not of breaking laws or endangering others.

SITUATION SEVEN

Coming to San Francisco alone, with no family in tow, you have taken a good job as a manager in a major bank. After you've been there a few weeks, your boss suggests you go out for drinks after work. You assume he wants to talk about business and your new job. When you get to the bar, however, it is clear he is interested in you personally, and after two cocktails he puts his hand on your leg and suggests you go back to his apartment for a "nightcap." What do you do?

❶ You are extremely attracted to the man, he seems very nice, and being new in town, you don't have a relationship at present. So you decide to go back to his apartment with him. He's also important in the bank, so a relationship with him might help you get ahead.

❷ You get very angry and tell him his behavior is inappropriate. You push his hand off your leg, and tell him if he ever does this again, you'll report him for sexual harassment.

❸ You thank him for the offer, but say firmly that it's not a good idea to have a personal relationship with a colleague. Then, after finishing your drink, you thank him again, say you'll see him at work tomorrow, and leave.

Comments

The answer is **❸**. It isn't a good idea to have a personal relationship with a colleague, and in fact, they rarely help someone get ahead in a company. And there's no point getting angry, if you want to stay happily in this new job. Instead of accepting a drink with him after work, which may well have had personal overtones that you didn't catch, you might have suggested a lunch instead. Yet sexual harassment is a tricky issue in the United States, and personal relationships in the office—including even the occasional friendly pat on the back—must be paid attention to. If you come from a culture where men and women friends are physically affectionate (kisses on cheeks, pats on backs, friendly hugs), you'll have to gauge each situation carefully in the United States. Shaking hands is always an accepted thing to do.

SITUATION EIGHT

Your family is visiting you. It's their first time in the United States and you want them to have a good time. You reserve at a typically-San Francisco restaurant near Union Square. Because your family is still tired from a long flight, you book early, imagining a nice leisurely dinner and lingering over a cup of coffee, hearing all the news and gossip from home. But at the end of the meal, just as you're finishing your coffee, the waiter comes over and asks, "Would you like anything else?" When you say, "No, thank you," he comes back immediately with the bill. It's clear that he intends for you to pay and leave, even though you're not ready. What do you do?

- **Ⓐ** You pay and leave. You're not happy with the situation and make a mental note not to come back to this restaurant again. You also leave a slightly smaller tip than you would have, had you not felt rushed.
- **Ⓑ** You say, "Thanks, but we're not quite ready to leave. We want to stay another fifteen minutes, or so." If the waiter responds nicely, you make a mental note to give him a large tip.
- **Ⓒ** You pay and ask whether there's a table at the bar where you can continue your conversation. If there isn't, you leave and find another place—perhaps a cocktail lounge or nice bar—where you can linger awhile.

Comments

In the United States, restaurants generally open early and expect to reseat the table several times in the evening, allocating a certain amount of time for each party to eat and then leave. This is called "turning" the tables. Waiters make most of their income on tips, so it is also to their advantage to have as many different parties of diners at a table as possible. Here the best answer is **Ⓑ**, and your waiter should be accommodating, since the time when the table will be free can be gauged. But if the server isn't happy with the idea, try answer **Ⓒ**. There may be a free table at the bar, but on a weekend night, don't count on it. Otherwise, just pay your bill and find somewhere else. But realize that the waiter is probably just following the policy of that restaurant—the same as in many others.

DO'S AND DON'TS

So, now you're in San Francisco, perhaps here to stay. Your belongings have arrived, your children are in school, you've most likely started to work at a job with new colleagues, and even your dog has made friends in the park. What comes next? That's clear: building your life in a city that may have civil laws, but seems to have few rules—or even guidelines—for individual behavior. But certainly, it must. Actually, there are very few, and San Franciscans, being an outspoken lot, will let you know when you've broken some—no doubt arcane—taboo. Pay attention to those around you, and ask if you have a question. Herewith just a few reminders of what San Franciscans know.

DO'S

- Do remember that the climate in San Francisco is ever-changing. Unless there is a definite heat wave, think about taking a jacket when you go out. And, because summer is a cool and foggy season, women don't usually wear white shoes and white clothing as though they were in the tropics. Do wear light-colored suits and shoes, if you like, but not necessarily white. The same holds true for men.
- Do understand that San Francisco accepts people for who and what they are. Thus, people's lifestyle choices—whether you approve of them or not—are their business and not yours. Don't show disapproval or in any way try to impede behavior that you think is inappropriate, unless it is obviously criminal, illegal, or endangering others.
- Do be careful when you are out late at night; petty crime, pick-pocketing, and purse snatchings do exist, especially in some peripheral areas South of Market or the Tenderloin. Do take the usual precautions that you would in any large city; stay on well-lighted, well-populated streets, and if you must go into a neighborhood that is "iffy," go in a group.
- Do realize that Americans may be casual, even in first encounters. Don't be offended if you are called by your

given name immediately upon meeting someone. This holds true even when you make a business call: expect to be called by your first name and don't insist on formality in response.
- Do remember that San Francisco has a high rate of HIV and Aids. If you meet someone and are considering an intimate relationship, do practice "safe sex," no matter how "safe" you think your new partner may be. Or, you and your partner might decide together to have AIDs tests; several clinics offer free and confidential testing. (*See page 156*.)
- Do be a generous tipper in a restaurant. Servers earn low salaries and depend on their tips. Generally, the tip is not included in the bill, so if the service is good, add somewhere between 15–20 per cent. If the service is not good, leave less or inform the management that you were not treated well. In some restaurants, a tip is included in the bill if the party has six people or more.
- Do be on time for a social engagement. San Francisco is an "early town," and even on weekends, you may well be invited to someone home for dinner at 7:00 or 7:30 pm. Both at someone's home or at a restaurant, arrive within ten minutes of the specified time. Call if you're going to be late. And, if you change your plans and can't eat where you've reserved, call to cancel the reservation. Don't just not show up.
- Do offer the person you're with a taste of your dinner when you're in a restaurant. That's what people do. And don't be offended if someone asks—or, heaven forbid!—even reaches over and spears something off your place. Do feel free to accept a taste of your friend's dinner when offered, but don't feel obliged, if you don't want to.
- Do remember that San Franciscans dress casually. It depends on your social group and where you're going, but it's often okay to wear jeans in the evening—if they're clean and you don't look sloppy.
- Do remember that smoking is illegal in all restaurants and bars and public spaces. This is one instance when you can admonish someone else: if they are smoking in

a prohibited area and it is offending you. Do be polite but firm.

DON'TS
- Don't call the city Frisco. Do call the city San Francisco, or The City. If a local asks whether you live in Marin, for example, you might answer, "No, I live in The City."
- Don't call the towns or the rest of the Bay Area "suburbs." Do refer to the areas as "The East Bay" (east); "Marin" (north); "The South Bay" or "The Peninsula" (south).
- Don't be upset if a new acquaintance who has expressed warm interest in knowing you doesn't call you to get together. This happens; people are busy in their lives and with their friends and colleagues. If this happens, wait a short while and then do take the initiative: call and suggest a definite day for a movie or a dinner or a hike—or whatever you have in common. You might say, "Would you like to see the film at the Roxie next Saturday?" Then you can negotiate a time. Or if the person doesn't seem interested, drop it and don't pursue it further.

RESOURCE GUIDE

EMERGENCIES
All dire emergencies	911
Electric/gas emergencies	(800) 743-5002
Poison Control	(800) 222-1222
Telephone operator	Dial 0

AMBULANCES
Bayshore Ambulance	(650) 525-9700
Fire Department	(415) 558-3200
King American Ambulance	(415) 931-1400
AMR/San Francisco Ambulance	(415) 922-9400
Saint Joseph's Ambulance	(415) 460-6020

24-HOUR HOSPITAL EMERGENCY ROOMS (BY AREA)

- **Castro / Hayes Valley / Mission**
  California Pacific Medical Center
  (Davies Campus)
  Castro Street at Duboce
  Tel: (415) 600-6000

- **Chinatown / North Beach**
  Chinese Hospital
  845 Jackson Street
  Tel: (415) 982-2400

- **Downtown**
  Saint Francis Memorial Hospital
  900 Hyde Street
  Tel: (415) 353-6000

- **Haight / Sunset**
  Saint Mary's Medical Center
  450 Stanyan Street
  tel: (415) 668-1000

- **Pacific Heights**
  California Pacific Medical Center (Women and Children's Center) 3700 California Street; tel: (415) 600-6000

- **Pacific Heights / Inner Richmond**
  California Pacific Medical Center (California Campus)
  3700 California Street
  Tel: (415) 600-6000 (Maternity emergencies only)
- **Mission / Potrero Hill**
  San Francisco General Hospital
  1001 Potrero Avenue
  Tel: (415) 206-8000
- **Sunset / Avenues**
  UCSF Medical Center
  505 Parnassus Avenue
  Tel: (415) 476-1000
- **Western Addition**
  Kaiser Permanente
  2425 Geary Boulevard
  Tel: (415) 833-2000 (For Kaiser members)

CRISIS HOTLINES

AIDS Nightline	(415) 434-2437
Alcoholics Anonymous	(415) 674-1821

WALGREENS 24-HOUR PRESCRIPTION PHARMACIES

- **Castro / NoeValley**
  498 Castro Street
  Tel: (415) 861-3136
- **Outer Richmond**
  25 Point Lobos, at 42nd Avenue
  Tel: (415) 386-0736
- **Marina / Cow Hollow**
  3201 Divisadero Street, at Lombard
  Tel: (415) 931-6415
- **Potrero Hill**
  1189 Potrero Avenue
  Tel: (415) 647-1397

TRAVEL INFORMATION

- San Francisco International Airport / SFO Airport
  Tel: (650) 821-8211; Website: http://www.flysfo.com

- Oakland International Airport
  Tel: (510) 563-3300
  Website: http://www.flyoakland.com
- Amtrak (trains)
  Tel: (800) 872-7245
  website: http://www.amtrak.com
- Greyhound (bus)
  Tel: (800) 231-2222
  website: http://www.greyhound.com
- All Bay Area Transportation Information
  Tel: 511
  Website: http://www.511.org
- CalTrans Road Conditions
  Tel: 511; or (800) 427-7623

TRAVELER'S AID

SFO Airport
Tel: (650) 821-2735
Website: http://www.travelersaid.org
Nonprofit organization that helps travelers in difficult straits: reunites families separated while traveling, provides food or shelter to people stranded without cash, offers emotional counseling as needed.

VISITOR INFORMATION

- San Francisco Visitor Information Center
  Corner of Market and Powell; lower level of Hallidie Plaza
  Tel: (415) 391-2000
  Website: http://www.onlyinsanfrancisco.com
  Open daily. Free advice on understanding and seeing San Francisco, hotel reservations, brochures.
- National Park Service Visitor Information
  102 Montgomery Street, in the Presidio
  Tel: (415) 561-4323
  Website: http://www.nps.gov
  The Park Service administers the National Historical Maritime Park, Alcatraz, and the Golden Gate National Recreation Area, including the Presidio and Crissy Field. Each attraction has its own visitor center.

FEDERAL INFORMATION
- National Federal Information: tel: (800) 333-4636; website: http://www.usa.gov
- Department of Homeland Security (Citizenship and Immigration) tel: (800) 375-5283; website: http://www.dhs.gov
- Internal Revenue Service: tel: (800) 829-1040; website: http://www.irs.gov
- Social Security Administration: tel: (800) 772-1213; website: http://www.ssa.gov

CITY INFORMATION
- Official website, City of San Francisco. http://www.sfgov.org
- City Customer Service Center. 24-hour telephone: 311
- City Hall. Tel: (415) 554-4000
- Police Department, non-emergencies. Tel: (415) 553-0123
- San Francisco Unified School District. Tel: (415) 241-6000

LOST CREDIT CARDS
- American Express
  Tel: (800) 992-3404
- Diners Club
  Tel: (800) 234-6377
- MasterCard
  Tel: (800) 627-8372
- Visa
  Tel: (800) 847-2911

TELEPHONE AREA CODES
For international calls, dial 011 before the country code and telephone number. For any American or Canadian number outside the 415 area code, dial the number 1 before the telephone number.

East Bay	510
Marin County	415
Napa/Sonoma	707
San Francisco	415
South Bay/Peninsula	650

Toll-free numbers start with: 800, 888, 866, 877. Numbers that start with 700 or 900 are not free. To reach the operator, dial 0.

CONVERSION TABLES

One U.S. gallon = 3.8 liters; .85 Imperial gallons
One kilo = 2.2 pounds
100 grams = 3.5 ounces
One liter = 1 quart, 2 ounces; about 4 cups
One teaspoon dry measure = about 5 grams
One tablespoon = 14.3 grams
One stone = 14 pounds
One centimeter = .39 inches
One meter = 39.3 inches; 3.3 feet; 1.1 yard
One kilometer = .62 miles; One mile = 1.6km
212° Fahrenheit = 100° Centigrade
32° Fahrenheit = 0° Centigrade
98.6° Fahrenheit = 37° Centigrade

DISCOUNTS ON GOODS AND SERVICES

- **The Entertainment Book**
  An annual publication that for a fee allows discounts to hundreds of restaurants, shops, car rentals, hotels, and services. Buy online at http://www.entertainment.com
- **San Francisco City Pass**
  If you're here for a week, consider the City Pass, which allows access to six of the city's attractions—De Young Museum and the Legion of Honor, Aquarium of the Bay, the Exploratorium, Museum of Modern Art, and one other: either the Asian Art museum, or California Academy of Sciences and Steinhart Aquarium, plus seven consecutive days of free public transportation including the cable car, and a Blue and Gold Fleet Bay Cruise Adventure.
  Tel: (888) 330-5008
  Website: http://www.citypass.com/sanfrancisco

  Currently all this costs only US$ 59 (reduced price for children) and is a real bargain, when you think that the cable car costs US$ 5 a ride. You can pick up the city pass at any of the above attractions or at the Tourist Office.

- **Go San Francisco Card**
  Unlimited admission to some 45 museums and attractions in San Francisco, and a few others in the wine country (including winery visits) and Monterey. Discounts can be enjoyed at some shops and restaurants. The card is issued in differing durations up to seven days, costing from US$ 49–149.
  Tel: (866) 628-9028
  Website: http://www.gosanfranciscocard.com

VOTER INFORMATION
- **Voter Registration**
  Tel: (415) 554-4375
- **Democratic Party**
  100 McAllister Street
  Tel: (415) 626-1161
  Website: http://www.cadem.org
- **Republican Party**
  110 Pacific Avenue
  Tel: (415) 989-1259
  Website: http://www.sfgop.org

LGBT RESOURCES
For a comprehensive look at the LGBT communities in San Francisco, visit A Different Light Bookstore (*See page 190.*), and take a walking tour of the Castro, which informs about the history of the area as well as its current life.
- Lesbian, Gay, Bisexual Transgender Community Center
  1800 Market Street
  Tel: (415) 865-5555
  Website: http://www.sfcenter.org
  Home to LGBT organizations, including a space for community events and performances, social support activities, art gallery, and film screening room.
- James C. Hormel Gay and Lesbian Center
  San Francisco Main Pubic Library
  100 Larkin Street
  Tel: (415) 557-4566 (Archives, books, periodicals)

- Bay Area Career Women
  1800 Market Street, #404
  Tel: (415) 865-5630
  Website: http://www.bacw.org
  World's largest lesbian volunteer organization formed to eliminate discrimination. This provides business networking opportunities, social events, etc.
- Women's Building
  3543, 18th Street
  Tel: (415) 431-1180
  Website: http://www.womensbuilding.org
  Multi-cultural center for women and girls, providing tools for full participation in society. Hosts events, meeting, and seminars for women.
- Eureka Valley-Harvey Milk Library
  1 José Sarria Court (at 16th, near Market)
  Tel: (415) 355-5616
  This Castro branch of the Public Library has a well-organized collection of materials for the LGBT communities.
- Pacific Center
  2712 Telegraph Avenue, Berkeley
  Tel: (510) 548-8283
  Website: http://www.pacificcenter.org
  LGBT resource and support center for the entire Bay Area.

MEETING PEOPLE BY VOLUNTEERING

You will meet people at work, at your gym, walking your dog in the parks, and through other means, especially by volunteering for community or non-profit organizations, often in the arts. For professional and business networking, see pages 340–341.

- The San Francisco Volunteer Center
  1675 California Street
  Tel: (415) 928-8999
  Website: http://www.thevolunteercenter.net
  Coordinates volunteers in community-wide projects.
- Project Homeless Connect
  60 Spear Street
  Website: http://www.sfconnect.org

A city-sponsored set of projects to help the San Francisco homeless.

- SFCASA (San Francisco Court Appointed Special Advocate Program)
100 Bush Street
Tel: (415) 398-8001
Website: http://www.sfcasa.org
You can aid some children in difficult circumstances and in need of help, by supporting them in different ways and guiding them through the court system, as necessary.
- Contemporary Extension
151 3rd Street
Tel: (415) 947-1155
Website: http://www.sfmomacx.org
Member-run organization for the young professional who wants to expand knowledge and take an active role in supporting the Museum of Modern Art (MOMA).
- Friends of the San Francisco Public Library
391 Grove Street
Tel: (415) 626-7500
Website: http://www.friendssfpl.org
Friends raise money for the Library, help operate the several bookshops, and support the library in other ways.
- San Francisco Gay Men's Chorus
1800 Market Street
Tel: (415) 865-3650
Website: http://www.sfgmc.org
The chorus presents major concers each year, plus outreach concerts for community groups. Audition for the chorus, or even if you can't sing, volunteers are always needed to keep track of wardrobe, ticket sales, production, etc.
- San Francisco Opera Guild Volunteer Program
301 Van Ness Avenue
Tel: (415) 565-6433
Website: http://www.sfopera.com/guild
Volunteer throughout the opera world: in the gift shop, administrative offices, costume shop, or in other ways behind the scenes. Bravo! is a young professionals' group

that participates in a variety of events related to the opera: receptions, benefits, etc.

- San Francisco Symphony Volunteer Council
  Davies Symphony Hall
  Tel: (415) 503-5500
  Website: http://www.sfsymphony.org
  Volunteer behind the scenes at the gift shop, in the office, with the Concerts for Kids Program, and more.

  Symphonix is the young professionals group. It offers meetings, musical programs, social events, discounts on dinner and concerts.
  Tel: (415) 281-0700
  Website: http://www.sfsymphonix.com

- San Francisco Ballet:
  455 Franklin Street
  Tel: (415) 553-4634
  A host of varied opportunities to volunteer and participate with this major ballet company, through the two programs:
  Bravo: Website: http:www.bravosfb.org
  Encore! Tel: (415) 865-6762; email: encore@sfballet.info.
  Website: http://www.sfballet.org

San Francisco offers something for everyone. Shopping is convenient and fun, no matter your age.

FURTHER READING

FICTION

Hammett, Dashiell. *The Maltese Falcon*.
- "Hard boiled" detective novel set in San Francisco in the 1920s. Novel was made into a classic film starring Humphrey Bogart.

London, Jack. *Call of the Wild*.
- Representative of London's work, this book chronicles the adventures of the sheepdog Buck, a sledge dog in the Klondike, adapting to survive.

London, Jack. *Martin Eden*.
- Semi-autobiographical novel of a poor boy who thinks to better himself by becoming a writer, only to be increasingly disillusioned as he succeeds.

Maupin, Armistead. *Tales of the City*.
- A cult favorite, bestselling six-volume series of witty novels (soap operas, actually) that recreate the atmosphere of San Francisco in the 1970s and 1980s.

Norris, Frank. *McTeague: A Story of San Francisco*.
- Writing at the same time as London, Norris' gritty tale of avarice and violence takes place in turn-of-the-century San Francisco.

Seth, Vikram. *The Golden Gate*.
- A novel in verse form, depicting the lives of a group of San Francisco yuppies.

Steinbeck, John. *The Grapes of Wrath*.
- Grim, Pulitzer Prize-winning novel of sharecroppers during the Great Depression, driven from their home by drought, joining migrant workers of California.

Tan, Amy. *The Joy Luck Club*.
- Charming novel, relating the interconnected woes and joys of four Chinese women who have immigrated to San Francisco, and their American-Chinese daughters.

Twain, Mark. *Roughing It*.
- Tales of frontier California and San Francisco in the 1860s. Descriptions of the Comstock Lode, the famous silver mines.

NON-FICTION

- Fracchia, Charles and Thomas Stauffer. *San Francisco: From the Gold Rush to Cyberspace*.

- Jacobson, Susan. *Getting the Public School You Want: San Francisco*.

- Starr, Kevin. *Americans and the California Dream, 1850–1915*.

- Starr, Kevin. *California: A History*.

- Sullivan, Charles L. *A Companion to California Wine: An Encyclopedia of Wine and Winemaking from the Mission Period to the Present*.

- Unterman, Patricia. *Patricia Unterman's Food Lover's Guide to San Francisco*.

- Zagat Survey. *San Francisco/Bay Area Restaurants*.

- Zagat Survey. *San Francisco Nightlife*.

ABOUT THE AUTHOR

Frances Gendlin has held leadership positions in magazine and book publishing. She was Editor and Publisher of Sierra, the magazine of the Sierra Club, a worldwide environmental organization, and was the association's Director of Public Affairs. As Executive Director of the Association of American University Presses, she represented the 100-member publishing houses to the public and fostered scholarly publishing interests. In 1997, she wrote *Rome At Your Door* (also published as *Living & Working Abroad: Rome*), a widely read guide to living in that city. In 1998, using the same format, she wrote *Paris At Your Door* (*Living & Working Abroad: Paris*).

While she was growing up, her family moved several times to different areas of the United States, each with its own characteristics and culture, climate, and cuisine. This has led her to appreciate new cultures, to wonder about their differences and similarities, and to try and understand them. All her life she has enjoyed travel and new adventures, meeting interesting people and making new friends.

After having lived in San Francisco for twenty years, Frances Gendlin now has moved to Paris. She feels fortunate to have lived in two of the most charming cities in the world. Her fictional memoir, *Paris, Moi, and the Gang: A Memoir... of Sorts* was published in January, 2010.

INDEX

A
accommodation 82, 83, 139, 333

airports
 Oakland International Airport (OAK) 158
 San Francisco International Airport (SFO) 157, 170, 351

apartments 80, 86–88, 90, 93–96, 99, 112, 140

B
banking 108, 109

Barbary Coast 10, 2

bars 260, 263–268

Bay Area 11, 13, 14, 38, 49, 50, 51, 53, 87, 88, 93, 99, 105, 107, 114. 116, 117, 129, 131, 136, 140, 144, 156, 161, 162, 169, 176, 189, 191, 192, 244, 246, 272, 274, 275, 278, 198, 336, 337, 338, 342, 343, 344, 346

Bay Bridge 23, 51, 159, 160, 284, 345
 161, 181, 189–191

business and employment
 currency 81, 109
 employment agencies 343, 344, 346
 job searching 342–344, 346
 networking 340–341
 office space 341–342
 pay 342–343
 setting up a business 337–340
 U.S. Small Business Administration (SBA) 339

C
children 19, 30, 32, 34, 46, 56, 57, 63, 92, 107, 113, 115, 118, 120–128, 130–133, 135, 136, 150, 155, 159, 164, 173, 182, 185, 190, 191, 194, 195, 196, 279, 280, 285, 289, 328

citizenship 78

climate 349

D
demographics 55–63

dental care 155, 156

districts and neighbourhoods
 Alamo Square 31, 32, 33, 96, 215
 Bayview 38, 47, 251
 Bernal Heights 15, 37, 38, 42, 46, 47, 61, 97, 150, 230, 268, 352
 Buena Vista 15, 33, 34, 46, 229, 270
 Castro 13, 15, 43–48, 52, 56, 61, 97, 114, 150, 155, 157, 166–169, 187, 190, 213, 228, 229, 230, 266, 267, 281, 288, 301, 303, 306, 309, 352
 Central Waterfront 39
 Chinatown 2, 3, 10, 15, 20, 21, 22, 23, 26, 35, 52, 56, 114, 115, 135, 168, 175, 184, 187, 207, 218, 219, 232, 234, 237, 238, 242, 247–249, 251, 254–256, 309, 332, 352
 Civic Center 17, 18, 86, 106, 146, 168, 175, 183, 190, 207, 214, 219, 226, 243, 251, 287, 290, 305–309
 Cow Hollow 14, 26, 28, 29, 96, 98, 136, 187, 207, 219, 224, 229, 239, 240, 256, 257, 261, 279, 352
 Crocker Amazon 37, 38
 Diamond Heights 46, 48, 93, 96, 166
 Embarcadero 6, 23, 39, 63, 84, 94, 132, 136, 167, 182, 185, 190, 210, 215, 217, 223, 225, 233, 244, 260, 262, 264, 268, 274, 276, 279, 280, 285, 304, 346
 Excelsior 37, 282
 Financial District 2, 18, 19, 20, 23, 26, 29, 42, 48, 55, 62, 94, 115, 169, 170, 175, 185, 207, 210, 218, 219, 230, 264, 270, 345, 352
 Haight 15, 32, 33, 34, 45, 61, 90, 115, 125, 143, 150, 155, 182, 190, 191, 220, 228, 230, 241, 242, 253, 267, 268, 269, 279, 352, 356
 Hayes Valley 18, 97, 150, 155, 190, 194, 214, 228, 230, 251, 260, 262, 264
 Hunters Point 38, 39, 90
 Japantown 31, 32, 45, 56, 84, 114, 168, 175, 190, 191, 232, 241, 249, 282, 301, 352
 Lakeshore 37, 195
 Marina 9, 28, 29, 30, 49, 51, 93, 94, 96, 97, 114, 129, 131, 170, 195, 215, 218, 223, 229, 240, 250, 279, 282, 283, 285, 307, 352
 Mission 9, 10, 12, 14, 15, 21, 39, 40–43, 46, 47, 49, 56, 61, 62, 66, 90, 94, 96, 99, 112, 116, 135, 142, 143, 150, 155, 158, 166, 167, 175, 183, 185, 186, 187, 190, 193, 210, 214, 219, 222–225, 228, 231, 240, 249, 250, 251, 253–255, 257, 261, 263, 265, 267, 268, 279. 280, 282, 286–288, 291, 294, 295, 300, 301,

307, 308, 309, 332, 337, 339, 342, 351, 352

Nob Hill 17, 19, 20, 21, 83, 85, 86, 93, 114, 166, 288, 352

Noe Valley 12, 43, 46–48, 61, 97, 117, 136, 152, 182, 194, 195, 217, 229, 230, 245, 252, 261, 265, 282, 286, 296, 297, 352

North Beach 2, 5, 6, 10, 17, 19–21, 23, 24, 26, 28, 34, 45, 94, 114, 115, 169, 175, 176, 182, 191, 203, 213, 223–226, 229, 230, 249, 251, 252, 255, 256, 262, 265, 266, 269, 270, 282, 288, 299, 309, 352

Oceanview Merced Ingleside (OMI) 36

Ocean Beach 35, 269, 272, 274, 275, 278, 283, 287

Pacific Heights 15, 28, 30, 35, 48, 53, 96, 97, 111, 114, 115, 150, 166, 203, 218, 222, 224, 225, 228, 229, 246, 252, 253, 352

Parkside 36, 282

Pine Lake Park 36

Portola 37, 160, 253

Potrero Hill 15, 39, 42, 43, 98, 183, 185, 188, 225, 229, 231, 262, 282, 285, 299, 300

Presidio Heights 10, 16, 21, 28, 29, 30, 35, 94, 97, 117, 150, 182, 183, 185, 187, 194–196, 229, 246, 274, 277, 278, 280, 284, 285, 287, 308, 352

Richmond 32, 34, 35, 151, 170, 176, 185, 187, 190, 212, 214, 221, 225, 230, 231, 237, 240, 242, 249, 252, 254, 270, 282, 352

Russian Hill 25–28, 93, 166, 196, 231, 260, 352

Saint Francis Wood 48

Sherwood Forest 48, 96

SoMa (South of Market) 12, 16, 39, 40, 61, 94, 105, 112, 176, 185, 187, 192, 196, 203, 207, 209, 217, 218, 222, 225, 228, 239, 247, 262, 269, 352

Sunset 21, 32, 34–36, 94, 98, 151, 183, 185, 188, 203, 219, 229–232, 236, 237, 239, 247, 249, 252, 254, 257, 282, 332, 352

Telegraph Hill 24–26, 93, 98, 281, 352

Tenderloin 18, 63, 83, 90, 116, 150, 155, 221, 241, 294, 333

Twin Peaks 43, 47, 48, 160, 255, 267

Union Square 2, 3, 16–19, 21, 38, 83, 84, 112, 114, 166, 172, 181, 182, 184, 187, 188, 192, 194, 196, 207, 210, 219, 228, 231, 257, 260, 266, 287, 292, 309, 352

Van Ness 17, 18, 28, 49, 83, 86, 94, 95, 96, 150, 161, 166, 167, 187, 189, 220, 221, 224, 227, 255, 262, 283, 287, 295, 296, 301

Visitacion Valley 37, 167, 197, 282

Western Addition 14, 15, 31, 32, 49, 62, 90, 94, 95, 215, 299, 352

Westwood Highlands 48

West Portal 48, 136

driving 171–179

driver's license 77, 92, 108, 125, 146, 176, 177, 178

parking 173–176

E

earthquakes 13, 107, 351

East Bay 50, 51, 91, 112, 114, 140, 169, 170, 197, 284, 284, 293, 326

education 120–146

F

films 300–303

fitness clubs and gyms 280–282

food 199–270

Asian food 232–242

bakeries 251–252

chocolates 257

foreign cuisines 220–224

fresh produce 243–245, 249, 250, 253–256

ice cream 230–231

pizza 224–225

seafood 211–215, 253–255

supermarkets 245–248, 254, 255

tea and coffee houses 229–230

vegetarian cuisine 218–219

foreign consulates and embassies 79–80

G

gays and lesbians 118, 266–268

Golden Gate Bridge 23, 28, 51, 52, 53, 132, 133, 159, 160, 169, 278, 290, 324, 326

Gold Rush 10, 14, 19, 22, 201, 213, 251, 291

H
HIV/AIDS 156–157
Housing 86–100, 139, 140

I
identification cards 108
immigration 72–78, 137
insurance
  automobile 177, 178
  earthquake 107
  health 148–149
  household 106–107
International Student Identity Card (ISIC) 145
Internet access 105

L
language 124, 125, 331–334
laundromats and dry cleaners 110–111
libraries 146

M
medical care 146–157
  hospitals 150, 151
Mission Dolores 10, 40, 116, 282, 291, 351
museums 289–292, 327

N
national holidays and local events 304–309
newspapers 113–115
North Bay 50, 51, 113

O
Oakland 49, 51, 91, 159, 160, 170, 302, 326, 338, 344

P
pets 23, 81, 92
postal service 105, 106
purchasing a car 178

R
real estate agents 91, 94, 95
religions and places of worship 115–118

S
San Jose 49, 51, 91, 114, 140, 170, 231, 330, 337
schools 120–132
  charter schools 128
  child care 131, 132
  Child Development Program 126
  English-language schools 125, 333
  preschools 126–128
  private schools 128–130
  public schools 123–126
  San Francisco Unified School District (SFUSD) 119
  Test of English as a Foreign Language (TOEFL) 137
shopping 181–198
  appliances and electronics 185–188
  clothing 192–196
  furniture rental 189
  shopping centers 184, 185
  sports clothing and gear 195, 196
Silicon Valley 51, 86–87, 330, 337
socializing 64–70
South Bay 50, 113
sports and fitness 272–286
storage lockers 111, 112

T
taxes 83, 110, 125, 177, 184
telephone services 101–104
television and radio 105
transportation 161
  BART 158, 165, 168, 169, 170, 179, 182
  buses 94, 134, 158, 164, 168–171, 179, 197
  cable cars 164–167, 179
  ferries 161, 169, 170, 179
  Muni (Municipal Railway) 164, 165, 166, 179 182
  San Francisco City Pass 165
  taxis 170–171

U
universities and specialized technical schools 137–144
utilities 100
  electricity 100
  water 100

V
visas 75–78
  student visa 137–139
vote 108

W
wine country 70, 259, 310–316

Titles in the CultureShock! series:

Argentina	France	Portugal
Australia	Germany	Russia
Austria	Great Britain	San Francisco
Bahrain	Hawaii	Saudi Arabia
Beijing	Hong Kong	Scotland
Belgium	India	Shanghai
Berlin	Ireland	Singapore
Bolivia	Italy	South Africa
Borneo	Jakarta	Spain
Brazil	Japan	Sri Lanka
Bulgaria	Korea	Sweden
Cambodia	Laos	Switzerland
Canada	London	Syria
Chicago	Malaysia	Taiwan
Chile	Mauritius	Thailand
China	Morocco	Tokyo
Costa Rica	Munich	Travel Safe
Cuba	Myanmar	Turkey
Czech Republic	Netherlands	United Arab Emirates
Denmark	New Zealand	
Ecuador	Pakistan	USA
Egypt	Paris	Vancouver
Finland	Philippines	Venezuela

For more information about any of these titles, please contact any of our Marshall Cavendish offices around the world (listed on page ii) or visit our website at:

www.marshallcavendish.com/genref